FOR A LATER GENERATION

The Transformation of Tradition in Israel, Early Judaism, and Early Christianity

Edited by

Randal A. Argall, Beverly A. Bow, and Rodney A. Werline

TRINITY PRESS INTERNATIONAL

Harrisburg, Pennsylvania

Trinity Press International, P.O. Box 1321, Harrisburg, PA 17105
Trinity Press International is a division of the Morehouse Group.

Cover design: Corey Kent

Cover art: *The Translation of Enoch*, Nicolas of Verdun, Klosterneuburg Abbey, Austria. Erich Lessing/ Art Resource, NY

Library of Congress Cataloging-in-Publication Data
For a later generation : the transformation of tradition in Israel, early Judaism, and early Christianity / edited by Randal A. Argall, Beverly A. Bow, and Rodney A. Werline.
    p. cm.
    Festschrift for George W.E. Nickelsburg.
    Includes bibliographical references and index.
    ISBN 1-56338-325-X
    1. Apocryphal books (Old Testament) – Criticism, interpretation, etc.
  2. Bible – Criticism, interpretation, etc. I. Argall, Randal A. II. Nickelsburg, George W. E., 1934- . Bow, Beverly A. IV. Werline, Rodney Alan, 1961-
BS1700 .F67 2000
220.6 – dc21
                                     00-037414

Printed in the United States of America

00   01   02   03   04   05   10 9 8 7 6 5 4 3 2 1

FOR A
LATER
GENERATION

George Nickelsburg   (photo: Jon Van Allen, UI foundation)

This book has been published thanks to the generous support of the School of Religion of The University of Iowa.

Contents

Foreword

During the 1950s and 1960s there was a wonderful window of opportunity in the history of Lutheran theological education in the United States. I remember how I felt, and often said, that arguably the most stimulating Lutheran seminary in the States was the Missouri Synod's Concordia in St. Louis. It was a joy to go there. The solid grounding in the sources and the languages that gave access to them paid off in theological creativity. Spring was in the air as the old branches blossomed. There was exuberance, not least in the field of biblical studies, so dear and sensitive to Missouri Lutherans. That made the excitement that much more palpable and it was of the kind that inspires smart students to consider the life of scholarship a calling for life.

In my mind and memory George Nickelsburg is linked to those heady and exhilarating days, before that synod chose to quench the spirit that scared them — but that is another story, and perhaps one factor that caused George's career to unfold, not in seminaries, but in a state university, albeit one with a unique and time-honored regard for religious studies.

So he came to us at Harvard Divinity School well prepared, highly motivated, and trained in a tradition in which truth matters and, hence, scholarship is serious business. As I got out of the Divinity School library the copy of his 1967 dissertation, I found a few lines that give me a key to the sustained quality of his scholarly contributions. The lines are found at the end of the one-hundred-page appendix, which was not included in the published edition.[1] Nickelsburg is discussing Oscar Cullmann's then-famous article in which he made doctrinal claims for resurrection of the body as against immortality of the soul. Nickelsburg sums up his response — and in a way the theological implications of his dissertation — as follows:

> Because of the close interrelations of these various aspects of theological formulation, one must ask: Does the Church reject a belief in immortality of the soul because it considers this to be in itself heretical anthropology? Does it reject the belief that the resurrection has already happened because

---

1. *Resurrection, Immortality, and Eternal Life in Intertestamental Judaism* (HTS 26; Cambridge: Harvard University Press, 1972). Actually, the printed edition has a very short appendix with a critique of Cullmann's views, 177–80. Nickelsburg has dipped into his original appendix from time to time, for example in his article in the Helmut Koester Festschrift (1991). My quote is from the original dissertation, pp. 464–65.

realized eschatology is in itself objectionable? Or are there other "heretical" theological elements concomitant with this anthropology or eschatology? Does realized eschatology encourage or discourage a concern for ethical behavior? Do those who maintain the immortality of the soul also deny God's creation of the body, and does this have ethical implications? Does an assumption Christology invite, or even imply, a kind of docetism, viz., a denial of the incarnation and the reality of Jesus' passion and death? The Church had to address itself to these practical ramifications and actual concomitants of a given anthropology or eschatology, when it defined between orthodoxy and heresy, and when it picked and rejected certain formulations. Such considerations have influenced the manner in which the various strata and cross-currents of theology were redacted, integrated, and, in some cases, squelched within the New Testament writings themselves. If, like Cullmann, one wishes to raise such questions once more, the task of choosing must be threefold: (1) As an historian, one must study the variety of theological expressions current in the primitive Church. (2) One also must study (even in the N.T.) the history of how and why the early Church dealt with the formulations. (3) The theologian can then ask himself whether and why he agrees or disagrees with the theological decisions of the early Church! Cullmann has spoken as historian and churchman. Our study here (albeit brief and preliminary) has suggested that Cullmann has over-simplified step one. Hence, step two was unnecessary for him. Therefore step three has not been properly informed.

In that passage I find much of what has inspired and sustained Nickelsburg's painstaking and careful work. He has stayed the whole time in the same realm in order to rescue us all from our often self-serving simplifications. He has continued to develop his fine sense of diversities and continuities, mutations and splicings. But somehow his analyses did not get out of hand and move toward boredom and pedantry; the secret was the underlying urge to make decisions of truth that were properly informed — be it in the scholarly community or in communities of faith.

His realm of study has been the multifaceted era of pre-canonical Judaism and Christianity, a field in which so-called data are exposed to unusually strong pulls by doctrinal magnets. Nickelsburg's scholarship has been of special significance also in its restraint from attempting the glittering grand schemes. He is trusted. I came to think of Paul's words: "Thus what one seeks for in stewards [of the mysteries of God] is that they be found trustworthy" (1 Cor. 4:2).

Harvard's unforgettable Arthur Darby Nock used to say: "In order to compare two things you must know one of them very well." And from the time one had to build a herbarium for the botany class, I remember my father saying: "If you really look, you will find all the sixty species you need in this one meadow." George's scholarly equivalent to the Benedictine *stabilitas loci* has paid off, not only as to his university venue but, more importantly, in his chosen area of research.

Thus he has become a sought-after contributor to symposia volumes and dictionaries and encyclopedias. When I read his articles in the *Anchor Bible Dictionary*, I have that deeply satisfying feeling which I had so eminently when I read Arthur Darby Nock: Every noun, adjective, and adverb could be footnoted with specific texts, some of which I knew and some of which I trusted to be there if I had known them. That is the sure hand of a true scholar who thinks that truth matters and who wants our choices and decisions to be "properly informed."

And now we eagerly await his *opus maximum*, his commentary to *Enoch*, those multilayered, multivalent, interacting strands of traditions. Just right for George.

KRISTER STENDAHL

Editors' Preface

We are proud to honor our professor, George W. E. Nickelsburg, with this volume at the occasion of his approaching retirement. Our joy as students was to watch him work with these early Jewish and Christian texts, which are now central to our own lives as professors. His skill as an interpreter, his careful methodology, and his knowledge of these texts always reminded us that we were, indeed, studying with a master of this area of religious studies.

The title of the volume plays with, or transforms, a phrase from 1 *Enoch* 92:1, the beginning of "The Epistle of Enoch": "Written by Enoch the scribe — this complete sign of wisdom — praised by all men and a leader of the whole earth, to all my sons who will dwell upon the earth, and *to the last generations* who will observe truth and peace." We hope that this volume will be a tribute to George and will be part of the testimony to later generations of his virtuosity as a scholar.

We have many people to thank. First, we express our gratitude to Hal Rast at Trinity Press for being willing to take on this project. We wish him the best as he moves into retirement. Thanks to Henry Carrigan, Hal's successor at Trinity, for seeing this project to the end. Along the way, Birger Pearson and Norman Petersen offered us their sage advice and guidance.

We extend our deepest gratitude to all those who contributed to this volume. Without them, of course, this volume would not have existed. Their contributions are, on the one hand, a compliment to George. On the other hand, these essays are a mark of the contributors' own collegiality and scholarship. Thanks to Krister Stendahl for contributing the foreword to this volume.

The University of Iowa gave a generous gift toward the publication of this volume. We thank the University for the gift and for the wonderful academic setting that the University provided us while we studied there. Thanks to the chair of the School of Religion at the University of Iowa, Robert Baird, for seeing the value of this volume and for his work toward its funding. Thanks also to his program assistant, Maureen Walterhouse, for her help.

We are all deeply indebted to Mindi Thompson, Rodney Werline's graduate assistant, for all her hard work. To her fell the work of George's bibliography and the retyping of some of the manuscripts that had electronic disk problems.

Thanks to Marilyn Nickelsburg for her encouragement during the work and for her advice. Thank you especially, Marilyn, for telling stories about George at social occasions. As anxious and scared graduate students, those stories gave us a different perspective on our mentor.

We are sad to see the time of retirement arrive for such a wonderful generation of scholars that included George, Birger Pearson, Norman Petersen, Robert Kraft, Hal Rast, and others. As graduate students, we admired this generation and wanted to be like them.

George, with all our gratitude, this book is for you.

RANDY, BEV, AND ROD

Abbreviations

AASOR	Annual of the American Schools of Oriental Research
AB	Anchor Bible
ABD	*Anchor Bible Dictionary.* Edited by D. N. Freedman. 6 vols. New York, 1992
AGJU	Arbeiten zur Geschichte des antiken Judentums und des Urchristentums
AJSR	*Association for Jewish Studies Review*
ALGHJ	Arbeiten zur Literatur und Geschichte des hellenistischen Judentums
ANF	*Ante-Nicene Fathers*
AnOr	Analecta orientalia
AOAT	Alter Orient und Altes Testament
APOT	*The Apocrypha and Pseudepigrapha of the Old Testament.* Edited by R. H. Charles. 2 vols. Oxford, 1913
ATANT	Abhandlungen zur Theologie des Alten und Neuen Testaments
AUU	Acta Universitatis Upsaliensis
BASOR	*Bulletin of the American Schools of Oriental Research*
BCNH	Bibliothèque copte de Nag Hammadi
BDB	Brown, F., S. R. Driver, and C. A. Briggs. *A Hebrew and English Lexicon of the Old Testament.* Oxford, 1907
BETL	Bibliotheca ephemeridum theologicarum lovaniensium
BG	Berlin Gnostic Codex
BHK	*Biblia Hebraica.* Edited by R. Kittel. Stuttgart, 1905–6, 1925[2], 1937[3], 1951[4], 1973[16]
BJS	Brown Judaic Studies
BN	*Biblische Notizen*
BTB	*Biblical Theology Bulletin*
CAH	Cambridge Ancient History
ConBNT	Coniectanea biblica: New Testament Series

CBQ	*Catholic Biblical Quarterly*
CBQMS	Catholic Biblical Quarterly Monograph Series
CD	Cairo Genizah copy of the *Damascus Document*
CG	Cairensis Gnosticus
CRINT	Corpus rerum iudaicarum ad Novum Testamentum
CSCO	Corpus scriptorum christianorum orientalium. Edited by I. B. Chabot et al. Paris, 1903–
CSEL	Corpus scriptorum ecclesiasticorum latinorum
DJD	Discoveries in the Judaean Desert
DSD	*Dead Sea Discoveries*
ErJb	*Eranos-Jahrbuch*
EstBib	*Estudios biblicos*
GCS	Die griechische christliche Schriftsteller der ersten [drei] Jahrhunderte
GKC	*Gesenius' Hebrew Grammar.* Edited by E. Kautzsch. Translated by A. E. Cowley. 2d ed. Oxford, 1910
HAT	Handbuch zum Alten Testament
HBC	*Harper's Bible Commentary.* Edited by J. L. Mays et al. San Francisco, 1988
HR	*History of Religions*
HSM	Harvard Semitic Monographs
HSS	Harvard Semitic Studies
HTR	*Harvard Theological Review*
HTS	Harvard Theological Studies
HUCA	*Hebrew Union College Annual*
IDBSup	*Interpreter's Dictionary of the Bible: Supplementary Volume.* Edited by K. Crim. Nashville, 1976
JAAR	*Journal of the American Academy of Religion*
JAC	Jahrbuch für Antike und Christentum
JAOS	*Journal of the American Oriental Society*
JBL	*Journal of Biblical Literature*
JEA	*Journal of Egyptian Archaeology*
JJS	*Journal of Jewish Studies*
JQR	*Jewish Quarterly Review*
JR	*Journal of Religion*

JSHRZ	*Jüdische Schriften aus hellenistisch-römischer Zeit*
JSJ	*Journal of the Study of Judaism in the Persian, Hellenistic, and Roman Periods*
JSNT	*Journal for the Study of the New Testament*
JSNTSup	Journal for the Study of the New Testament: Supplement Series
JSOT	*Journal for the Study of the Old Testament*
JSOTSup	Journal for the Study of the Old Testament: Supplement Series
JSP	*Journal for the Study of the Pseudepigrapha*
JSPSup	Journal for the Study of the Pseudepigrapha: Supplement Series
JTS	*Journal of Theological Studies*
NHC	Nag Hammadi Codices
NHMS	Nag Hammadi and Manichaean Studies
NHS	Nag Hammadi Studies
NIB	*The New Interpreter's Bible*
NovTSup	Novum Testamentum Supplements
NPNF	*Nicene and Post-Nicene Fathers*
NTApoc	E. Hennecke and W. Schneemelcher, eds., *New Testament Apocrypha*, 2 vols. Philadelphia, 1963
NTOA	Novum Testamentum et Orbis Antiquus
NTS	*New Testament Studies*
Or	*Orientalia*
OTL	Old Testament Library
OTP	*Old Testament Pseudepigrapha*. Edited by J. H. Charlesworth. 2 vols. New York, 1983
PE	Eusebius, *Praeparatio Evangelica*
PG	Patrologia graeca [= Patrologiae cursus completus: Series graeca.] Edited by J.-P. Migne. 162 vols. Paris, 1857–86
PO	Patrologia orientalis
PSB	*Princeton Seminary Bulletin*
RAC	*Reallexikon für Antike und Christentum*. Edited by T. Kluser et al. Stuttgart, 1950–
RB	*Revue biblique*
RelSRev	*Religious Studies Review*
RevQ	*Revue de Qumran*
RHPR	*Revue d'histoire et de philosophie religieuses*

SAC	Studies in Antiquity and Christianity
SBLDS	Society of Biblical Literature Dissertation Series
SBLEJL	Society of Biblical Literature Early Judaism and Its Literature
SBLMS	Society of Biblical Literature Monograph Series
SBLSCS	Society of Biblical Literature Septuagint and Cognate Studies
SBLSP	*Society of Biblical Literature Seminar Papers*
SBLTT	Society of Biblical Literature Texts and Translations
SCS	Septuagint and Cognate Studies
Sem	*Semitica*
SNTU	Studien zum Neuen Testament und seiner Umwelt
SPB	Studia postbiblica
STDJ	*Studies on the Texts of the Desert of Judah*
SUNT	Studien zur Umwelt des Neuen Testaments
SVTP	Studia in Veteris Testamenti pseudepigrapha
TDNT	*Theological Dictionary of the New Testament.* Edited by G. Kittel and G. Friedrich. Translated by G. W. Bromiley. 10 vols. Grand Rapids, 1964–76
TLZ	*Theologische Literaturzeitung*
TS	*Theological Studies*
TSAJ	Texte und Studien zum antiken Judentum
TU	Texte und Untersuchungen
VC	*Vigiliae christianae*
VT	*Vetus Testamentum*
VTSup	Vetus Testamentum Supplements
WBC	Word Biblical Commentary
WUNT	Wissenschaftliche Untersuchungen zum Neuen Testament
WW	*Word and World*
ZAW	*Zeitschrift für die alttestamentliche Wissenschaft*
ZNW	*Zeitschrift für die neutestamentliche Wissenschaft und die Kunde der älteren Kirche*

1

The Suda and
the "Priesthood of Jesus"

William Adler

North Carolina State University

The Suda Lexicon, a Byzantine lexicon dating to the twelfth century, contains an unexpected entry *sub voce* Ἰησοῦς ὁ χριστὸς καὶ θεὸς ἡμῶν.[1] Instead of a biographical sketch of Jesus' life drawn from the canonical Gospels, the entry records a discussion between a Christian named Philip and a Jew named Theodosius. Set during the reign of the emperor Justinian, the story recounts Philip's sincere efforts to convert his friend to Christianity. Theodosius is not an intransigent unbeliever. To the contrary, he confides in Philip that for some time he has been convinced of the truth of Jesus' divine sonship. The only reason he wavers in his decision to convert is because he would have to sacrifice the power, luxuries, and privileges afforded him by the Jewish community.

Theodosius arrives at his conviction about Jesus' divinity not only through the Law and the Prophets. As an influential figure in the community, he has learned of a "secret" revealed only to a select few. The secret is preserved in a "codex [*sic*]" kept by the priests in the temple and hidden in Tiberias after the destruction of Jerusalem in 70 C.E. The codex, a registry of the names of Jewish priests along with the names of their parents, included the name of Jesus, described here as the son of the "virgin Mary and the living God."

A parallel version of this story, with some significant deviations, exists in the Arabic version of the *History of the Patriarchs of the Coptic Church of Alexandria* (hereafter *HP*). Entitled "The Priesthood of Christ," it was translated into English by B. Evetts and published in Patrologia orientalis.[2] The Suda's version (hereafter S.) was noted by A. Vassiliev in his *Anecdota Graeco-Byzantina*. In addition to this version, Vassiliev published two other versions: (1) a shorter version found

---

1. A. Adler, ed., *Suidae Lexicon* (Leipzig: Teubner, 1931), 2.620–25.
2. "The Priesthood of Christ" (trans. B. Evetts), in *History of the Patriarchs of the Coptic Church of Alexandria* (PO 1; Paris: Firmin-Didot, 1907), 120–34.

1

in *Cod. Otthobonian.* 408, fol. 170–72 (fifteenth to sixteenth century) (hereafter Gr. α); (2) *Cod. Mosquensis* X, fol. 85–88 (twelfth century) (hereafter Gr. β). This latter version is so close in content to the Suda's that Vassiliev published them in parallel columns.[3]

Despite the late date of the several recensions and the numerous amusing anachronisms, the story has interest for several reasons, not the least of which is its attempt to establish the legitimacy of Jesus' hereditary claim to the Jewish priesthood. To my knowledge, none of the Greek versions is available in English translation. In what follows, I offer an English translation of the Suda's entry, based on the text in Adler's edition of the lexicon. After that, I append some comments on its relationship to the other Greek versions as well as the Arabic version, and the complex of traditions that underlies the story.

Translation

Jesus, the Christ and our God: In the time of the most holy emperor Justinian there was a certain man, a leader of the Jews, whose name was Theodosius. He was known to a very great number of the Christians, including the aforementioned emperor himself, a believer. Around that time, there was a certain man, a Christian (whose name was Philip), a banker by trade.[4] He was aware of Theodosius's situation; and as he was holding him in great honor, he began to urge him on and advise him to become a Christian. One day, then, the previously mentioned Philip said the following to this Theodosius: "Why on earth do you, a man who is wise and possessed of an unerring understanding of what the Law and the Prophets proclaimed about the Lord Christ, not believe in him and become a Christian? For I am convinced concerning you, that although you are not unaware of what divinely inspired scriptures have proclaimed concerning the public advent of our Lord Christ, you beg off from becoming a Christian. Take care, then, to save your own soul, believing in the Savior and our Lord Jesus Christ, lest continuing in unbelief you might make yourself liable for eternal judgment."

After hearing what was said by the Christian to him, the Jew received him favorably, verbally expressed his gratitude to him, and responded to him as follows: "I accept your love by the favor of God, because you exert yourself out of your concern for the salvation of my soul, admonishing me to become a Christian. Therefore, as in the presence of God who knows the secrets of the hearts, and who sees guilelessly and without dissembling and with all truth, I will make this assertion to you: 'The Christ who was proclaimed in advance by the Law and

---

3. A. Vassiliev, *Anecdota Graeco-Byzantina* (Moscow, 1893), 1.58–72. Another version of the legend, apparently unknown to Vassiliev, is found in John of Euboea, *Sermo in conceptionem deiparae* (PG 96.1489B–1491B).

4. Text: τὴν μέθοδον ἀργυροπράτης; Gr. β: ἀργυροπράτης τὴν τέχνην.

the Prophets, the one who is worshiped by you Christians, has come.' Of this I am convinced and I confess it boldly, as to my genuine friend, and to one who is also constantly concerned to do good things for me. But because I am under the sway of human intention, I am not becoming a Christian and for this I condemn myself. For currently I am a Jew, a prince of the Jews, and enjoy great honor and many gifts and all the necessities for this life. Now I imagine that if I were to become a patriarch of the Catholic Church or to receive greater powers and dignities from you, I would not be deemed worthy of such treatment. To keep from losing, then, what are considered pleasures in this life, I disdain the life to come and in so doing act badly. But in order that I might show that my statement to you, my beloved friend, is truthful, I will entrust to you a secret, which has been kept hidden by us Hebrews. From it we know exactly that the Christ who is worshiped by you Christians is the one who has been proclaimed in advance by the Law and the Prophets; this we know not only from what has been publicly written, but from the secret that has been registered and hidden by us. The story of this secret is as follows:

"In ancient times, when the temple was established in Jerusalem, there was a practice among the Jews to arrange it that the priests in the temple were equal in number with the twenty-two letters of our alphabet. For this reason, we also number twenty-two divinely inspired books. There was, then, a codex (κῶδιξ) in the temple, in which were recorded the name of each of the twenty-two priests, and the name of his father and mother. Thus, when one of the priests died, the remaining priests would assemble in the temple, and from a common vote would appoint another priest in place of the priest who had died, thereby completing the number of the twenty-two priests. And it would be recorded in the codex, that on that day priest 'so and so' had passed away, the son of 'such and such' man and woman, and in his place priest 'so and so' was appointed. Now this custom was in force in the Jewish nation; and it so happened that at that time, during which Jesus was residing in Judea, one of the twenty-two priests died, before Jesus began to make himself known and to teach men to believe in him. So the remaining priests assembled to appoint another priest in place of the priest who died. When each priest proposed someone he believed worthy of becoming priest, the others rejected him for being deficient in virtue, on the basis of which he should be appointed priest. For if he was wise, and worthy both in his moral character and mode of life, but proved to be ignorant of the Law and the Prophets, he was judged unsuitable for the priesthood. So when many priests were in this way voted on and all were rejected, a certain priest stood up in their midst and said to the others: 'Look, many were nominated by us and found unfit for priesthood. Hear me, then, as I speak about one man who should be selected in place of the priest who died. For I suppose that none of you will be displeased by the vote cast by me.' When the remaining priests granted him permission, he said, 'It is my wish that Jesus, the son of Joseph the carpenter, replace the priest who died. Granted, he is a young man, but he is equipped in reason, mode of life, and worthy moral traits. And I suppose that there has never appeared a man such as him in reason, mode of life, or moral traits. And I think also that for all of you who live in Jerusalem, this is recognized and undeniable.'

"When they heard this statement, the other priests accepted the man and confirmed it by a vote, having said that Jesus was fit for priesthood more than any other man. Now some began to say of him that he was not from the tribe of Levi, but rather from the tribe of Judah. And under the assumption that he was the son of Joseph (for this was the way he was known by name among the Jews), everyone attested that Joseph was from the tribe of Judah, not from the tribe of Levi. And for this reason, since it was thought that he was not from the Levitical tribe, they prevented him from becoming a priest. Then the priest who nominated him replied to them that he was of mixed ancestry. For long ago, among the families of old, there was intermingling of the two tribes, and it was from this that the family of Joseph traced its lineage. So upon hearing this, the other priests consented to a vote. And by common consent all the priests who assembled determined to appoint Jesus as a replacement for the priest who had died. Now since there was a custom not only to register the name of the new priest in the codex, but the name of his father and mother as well, some of them said that they had first to call his parents and to learn from them their names, and to get a deposition from them that the one being chosen for the priesthood was their son. This was acceptable to all of them. The priest, then, who had previously nominated Jesus to be priest, said that his father Joseph had died, and that only his mother was still alive. So all of them agreed to bring his mother to the council (συνέδριον) and learn from her if she was the mother of Jesus and if she gave birth to him, and to hear the name of her husband, from whom she gave birth to Jesus. Since this was in fact agreeable to everyone, they summoned the mother of Jesus and said to her, 'Inasmuch as priest "so and so," the son of "so and so," has died, and we want to make your son Jesus his replacement, there is a practice that the name of the mother and father be registered. Tell us if Jesus is your son, and if you gave birth to him.' Now Mary heard this and answered the priests, 'Jesus is my son, this I acknowledge. For I gave birth to him, and both men and women can be found who will attest that I gave birth to him. But he does not have a father on this earth — let me assure you of this, since you want to know. For I was a virgin and living in Galilee; and an angel of God, when I was awake and not sleeping, came into the house where I was, and proclaimed the good news to me that I would give birth to a son from the Holy Spirit. And he instructed me to call him by the name Jesus. And even though I was a virgin, after seeing this vision I conceived and gave birth to Jesus, remaining a virgin up to now and after I gave birth.'

"Upon hearing this, the priests ordered trustworthy midwives to come and directed them to conduct an examination, to determine whether Mary was still really a virgin. And they were fully assured from their work and confirmed that she was a virgin. Now women were also discovered who had witnessed her giving birth, attesting that Jesus was her son. The priests were shocked at what was said by Mary and by those who had given witness concerning her giving birth. And they replied to Mary, 'Tell us frankly, that we might hear from your mouth, from whom he comes and whose son he is, so that we might thereby register him. The parents whom you tell us, we will register them, and no one else.' And she answered, 'I was the one who really did give birth to him; I did not know his father on this earth, rather I heard from the angel that he is the Son of God. So he is the son of me, the one named Mary, and the Son of God, and I am unmarried and a virgin.' When they heard this, the priests brought forth the codex and added the following in writing: 'On this day, priest "so and so" died, the son of "so and so," and by common vote of all of us, Jesus has become a priest in his place, Jesus the Son of the living God and Mary the virgin.' And this codex was rescued from the temple through the exertion of those among the Jews who were taking out the primary objects at the time of the capture of the temple and Jerusalem, and it was deposited in Tiberias. And this secret was made known to very few and to the believers of our nation. Therefore, it was also revealed to me, since I am a leader and teacher of the Jewish nation. For it is not only from the Law and the Prophets that we are assured that the Christ who is worshiped by you Christians is himself the Son of the living God, who came to earth for the salvation of the world; but we also have this assurance from the register, which is preserved even up to this very day and is deposited in Tiberias."

Now the Christian, after hearing what was said to him by the Jew, was moved by divine zeal and said to the Jew, "I am reporting what you said right away to the believing and pious emperor, so that he might send to Tiberias and make known the codex, of which you speak, so as to refute the unbelief of the Jews." But the Jew said to the Christian, "Why do you want to bring judgment on his soul and report this to the emperor and then not obtain the desired object? For if something like this happens, a great war is bound to occur, and bloodshed will immediately ensue. And then, if they see themselves being subdued, they will set fire to the place in which the codex is stored, and we will labor in vain in not succeeding in obtaining the desired object; rather, we shall only be the cause of bloodshed. For out of love for you, and since you are a genuine friend, I have revealed these things to you, so that I might assure you that I do not reject Christianity out of ignorance, but out of empty glory." After hearing this from the Jew, the Christian was also confident that what he said was true. But he did not reveal this story to the emperor Justinian, a believer; this was so that, incited by zeal, that great emperor, a man of faith, might not cause bloodshed, without the desired object then being successfully obtained. But to many of his acquaintances and friends, he did reveal this story.

We have learned the story from those who heard it from the aforementioned

Philip the banker, and have expended not a little care in our desire to know if in fact the Jew uttered the truth in his story about such a registry. So we have found that Josephus, the author of the *Conquest of Jerusalem*, whom Eusebius Pamphilou recalls at length in his *Ecclesiastical History*, says clearly in his memoirs of the captivity that Jesus officiated in the temple with the priests. Having thus discovered that Josephus, a man of antiquity, who was not long after the time of the apostles, says this, we searched to find this story confirmed as well from divinely inspired scriptures. So we found in the Gospel according to Luke that Jesus entered into the Jewish synagogue and a book was given to him, and he read the prophet Isaiah which says, "The spirit of the Lord is upon me, because he anointed me to proclaim good news to the poor" (Luke 4:18). Now we have deduced that if the Christ Jesus did not have some position of service among the Jews, a book would not have been given to him in the synagogue to read for the hearing of the people. For among us Christians, it is not possible for someone to read in the churches books of divinely inspired scriptures to the laity, unless he is enrolled in the clergy. And from what was written by Josephus and recorded by the evangelist Luke, we know that Theodosius the Jew, when he told the aforementioned story to Philip the banker, did not fabricate it. Rather he truthfully confided in Philip, since he was a true friend, the secret hidden among the Jews. (But Chrysostom does not accept at all this priesthood for Jesus.)

Commentary

Context, Date, and Characterization

Although all four versions clearly share a common origin, there are notable differences in specifics. Gr. α gives only the core story of Jesus' appointment as priest, without the framing narrative about Theodosius and Philip and the former's revelation of the priestly registry stored in Tiberias. In *HP*, Theodosius is a priest, whereas the other two Greek versions (S. and Gr. β) describe him only as a leader in the Jewish community. His Christian counterpart, Philip, a banker in the two Greek versions, is identified as a silversmith in *HP*. Unlike the Greek versions, which provide no location for their meeting, HP fixes the location of their conversation in Syria, after Philip had sailed there. The date of their meeting is also different. *HP* assigns their meeting to the time of Julian, "the unbelieving prince." This dating is curiously inconsistent with Philip's subsequent plan to reveal the existence of the secret codex to "our religious prince, so that he may send and bring to light the genealogy written in the register and the Jews' want of faith."[5] The two Greek versions (S. and Gr. β), which put their meeting in the time of the emperor Justinian, produce a more acceptable resolution to the story. Naturally, the pious emperor Justinian would be keenly interested in recovering the

---

5. *HP* 131.

codex for the strengthening of the Christian faith. On the other hand, the discussion of the bloodshed bound to occur if Justinian were to attempt to recover the "codex" raises the possibility that the version of the story known to the Suda was composed at a time when Palestine was no longer under the control of the Byzantines.

The several forms of the story present a cordial relationship between the Jew and the Christian, repeatedly stressing their mutual affection. While the Greek versions state that Theodosius's reasons for avoiding conversion are strictly material and self-interested, they inject a touch of pathos into the story by having Theodosius rue this character flaw to his friend. The representation of Theodosius in *HP* is more sympathetic. As in the Greek versions, Theodosius acknowledges that at the root of his failure to convert is a defect in his character born of materialism. But the author heaps much of the blame on the Christian community. The "greater part of the Jewish community," Theodosius says, "believes in the truth of the Messiah and in his miracles more firmly than you do.... We know and believe in Christ's miracles and works more firmly than you Christians." What prevents en masse baptism of the Jews is the hostility of Christians themselves, many of whom liken the baptism of Jews to the baptism of asses. And why convert to Christianity, when Christians conduct themselves so poorly and have been "to this day" so unsuccessful in bringing Gentiles into the church?[6] *HP* evidently meant these words, placed in the mouth of a learned and influential Jew, to improve internal discipline, to chastise Christians about their anti-Jewish feeling, and to redouble their missionary efforts.

Jesus' Priesthood and the Secret Jewish Codex

S. states expressly that Jesus' selection as priest occurred in Judea before he began his public ministry.[7] The purpose of this statement is to explain how, in the Gospels, Jesus appropriated for himself the privileges of priesthood. As an example of this, *HP* mentions his conduct in the Jerusalem temple, in which he makes a scourge of cords and drives out the temple traffickers.[8] One other example, found only in the Greek versions, concerns Luke's story of Jesus' appearance in the synagogue in Nazareth and his recitation of a passage from the Book of Isaiah (Luke 4:14–22). S. and Gr. β assume anachronistically that, since only priests can read passages from scriptures to Christian laity, then this same prohibition must have applied to Jewish practice as well. This explanation demonstrates that the authors

---

6. *HP* 121–22.

7. But cf. Gr. β (Vassiliev, *Anecdota Graeco-Byzantina*, 1.64), which states that the vote to appoint Jesus as priest occurred when Jesus' ministry was already beginning.

8. *HP* 133. See also Gr. α (in Vassiliev, *Anecdota Graeco-Byzantina*, 1.59): "If he [Jesus] were not a priest, he would not have cast out the vessels of food from the temple and said to the priests, 'You shall not make the house of my father a house of utensils.'" The same text mentions Jesus' teaching in the temple, when he was asked about the woman caught in adultery (John 8:1–11).

no longer grasped the connection of Jesus' actions with priesthood. The Isaiah passage that Jesus reads refers to an "anointing by the Spirit of the Lord" (Isa. 61:1). Among certain Christian interpreters (including Eusebius), the anointing described in Luke proved Jesus' superiority to the Jewish high priesthood.[9] But here, the passage from Luke is cited to demonstrate that when Jesus' ministry began he had already been consecrated as a priest according to Jewish law.

In the actual story of Jesus' consecration as priest, all the versions speak anachronistically of a temple "codex" containing the names of the priests, and its subsequent removal to Tiberias after the conquest of Jerusalem.[10] They also contain the same peculiar details about the twenty-two priests, although only S. and Gr. β explain this number as equal to the letters of the Hebrew alphabet and the canonical books of the Hebrew Bible. The enumeration of twenty-two priests was probably derived from a reference in the Book of Nehemiah (12:1–7, 12–21) to twenty-two postexilic priests and twenty-two priestly heads.

The Jewish priests initially resist Jesus' consecration as priest on the grounds that Joseph was from the tribe of Judah and Mary was descended from David. To answer this objection, the story in all its forms appeals to the idea of mixing between the two tribes in ancient times. *HP* gives a precise example of this intermingling when it mentions an "alliance by marriage between Aaron and the tribe of Judah, to which the prophet David bore witness."[11] This is obviously a reference to the marriage of Aaron and Elisheba (Exod. 6:23), which is cited here to show that from the very beginning the offspring of Aaron were of mixed Levitical and Judahite descent.

But there are notable differences in presentation. In the Greek versions, the legitimation of Jesus' Levitical heritage arises from Joseph, who is said to be of mixed Levitical and Judahite heritage. *HP* presents the matter quite differently. In this latter case, it is Mary who is "connected with both tribes." In certain respects, *HP* presents a more consistent picture. Since the registration of Jesus as priest named only Mary as Jesus' earthly parent, Joseph's alleged mixed Levitical/Judahite lineage would have little probative value. It would also be difficult to see how the Davidic genealogies of Joseph found in the canonical Gospels reflect ancient mixing between the two tribes. By contrast, the Levitical lineage of Mary is at least intimated by the Gospel of Luke; this work names Mary as a relative of Elizabeth, the latter of whom is described as a "daughter of Aaron" (Luke 1:5, 36). At the same time, Mary's mixed lineage would hardly be conclusive proof of

---

9. See Eusebius, *Ecclesiastical History* (hereafter *HE*) 1.3.13–14. See also below, p. 10.

10. In the version of John of Euboea (PG 96.1492A), the author refers to the registry not as a codex, but as a τόμος (which could mean either a "scroll" or "volume"). The author also states only that the registry is preserved "up to this day" among the Jews, without specifically naming Tiberias. He also adds that at the second coming of Christ, the registry will be opened and read as a refutation of the Jews.

11. *HP* 125.

Jesus' fitness for priesthood. Since fitness for this office was established paternally, there was no requirement that priests marry a woman of the tribe of Levi.[12]

After receiving Theodosius's account of Jesus' priesthood, Philip seeks to confirm it from other sources. In addition to the Gospels, he finds further corroboration in Josephus's *Jewish War*.[13] According to *HP*, Josephus wrote that "Jesus was seen to enter the temple with the priests at the time of the sanctification."[14] S. and Gr. β attribute to Josephus the claim that Jesus "officiated in the temple with the priests." Statements to this effect do not appear in the text of Josephus's *Jewish War*, and it is thus likely that this report originated in an interpolated version of Josephus's history.

The Jewish Christian Provenance of the Story

The central contention of the story, namely Jesus' hereditary fitness for the Levitical priesthood, is actually well-documented in Byzantine Greek sources.[15] The tradition, however, did not command universal assent. Gr. α obliquely acknowledges this in asserting that "many are unaware" of Jesus' enrollment in the temple as a Levitical priest. S. also acknowledges some misgivings about the truth of the whole story, appending to it the comment that John Chrysostom (a highly esteemed figure in Byzantine Christianity) "does not accept this priesthood for Jesus."[16] The Byzantine chronicler Michael Glycas registers even greater skepticism. Since in his view Jesus was unknown when his public ministry began, Glycas wonders how his reputation could have already been so widely celebrated. "[I]f before his baptism he was entirely unknown," Glycas writes, "then as to those stories (wherever they turn up) about the alleged water of the conviction (ἐλεγμοῦ) and the actual high priesthood which they say Christ received from the Jews, think nothing of them and throw them away."[17]

---

12. In Gr. α (Vassiliev, *Anecdota Graeco-Byzantina*, 1.58), the Jewish temple priests initially reject Jesus' appointment as priest for the following reason: "But Joseph is not from Levi, and Mary is descended from David (for the mother of God [θεοτόκος] was called ἐξότονος)." Since the priests had not yet learned that Mary was the "mother of God," this statement was probably inserted as a parenthetical remark. The word ἐξότονος is a *hapax legomenon*, and its significance in the present context is unclear.

13. In describing Josephus as the author of the *Conquest of Jerusalem* (τῆς ἁλώσεως Ἰεροσολύμων), S. is simply following the conventional title found in most of the Greek manuscripts of the *Jewish War*.

14. *HP* 133.

15. For the relevant sources, see R. Laurentin, *Maria Ecclesia Sacerdotium* (Paris: Nouvelles Éditions Latines, 1952), 66–73.

16. S. does not specify where Chrysostom rejected this view. In several places in his writings, however, Chrysostom polemically asserts that Jesus was a non-Levitical priest. See, for example, *Against the Jews* 7.4–5 (PG 48.922).

17. Michael Glycas, *Annales* (ed. I. Bekker; Bonn: Weber, 1836), 394.12–16. "The water of conviction" refers to the test to determine if a woman is guilty of adultery (Num. 5:16–28). The version of the story that Glycas knows apparently recounted the administering of this test by the priests to determine if Mary was speaking the truth about Jesus' father. For the administering of this test to

Disputes arising from the claim that Jesus possessed a mixed Judahite and Levitical lineage qualifying him for the temple priesthood have roots in the early Church. In his *Epistle to Aristides* (third century), Julius Africanus speaks con-temptuously about a school of interpreters who had claimed, falsely in Africanus's view, that the discrepancies between the genealogies of Jesus in the Gospels of Matthew and Luke reflected Jesus' mixed Levitical and Judahite heritage; in this way, they revealed a veiled message about his dual role as priest and king.[18] By the fourth century, the idea that Jesus was of mixed priestly and royal descent was well-known; according to Eusebius, it was held by many men of renown.[19] Since Eusebius himself personally rejected this view, it is thus all the more striking that three of the versions of Jesus' enrollment as temple priest cite Eusebius's *Ecclesiastical History* as a corroborating witness.[20] In that work, Eusebius does speak at length of Jesus' priesthood. But this is only in the context of demonstrating that Jesus' priesthood both differed from and exceeded the traditional Jewish priest-hood. Jesus, Eusebius writes, "received from none the symbols and types of the high priesthood, nor did he trace his physical descent from the race of priests." Whereas our story of Jesus' priesthood cites his reading from Isaiah as evidence that Jesus had been previously consecrated as a temple priest, Eusebius cites the same episode to prove that Jesus' anointing "indicated his peculiar distinction and superiority to those who in the past had been more materially anointed as types."[21] One conspicuous difference concerns their respective interpretations of Ps. 110:4. Two of the versions (Gr. α and *HP*) state that Jesus' appointment as priest in the Jerusalem temple fulfilled the famous verse in Psalm 110, "You are priest forever after the order of Melchizedek."[22] By contrast, Eusebius, following the Epistle to the Hebrews, cites precisely the same verse as proof that Jesus was not "anointed physically by the Jews or even that he was of the tribe of those who hold priesthood."[23] The pronounced difference in perspectives invites the conclusion that the representation of Jesus as Levitical priest arose in heterodox circles dating at least to the early third century C.E.

In his brief comments on the three Greek recensions of the story, Vassiliev

---

Mary by the temple priests, see also the *Protevangelium of James* 16.1 (trans. R. McLean Wilson), in *New Testament Apocrypha*, ed. W. Schneemelcher (Louisville: Westminster/John Knox, 1991), 1.432.

18. Julius Africanus, *Epistle to Aristides* 54.25–55.1 (ed. W. Reichardt; TU 34.3; Leipzig: Hinrichs, 1909).

19. See Eusebius, *Supplementa Quaestionum ad Stephanum* (PG 22.973AB).

20. The Greek versions state only that Eusebius mentions at length Josephus's account of the fall of Jerusalem in his *Ecclesiastical History*; in doing so they were only attempting to assert the reliability of Josephus as a historian. *HP* goes a bit farther. In this version, Philip takes the report of the hidden codex to an assembly of the church, including bishops and monks. They confirm the story of Jesus' priesthood, not only from Josephus, but from Eusebius as well, who, they say, "mentions this matter in several passages in the history of the Church" (133).

21. Eusebius, *Hist. eccl.* 1.3.13–15.

22. *HP* 131; Gr. α (Vassiliev, *Anecdota Graeco-Byzantina*, 1.69).

23. Eusebius, *Hist. eccl.* 1.3.18.

noted that the claims about Jesus' mixed Judahite and Levitical lineage bear certain similarities with portions of the *Testaments of the Twelve Patriarchs*. He conjectured that the story was rooted in a legend much earlier than its present setting in the age of Justinian.[24] Independently of him, Theodor Zahn argued that the Christology of Jesus' mixed Levitical/Judahite ancestry underlying the story originated in a very ancient Jewish Christian tradition of the Jerusalem church, which in Zahn's words had been deformed into nonsense by subsequent efforts to integrate it with the developing doctrine of Jesus' Davidic ancestry.[25] There is no need to rehearse all the evidence in support of that claim, which I have set forth in a previous article.[26] One tradition, however, about Jesus' brother James is especially relevant for our present purposes. According to an ancient tradition already attested in the second century, James made regular intercession on behalf of his people in the Jerusalem temple.[27] In attempting to explain how James, the brother of Jesus, was permitted to enter the holy of holies once a year and wear the priestly miter, Epiphanius reports that James was a "distinguished member of the priesthood, because the two tribes were linked exclusively to one another (αἱ δύο φυλαὶ συνήπτοντο μόναι πρὸς ἀλλήλας), the royal tribe to the priestly one and the priestly to the royal, just as earlier, in the time of the exodus, Nahshon the phylarch took as his wife the Elisheba of old, [the] daughter of Aaron [sic]."[28] The striking symmetry in pedigree between Jesus and James again points to the existence of an early Jewish Christian tradition about their respective qualifications to discharge sacerdotal functions in the Jerusalem temple.

There is thus much to commend Vassiliev's conjecture that the story about Jesus' consecration as temple priest owes its origins to a Jewish convert to Christianity. Other features of the story point in the same direction. In contrast to the critique of Gentile Christians for their disdain of baptized Jews, Jews with leanings to Christianity are depicted sympathetically.[29] Of particular interest is Theodosius's revelation about the temple registry hidden in Tiberias. By the fourth century, Tiberias had gained a reputation for its repositories of secret Jewish books, some of them corroborative of Christian doctrine. In his *Panarion*, Epipha-

---

24. Vassiliev, *Anecdota Graeco-Byzantina*, 1.xxv–xxvi, echoing a statement made earlier by J. K. Thilo, *Codex apocryphus Novi Testamenti* (Leipzig: Vogel, 1831), 375. On the messiah of mixed Levitical and Judahite lineage in the *Testaments of the Twelve Patriarchs*, see *T. Gad* 8.1–2: "Honor Judah and Levi, because from them the Lord will raise up a Savior for Israel"; also *T. Dan* 5.10; *T. Sim.* 7.1–3; *T. Levi* 2.11.

25. T. Zahn, *Forschungen zur Geschichte des neutestamentlichen Kanons* (Leipzig: A. Deichert, 1900). 6.329 (n. 2).

26. W. Adler, "Exodus 6:23 and the High Priest from the Tribe of Judah," *JTS* 48 (1997): 24–47.

27. See Eusebius, *Hist. eccl.* 2.23.6 (quoting the second-century Jewish Christian Hegesippus).

28. Epiphanius, *Panarion* 78.11.13.5–6 (ed. K. Holl; GCS 37; Leipzig: Hinrichs, 1933). On James's supplication in the Jerusalem temple on behalf of the Jewish nation, see also Eusebius, *Hist. eccl.* 2.23.6 (quoting Hegesippus). Notice Epiphanius's misrepresentation of the Judahite phylarch Nahshon (not Aaron) as Elisheba's husband. For the same error, see the Suda, s.v. "Ναασσών" (Adler), 3.342.

29. See above, pp. 5–6.

nius writes of Jews in Tiberias who, like Theodosius, concealed their Christian sympathies out of fear, obstinacy, or high standing in the Jewish community. The path to their conversion allegedly began with books preserved in Jewish storehouses in Tiberias. As an example of one such Jewish convert to Christianity, Epiphanius's refutation of the Ebionites mentions a certain Joseph. After becoming progressively more interested in and troubled by Christianity, Joseph witnessed the deathbed baptism of the Jewish patriarch. Later, to satisfy his curiosity, he opened a sealed treasury in Tiberias, and found there Hebrew versions of Matthew, John, and Acts of the Apostles. Yet he remained obstinate, even after experiencing two visions of Jesus and curing an insane man of his afflictions by performing Christian rites. The parallels between the stories of Joseph and Theodosius are arresting. Like Theodosius, Joseph is a man of standing and integrity, who in his capacity as "apostle" served as adviser to the Jewish patriarch in Tiberias. Even in the face of overwhelming evidence of the truths of Christianity, his high office in the Jewish community of Tiberias of the fourth century initially deterred him from converting. The only difference between the two figures is in the resolution of their spiritual conflicts. Finally won over to the faith, Joseph receives baptism; appointed to high office by Constantine, he receives authorization from the emperor to build a church in Tiberias. Theodosius, on the other hand, keeps his Christian sympathies to himself. Preferring to retain the pleasures of his present life, he shuns both the honors bound to come his way from the emperor and the Christian community, as well as the rewards of the life to come.[30]

---

30. Epiphanius, *Panarion* 30.8.1–12.10 (ed. K. Holl; GCS 25 Leipzig: Hinrichs, 1915).

2

A Hellenistic Jewish
Source on the Essenes in
Philo, *Every Good Man Is Free* 75–91
and Josephus, *Antiquities* 18.18–22

———— ◆ ————

Randal A. Argall
Jamestown College

The importance of engaging in a literary and source analysis of the Essene passages known to us from antiquity has long been recognized. Jerome Murphy-O'Connor wrote in 1986 that "a serious literary analysis of all the ancient texts referring to the Essenes . . . is a prerequisite for any valid comparative study. Sources and supplements need to be determined and not merely speculated about."[1] Murphy-O'Connor was impressed by the contribution of Morton Smith in arguing that Josephus, *J.W.* 2.119–61, and Hippolytus, *Haer.* 9.18–28, go back to a common

I presented some of these ideas in a paper for the Hellenistic Judaism Section at the AAR/SBL meeting in Orlando, Florida, in 1998. I must thank my colleague, Stephen Reed, for offering insightful criticism.

1. "The Judean Desert," in *Early Judaism and Its Modern Interpreters* (ed. Robert A. Kraft and George W. E. Nickelsburg; Philadelphia: Fortress, 1986), 125. The ancient texts in view have been reproduced in G. Vermes and M. D. Goodman, *The Essenes: According to the Classical Sources* (Sheffield: JSOT, 1989). That Todd Beall did not heed Murphy-O'Connor's advice casts a shadow over his exhaustive comparison between the Essene material in Josephus and the Qumran literature. Beall writes, "While mention will be made of sections in Philo that correspond to each passage in Josephus, a detailed comparison between Philo and Josephus . . . is beyond the scope of this study" (*Josephus' Description of the Essenes Illustrated by the Dead Sea Scrolls* [Cambridge: Cambridge University Press, 1988], 11). But if Josephus is editing one source used also by Hippolytus and a second shared also with Philo, how can one go directly to the Qumran texts without attempting to first reconstruct these two sources? Much better is the methodology of Gabriele Boccaccini, *Beyond the Essene Hypothesis: The Parting of the Ways between Qumran and Enochic Judaism* (Grand Rapids: Eerdmans, 1998), who first analyzes the Essenes as they are portrayed in ancient historical narrative (21–49) before attempting a comparative study with Enochic and Qumran literature (165–96).

source.[2] In his seminal essay, Smith also suggested that Josephus, *Ant.* 18.18–22, and Philo, *Every Good Man* 75–91, derive from a common source rather than that Josephus is dependent on Philo.[3] It is this suggestion that I wish to investigate. The recent work of Stephen Goranson and Roland Bergmeier will be utilized to advance our understanding of the source behind *Ant.* 18.18–22 and *Every Good Man* 75–91. A minimalist reconstruction of the *topoi* contained in the source will be offered at the end of this article.

Goranson suggests that Philo and Josephus "got some of their reports on Essenes from Strabo, who in turn drew on Posidonius."[4] The source of the account in Pliny's *Natural History* 5.73 is Marcus Vipsanius Agrippa.[5] These suggestions offer us a good starting point, but the source history is probably a bit more complex. First, it seems likely that a major report from Strabo was edited and expanded by a Hellenistic Jewish author before coming into the hands of Philo and Josephus.[6] That is, the content and character of the source shared by Philo and Josephus reflect the interests of Hellenistic Judaism and offer much more than we might expect even from a sympathetic Stoic philosopher and geographer. Second, there are some intriguing possible connections between the source in Pliny and the putative Hellenistic Jewish source known to Philo and Josephus. The connections could be explained by the fact that Strabo used the work of Marcus Agrippa, in addition to that of Posidonius.[7] A diagram of the source history would then look like that on the following page:

---

2. Morton Smith, "The Description of the Essenes in Josephus and the Philosophumena," *HUCA* 29 (1958): 273–313. Smith's conclusion is accepted by John J. Collins, "Essenes," *ABD* 2.619–26. See also Matthew Black, in "The Account of the Essenes in Hippolytus and Josephus," *The Background of the NT and its Eschatology* (ed. W. Davies and D. Daube; Cambridge, 1956), 172–75.

3. Smith, "Description of the Essenes," 278–79. Louis H. Feldman, in a footnote to his Loeb translation of *Antiquities,* suggested that Josephus in *Ant.* 18.18–22 may have drawn upon Philo, *Every Good Man* 75–91 (*Josephus IX* [LCL; Cambridge: Harvard University Press, 1965], 15, n. d). Later, when commenting on F. H. Colson's Loeb translation of Philo's *Every Good Man,* Feldman wrote that the similarities between Josephus and Philo, which Colson had listed in an appendix, may derive from a common source (*Josephus and Modern Scholarship (1937–1980)* [New York: Walter de Gruyter, 1984], 593). For the argument that Josephus in *Ant.* 18 is dependent upon Philo's account in *Every Good Man,* see Tessa Rajak, "Ciò Che Flavio Giuseppe Vide: Josephus and the Essenes," in *Josephus and the History of the Greco-Roman Period: Essays in Memory of Morton Smith* (ed. Fausto Parente and Joseph Sievers; SPB 41; Leiden: Brill, 1994), 141–60, esp. 147. Rajak also believes that the long Essene passage in *J.W.* 2 reflects Josephus's own experience and was organized and shaped by his own hand (contra Smith).

4. Stephen Goranson, "Posidonius, Strabo, and Marcus Vipsanius Agrippa as Sources on Essenes," *JJS* 45 (1994): 295.

5. Ibid., 297–98.

6. See my treatment of Bergmeier below.

7. Goranson points out that Pliny and Strabo used Agrippa's work (Goranson, "Posidonius, Strabo, and Marcus Vipsanius Agrippa," 297).

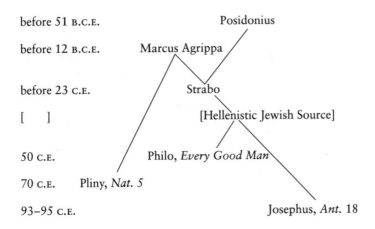

before 51 B.C.E.   Posidonius

before 12 B.C.E.   Marcus Agrippa

before 23 C.E.   Strabo

[   ]   [Hellenistic Jewish Source]

50 C.E.   Philo, *Every Good Man*

70 C.E.   Pliny, *Nat. 5*

93–95 C.E.   Josephus, *Ant.* 18

What evidence exists to support this reconstruction of the source history? Let us consider the following parallels:

Pliny, *Nat.* 5.73	Philo, *Every Good Man* 77	Josephus, *Ant.* 18.20
On the west side of the Dead Sea, but out of range of the noxious exhalations of the coast, is the solitary tribe of the Essenes, which is remarkable beyond all the other tribes in the whole world, as it has no women and has renounced all sexual desire, has no money, and has only palm trees for company. Day by day the throng of refugees is recruited to an equal number by numerous accessions of persons tired of life and driven thither by the waves of fortune to adopt their manners. Thus through thousands of ages (incredible to relate) a race in which no one is born lives on forever; so prolific for their advantage is other men's weariness of life!	For while they stand almost alone in the whole of mankind in that they have become moneyless and landless by deliberate action rather than by lack of good fortune, they are esteemed exceedingly rich, because they judge frugality with contentment to be, as indeed it is, an abundance of wealth.	They deserve admiration in contrast to all others who claim their share of virtue because such qualities as theirs were never found before among any Greek or barbarian people, nay not even briefly, but have been among them in constant practice and never interrupted since they adopted them from of old. Moreover, they hold their possessions in common, and the wealthy man receives no more enjoyment from his property that the man who possesses nothing.

These passages display a cluster of similar *topoi*. The subject matter itself is common to the ethnography and moralizing tendency of the time.[8] (1) The Essenes are

---

8. Some of the similarities between Pliny on the one hand, and Philo and Josephus on the other, are noted by M. Stern, *Greek and Latin Authors on Jews and Judaism* (3 vols., Jerusalem: Israel Academy

praised. (2) The uniqueness of the sect is emphasized in comparison to all other peoples. (3) The absence of money (or in Josephus, the usual function of wealth) is stated. (4) The issue of whether sect membership is voluntary or involuntary is raised. Philo and Josephus use the same word (ἐπιτηδεύσει/ἐπιτηδεύεσθαι) for the voluntary decision to join the sect. Pliny has no Latin term for "adoption," but he is clearly describing people who have committed to certain customs (*ad mores*). Moreover, in Pliny's source this commitment is regarded as involuntary since the Essenes are said to have been driven (*agitat*) to these customs "by the waves of fortune" (*fortunae fluctibus*).[9] Interestingly, the Philo passage states that the Essene practices come from deliberate action rather than "by lack of good fortune" (ἐνδείᾳ εὐτυχίας). Is Philo reproducing his source on this particular point? If so, the Hellenistic Jewish author upon whom Philo depends had already corrected the older core material that is reflected in Pliny. (5) The antiquity of the sect is stated. This topic is missing in the Philo passage printed above, but appears later in a section in which Philo is freely creating while at the same time drawing upon some source material (*Every Good Man* 80–84). Philo mentions that Essenes are trained by the "laws of their fathers" (80) and in their philosophical study "they emulate the tradition of the past" (82; cf. *Ant.* 18.11).

The similarities in content between these three passages could simply be attributable to the fact that such *topoi* are common to the literary form of ethnographic descriptions. However, there are a couple of tantalizing literary clues which may indicate the presence of a core of older material. Philo and Josephus use the same word to describe the decision to commit to the practices of the sect. This could be regarded as a coincidence, until we notice that the description of the voluntary decision continues in Philo with the language of "fortune," which directly contravenes what is written in Pliny. These facts at least raise the possibility that the Hellenistic Jewish source known to Philo and Josephus contained a core of older material also used by Pliny. This older material identified the Essenes with the Qumran community. It praised them for their uniqueness, absence of money, and celibacy (see below). This core material also seems to have poked some lighthearted fun at the sect in ways that called into question both its voluntary nature and its antiquity (see Pliny). Ultimately, this older core material may derive from Marcus Agrippa, as suggested by Goranson. The Hellenistic Jewish source, reflected in Philo and Josephus, gives evidence in at least two basic ways of editorial work on the older material. First, as I have just argued, it stressed the

---

of Sciences and Humanities, 1974–84), 1.479–81. On the standard *topoi* of ethnographic descriptions, see Gregory Sterling, "'Athletes of Virtue': An Analysis of the Summaries in Acts (2:41–47; 4:32–35; 5:12–16)" *JBL* 113 (1994): 679–96, who treats several classical texts, including the Essene descriptions of Philo and Josephus.

9. Contra Boccaccini, *Beyond the Essene Hypothesis*, 23: "With much admiration Pliny also emphasizes that nothing else but a personal choice leads to membership: 'those whom, wearied by the fluctuations of fortune, life leads to adopt their customs, stream in great number' (*Nat.* 5.73)." But the verb translated "leads" (*agitat*) means to "drive on, impel" and is commonly used for cattle!

voluntary nature of the sect. Second, it eliminated the geographical references to the vicinity of the Dead Sea. This was done for an obvious reason. The Hellenistic Jewish author was aware that the Essene movement was much larger and broader than the solitary community which lived by the Dead Sea. In fact, it was this author who supplied the number 4,000 for the size of the sect and placed them in communities (plural).

This last point raises the issue of the ways in which the Hellenistic Jewish author expanded the older material. A literary analysis of the similarities between Philo, *Every Good Man* 75–91, and Josephus, *Ant.* 18.18–22, which have no parallels in Pliny, should reveal the contributions of this author. Much of this literary work has been done by Bergmeier, although he comes at the task from a different direction. Bergmeier sets out to investigate the Essene sources used by Josephus and concludes that there are four:

1. An anecdotal source which, since it does not reflect a Jewish standpoint, probably derives from the world history of Nicholas of Damascus. It includes the stories of a certain Judas of the Essene group (*Ant.* 13.311–13) and a certain Simon of the sect of the Essenes (*J.W.* 2.113). Another anecdote, that of a certain Essene named Manaemus = Menahem (*Ant.* 15.373–79) is different in that it displays a Hellenistic Jewish spirit and an Alexandrian Jewish manner of speech.

2. A three-school source which described the three philosophies of the Jews in the sequence Pharisees, Sadducees, and Essenes (*J.W.* 2.119; *Ant.* 13.171; 18.11). In content, this source contained doxographical elements concerning fate, the soul, and character.

3. A Hellenistic Jewish Essaean source was used by Josephus in *J.W.* 2 and *Ant.* 18, and by Philo in *Every Good Man* 75–91 and *Hypothetica* 11.1–18.

4. A Pythagorean-Essene source is detectable in Josephus, *J.W.* 2, and in Philo's account of the Therapeutae in *The Contemplative Life*, as well as in Pliny's *Nat.* 5.15.73.

It is only the Hellenistic Jewish Essaean (=Essene) source which concerns us here.[10] The profile of this source has been sketched by Bergmeier, and in his view it displays the following structure and content. The opening includes an etymology of the name "Essene" and commends the sect for striving for virtue. The body of the source presents details related to several topics: celibacy; the numerical size of the sect and its existence in villages and cities; farming and

---

10. For a thorough review of the book, see John J. Collins, review of Roland Bergmeier, *Die Essener-Berichte des Flavius Josephus, JBL* 113 (1994): 525–26. I will simply use the name "Essenes" and not raise the question whether the source named the sect *Essenoi* as in *Ant.* 18 or *Essaioi* as in the Philo texts.

crafts; rejection of commerce and renunciation of possessions, including slaves; elected officers, including the treasurer; community meals; mutual service; a love of peace and rejection of force; an unconditional love of truth; prohibition on the swearing of oaths; adherence to the laws of the fathers/holy scripture; and special Sabbath observance. The source concludes with references to the responses of political powers to the community. The powers-that-be both honor and persecute the Essenes. The persecution of the Essenes is portrayed in the language of the martyr theme known from the Books of the Maccabees. The final note of the source sounds the theme of the opening, i.e., praise for the high excellence of the sect.

I wish to make a general observation on the topics Bergmeier has included in the Hellenistic Jewish source and then to argue specifically for one topic he has omitted but that should be included. First, the profile of the source is somewhat richer than might have been expected because Bergmeier has included Josephus, *J.W.* 2, and Philo, *Hypothetica* 11.1–18, in his attempt to sketch it. It is possible that Josephus was acquainted with the Hellenistic Jewish source earlier than 93–95 c.e. (when he wrote the *Antiquities*) and that some elements from it appear in the *War*, although the latter is drawn largely from a different source (shared with Hippolytus). Philo, for his part, did in all likelihood use the same source when writing *Hypothetica*, and may well include some topics in *Hypothetica* which he passed over in *Every Good Man.* A good example of the last point is the reference to celibacy. In fact, one of Philo's statements on celibacy in *Hypothetica* (if we extract his commentary) is conceptually close to the statement in Pliny:

Philo, *Hypothetica* 11.14	"they eschew marriage . . . because they particularly practice continence."
Pliny, *Nat.* 5	"it has no women and has renounced all sexual desire."

The picture in Josephus is not as simple because he corrects his sources on the subject of women in the Essene community. His statement in *Ant.* 18.21 ("they do not admit wives to the community . . .") could represent his correction of the Hellenistic Jewish source. In short, the reference to celibacy among the Essenes was present in the older core material which goes back to Marcus Agrippa, was repeated in the Hellenistic Jewish source known to Philo and Josephus, and was modified significantly by Josephus.[11]

But if including *J.W.* 2 and *Hypothetica* 11.1–18 offers some intriguing new possibilities for enriching our understanding of the source and its history, it also

---

11. See Harmut Stegemann, *The Library of Qumran: On the Essenes, Qumran, John the Baptist, and Jesus* (Grand Rapids: Eerdmans, 1998), 193–98, for an explanation of how the mistaken notion that the Essenes were celibate arose and was perpetuated.

presents some pitfalls. After all, as we shall see below, specific pieces of information in *Ant.* 18.18–22 and *Every Good Man* 75–91 occur in similar clusters and in much the same relative order. This suggests the presence of a well-knit common source. But some of the data Bergmeier derives from *J.W.* 2 and, to a lesser extent, from *Hypothetica* 11.1–18 must be pulled out from their contexts and treated as though they were loose threads. For example, Bergmeier states that the Hellenistic Jewish source contains a statement on the special Sabbath observance of the sect. In support, he cites *Every Good Man* 81 and *J.W.* 2.147.[12] However, the former passage reads much like what Philo also writes about the Sabbath observance of the Therapeutae (*Contemplative Life* 30–31) and of the Jewish nation as a whole (*Hypothetica* 7.12–13) and should therefore be regarded as coming from his own hand.[13] The latter passage, *J.W.* 2.147, is very different in content from Philo and much closer to Hippolytus, *Haer.* 9.20.[14] We may assume that it comes from the source Josephus shares with that document. If this is correct, then the Hellenistic Jewish source shared by Philo and Josephus does not contain a statement about the special Sabbath observance of the Essenes.

We are on much firmer ground in our reconstruction of the source when we can demonstrate parallels between *Every Good Man* 75–91 and *Ant.* 18.18–22. In terms of such literary and conceptual ties, there is one topic Bergmeier has not included in the Hellenistic Jewish source which probably belongs there. I refer to the peculiar practice of sacrifice among the Essenes. The relevant passages are:

Philo, *Every Good Man* 75	Josephus, *Ant.* 18.19
Palestinian Syria, too, has not failed to produce high moral excellence. In this country live . . . Essenes. Their name . . . is given them, because they have shown themselves especially devout in the service of God, not by offering sacrifices of animals, but by resolving to sanctify their minds.	They send votive offerings to the temple, but perform[15] their sacrifices employing a different ritual of purification. For this reason, they are barred from those precincts of the temple that are frequented by all the people and perform their rites by themselves. Otherwise, they are of the highest character. . . .

12. Roland Bergmeier, *Die Essener-Berichte des Flavius Josephus: Quellenstudien zu den Essenertexten im Werk des Jüdischen Historiographen* (Kampen: Kok Pharos, 1993), 70.

13. F. H. Colson noted that what Philo writes about the Sabbath observance of the Essenes in *Every Good Man* 81 is not at all distinctive to that sect, *Philo IX* (LCL; Cambridge: Harvard University Press, 1941), 514. In addition, it occurs in a section in which Philo is freely creating (80–84).

14. The helpful appendix to Smith's article lists four parallels (nos. 128–31) between *J.W.* 2.147 and *Haer.* 9.20 on the subject of the Sabbath. Of these four, two display substantial verbal agreement. See Smith, "Description of the Essenes," 304–5.

15. The epitome of Josephus and the Latin version place a negative before the verb: "*do not* perform sacrifices since they employ a different ritual of purification." See the references in Boccaccini, *Beyond the Essene Hypothesis*, 183, n. 21.

The idea of offering sacrifices is present in both texts, although the vocabulary differs (Philo: οὐ ζῷα καταθύοντες; Josephus: θυσίας ἐπιτελοῦσιν). However, it should be noted that Josephus's emphasis on the importance of "ritual purity" (ἀγνεία) is present at a later point in the Philo passage ("Their love of God they show...by religious purity [ἀγνεία]," *Every Good Man* 84). While this term can cover a broad range of cultic acts, it does help support the possibility that Philo and Josephus are describing the same characteristic of the sect in the passages printed above.[16] It would be very problematic and highly unlikely for Philo to be commending the sect in *Every Good Man* 75 for abandoning the practice of sacrifice for a higher intellectual or spiritual exercise. In Philo's view, one must practice the literal prescriptions of the law and have regard for the law's deeper spiritual meaning (cf. *Migration* 89–93). In *Every Good Man* 75, Philo is commending the sect for the peculiar ritual of sacrifice mentioned in his source.

Josephus, on the other hand, has a problem with this different ritual of purification. Bergmeier called our attention to the fact that the Hellenistic Jewish source opened with a reference to the moral excellence of the Essenes. Notice, however, that in *Ant.* 18.18–19 Josephus has postponed this opening reference until after he mentions their peculiar sacrifices and can thereby express his disapproval ("Otherwise, they are of the highest character..."). Josephus cannot commend a group that has been barred from the precincts of the temple. Philo has understandably passed over the source's reference to separation from the temple since it reflects negatively on the group he seeks to commend.

The analysis above assumes that there is a statement about sacrifice, ritual purity, and separation from certain of the temple sacrifices in the source used by Philo and Josephus.[17] Bergmeier argues that this is not the case. He believes that the statement about sacrifice in Josephus, *Ant.* 18, is drawn from a different source, which he designates the Pythagorean-Essene source. This source pictured the Essenes as a Pythagorean congregation which had its center in a sanctuary. In Bergmeier's view, *Ant.* 18.19 actually contains reference to two separate holy places: the sanctuary of the Essenes, where they perform their cultic rites, and the Jerusalem temple from which the Essenes "barred themselves" (middle voice). He suggests that *Ant.* 18.19 be translated as follows:

---

16. Stegemann concludes that Philo and Josephus make the same point with respect to sacrifice. "Therefore both these ancient writers should be regarded as witnesses to the Essenes' non-participation in the temple offerings of their times, however their own offerings might have been performed" ("The Qumran Essenes — Local Members of the Main Jewish Union in Late Second Temple Times," in *The Madrid Qumran Congress: Proceedings of the International Congress on the Dead Sea Scrolls, Madrid, 18–21 March 1991* [ed. Julio Trebolle Barrera and Luis Vegas Montaner; Leiden: Brill, 1992], 1.122–23).

17. Separation from the temple was not absolute, but related only to those Sabbath and feast day sacrifices that were dictated by the solar calendar followed by the Essenes (Stegemann, *The Library of Qumran*, 166–76).

When they return to their sanctuary with votive offerings, they perform the cultic observances with different rites of purification which are valid for them. On this account, they bar themselves from the temple common to all and celebrate their cultic observances by themselves.[18]

Bergmeier is quick to point out that this interpretation does not require that the Essenes had an independent sacrificial cult nor even a separate area in the temple complex as their own place of sacrifice. The expression "to offer sacrifices" could simply refer to "performing cultic observances" (as he translated *Ant.* 18.19) in a synagogue service.

Bergmeier's suggestion is highly speculative and ultimately unnecessary. The very existence of a Pythagorean-Essene source, one of Bergmeier's four sources for Josephus's information on the Essenes, is unlikely for reasons indicated by John Collins.[19] But beyond this, the hypothesis that material was inserted in *Ant.* 18.19 from a different source is belied by the fact that this material can be explained solely on the basis of the Hellenistic Jewish source. As we have seen, there is a reference to offering sacrifices in Philo, *Every Good Man* 75, that is, at about the same position in the source shared with Josephus. Both Philo and Josephus edit this material in their own way, but they do so at this precise place in their respective accounts because the information was present at this place in their common source.

In sum, we should include in our reconstruction of the Hellenistic Jewish source the peculiar Essene practice of offering sacrifices. This appears to have been one of the first characteristics of the sect mentioned in the body of the source.

I am now in a position to offer my own minimalist reconstruction of the Hellenistic Jewish source used in *Every Good Man* 75–91 and *Ant.* 18.18–22. This source will include *topoi* shared with Pliny as well as the editorial contributions of the Hellenistic Jewish author. I call my reconstruction "minimalist" for two reasons: (1) I will not include data that is missing from these texts but that one may find in *Hypothetica* or *War*, and (2) with very few exceptions, the pieces of information must be present in both *Every Good Man* 75–91 and *Ant.* 18.18–22. One caveat is in order. As Bergmeier stated, Philo creates from the source document with greater freedom than does Josephus, so it is often very difficult to determine where the source ends and Philo begins.[20] However, most of Philo's sustained creative work appears to be concentrated in *Every Good Man* 80–84 and includes: (1) the division of philosophy into three parts (80); (2) the description of Sabbath observance (81–82); and (3) the threefold schema of paraenesis (83–84). There are individual words or phrases in this creative block that have parallels in *Ant.* 18.18–22 and therefore may derive from the source (e.g., references to the

---

18. Bergmeier, *Die Essener-Berichte*, 41 (my translation).
19. Collins, review of Roland Bergmeier, 525–26.
20. Bergmeier, *Die Essener-Berichte*, 39.

topoi	Philo, *Every Good Man*	Josephus, *Antiquities* 18
1. identification of that part of the Jewish nation which will be described	a considerable part of the very populous nation of the Jews …called Essenes (75)	[The Jews, from the most ancient times, had three philosophies pertaining to their traditions, that of the Essenes…(11)]
2. moral character	high moral excellence (75)	Otherwise, they are of the highest character (19)
3. numerical size	more than four thousand in number (75)	number more than four thousand (20)
4. distinctive doctrine	*their belief that the Godhead is the cause of all good things and nothing bad* (84)	The doctrine of the Essenes is wont to leave everything in the hands of God (18)
5. distinctive sacrifices	not by offering sacrifices of animals (75) *by religious purity* (84)	perform their sacrifices employing a different ritual of purification…barred from the temple precincts (19)
6. agricultural practice	Some of them labor on the land and others pursue such crafts as cooperate with peace (76)	devoting themselves solely to agricultural labor (19)
7. uniqueness	they stand almost alone in the whole of mankind (77)	such qualities as theirs were never found before among any Greek or barbarian people (20)
8. do not use money, revenues go into a common stock for disbursements as needed	They do not hoard gold or silver or acquire great slices of land because they desire the revenues therefrom, but provide what is needed for the necessary requirements of life. (they have become moneyless and landless [76–77; cf. 86])	Moreover, they hold their possessions in common, and the wealthy man receives no more enjoyment from his property than the man who possesses nothing (20)
9. voluntary practice	by deliberate action rather than by lack of good fortune (77)	they adopted them (20)

antiquity of the sect, as we saw above). These words and phrases are highlighted in italic type in the chart above. Also, notice that this block of material in *Every Good Man* 80–84 ends on the subject of fellowship, at which point Philo returns more directly to his source in 85–87 as indicated by the parallels with *Ant.* 18. Philo may even offer a literary hint that he is returning to his source ("their spirit of fellowship, which defies description, although a few words on it will not be out of place. First of all then…" [84–85]).

From the perspective of the methodology and observations outlined above, the Hellenistic Jewish source would include the elements indicated in the table above.

topoi	Philo, Every Good Man	Josephus, Antiquities 18
10. antiquity of their practice/ philosophy	they emulate the tradition of the past (82)	from of old (20) cf. *Ant.* 18.11 above
11. celibacy	[cf. *Hypothetica* 11.14: they eschew marriage]	they neither bring wives into the community (21)
12. slave ownership	Not a single slave is to be found among them... injustice (79)	nor do they own slaves... contributes to injustice (21)
13. live in communities	they dwell together in communities (85); cf. *Hypothetica* 11.1, 5	they live by themselves (21); a plurality of groups is implied as indicated by the plurals "good men" and "priests" in nos. 14 and 15
14. single treasury	they all have a single treasury and common disbursements (86); cf. *Hypothetica* 11.10: Each branch when it has received the wages of these so different occupations gives it to one person who has been appointed as treasurer	They elect by show of hands good men to receive their revenues and the produce of the earth (22)
15. common food/meals	also their food through the institution of public meals (86)	and priests to prepare bread and other food (22)
16. serve one another	exchanging services with each other (79), illustrated by their care of the sick and elderly (87)	and perform menial tasks for one another (21); no illustrations
17. final note of praise	high excellence of these people (91)	implicitly praised by way of comparison to another tribe (material which Josephus has incorporated from elsewhere, since it contradicts no. 7 above)

Several observations are in order. First, for the most part the individual topics are presented in the same approximate order. The few variations in order can be attributed to the redaction work of Philo and Josephus. The presence of this order is surely significant. When commenting on the literary form of a number of classical texts, including the two outlined above, Sterling wrote: "The literary shape of each of these texts is an eclectic résumé. There is no discernible pattern or consistent order in the descriptions. The specific shape which each assumes depends on a number of factors, including the sources of information and the requirements of the larger narrative."[21] I would modify this conclusion. As illustrated above, *Every Good Man* 75–91 and *Ant.* 18.18–22 do display a relatively

---

21. "'Athletes of Virtue,'" 693.

consistent order. This particular order is not characteristic of a literary form or genre; rather, it is best attributed to a common source of information, namely, the Hellenistic Jewish source. In addition, we saw earlier that nos. 7–11 in the chart were descriptions shared with Pliny. This cluster of *topoi* or older core material was incorporated by the author of the Hellenistic Jewish source after his description of agricultural practice and before his description of the prohibition of slavery.

A second observation from the parallels listed above is that the Hellenistic Jewish author has colored his own contributions to the Essene report with a moralizing commentary. For example, he writes that the Essenes regard slavery as an injustice. The likelihood is that the prohibition on slavery had more to do with making purity obligations easier than advancing the claims of human justice. According to the Mishnah, purity obligations were extended to slaves (*m. Zabim* 2:1; *m. Ker.* 1:3). But the author of this Essene report sees only a moral reason for not owning slaves. Along the lines of this moralizing tendency, it is also possible that a couple of terms shared by Philo and Josephus, such as "virtue" (*Every Good Man* 83–84; *Ant.* 18.20) and "righteousness" (*Every Good Man* 83; *Ant.* 18.18), were present in their common source.

Third, if we compare these *topoi* with those discussed by Bergmeier, it is apparent that our list is significantly shorter. For example, Bergmeier has included in the Hellenistic Jewish source such subjects as the striving for virtue, a locale in villages and cities, crafts, rejection of commerce, a love of peace and rejection of force, an unconditional love of truth, a prohibition on the swearing of oaths, adherence to law/scripture, special Sabbath observance, and the responses of political powers. While it is true that all of these topics are present in Philo, *Every Good Man* 75–91, they are missing in Josephus, *Ant.* 18.18–22. The presence of this data in the source is often conjectured on the basis of parallels in *War.* However, as we saw above with respect to the observance of the Sabbath, the supposed parallels in *War* are actually much closer to the text and context in Hippolytus than they are to the text in Philo. In sum, while these additional *topoi* may be present in the Hellenistic Jewish source as reflected in *Every Good Man* 75–91, there appears to be no literary basis for including them. Some of this material may have been added by Philo himself based on personal knowledge or secondhand reports.

There is much literary analysis and comparative work that remains to be done on the Essene reports in Philo and Josephus. I have attempted to show that Philo, *Every Good Man* 75–91, and Josephus, *Ant.* 18.18–22, share a literary source, called the Hellenistic Jewish source, which itself reflects a core of older material in common with Pliny, *Nat.* 5.73. I have tried to take seriously Murphy-O'Connor's injunction mentioned at the outset. Hopefully the discussion was moved forward, however slightly.

3

Prophetic Rhetoric in 6 Ezra

——— ◆ ———

Theodore A. Bergren
University of Richmond

It is well-known that 6 Ezra (2 Esdras 15–16 or 4 Ezra 15–16), an anonymous Christian writing of the third century, probably from Asia Minor, utilizes prophetic rhetoric much like that of the Hebrew Bible to advance its message.[1] However, the means by which the author has accomplished this, and the precise forms of literary and rhetorical relationship between the classical Hebrew prophets and 6 Ezra, have never been systematically studied. I am honored to be able to offer the present effort in this direction to George W. E. Nickelsburg, one of the most astute and personable biblical scholars of his generation, with heartfelt thanks for the help that he has consistently and selflessly offered to junior scholars like myself.

Our first desideratum is to survey the types of prophetic language and style that characterize 6 Ezra. This will provide a ready basis for comparison with the classical biblical prophets.

The text of 6 Ezra may be read in two parts. In the first, 15:1–16:34, an unnamed prophet speaking on God's behalf delivers a grandiloquent prediction of "evils" that will strike the world as a whole, and certain specific parts of it, as punishment for human sin. In the second, 16:35–78, the prophet moves to paraenesis and encouragement of a group called God's "elect" or "chosen," pleading with them to remain firm in the face of coming persecution. The boundary between these sections is fluid, as the two themes interplay to some extent in both sections.

Moving to specifics, the book, which is not particularly long, begins with a commissioning of the prophet by God in classical style (15:1–4; cf. esp. Jer. 1:7–9 and Hab. 2:2). The author then immediately brings out the main themes of the introductory section: "Behold, says the Lord, I am bringing evils upon the

---

1. For 6 Ezra, see T. A. Bergren, *Sixth Ezra: The Text and Origin* (New York and Oxford: Oxford University Press, 1998).

world...because iniquity has overwhelmed the whole earth" (15:5–6). This introductory section, or preamble, spans roughly 15:5–27. Besides laying out the principal themes of the book, this section also picks up a number of important subthemes, such as the wrongful persecution of innocent people (15:8–11), excoriation of "sin" and "sinners" (15:20–27), and particular focus on one part of the world, here Egypt (15:10–19). The narrative in 15:5–27 is delivered mainly by God in the first person through the prophet, and consists chiefly of pronouncement sayings predicting future events; it also utilizes classical prophetic discourse formulae ("says the Lord" [15:1, 5, 7, 9, 20, 24]; "Thus says the Lord God" [15:21]).

The next main section, 15:28–64, comprises detailed descriptions of two major "visions" witnessed by the seer. These are introduced rather vaguely, without details of the seer's physical or psychological condition. In these visions, the narrative mode of first-person address by God found in 15:1–27 continues, but the prophet himself also begins to take on a more significant speaking role (the prophet's voice can probably be assumed, for example, in 15:28–33). The first vision (15:28–33; "Behold, a terrible vision and its appearance from the east..." [15:28]) narrates a frightful chain of events witnessed by the seer, the clash of two opposing military forces, the "Arabians" and "Carmonians." Some of the fighting takes place in "Assyria" as well.

The second vision (15:34–64), which is longer and more complex, describes the movement and clash of titanic, frightful storm clouds that visit violence and destruction on the earth. The vision focuses on the clouds' origination from various points of the compass and their eventual movement to destroy "Babylon" (almost certainly a cipher for Rome). A major interlude in this section, spanning 15:46–60, involves a vehement prophetic invective against "Asia," who has "imitated that hateful one [Babylon]" (15:48). Asia, like Egypt in the first section, has killed and persecuted God's elect, and will receive a fitting punishment from the wrathful storm clouds as they return from having destroyed "Babylon." In this second vision, although the earlier part (15:34–45) seems to be narrated by the prophet, the interlude of invective against Asia returns to first-person address by God, imparting emphasis. In this section, God delivers "woes" against Asia and announces how Asia will be punished; the address is punctuated with rhetorical questions and exclamatory statements by God.

The first chapter (chap. 15) is marked by visions of the prophet and by focus on particular locales (in succession: Egypt, Arabia, Carmonia, Assyria, Babylon, Asia). In chapter 16, the seer's vision becomes more universal in scope and somewhat more rhetorical in style; in addition, there is an increasing emphasis on exhortation of God's people. First, however, the narrator skillfully reprises the first chapter: "Woe to you, Babylon and Asia! Woe to you, Egypt and Syria! Gird yourselves with sackcloth, wail for your sons...because your dismay has drawn near" (16:1–2).

The author then moves quickly to an exquisite rhetorical evocation of God's power and the inevitability of his instruments of destruction (16:3–17). Parallel statements are repeated time and again with slight variation, and complementary themes, images, and rhetorical devices are skillfully woven into the discourse. The result is a complex mesh of interconnected images and rhetorical styles, all undergirding the main points of God's power and that the means by which God destroys the earth are indomitable. In narrative terms this section is clearly an address by the prophet himself; God appears consistently in the third person. The section ends with a plaintive prophetic apostrophe: "Woe to me, woe to me! Who will save me in those days?" (16:17).

The next subsection, 16:18–20, continues the prophetic address and rhetorical force of 16:3–17, but with a new rhetorical framework. Like what comes before, it involves prediction of woes and a focus on human helplessness in their wake. Verse 16:20 again sets forth a final, direct comment by the prophet.

In 16:21–36 the narrative shifts to a graphic, physical description of the eschatological scenario. The focus is on death and desolation. Again, the prophet himself seems to be the speaker; God as narrating voice has moved to the background. The address is general, directed neither specifically against sinners (as in what came before) nor toward God's chosen (as in what follows). After a brief rhetorical flourish in vv. 33–34, however, the narrative moves suddenly to direct address of the "servants of the Lord": "This is the word of the Lord: receive it!" (16:36). The discourse continues with an extended, third-person metaphor comparing the inevitability — indeed, the imminence — of the coming end time with a woman in childbirth (16:37–39).

The author launches another major section characterized by extended rhetorical parallelism (16:40–46). Here, however, the theme of the rhetoric is paraenesis of God's chosen: in the face of the coming evils, they should act "like strangers on the earth" (16:40). The author evokes all the great metaphors of worldly activity — buying, selling, building, planting, marriage — decrying their uselessness in the face of the imminent catastrophes. This section marks a return to a first-person address by God that will continue, with sporadic interruptions, to the end of the book.

The author segues into a major section of polemic against sin and sinners (16:47–67). At first God advances the polemic. However, the discourse soon moves into a disquisition on God's omnipotence and omniscience (16:54–62), with God now in the third person. The point of the discourse is that sin is futile and that sinners are misled because God, as creator of the vast cosmos, obviously knows what is in human hearts. The interlude on God as omniscient creator closes with severe warnings to sinners by the prophet (16:63–67).

The book's final section (16:68–78), predicated mainly as a first-person address by God, predicts persecution and contains a final exhortation to the elect to remain sinless. At first, specific details of the coming persecution are given

(16:68–72). The point, God says, is to "prove" God's elect, as fire proves gold. In typical form, the book closes with a "woe" against sinners, using the analogy of an overgrown field that is destined to be shut off and burned (16:77–78). This note, directed toward sinners on a personal level, forms a fitting "inclusio," not only with 16:68 (the "burning wrath" of the persecutors), but also with earlier portions that also feature "burning" on a more cosmic, universal level. Thus microcosm (personal judgment) is tied to macrocosm (universal judgment).

The first and most important point about 6 Ezra is the extent to which it is, through and through, a writing in the classical, biblical, prophetic style. In virtually every aspect — content, types of discourse, morality, modes of address, use of imagery, how the audience is envisioned and addressed, use of rhetoric and rhetorical devices, mix between general postulates and specific cases, admixture of the personal element, use of visual and visionary elements, and balance between threat of condemnation and consolation — this work evokes and, given its period, one might even say mimics the biblical prophets. There are, certainly, some distinctions to be drawn, and these will occupy us below. But in the main, it is 6 Ezra's close similarities with classical prophecy that dominate.

Curiously, 6 Ezra as an evocation of classical prophecy is virtually unique in its period, in either the Jewish or Christian spheres. One searches in vain for works from the first centuries c.e. that come as close to the biblical prophets as 6 Ezra does. One could mention the *Sibylline Oracles,* which display some of the same characteristics and rhetorical devices, but their style is distinctive: the standard, easily recognizable "Sibylline oracular" genre, poetic meter, and so forth dominate. Another writing similar to old-style biblical prophecy is 5 Ezra, but the second half of the book features themes and modes of expression that are characteristic of its period and that have no strong analogues in the classical prophets. We are faced then with 6 Ezra as a type of formal anomaly, a "prophetic thunderbolt," a writing evoking rhetorical styles and literary and contextual elements of a genre that had long since passed away, and adding, it might be said, little new in the process. What are the implications?

One could explain the dearth of "prophetic"-style writings in the postbiblical period by evoking the traditional notion that "prophecy had ceased"; that after Haggai, Zechariah, and Malachi, God had somehow withdrawn the prophetic spirit, either for a time or permanently, and that authors accepted this notion. In contradistinction to this idea one notes the exceptions of apocalyptic prophecy, the Qumranites, and the early Christian prophets. Furthermore, the notion of prophecy having ceased only reconfigures the question: what, then, did the author of 6 Ezra think he was doing? Was he the *only* one who hadn't heard that "prophecy" in the classical, biblical, literary style had "ceased"? If not, how did he envision himself and his message; why did he adopt so literally this literary genre that had been out of currency for so long? These are questions that cannot be answered in this abbreviated format, but they are worth asking.

Noteworthy in this context is that the author of 6 Ezra had no lack in his immediate environment of literary models from which to choose. The Book of Revelation, the *Ascension of Isaiah*, and the prophecies of the "New Prophecy" ("Montanism") all offered models within Asia Minor with which our author was clearly (as in the case of Revelation) or at least potentially familiar. Yet he chose deliberately not to evoke an "apocalyptic" style, nor to adopt the stance of a visionary (ecstatic or otherwise) claiming personal charisma, nor to write of a heavenly ascent during which he obtained his insights. Instead, the insights come in a deliberately old-fashioned style: "...says the Lord God," repeated some thirteen times. What is the significance of this decision?

Into this mix we may add another, most curious phenomenon: this author, who was almost certainly a "Christian,"[2] chose deliberately to write a prophetic, soteriological, eschatological treatise in which "Christian" elements are completely suppressed. This fact is more significant than it might first appear. We know from the vast bulk of early Christian literature that distinctively "Christian" elements are at the core of Christian soteriology and end-time speculation. Even books as "Jewish" as the Book of Revelation prove the point. What, then, does the author of 6 Ezra mean to say by suppressing virtually every sign of Christian ideology or symbology and presenting us with a treatise that could just as well be Jewish?

This question might, I think, have a more ready answer than those posed above. Although 6 Ezra in its present form is anonymous, there is some evidence that it might originally have had a longer beginning than that which is currently preserved.[3] Thus, a more original form of the book might have preserved the *name* of a prophet. If this was the case, and if that prophet was a Jewish, biblical figure, we have a logical answer to the question why the book is not overtly "Christian," namely, the pseudonymous author's desire to preserve historical verisimilitude. Although this explanation may seem simplistic, it is, I think, plausible.

What, then, of the issue raised above — the points at which 6 Ezra *differs* in style or content from the classical prophets? There are a number of such points.

One important issue of a general, conceptual nature is that the discourse of 6 Ezra tends to be more abstract, more generalized, and less personalized than that of most of the biblical prophets, especially books like Jeremiah and Ezekiel. Not only is the personal element missing, but 6 Ezra lacks the nationalizing and historicizing characteristics that loom so large in the classical prophets. The text has little reference to actual historical events, and none of the strong ethnic focus on "Zion," the Jewish people, or Jerusalem; in short, its author lacks the strong national identity of the biblical prophets. This obviously reflects a different *Sitz*

---

2. While aware of the complications that attend the terms "Jew" and "Christian" in this period and in this region, I use the term simply to designate what we know about the author. We know nothing about his position vis-à-vis Judaism, but we do know, with some certainty, that he was a "Christian" (see Bergren, *Sixth Ezra*, chap. 6).

3. Ibid., 6.

im Leben; we are dealing here not with a Jewish prophet of the First or Second Commonwealth, but with an author who feels himself part of a larger and more anonymous historical setting.

A second, structural point, with elements of similarity as well as difference between 6 Ezra and the prophets, is that 6 Ezra manifests a distinct shift from prediction of woe and desolation in the first part of the book to earnest paraenesis in the second. In a sense, this does mirror the structure of the present form of many of the classical prophetic writings. Isaiah, Ezekiel, LXX Jeremiah (to some extent), Joel, Zephaniah, and Zechariah in their canonical forms all manifest, whether arbitrary or not, a similar shift from wrath and warning to consolation and restoration. The difference is that the paraenesis of the second part of 6 Ezra is not the same as the consolation and restoration of the Hebrew prophets. In many of the latter, there is trumpeting of salvation, a tone of exultation, a feeling that God has really and finally changed his mind to save his people. The text of 6 Ezra, on the other hand, displays a more stable and fixed, but also a less optimistic, ethos — the book's paraenesis has a tone of warning, not rejoicing, and stems from the conviction that the book's community is in a real and immediate position of ethical crisis. Again, this is no doubt related to the book's Sitz im Leben; the author perceived his audience as living in a situation in which individuals' moral choices would directly affect their condition of "salvation." This attitude is, on the whole, distinctly different from the ethos of the classical prophets.

A third point, related to the second, is that in 6 Ezra the people excoriated by the prophet are not the same as the book's target audience, the latter being referred to variously as God's "chosen" or "elect." In the Hebrew prophets, it is normal for the people targeted for wrath and warning within the Jewish nation — usually the people of Israel as a whole — to be precisely the group which, later in the book, is comforted, consoled, and promised a turnabout in God's attitude, given a proper attitude of repentance on their part. In 6 Ezra, on the contrary, the real audience of the book, God's "chosen," is never directly criticized or threatened; they are just warned and exhorted. The book's "enemy" is always other people. Indeed, the idea of the "elect" as a subsection of the author's larger community, so prominent in 6 Ezra, is largely absent in the prophets. This probably derives from the fact that 6 Ezra's "inner" community — the Christians — is, unlike the audience of the prophets, a small and persecuted minority within a larger, pagan social setting. The result is that the lines between "in-group" as good and "out-group" as evil are much more strongly drawn in 6 Ezra.

A fourth point concerns the prophetic discourse of 6 Ezra. As noted above, the discourse is often, perhaps normally, set in the third person: the prophet tends to avoid the first person, refers to God in the third person, and addresses other groups (sinners; the "elect") in the second person. This is not ubiquitous, since God does appear in the first person. This general practice contrasts with most of the classical prophets, in which God in the first person tends to dominate. In this regard 6 Ezra is more consonant with the writings of First Isaiah and Habakkuk, for example.

Fifth, it is useful to compare the rhetorical arsenals — use of rhetorical devices, extended literary parallelism, and so on — of the two corpora. In my review of 6 Ezra, it became clear that this author possesses a highly developed literary-rhetorical consciousness. This is most evident in 16:3–17, 16:18–20, 16:40–46, and 16:54–63. Each of these passages features extended and highly effective use of devices like literary parallelism, rhetorical questions, and repetitive but slightly varied word usage. Taken together, these passages indicate a self-conscious and relatively skilled literary stylist.

The classical biblical prophets, notwithstanding their rhetorical urgency, tend to lack the sorts of literary rhetorical devices mentioned above. There are exceptions, of course, but they illustrate the rule. Amos is probably the most literarily conscious of the group (cf. 3:3–8; 4:7–11; 5:18–20; 7:1–6; 9:1–4); we also note Obad. 12–14; Mic. 6:14–15; and Isa. 33:14 and 40:12–15.

A sixth point concerns the occurrence of "visions" in the two corpora. The first chapter of 6 Ezra is dominated by two visions of the prophet, in 15:28–33 and 15:34–63. As described above, both of these focus on violence and the clash of opposing forces, and apparently are meant to inculcate "fear and trembling" in the reader. Regardless of the content, however, the point is that "visions" of any sort are relatively rare in the classical prophets. Again, we can note exceptions: the most prominent are Zechariah 1–6 and Ezekiel 40–48 (see also Ezekiel 8). The relative preponderance of visions in 6 Ezra, both of which resemble narratives in those *Sibylline Oracles* contemporary with 6 Ezra, suggests that the author was writing in a literary environment in which such elements were more highly prized than they might have been during the periods of Hebrew prophecy.

In concluding, we note several other, more minor parallels and differences between 6 Ezra and the classical prophets. First, it is noteworthy that the "oracles against foreign nations" genre, so dominant in many of the prophets, is faithfully preserved in 6 Ezra (chap. 15, passim). Second, the classical prophets feature no significant warnings of persecution that will be directed toward a specific, select group, as we find in 6 Ezra 16:68–73. Third, concerning the heavy emphasis on whores and harlotry in 6 Ezra, although this theme is certainly present in the prophets (see esp. Hosea, Ezekiel 16 and 23, and Nah. 3:4–11), 6 Ezra probably derives it more directly from the Book of Revelation (chaps. 17–19). And fourth, the sudden, atypical first-person "apostrophe" of the prophet in 6 Ezra 16:17 is paralleled in such passages as Isaiah 50; Jer. 4:19–26; 15:10–18; and Mic 7:1.

The text of 6 Ezra clearly was written by an author who cherished the words and literary forms of the classical Hebrew prophets and who to some extent strove to imitate them in his own work. Besides the more general parallels noted above, there are numerous passages in 6 Ezra that either echo, or directly borrow, the wording of one of the classical prophets. At the same time, however, this author was inevitably a product of his own time, and much of what he produces — especially the notion of an "elect," the de-historicizing and de-nationalizing trend, and the focus on paraenesis rather than consolation or national restoration — reflects the worldview and *Sitz im Leben* of the later period in which he writes. But especially noteworthy is his "reversion," if we may call it that, to the classical prophetic form in a world that had long since "converted" to apocalypses, heavenly journeys, gnosis, and more personal and exhibitionistic forms of prophetic experience. Why the author chose to write as he did is ultimately, perhaps, beyond our knowledge; doubtless it had something to do with his personality and the expectations of the society within which he spun his craft.[4]

---

4. I am indebted to Prof. David Frankfurter for his thoughtful comments on this essay. Important discussion of these same issues is found in his book *Elijah in Upper Egypt: The Apocalypse of Elijah and Early Egyptian Christianity* (SAC; Minneapolis: Fortress, 1993), 31–34, 79–94.

4

Melchizedek's Birth Narrative in
2 Enoch 68–73: Christian Correlations

——————— ◆ ———————

Beverly A. Bow
Cleveland State University

The story of Melchizedek's birth at the end of 2 Enoch is an inventive expansion of the few biblical references to Melchizedek. 2 Enoch itself is a difficult but intriguing text. The manuscript tradition is complicated, and questions of original language, date of composition, and provenance have never been satisfactorily answered.[1] Whatever the provenance of the rest of 2 Enoch, if we consider Melchizedek's birth narrative independently, as an appendix, this part of the story has its closest affinities with Christian texts and Christian themes.

2 Enoch 68–73 as an Appendix

The birth story appears to be an appendix for several reasons. First, most manuscripts of 2 Enoch do not include the section on Melchizedek's birth. Second, the birth story is a different type of writing than the rest of 2 Enoch. Third, the person Enoch is virtually absent in the birth story, in which new characters appear and take center stage. Finally, a new thematic emphasis occurs in the birth story.

Manuscripts. Of the twenty known manuscripts of 2 Enoch, Melchizedek's birth story appears in only six, some of which have only parts of the birth story. Although these six manuscripts represent all four recensions delineated by Francis

---

1. See F. I. Andersen, "2 (Slavonic Apocalypse of) Enoch," in *Old Testament Pseudepigrapha* (ed. J. H. Charlesworth; Garden City, N.Y.: Doubleday, 1983), 1.92–100; J. J. Collins, *The Apocalyptic Imagination: An Introduction to Jewish Apocalyptic Literature*, 2d ed. (New York: Crossroad, 1998), 243–47; G. W. E. Nickelsburg, *Jewish Literature between the Bible and the Mishnah* (Philadelphia: Fortress, 1981), 185–88; E. Schürer, *The History of the Jewish People in the Age of Jesus Christ* (Edinburgh: T. & T. Clark, 1987), 2.746–49; A. Pennington, "2 Enoch," in *The Apocryphal Old Testament* (ed. H. F. D. Sparks; Oxford: Clarendon, 1984), 321–26; A. Vaillant, *Le livre des secrets d'Hénoch: Texte slave et traduction française* (Paris: Institut d'études slaves, 1952), iii–xxvi.

Andersen, and the story never appears as an individual text,[2] the majority of the manuscript evidence does not include the section on Melchizedek's birth.

Genre. The first sixty-seven chapters[3] of *2 Enoch* have elements characteristic of the apocalypse:[4] revelation and exhortations based on it, a heavenly journey with a supernatural guide, an interest in cosmology and calendars, eschatological judgment. Melchizedek's birth story (chaps. 68–73),[5] however, is primarily a narrative about the events between the day of Enoch's disappearance and forty days after Melchizedek's birth. While there is one dream vision and an angelic visitor in the birth story, it is not an account of an otherworldly journey, and there are no paraenetic, cosmological, or calendrical aspects, and very little that is eschatological.

Characters. Melchizedek's birth story occurs at the end of a text that already ends satisfactorily when Enoch is taken back to heaven for the second and final time, and everyone who has gathered to hear his teachings goes home (67:2–3). That is, Enoch's story ends. The placement of the birth story at this point in *2 Enoch* parallels that of Noah's birth story at the end of *1 Enoch;*[6] but in *1 Enoch,* Enoch himself is still an integral part of the story, for Methuselah journeys to seek Enoch's advice when Lamech is bewildered by the strange appearance of Noah. In *2 Enoch,* although Enoch's name is mentioned a few times in Melchizedek's birth story,[7] the primary figure of the apocalyptic section is now only an ancestor, a memory. The birth story focuses first on Methuselah, then on Nir and Melchizedek.

Theme. The predominant theme in the birth story is the priesthood, while, aside from a few references in *2 Enoch* 18–19 to the failure of the Grigori in the fifth heaven to perform liturgy, there is hardly anything that can be connected to the priesthood in the earlier chapters.[8] After Enoch vanishes, suddenly there is great concern to find a priest for the people, as if Enoch's absence had left a vacancy in that position (69:2).[9] But the earlier chapters have never identified Enoch as a priest. The first line of *2 Enoch* introduces Enoch as "a wise man, a great scribe" (*muža mudrago, knižnika velikago*), and that is how the text presents

---

2. Andersen, "2 Enoch," 93–94.

3. Using the chapter-and-verse enumeration of Andersen, *"2 Enoch."*

4. On the apocalyptic genre, see Collins, *Apocalyptic Imagination,* 1–42; on *2 Enoch* as apocalypse, see Nickelsburg, *Jewish Literature,* 185–87.

5. The first four verses of chapter 68, which appear only in two manuscripts of the long recension, seem to be a transition between Enoch's and Melchizedek's stories.

6. As Nickelsburg (*Jewish Literature,* 188) points out.

7. E.g., references to "the sons of Enoch" in chapter 68, "your [Methuselah's] father Enoch" in chapter 69; after 69:5 the name appears only once, in a list of names (71:32).

8. When Enoch returns from his heavenly journey, he tells his children that God does not need sacrifices (45:3), and later includes one general instruction about clean sacrifices (59:2; cf. 2:2).

9. The only place Enoch is called a priest is when he is included among those in 71:32 as "priests" (*ierei*), but this occurs only in manuscript R, the sole representative of the long recension after 71:4; the short recension has "servants" (*raby*).

him: he writes down what God instructs him to write and passes along his wisdom to his children.

2 Enoch 68–73 Compared with Other Birth Stories

Jewish, Greco-Roman, and Christian texts tell standardized stories of the births of remarkable or significant figures. The standard formula in Hebrew Bible birth stories and in postbiblical retellings[10] is that God opens the womb of a barren woman, after which she is impregnated by her husband; the birth stories generally serve as introductions to the stories of the offspring (Isaac, Jacob, Joseph, Samson, Samuel). Postbiblical accounts of births not involving barren women usually include an anomaly at birth (extraordinary beauty, strange appearance, bright light) which indicates future eminence, but not divine siring.[11] In Greco-Roman stories, deities physically mate with humans;[12] one repeated pattern is that a male god spots a beautiful young girl and rapes her or tricks her into sleeping with him. This results in the birth, often anomalous, of a god or hero (e.g., Dionysus, Asclepius, Heracles, Achilles). Christian stories of Jesus' birth tell of a virgin who conceives without the involvement of a man, producing the Christ; other births (John the Baptist, Mary) related in Christian texts follow the biblical barren-woman type. Melchizedek's birth story, though, does not precisely fit any of the patterns found in these traditions, yet shares some similarities with each.

Jewish. There are more differences than similarities between Melchizedek's birth story and the birth stories of biblical figures. Of the five barren women in the Hebrew Bible, Sopanim most resembles Sarah: she is not only barren, but also past childbearing age (71:1–2). But common elements in the Hebrew Bible story type are missing in 2 Enoch. There is no pre-birth annunciation about Melchizedek, as there is for Isaac, Jacob, and Samson. The five Hebrew Bible stories (and retellings) indicate explicitly that God reverses the woman's barrenness (e.g., by noting that God "remembered" the woman or "opened her womb"), and both biblical and postbiblical texts make plain that the woman's husband fathers her child. In contrast, 2 Enoch gives no explanation at all for how Sopanim got pregnant, but Nir is clearly not Melchizedek's father since he has not slept with Sopanim since Methuselah died (71:2). Nor does the birth story introduce an account of Melchizedek's life; rather, the child himself is taken away from Nir after "forty days" (72:1), and predictions about his role in a distant future are made only after his birth (71:28–37; 72:5–7).

---

10. E.g., Josephus, Philo, *Midrash Rabbah*, Pseudo-Philo, *Jubilees.*

11. Moses in Josephus, Philo, *Midrash Rabbah*, Pseudo-Philo; Noah in *1 Enoch, Genesis Apocryphon.*

12. For all the classical myths, see Ovid's *Metamorphoses* or Apollodorus's *Biblioteca*; references to various divine/hero births are found everywhere, including Homer, Hesiod, Pausanius, Euripides, Virgil, Pindar.

Greco-Roman. Melchizedek's birth story is also largely dissimilar to the typical pattern found in Greco-Roman stories of heroes' births. There is no description of a divine being mating with Sopanim,[13] and she is not the beautiful, young, fertile virgin one most often finds mating with gods in Greco-Roman myths. However, the unusual birth of Melchizedek from the corpse of Sopanim (71:17), who drops dead when Nir accuses her of being unfaithful (71:6–9), resembles the story of Asclepius's birth.[14] Apollo argues with Coronis about her unfaithfulness, kills her, then rescues Asclepius from her womb and takes him elsewhere to be raised.[15] Ovid's version of the story includes a postbirth prediction about Asclepius's distant future. In a similar story, Zeus, after his lightning bolt kills Semele, takes the unborn Dionysus from his mother's womb and sews the fetus into his own thigh until he is born.[16]

Christian. The birth story in *2 Enoch* differs most obviously from Christian birth stories in that it is about neither Jesus nor anyone who lived during his lifetime, while Christian texts describe the births of Jesus, John the Baptist, and Mary.[17] However, there are some interesting similarities between Melchizedek's birth and several Christian birth narratives. Like Mary, Sopanim conceives Melchizedek without having sex, although Sopanim is not a virgin. Variant readings of Anna's conception of Mary in the *Gospel of James* suggest that Anna, a barren nonvirgin, conceives Mary without having sex, while her husband is away (4:2).[18] Of all the mothers in all three traditions, Sopanim is most like Luke's Elizabeth, who is barren, old, and married to a priest.[19] Further, Elizabeth secludes herself for five months, remarking that God took away her reproach (ὄνειδος), while Sopanim, ashamed (*ustydě*), hides herself during the whole pregnancy (71:3). Joseph's accusation upon finding Mary pregnant and her response in *Gospel of James* 13:2 are very similar to Nir's accusation and Sopanim's response in *2 Enoch* 71:6–7, although Mary, of course, does not drop dead.[20] Finally, Melchizedek's abrupt

---

13. In manuscript R of the long recension, the Lord refers to Melchizedek as "my" child in 72:1, but one cannot conclude from that that God is Melchizedek's father. Earlier in the same manuscript Noah and Nir say, "God is renewing the priesthood from blood related to us" (71:19), even though Nir is not the child's father, either. *2 Enoch* never gives a clear indication of the identity of Melchizedek's father.

14. Apollodorus, *Biblioteca* 3.10.3; Ovid, *Metamorphoses* 2.542–47, 596–648; Pindar, *Pythian Odes* 3.

15. The centaur, Cheiron, raises Asclepius and teaches him the healing arts.

16. Ovid, *Metamorphoses* 3.320–12; Euripides, *Bacchae* 89–98, 523–27; cf. Apollodorus, *Biblioteca* 3.4.2; Pindar, *Olympian Odes* 3.

17. John the Baptist in Luke; Mary in *Gospel of James*, *Latin Infancy Gospel*, Pseudo-Matthew.

18. See Oscar Cullmann, "The Protevangelium of James," in *New Testament Apocrypha* (ed. E. Hennecke, W. Schneemelcher, and R. Wilson; Philadelphia: Westminster, 1963), 1.376.

19. Elizabeth is herself patterned after Sarah. See R. E. Brown, *The Birth of the Messiah* (New York: Doubleday, 1977, 1993), 269. Similarly, the *Gospel of James* explicitly compares Anna to Sarah (2:4) although it does not mention Anna's age.

20. Joseph asks, "Why have you done this?" mentions humiliation, and asks from where "this thing" in her womb has come; Mary says she does not know. Nir asks, "What have you done?" and

appearance in *2 Enoch* resembles Jesus' arrival in *Ascension of Isaiah* 11:8, where Jesus is in the womb one minute, then suddenly sitting beside Mary on the bed.

The Function of *2 Enoch* 68–73

Melchizedek's birth story has one function: to legitimate the priesthood of Melchizedek. The appendix emphasizes the priesthood from the beginning, when Methuselah and his brothers construct the first altar mentioned in *2 Enoch* and offer sacrifices on it (68:5). God then appoints Methuselah as priest to fill the implied vacancy left by Enoch's disappearance (69:2–5). The elders dress Methuselah in priestly (literally, "choice") garments (*v rizou izrędnou,* 69:8) and he makes his first sacrifice as priest, the knife leaping into his hand to confirm his office (69:12–16). Ten years later, God chooses as Methuselah's successor his grandson Nir, Noah's younger brother (70:3–4). He too is clothed "in garments of consecration" (*v rizy svęštenyja*) and performs a sacrifice (70:4, 13, 19–21). Melchizedek is born into this priestly family, clothed and wearing the "seal of consecration" (*pečat[i] svętitelĭstva*) on his chest; he immediately blesses God (71:17–19). Noah and Nir conclude that this strange child is God's way of continuing the priesthood after them (71:20). Nir has a dream vision from God and an angelic visitation to tell him that Melchizedek will be taken away to escape the destruction of the impending flood and that Melchizedek will have a priestly role as "priest to all priests" (*erěi erěemi*) or "head of priests" (*glava ierěemi*) at some future time (71:27–37; 72:1–7). The entire appendix leads to God saving Melchizedek from the flood so that this particular priestly line, commissioned by God in the first place, will not perish in the flood, but will continue and be preeminent in the future.

Thus the text legitimates a non-Levitical priesthood by making it pre-date the flood. Noah will also survive the flood, as the appendix knows (71:37; 73:1–9), and his descendants will include Levi. But Levi's priestly line will be overshadowed by Melchizedek's, because God inaugurated Melchizedek's priesthood first and because Melchizedek will be "head of priests" in the future.

Connections to Other Melchizedek Traditions

The Hebrew Bible mentions Melchizedek in only two texts, which are ultimately the origin of any speculation about him. And quite a few Jewish and Christian texts do speculate about this mysterious figure.[21] Compared to other Melchizedek

---

mentions disgrace; Sopanim says she does not know how she conceived. In the fragmentary Jewish text, *Genesis Apocryphon,* Lamech similarly accuses Bitenosh, but she knows exactly how and when Lamech fathered Noah, as her response indicates.

21. See F. L. Horton, *The Melchizedek Tradition* (Cambridge: Cambridge University Press, 1976).

traditions, the Melchizedek depicted in *2 Enoch* 68–73 has the most correlations to one Christian tradition about him.

Hebrew Bible. The birth story in *2 Enoch* has little relation to the Hebrew Bible texts that mention Melchizedek. Gen. 14:18–20 identifies Melchizedek as the king of Salem and priest of El Elyon (identified in 14:22 as YHWH), who blesses Abram and to whom Abram gives a tithe. In Ps. 110:4, YHWH swears to the appointed king that he will be forever a priest "according to the order of" (*'al dibrātî*) Melchizedek. Only his name and his role as priest connect *2 Enoch*'s Melchizedek directly to the references in Genesis and Psalms.

Qumran. There is even less connection between the Melchizedek in *2 Enoch* and the figure of the same name in the fragmentary Melchizedek document from Qumran Cave 11.[22] In 11QMelchizedek, Melchizedek is an eschatological heavenly warrior-judge who makes atonement. He is not called a priest,[23] although the atonement reference might suggest a priestly role.[24] In *2 Enoch*, Melchizedek is an otherworldly figure only in the sense that an angel takes him to the paradise of Eden forty days after his birth to save him from perishing in the flood. His future as a priest is mentioned repeatedly, but nowhere does the appendix speak of atonement or judgment, or refer to Melchizedek as a heavenly warrior.

Rabbinic Texts. The function of *2 Enoch*'s Melchizedek appendix is negated by rabbinic texts. Rabbinic literature identifies Melchizedek with Noah's son Shem,[25] whose descendants eventually lead to Levi. Melchizedek's priesthood, then, would in effect become the Levitical priesthood through the family line. Some texts go further by taking the merit of starting the priestly line away from Melchizedek-Shem and giving it to Abraham, because, in Genesis 14, Melchizedek names Abram before naming God.[26] This demotion of Melchizedek may be anti-Christian polemic because of Melchizedek's prominence in Hebrews and certain patristic writings.[27] The rabbinic version of Melchizedek controverts the depiction of his priesthood in *2 Enoch*, in which Melchizedek is not actually related to Noah's family since Nir is not his biological father. In *2 Enoch*, Melchizedek's priesthood continues apart from the fates of Noah and his sons, and he is to prevail over other future priests.

---

22. As Andersen ("2 Enoch," 97) also notes.

23. M. de Jonge and A. S. van der Woude, "11QMelchizedek and the New Testament," *NTS* 12 (1966): 306; Joseph A. Fitzmyer, "Further Light on Melchizedek from Qumran Cave 11," *JBL* 86 (1967): 29–31.

24. G. W. E. Nickelsburg and M. E. Stone, *Faith and Piety in Early Judaism* (Philadelphia: Fortress, 1983), 185.

25. E.g., *Targum Yerushalmi, Pirqe Rabbi Eliezer, b. Nedarim* 32b, *Targum Pseudo-Jonathan.*

26. *b. Nedarim* 32b, *Midrash Wayyiqra' Rabbah* 25.6.

27. See Gustave Bardy, "Melchisédech dans la tradition patristique," *RB* (1926): 498; M. Simon, "Melchisédech dans la polémique entre juifs et chrétiens et dans la légende," *Revue d'Histoire et de Philosophie religieuses* (1937): 63–69; R. Travers Herford, *Christianity in Talmud and Midrash* (Clifton, N.J.: Reference Book Publishers, 1966), 265–66; 339–40.

Christian Gnosticism. Second Enoch's Melchizedek has almost nothing in common with the figure in Christian gnostic texts, which associate him in some way with Jesus. In *Pistis Sophia* 25, Jesus explains to his disciples Melchizedek's role in the making of souls, as the Receiver of Light or Light Purifier. The Nag Hammadi text *Melchizedek* refers to Melchizedek as "priest of God Most High," as in Genesis 14. The text, while extremely fragmentary, seems to identify Melchizedek with Jesus.[28] "I, Melchizedek, the Priest of [God] Most High" (15.9–10) is separated by only a few lines from "I have offered myself up to you as a sacrifice" (16.7–8). Later, Melchizedek says in his second revelation,[29] "[you crucified me] from the third hour [of the sabbath eve] until [the ninth hour]. And after [these things I arose] from the [dead]" (25.5–9). 2 *Enoch* gives Melchizedek no task having to do with light; nor does it allude to crucifixion, expiatory death, or Jesus.

Hebrews. As with Christian gnostic texts, Hebrews 7 makes an association between Jesus and Melchizedek. The passage, a midrash on the Hebrew Bible references to Melchizedek,[30] connects those references to Jesus. The author explains that Melchizedek resembles the Son of God in that he is a priest forever (7:3), and shows that Melchizedek is superior to Abraham and the Levitical priesthood (7:4–14). The second half of the chapter turns to Jesus, whose priesthood is of the order of Melchizedek, and the author shows that Jesus as high priest is greater than the Levitical priesthood (7:15–28).[31] Melchizedek resembles Jesus (7:3), whose priesthood resembles Melchizedek's (7:15), but it is clear that Jesus, who preexisted (1:2) and who is superior to the angels (1:4), is greater than Melchizedek.[32]

There are intriguing correlations between the 2 *Enoch* appendix and Hebrews. Hebrews describes Jesus' exalted priesthood, and 2 *Enoch* describes Melchizedek's exalted future priesthood. A more direct affinity is that both Hebrews and 2 *Enoch* elevate Melchizedek's priesthood over the Levitical priesthood. The claim in Heb. 7:3 that Melchizedek is without father, mother, and genealogy is interesting in light of the story in 2 *Enoch* where Melchizedek has no identifiable father and his mother died before he was born.[33]

28. B. A. Pearson, "Melchizedek," in *The Nag Hammadi Library in English* (ed. James M. Robinson; San Francisco: Harper & Row, 1977), 399.

29. Ibid.

30. See Joseph A. Fitzmyer, "Now This Melchizedek...," *CBQ* 25 (1963): 305–21; de Jonge and van der Woude, "11QMelchizedek," 318–23.

31. On this comparison, see David deSilva, "Exchanging Favor for Wrath: Apostasy in Hebrews and Patron-Client Relationships," *JBL* 115 (1996): 97–100.

32. Fitzmyer, "Now This Melchizedek...," 317; de Jonge and van der Woude, "11QMelchizedek," 321–22.

33. James H. Charlesworth sees Melchizedek's birth story and Heb. 7:3 as parallel (*The Old Testament Pseudepigrapha and the New Testament* [Cambridge: Cambridge University Press, 1985], 85); he cites F. Andersen as seeing 2 *Enoch* as contradictory to Hebrews because Melchizedek has a mother (105). For the view that Hebrews is referring to Melchizedek's and Jesus' lack of priestly (Levitical) genealogy (which could also be said about 2 *Enoch*), see Fitzmyer, "Now This Melchizedek...," 314–

Church Fathers. Patristic writings include various views about Melchizedek, none of which seems especially connected to 2 *Enoch*. Early on, the church fathers glorify Melchizedek over and against Judaic values, as Hebrews does. For example, Justin Martyr notes that Melchizedek was a "priest of those in uncircumcision" who blessed the (subordinate) circumcised Abraham, in order to defend Jesus as also a priest to the uncircumcised.[34] Some patristic figures regard Melchizedek as an angel, including Origen, according to Jerome.[35] Epiphanius mentions a sect of Melchizedekians, heretics who held Melchizedek in higher esteem than Christ.[36] While it might go a long way toward explaining the Melchizedek birth story, the evidence for a sect devoted to him is not firm.[37] Justin's view comes close to 2 *Enoch's* Melchizedek, but no more so than Hebrews, on which Justin's remarks are based.

Conclusions

As a birth story, 2 *Enoch* 68–73 is more similar to Christian birth stories than to Jewish or Greco-Roman stories (except for the corpse aspect). Melchizedek's mother is most like Elizabeth in Luke; the circumstances of the conception most like Anna's in the *Gospel of James*; the accusation of wrongdoing and response most similar to Joseph and Mary in the *Gospel of James*. Andersen points out that Melchizedek's birth story is not an imitation of Jesus' birth story, and goes on to claim that "no Christian could have developed such a blasphemy."[38] The latter does not necessarily follow from the former. Attributing a miraculous conception and birth (ridiculous or not) to Melchizedek does not impugn the unique circumstances of Jesus' conception, no more than Anna's conception of Mary in the *Gospel of James* imitates or impugns Jesus' conception, even in the version in which Joachim is absent when it occurs.

When compared to other traditions about Melchizedek, 2 *Enoch* 68–73 is most similar to the tradition found in Hebrews. Both the birth story and the first half of Hebrews 7 focus on the primacy of Melchizedek's priesthood over the Levitical (or any) priesthood. If whoever concocted the bizarre birth story in 2 *Enoch* was a Christian familiar with the claims made in Hebrews, Melchizedek's birth story could be understood as an explanation of how this primacy came about. It makes

---

18. For the view that Heb. 7:3 indicates that the author considered Melchizedek an angel, see de Jonge and van der Woude, "11QMelchizedek," 320–21.

34. Justin, *Dialogue with Trypho* 33. See the discussion in Bardy, "Melchisédech dans la tradition patristique," 499–500.

35. Jerome, *Epistulae* 73. See the discussion in de Jonge and van der Woude, "11QMelchizedek," 323–26.

36. Epiphanius, *Refutation of All Heresies* 55; see Bardy, "Melchisédech dans la tradition patristique," 505–9; de Jonge and van der Woude, "11QMelchizedek," 325.

37. Bardy, "Melchisédech dans la tradition patristique," 509; cf. Andersen, "2 Enoch," 96.

38. Andersen, "2 Enoch," 97.

his priesthood not only older than the Levitical priesthood, which Genesis 14 does, but also engineered by God through a miraculous conception and birth and preserved by God from the flood to be preeminent in some distant future. Of course, Hebrews goes on to indicate that Jesus' high priesthood, patterned upon Melchizedek's, is the highest of all, and *2 Enoch* does not.

There is nothing clearly, identifiably Christian in Melchizedek's birth story — nothing that points to a Christian redeemer, no mention of Jesus or any Christian figures. But why would there be, if all a hypothetical Christian author wanted to do was address how Melchizedek's priesthood got to be greater than Levi's? As mentioned above, there is evidence of a conflict between Jews and Christians over Melchizedek's priesthood in relation to the Levitical priesthood in rabbinic literature, which can also be seen in Hebrews. The function of the birth story focuses on this very issue.

5

When Did They Pray?
Times for Prayer in the Dead Sea Scrolls
and Associated Literature

—————— ◆ ——————

Esther Chazon

The Hebrew University of Jerusalem

This study addresses the fundamental question of when people prayed in antiquity, both individually and communally. The focus will be on the contribution of the Dead Sea Scrolls to our knowledge of this aspect of religious practice during the Second Temple period. The presentation will help illuminate the historical background against which prayer times were established in the Jewish and Christian liturgical traditions as well as the larger matrix out of which Jewish and Christian liturgy emerged.

The Dead Sea Scrolls provide more than two hundred previously unknown prayers, including several liturgical collections which explicitly state the time of their daily or weekly recitation and a few hymns which refer to fixed times of prayer.[1] This small core of texts provides the basis for our investigation of prayer times as reflected in the scrolls. Indeed, it constitutes our best available evidence for this phenomenon since the scrolls themselves preserve neither records of prayer practice nor laws regulating prayer times, with the exception of the

---

It is with great joy that I dedicate this article to George Nickelsburg. George was an active participant in the discussion on this paper at the 1997 Annual Meeting of the Society of Biblical Literature. The research was carried out and presented in spring 1997 while I was a fellow at the Institute of Advanced Studies at Hebrew University. I wish to thank the institute for providing that opportunity as well as my colleagues there for their helpful comments.

1. For this figure and an outline of the corpus, see E. G. Chazon, "Prayers from Qumran and Their Historical Implications," *DSD* 1 (1994): 265–84. A history of research and a catalog of the prayers is given in E. G. Chazon, "Hymns and Prayers in the Dead Sea Scrolls," in *The Dead Sea Scrolls after Fifty Years: A Comprehensive Assessment* (ed. P. W. Flint and J. C. VanderKam; Leiden: Brill, 1998), 1.244–70.

Community Rule's prescription "to bless together" during one-third of every night (1QS VI, 7–8).[2]

The texts examined in this study divide into two broad categories with respect to how they conceptualize and express the times for prayer. In *category A*, prayer follows natural time and prayer times are coordinated with the movements of the heavenly lights, particularly with their changes at sunrise and sunset. In *category B*, prayer follows sacrificial time and prayer times are coordinated with the hours when the daily, Sabbath, and festival sacrifices were offered at the temple. In view of the Qumranites' rejection of the temple cult as it was practiced in their own day, prayer's coordination with sacrifice undoubtedly functioned differently at Qumran than it did among nonseparatist groups, and this special function is also discussed in this study.

Before examining these two categories, it is important to note that the categorization according to different models of prayer time entails grouping together prayers of different types and of different origins (that is, Qumranic and non-Qumranic). As I discuss each text, however, I shall point out its genre, function, and provenance. Moreover, the extent to which the differences in prayer type, function, and provenance are relevant to the question of when people prayed will be considered in the conclusion.

Category A: Natural Time — Prayers at the Interchange of the Heavenly Lights

An obvious starting point for our discussion is the well-known personal hymn which concludes some recensions of the *Community Rule* and has a close parallel in the *Hodayot*.[3] This hymn declares the poet's commitment to praise God during the course of the day, the year, and the sabbatical cycles. A central feature is its specification of the times for such praise according to what Bilhah Nitzan aptly calls the "renewal of astronomical and calendric phenomena"[4] — that is, the daily appearance of the luminaries, the new moons, the four annual seasons, the yearly

---

2. In Shemaryahu Talmon's view the hymn at the end of the *Community Rule* (1QS IX, 26–XI, 15) prescribed prayer times and prayers to be said at those times ("The 'Manual of Benedictions' of the Sect of the Judaean Desert," *RevQ* 2 [1960]: 475–500; "The Emergence of Institutionalized Prayer in Israel in Light of Qumran Literature," in *The World of Qumran from Within* [Jerusalem: Magnes; Leiden: Brill, 1989], 200–43; see my critique in Chazon, "Hymns and Prayers," 244–46). This hymn is one of the texts analyzed below.

3. The hymn is preserved in 1QS, 4QS[b,d,f,j], and in 1QH[a] XX=Sukenik XII, 4QH427 3 ii; compare also 1QM XIV, 12–14. For the recensional history of the *Community Rule*, see S. Metso, *The Textual Development of the Qumran Community Rule* (STDJ 21; Leiden: Brill, 1997). On the different *Hodayot* collections, see E. Schuller, "The Cave Four Hodayot Manuscripts: A Preliminary Description," *JQR* 85 (1994): 137–50.

4. B. Nitzan, *Qumran Prayer and Religious Poetry* (STDJ 12; Brill: Leiden, 1994), 59.

festivals, and the new years. The language emphatically stresses the beginning of each time period and also its completion and transition to the next period.

This emphasis is apparent in the hymn's opening lines, which also indicate times for daily prayer:

> At the times ordained by Him: at the *beginning* (*bršyt*) of the dominion of light, and at its *coming round* (*tqwptw*) when it *retires* (*bh'spw*) to its appointed place; at the *beginning* of the watches of darkness when He unlocks their storehouse and spreads them out, and also at their *coming round* when they *retire* before the light.[5]

Although the threefold language — "beginning," "coming round," and "retire" — led Shemaryahu Talmon and others to argue that the hymn refers to a threefold division of daylight,[6] I agree with those who claim that it specifies only two times for daily prayer: the two times a day when the luminaries interchange, at the beginning of the morning and at the beginning of the evening. As Nitzan and others before her have noted,[7] such an interpretation suits the meaning of *tequpah* as the coming around of a circuit as well as the passage's concern with the beginning and end of the dominions of light and darkness. This concern is particularly evident in the summation, "when the luminaries *appear* from the holy abode and when they *retire* to the place of Glory" (1QS X, 2–3).

This hymn's emphasis on divinely appointed times and on the annual seasons, their renewal and transmission at the equinoxes and solstices,[8] all point to this poet's adherence to the sectarian solar calendar and the conviction that it alone embodies what Nitzan has called "the divine law of time."[9] However, I shall demonstrate below that aligning prayer with astronomical renewal is not an exclusively sectarian practice but rather a broader religious phenomenon. Similarly, the natural times for prayer specified in this hymn are not unique to this poet or to the *Yahad* community but are also attested outside of Qumran and in nonsectarian works.

Indeed, none of the other scrolls in this category of natural prayer times is distinctively sectarian in character, and a non-Qumranic provenance has in fact

---

5. This translation of 1QS X, 1–2, basically follows G. Vermes (*The Dead Sea Scrolls in English* [London: Penguin, 1995], 83), but I have substituted "coming round" for Vermes' translation of *tqwph* as "end." The emphasis is my own.

6. Talmon, "'Manual of Benedictions,'" 481–83; "Emergence," 215–19. Talmon also saw here a reference to a threefold division of the night. Compare J. Licht, *The Rule Scroll* (Jerusalem: Bialik, 1965), 123 (in Hebrew).

7. Nitzan, *Qumran Prayer*, 53–55, and the literature cited there.

8. The seasons are clearly listed in 1QS X, 7. Some scholars surmise that they are also mentioned in lines 3b–5a (see, e.g., Nitzan, *Qumran Prayer*, 57, and especially Licht, *Rule Scroll*, 209–10).

9. Nitzan, *Qumran Prayer*, 61; see also 52, 59–60.

been suggested for each.[10] If this assessment is correct, they would directly reflect religious practice outside the confines of the Qumran community.

Of the other scrolls in this category, the *Daily Prayers* in 4Q503 provide the most information about the times for prayer and the reasons for them. The text of 4Q503 preserves a liturgy comprised of short blessings for each evening and morning of the month. The introductory rubrics instruct the worshipers to recite each prayer "on the x of the month, in the evening (*b'rb*)" and "when the sun goes forth to shine on the earth." Significantly, these rubrics specify the hour of morning prayer as sunrise, thereby implying that the evening prayer took place at an analogous time, namely, sunset. The hour for evening prayer would then be at the beginning of the new day which, according to this text, began in the evening.[11]

Recitation at sunrise and sunset is basic to the blessings' purpose, which is to offer praise for the daily renewal of the heavenly luminaries and for each diurnal change in their light. In keeping with this purpose, each prayer not only mentions the sun's daily reappearance but also counts the daily changes in the portions ("lots") of lunar light and darkness as the moon waxes and wanes. The coordination between daily solar and lunar movements is also marked by counting the incremental change in the moon's phases at each sunrise. This is expressed by the term "banners of light."[12]

The angelic praise described in these blessings displays a similar content and purpose. This can readily be seen in the choice of angelic epithets such as "troops of *light*,"[13] and in the descriptions of joint praise such as "[we] praise your name, *God of lights*, in that you have *renewed* [. . .] *gates of light* and with us in praises of your glory" (4Q503 frg. 30). The incorporation of angelic praise within the blessings said by the human worshipers implies that praise in unison with the angels was thought to take place during the course of reciting these blessings at sunset as well as sunrise.[14]

---

10. Chazon, "Prayers from Qumran," 281–82.

11. The listing of each day's date ("on the x of the month") before the evening prayer but not before the morning prayer indicates that this liturgy reckoned the day from the evening. Compare 4Q334 which specifies the number (but not the content) of the praises for each "night" (*lylh*) and "day" (*ywm*).

12. The astronomical terminology is explained in J. Baumgarten, "4Q503 (*Daily Prayers*) and the Lunar Calendar," *RevQ* 12 (1986): 399–406, and M. Abegg, "Does Anyone Really Know What Time It Is? A Reexamination of 4Q503 in Light of 4Q317," in *The Provo International Conference on the Dead Sea Scrolls* (ed. D. W. Parry and E. Ulrich; STDJ 30; Leiden: Brill, 1999), 396–406.

13. For example, 4Q503 frgs. 8–9, 10 (see also Nitzan, *Qumran Prayer*, 56, n. 29). Note that this angelic epithet is identical with the astronomical term "banners of light" (*dgly 'wr*).

14. Compare Job 38:7, *Jub.* 2:2–3, Sir. 42:16–17, and the *Hymn to the Creator* in 11QPs^a, which refer to angelic praise at sunrise; angelic (and perhaps joint praise) in the evening and morning is referred to in the *Ritual of Marriage*, 4Q502 27. For a fuller treatment of the angelic praise in 4Q503, see E. G. Chazon, "The Function of the Qumran Prayer Texts," in *The Dead Sea Scrolls — Fifty Years after Their Discovery* (ed. L. H. Schiffman, E. Tov, and J. C. VanderKam; Jerusalem: Israel Exploration Society, forthcoming), 217–25.

One further aspect of this text's conception of prayer times should be noted. It concerns the evening and morning blessings for the four Sabbaths and the one festival which fell during the month.[15] These blessings are essentially identical in form, content, and function to those said on ordinary days. In other words, they also depict the diurnal changes in solar and lunar light but simply incorporate special motifs for those days such as rest, joy, and election within the set pattern used for all the daily prayers. Natural time and astronomical themes are thus supplemented but not replaced by historical time and holiday themes. It is also noteworthy that neither sacrifice nor sacrificial time is mentioned in these prayers.

Finally, it is important to note that the moon's movements as well as the sun's are praised in this liturgy, which apparently followed the fixed solar calendar of 364 days.[16] This phenomenon is analogous to the praise for the sun's creation and daily renewal pronounced in the traditional "Blessing on the Heavenly Lights," which was obligated by the rabbis who, as is well-known, fought against the solar calendar vehemently.[17] This somewhat paradoxical situation apparently arises naturally from human observation of the universe and the resulting urge to praise the creator for all created things, not the least of which are the luminaries and their workings.

Although no other copies of this liturgy of daily prayers have survived, the liturgical practice of praising God for the luminaries' renewal at the time that renewal takes place daily is amply documented in antiquity, in both sectarian sources like the hymn closing the *Community Rule* and nonsectarian sources such as the rabbinic "Blessing on the Heavenly Lights."[18] It is now further attested by another fragmentary scroll, which, like 4Q503, may be of non-Qumranic origin. This text, 4Q408, also contains a communal liturgy of morning and evening blessings in which worshipers bless God for the daily appearance of light and darkness and for the creation of the luminaries who are said to bless God.[19] The introductory rubric, opening blessing, specific content, and liturgical function as morning and evening prayers resemble 4Q503, but there are also differences in detail such as the blessing formula and the order in which morning and evening are mentioned. These two different liturgies, therefore, independently attest a similar practice in the same historical period.

---

15. For the identification of this month, the festival which falls in it, and the Sabbath prayers, see Chazon, "Function of the Qumran Prayer Texts."

16. Abegg, "Does Anyone Really Know What Time It Is?" and Chazon, "Function of the Qumran Prayer Texts."

17. This calendar controversy is reflected, for example, in m. *Menaḥ.* 10:3. Cf. Sir. 43:1–10.

18. The range of ancient sources for both natural and sacrificial prayer times is discussed in the conclusion.

19. A. Steudel, "4Q408: A Liturgy on Morning and Evening Prayer, Preliminary Publication," *RevQ* 16 (1994): 313–34. "408. 4QApocryphon of Moses," in *Qumran Cave 4 XXVI, Cryptic Texts and Miscellanea, Part 1* (ed. P. Alexander et al., DJD 36; Oxford: Clarendon, 2000). J. Baumgarten ("Some Notes on 4Q408," *RevQ* 18 [1997]: 143–44) has recently argued that the phrase "you created them to bless Your holy name" in 4Q408 1, 9, 11, refers to human rather than angelic blessing.

Before concluding this discussion of natural times of prayer, I would like to propose that the weekly liturgy entitled *Dibre Hamme'orot* (The words of the luminaries) should be included in this category. As I have suggested in previous studies, this title, which is inscribed on the back of the oldest copy (4Q504), seems to reflect the text's liturgical function so that each day's prayer would have been recited at one or both of the hours when the luminaries' light interchanges daily.[20]

Category B: Sacrificial Time — Prayers at the Times of Temple Sacrifices

The scrolls' most comprehensive description of prayer's coordination with temple sacrifices occurs in the prose inset known as *David's Compositions*, which comes near the end of the large Psalms scroll from Cave 11 (11QPs[a] XXVII, 4–8):

> And he [David] wrote 3,600 psalms; and songs to sing before the altar over the whole-burnt *tamid* offering every day, for all the days of the year, 364; and for the *qorban* [offering] of the Sabbaths, 52 songs; and for the *qorban* [offering] of the New Moons and for all Solemn Assemblies and for the Day of Atonement, 30 songs.[21]

This inset ascribes to David the psalms within this collection and many more, credits him with creating liturgical accompaniment to the temple sacrifices, and lends Davidic authority to the 364-day solar calendar with its fifty-two Sabbaths.[22]

Despite the inset's tendentious character, it may nevertheless reflect some religious practice during the period in which it was composed. This seems to be the case at least with respect to the Levitical song concluding the daily service at the Second Temple, cited by 1 Chron. 23:30–31, Sir. 50:18, and *m. Tamid* 7:3.[23] The latter two sources as well as Acts 3:1 and Luke 1:10 also attest popular prayer at that hour in the temple precincts.[24] Other sources such as Ezra 9:5, Dan. 9:21, Jdt. 9:1,

---

20. E. G. Chazon, "A Liturgical Document from Qumran and Its Implications: 'Words of the Luminaries' (4QDibHam)," (Ph.D. diss., Hebrew University, Jerusalem, 1991), 68 (in Hebrew); idem, "Hymns and Prayers," 259. For the custom of repeating one and the same prayer twice a day at these hours, compare the prose inset in the *Psalms Scroll*, discussed below (under category B), and the Levitical song accompanying the perpetual offerings as described in *m. Tamid* 7:3–4 (the fourth Mishnah, which enumerates the Levitical songs for each day of the week, is a late addition to this tractate).

21. J. A. Sanders, *The Psalms Scroll of Qumran Cave 11 (11QPs[a])* (DJD 4; Oxford: Clarendon, 1965), 92. The bracketed additions are my own.

22. Peter Flint has recently proposed that the entire collection was organized around these two principles of Davidic emphasis and the solar calendar, arguing that it "originally contained 52 Psalms plus 4 pieces that assert Davidic authorship" (*The Dead Sea Psalms Scroll and the Book of Psalms* [STDJ 17; Leiden: Brill, 1997], 192–94).

23. The biblical and Mishnaic sources mention the Levites explicitly. Ben Sira and the Mishnah, which are strikingly similar in their details, specify that the songs were sung during the concluding part of the service; this apparently was also the situation in the Chronicler's times (cf. 2 Chron. 29:30).

24. Josephus, *Against Apion* 2.196, seems to attest the same practice as may *Jub.* 6:14 (if the verbs refer to atonement through prayer and not just to sacrifice; for different interpretations of the hour

and Acts 10:30 refer to popular prayer outside of the temple at the hour of the daily, afternoon sacrifice.[25] Unlike *David's Compositions,* however, none of these sources speak of prayer before the altar (*lpny hmzbh*); rather, they indicate that prayers said at the temple remained on its periphery both geographically and culticly.[26]

In light of the foregoing, it is tempting to see the inset as creating a framework for an ideal liturgy either to accompany temple sacrifices or to be recited outside the temple in lieu of the sacrifices. However, we should bear in mind that the inset speaks only of the temple context and does not suggest this Psalms scroll was intended as a liturgical substitute for sacrifice, although the Qumran community may have used it that way later. In this connection, we should also note that 11QPs[a] does not appear to have been compiled within the Qumran community but rather among other, pre-Qumranic proponents of the solar calendar.[27]

Two other works specify praise at the time of temple sacrifices, both of which also follow the solar calendar. One of these, the fragmentary manuscript of 4Q409, I shall just mention briefly. It is a hymn calling for praise on festivals and apparently also for praise accompanying the festival offerings. The precise nature of the connection between the praise and the offerings "on the altar" can no longer be detected.[28]

The final text to be analyzed in this study is a major liturgical collection which raises some interesting possibilities concerning how prayer outside the temple was coordinated with sacrifice and how such prayer may have functioned in a sectarian context. This collection is the important work entitled the *Songs of the Sabbath Sacrifice.*

The collection comprises songs for the first thirteen Sabbaths of the year. The dated titles such as "song of the sacrifice of the seventh Sabbath on the sixteenth of the month" indicate both the liturgy's adherence to the 364-day solar calendar and some connection to the Sabbath sacrifice (*'Olat HaShabbat*). The songs' form and content suggest what the nature of that connection might be.

The songs invite the angels to praise God and describe angelic worship in the heavenly temple. Climaxes are the seventh song's sevenfold calls to praise, the twelfth song's description of the divine *merkabah* chariot throne, and the final depiction of the angelic priests offering sacrifices in the thirteenth song.

---

and sacrifices mentioned in 6:14a, see C. Werman, "The Story of the Flood in the *Book of Jubilees,*" *Tarbiz* 54 [1995]: 201 (in Hebrew).

25. Cf. 1 Kings 18:36; Ps. 141:2.

26. See I. Knohl, "Between Voice and Silence: The Relationship between Prayer and Temple Cult," *JBL* 115 (1996): 17–30, and the literature cited there. The ostensible discrepancy between *David's Compositions* and the other sources is obviated if the words "before the altar" are taken as a general designation for the temple or as a reference to the area on the far side of the altar, closer to the outer courts rather than to the holy of holies (Knohl, private communication).

27. The evidence is summarized by Flint, *Dead Sea Psalms Scroll,* 198–99.

28. E. Qimron, "Times for Praising God: A Fragment of a Scroll from Qumran (4Q409)," *JQR* 80 (1990): 341–47; "408. 4QLiturgical Work A," in *Qumran Cave 4 XXVI, Poetical and Liturgical Texts, Part 2* (ed. B. Nitzan et al., DJD 29; Oxford: Clarendon, 1999), 63–67.

The striking descriptions of the angelic priests and their sacrifices in the heavenly temple lend credence to A. S. van der Woude's suggestion that the songs served as a means of participating in the heavenly cult.[29] The songs' numinous quality and their progression from the heavenly temple's outer vestibules to its innermost sanctum led Carol Newsom to propose that their purpose was to create an experience of "being in the heavenly sanctuary and in the presence of the angelic priests and worshippers."[30] She explains that that experience would have been timed to coincide with the Sabbath sacrifice mentioned in the songs' titles. Johann Maier takes issue with Newsom's proposal for a "mystical" function and posits instead that the songs served as substitutes for the sacrifices in the earthly temple.[31]

What the different theories have in common is a recognition that these songs, with their solar-calendar and heavenly orientation, were probably not intended for use in the contemporary Jerusalem temple, and that their connection with the Sabbath sacrifice therefore had a different purpose, one rooted in the historical context(s) in which they were composed and transmitted. No matter what their origin, it is reasonable to assume that at Qumran these songs would have filled a cultic void and, at the same time, would have validated that Community's own priestly claims.[32] Whether one sees the *Songs of the Sabbath Sacrifice* as a substitute for the Jerusalem cult, as liturgical accompaniment to the heavenly cult, or as a vehicle for an experience of the heavenly temple and communion with the angels ministering there, it is highly plausible that they were recited at the hour when the Sabbath sacrifice was offered.

---

29. A. S. van der Woude, "Fragmente einer Roller der Lieder für das Sabbatopfer aus Hohle XI von Qumran (11QSirSabb)," in *Von Kanaan bis Kerala* (van der Ploeg Festschrift; ed. W. C. Delsman et al.; AOAT 221; Kevelaer, Germany: Butzon & Bercker; Neukirchen-Vluyn: Neukirchener Verlag, 1982), 332.

30. Newsom refers to this as "the praxis of something like a communal mysticism" and suggests that the songs were the Qumran community's "vehicle for the experience of communion with the angels" (*Songs of the Sabbath Sacrifice: A Critical Edition* [HSS 27; Atlanta: Scholars Press, 1985], 17–20, 59). For the text one should also consult her revised edition, "Shirot 'Olat Hashabbat," in *Qumran Cave 4 VI, Poetical and Liturgical Texts, Part 1* (ed. E. Eshel et al.; DJD 11; Oxford: Clarendon, 1998), 173–401.

31. J. Maier, "Shire 'Olat hash-Shabbat: Some Observations on Their Calendric Implications and on Their Style," in *The Madrid Qumran Congress* (ed. J. Trebolle Barrera and L. Vegas Montaner; STDJ 11; Leiden: Brill; Madrid: Editorial Complutense, 1992), 552–53. See also Nitzan, *Qumran Prayer*, 285–93.

32. For the latter social function see especially C. A. Newsom, " 'He Has Established for Himself Priests': Human and Angelic Priesthood in the Qumran Sabbath *Shirot*," in *Archaeology and History of the Dead Sea Scrolls* (ed. L. H. Schiffman; JSPSup 8; Sheffield: JSOT, 1990), 113–20, and idem, *Songs of the Sabbath Sacrifice*, 51–72. The nine Qumran copies of the songs indicate their importance for the Qumran community, but the possibility of non-Qumranic origin has now been entertained by Newsom, " 'Sectually Explicit' Literature from Qumran," in *The Hebrew Bible and Its Interpreters* (ed. W. Propp, B. Halpern, and D. N. Freedman; Winona Lake, Ind.: Eisenbrauns, 1990), 167–87. The Masada copy suggests a usage outside of Qumran by the close of the Second Temple period.

Conclusion

This study of the evidence from the scrolls for prayer times has shown that both patterns, the one following natural time and the other following sacrificial time, were used at Qumran for daily, Sabbath, and festival prayer. Thus, although we might have expected the Qumran community to follow only natural time and to reject a prayer model based on temple sacrifices, this was clearly not the case. Rather, the community added a sectarian dimension to each pattern by linking each with the sectarian calendar and by attributing a special function to prayer coordinated with sacrifice.[33]

The Dead Sea Scrolls thus teach us that despite ostensible ideological and functional differences, these two patterns of prayer actually cut across societal divisions and functioned together in the life of a single community. Moreover, by providing a windfall of new texts, including many of non-Qumranic provenance, the scrolls enable us to better appreciate how the natural and sacrificial prayer times coexisted not only at Qumran but probably also at other locales and among other groups during this period.[34]

The Scrolls now show more of a balance and interplay between the two patterns of natural and sacrificial prayer times than was discernible in the past. Previously known sources on Second Temple prayer were weighted in favor of prayer's coordination with sacrifice.[35] Thanks to the discovery among the scrolls of non-Qumranic daily liturgies for recitation when the luminaries exchange their light, such isolated statements about prayer at dawn as those found in several psalms and apocryphal books can now be viewed in a broader historical framework.[36] In this way both patterns of prayer times, the pattern of natural time and the pattern of sacrificial time, served as existing models in the rabbinic and early Christian periods, available and ready to be adopted (or rejected) during those crucial centuries of liturgical development.

---

33. For the latter see the discussion above on the function of the *Songs of the Sabbath Sacrifice* at Qumran. For the former see especially the *Community Rule*'s closing hymn, which connects natural prayer times with the sectarian calendar. 4Q503's evening and morning liturgy evidently also espouses that calendar as do all the scrolls which coordinate prayer with sacrifice (*Sabbath Songs*, 4Q409, and 11QPs^aDavComp; on these Scrolls see also the next note).

34. Although 4Q503 *Daily Prayers*, the *Songs of the Sabbath Sacrifice*, 4Q409 *Times for Praising God*, and 11QPs^aDavComp may have originated outside of the Qumran community, these texts all follow the fixed solar calendar and, therefore, came from the same wing of Judaism. On the non-Qumranic provenance and early date of the *Words of the Luminaries* (4Q504–6), see Chazon, "Prayers from Qumran," 271–73, and the literature cited there.

35. See the numerous sources cited above in the discussion of category B (nn. 23–25). For the rabbinic institution of obligatory daily prayer at the hours when the morning and afternoon *tamid* sacrifices were offered at the temple, see *t. Ber.* 3:1 and the Talmudic sources discussed below.

36. For example, Ps. 55:17 (cf. Dan. 6:11); Pss. 57:8–9; 88:14; Sir. 39:5; Wis. 16:28; *Sib. Or.* 3:591–93. The rabbinic sources on the prayer of the *Vatikin* at sunrise (*b. Ber.* 9b; cf. *t. Ber.* 1:2) and of those who pray "with the dim sunlight" (*dmdwmy ḥmh*; *y. Ber.* 4:1, 7b) may reflect ancient practices among certain segments of the population, as suggested by Shlomo Naeh and Aaron Shemesh in their helpful comments on a draft of this article.

Significantly, in actual religious practice or, when people really prayed, the disparity between these patterns might not have been as great as our theoretical models, or those of the rabbis, might suggest. Indeed, the Talmudic passage which sets up the kind of distinction I have made here assumes one *realia* of morning, afternoon and evening prayer regardless of which explanation is offered for this practice — correspondence with the times of the daily (*tamid*) sacrifices or "over against the three times when the day changes for all created beings" (*y. Ber.* 4:1, 7a–b).[37] Although this passage is relatively late and reflects three rather than two obligatory prayer times, it is instructive because it presents both models[38] and goes to the heart of the issue of when people worshiped God and why.

To conclude, I suggest that not only are the natural and sacrificial prayer times not so far apart in "real time" but that originally, and probably throughout most of the Second Temple period, sacrificial time was designed to correspond with natural time.[39] The twice-daily *tamid* sacrifices were to be offered in the morning (*bbqr*) and "between the two evenings" (*byn h'rbym*), that is, probably at twilight (Exod. 29:39 and Num. 28:4).[40] This pentateuchal language is echoed in the sources from the Persian and Hellenistic periods, which also refer to prayer at the time of the morning and especially the evening sacrifice (*mnht 'rb*; for example, Ezra 9:5 and Dan. 9:21; cf. Jdt. 9:1). Even the rabbinic sources which stipulate that the second daily sacrifice and corresponding prayer had to be offered "by the evening" (*'d h'rb*; *m. Ber.* 4:1, *t. Ber.* 3:1; cf. *m. Pes.* 5:1, *b. Pes.* 58a; Acts 3:1, 10:30; Josephus, *Ant.* 14.65), still reflect a basic connection with the waning of the day. Thus, the two times a day when light and darkness intermingled as the luminaries exchanged their dominion were evidently considered appropriate hours to give thanks to the Creator and particularly propitious times for worshiping the Lord.

---

37. Similar to the latter is the third model presented by this Talmudic passage; it is based on the forefathers' activities during the day. Compare the parallel passage in the Babylonian Talmud (*b. Ber.* 26b), which presents only the forefathers' model and that of the sacrifices.

38. Each of the two models occurs separately in other rabbinic sources (see nn. 35–36 above). For the two obligatory prayers, see *m. Ber.* 4:1 and *t. Ber.* 3:1.

39. D. K. Falk (*Daily, Sabbath, and Festival Prayer in the Dead Sea Scrolls* [STDJ 27; Leiden: Brill, 1998], 47) argues for maintaining the distinction between these two patterns of prayer while acknowledging that they are "sometimes blurred, not least because sacrifices were offered at daybreak and evening."

40. For this interpretation of *byn h'rbym*, see, for example, N. Sarna, *Exodus* (JPS Torah Commentary; Philadelphia and New York: Jewish Publication Society, 1991), 55, 192; J. Milgrom, *Numbers* (JPS Torah Commentary; Philadelphia and New York: Jewish Publication Society, 1990), 67, 239, 487; and O. Holtzmann, "Die täglichen Gebetsstunden im Judentum und Urchristentum," *ZNW* 12 (1911): 101 (I thank Joseph Tabory for this bibliographical reference). Holtzmann argued that the shift to offering the evening (*minhah*) sacrifice earlier in the day, that is, from the ninth hour of daylight on, occurred in the Herodian temple (compare Falk, *Daily, Sabbath, and Festival Prayer,* 47).

6

Reinventing Exodus:
Exegesis and Legend
in Hellenistic Egypt

◆

John J. Collins
Yale University

The story of the exodus occupies a foundational place in the Hebrew Bible and in Jewish tradition. While the ultimate origin of that story has been called into question in recent years,[1] it was certainly well established in the Hellenistic period. The retelling of the story has been viewed in two distinct, although not necessarily incompatible, ways in recent scholarship. On the one hand, James Kugel has argued that the return of the Jewish exiles in the Persian period ushered in "the age of interpretation," which came to full bloom in the Hellenistic and Roman periods.[2] Whereas Louis Ginzberg in an earlier generation wrote of *The Legends of the Jews,* Kugel writes of interpretations of biblical texts — interpretations of the Jews, so to speak. On the other hand, Erich Gruen has noted the frequency with which Hellenistic Jewish authors "simply rewrote scriptural narratives, inventing facts or attaching fanciful tales." He concludes that "the Bible served here less as a text for exegesis than as a springboard for creativity."[3] That creativity drew on many sources from the Gentile world in addition to the Bible. Gruen does not deny that exegesis plays a part in the process, nor does Kugel claim that it is the only factor. Their work can be viewed as complementary, but their perspectives are distinct and both are necessary.

---

1. See especially E. Blum, *Studien zur Komposition des Pentateuch* (BZAW 189; Berlin: Walter de Gruyter, 1990); H. Shanks, ed., *The Rise of Ancient Israel* (Washington, D.C.: Biblical Archaeology Society, 1992).

2. J. Kugel, *The Bible as It Was* (Cambridge: Harvard University Press, 1997), 2; for interpretations of the exodus see pp. 285–460. See also his more detailed volume, *Traditions of the Bible* (Cambridge: Harvard University Press, 1998).

3. E. Gruen, *Heritage and Hellenism: The Reinvention of Jewish Tradition* (Berkeley: University of California Press, 1998), 137.

The Exodus in Artapanus

The most colorful and creative account of the exodus from an ancient Jewish author is undoubtedly that of Artapanus. Artapanus is known to us only from fragments preserved by Eusebius and Clement,[4] who cited them from the work of Alexander Polyhistor, a native of Miletus who was brought to Rome by Sulla and given his freedom in about 80 B.C.E.[5] Alexander wrote a work, "On the Jews," which was a compilation of quotations from Hellenistic Jewish authors. The authors cited must have written no later than the early first century B.C.E. The fragments of Artapanus deal with Abraham, Joseph, and Moses. All, including the Abraham fragment, are set in Egypt, and there can be little doubt that this is where Artapanus wrote. He certainly belonged to the Ptolemaic era rather than the Roman, and he may have written as early as the end of the third century.[6] It is his account of the exodus that will concern us here.

Artapanus's account agrees with the biblical story in several details. Moses is introduced as a Jewish child, adopted into the family of an Egyptian ruler. He kills an Egyptian, but in self-defense, and flees to Arabia, where he marries the daughter of Raguel. He witnesses miraculous fire "kindled from the earth" that burns without wood, and he hears a divine voice from the fire. He returns to Egypt and performs signs for the king, including the transformation of a rod into a snake, and afflicts the Egyptians with plagues. He notes that the Jews despoiled the Egyptians and crossed the Red Sea when Moses struck it with his rod and divided it. From the form of the proper names (e.g., Raēouēlos, Raguel) and verbal echoes, it is apparent that he knew the biblical story of the exodus in its Septuagintal form.[7] He tells it, however, with numerous embellishments, and adds stories about the early career of Moses that have no basis in the biblical text. Moses is identified with Mousaeus and the teacher of Orpheus. He is credited with various inventions for the benefit of the Egyptians, including most notably the cult of various animals, including the Apis bull. His successes arouse the envy

---

4. Three fragments of Artapanus are preserved by Eusebius in PE 9.18, 23, and 27, dealing with Abraham, Joseph, and Moses respectively. The Moses fragment is partially paralleled in Clement, *Stromateis* 1.23.154, 2–3. See C. R. Holladay, *Historians* (vol. 1 of *Fragments from Hellenistic-Jewish Authors*; Chico, Calif.: Scholars Press, 1983), 199–232. Annotated translations can also be found in J. J. Collins, "Artapanus," OTP 2.889–903, and N. Walter, *Fragmente jüdisch-hellenistischer Historiker* (JSHRZ 1/2; Gütersloh: Mohn, 1976), 121–43.

5. On Alexander Polyhistor see the classic work of J. Freudenthal, *Hellenistische Studien I–II, Alexander Polyhistor und die von ihm erhaltenen Reste judäischer und samaritanischer Geschichtswerke* (Breslau: Skutsch, 1875); J. Strugnell, "General Introduction, with a Note on Alexander Polyhistor," OTP 2.777–79, and G. E. Sterling, *Historiography and Self-Definition: Josephos, Luke-Acts, and Apologetic Historiography* (Leiden: Brill, 1992), 144–52.

6. On the date of Artapanus, see Collins, "Artapanus," 890–91; M. Goodman, "Jewish Literature Composed in Greek," in *The History of the Jewish People in the Age of Jesus Christ* (ed. E. Schuerer; revised and edited by G. Vermes, F. Millar, and M. Goodman; Edinburgh: T. & T. Clark, 1986), 3.523–24.

7. For the correspondences, see Sterling, *Historiography and Self-Definition*, 174.

of the king, Chenephres, who sends him on a campaign against Ethiopia with a makeshift army. Moses nonetheless succeeds and even teaches the Ethiopians circumcision. The continued plotting of Chenephres, however, eventually causes Moses to flee to Arabia, and this is the occasion of the killing of the Egyptian. At first Moses restrains Raguel from invading Egypt, but eventually he is instructed by the divine voice from the fire to wage a campaign and rescue the Jews. From this point on, Artapanus's narrative is closer to that of Exodus, but there are still numerous embellishments. For example, the Egyptians dedicate the rod to Isis because of the wonders that Moses works with it.

Gruen has rightly celebrated the ingenuity of this concoction, which transfers to Moses exploits elsewhere attributed to Semiramis, Sesostris, and other legendary heroes.[8] Indeed, it is so creative that Gruen feels obliged to reassure us that "Jews would certainly not take it seriously."[9] But this is to dismiss the evidence of the text without warrant. We do not know where in Egypt Artapanus lived or what kind of Judaism he represents, except insofar as that Judaism is revealed in his text. The idea that Moses created the animal cults for the benefit of the Egyptians would undoubtedly have been as offensive to many Jews as it surely would have been to Egyptians, but Artapanus was clearly not constrained by Deuteronomic orthodoxy. Indeed, it is striking that he fails to credit Moses with the accomplishment for which he was most famous in the Hellenistic world, the giving of the law. However difficult it may be for a modern scholar to take it seriously, the claim that Moses founded the Egyptian animal cults was for Artapanus a source of ethnic pride, and this was evidently more important to him than scruples about violating the Torah.

It is also apparent that Artapanus "worked with more than scripture and his imagination."[10] Much light is shed on his account by comparison with a passage attributed to Manetho by Josephus.[11] Manetho claimed that Jerusalem was built "in the land now called Judaea" by the Hyksos, after they had been expelled from Egypt, and the claim is accepted by Josephus, who says that "up to this point he followed the chronicles."[12] But then "by offering to record the legends and current talk about the Jews, he took the liberty of interpolating improbable tales in his desire to confuse with us a crowd of Egyptians, who for leprosy and other maladies

---

8. Gruen, *Heritage and Hellenism*, 158. On the "competitive historiography" of Artapanus, see J. J. Collins, *Between Athens and Jerusalem: Jewish Identity in the Hellenistic Diaspora* (rev. ed.; Grand Rapids: Eerdmans, 1999), chap. 1; Sterling, *Historiography and Self-Definition*, 176–80.

9. Gruen, *Heritage and Hellenism*, 158.

10. Sterling, *Historiography and Self-Definition*, 181. Cf. P. W. van der Horst, "The Interpretation of the Bible by the Minor Hellenistic-Jewish Authors," in *Essays on the Jewish World of Early Christianity* (Göttingen: Vandenhoeck & Ruprecht, 1990), 187–219 (200–205 on Artapanus).

11. *Ag. Ap.* 1.228–52; M. Stern, *Greek and Latin Authors on Jews and Judaism* (Jerusalem: Israel Academy of Arts and Sciences, 1974), 1.78–86.

12. A separate account of the Hyksos, their expulsion from Egypt and occupation of Judea, is found in *Ag. Ap.* 1.73–91; Stern, *Greek and Latin Authors*, 1.68–69.

had been condemned to banishment from Egypt." According to this account, a king named Amenophis "conceived a desire to behold the gods" and was advised by a sage, also named Amenophis, that this would be possible "if he cleansed the whole land of lepers and other polluted persons." The king assembled some eighty thousand of these people, including some learned priests, and set them to work in the stone quarries, segregated from the ordinary Egyptians. After they had suffered there for a considerable time they were allowed to occupy the deserted city of the Hyksos, Avaris, which was dedicated to Typhon (the Egyptian Seth) according to religious tradition. They appointed one of the priests of Heliopolis, named Osarseph, as their leader. He made a law "that they should neither worship the gods nor refrain from any of the animals prescribed as especially sacred in Egypt, but should sacrifice and consume all alike, and that they should have intercourse with none save those of their own confederacy." He then rebelled against the king and summoned the Shepherds (Hyksos) to his aid from Jerusalem. The Shepherds then invaded Egypt. King Amenophis gathered the sacred animals to protect them and hid the images of the gods. Instead of engaging the Hyksos in battle, he withdrew to Ethiopia. While he was in exile, "the Solymites made a descent along with the polluted Egyptians and treated the people so impiously and savagely that the domination of the Shepherds seemed like a golden age to those who witnessed the present enormities. For not only did they set towns and villages on fire, pillaging the temples and mutilating images of the gods without restraint, but they also made a practice of using the sanctuaries as kitchens to roast the sacred animals which the people worshipped; and they would compel the priests and prophets to sacrifice and butcher the beasts, afterwards casting the men forth naked." The leader, concludes Manetho, was "named Osarseph after the god Osiris, worshiped at Heliopolis, but when he joined this people, he changed his name and was called Moses." Eventually, Amenophis and his son returned from Ethiopia and drove the Shepherds and the lepers out of Egypt, as far as the borders of Syria.

Most students of Artapanus have agreed that his account of Moses is a rebuttal of this unflattering account attributed to Manetho.[13] Manetho had alleged that Moses forbade his people to worship the gods or to abstain from the flesh of the sacred animals. Artapanus claimed that it was Moses who established these cults. Manetho alleged that Moses had instigated the Hyksos to invade Egypt. Artapanus claimed that Moses restrained Raguel and the Arabs from invading and only launched a campaign when he was directly commanded by a divine voice. According to Manetho, the Pharaoh had to protect the sacred animals from Moses; Artapanus claims that the Pharaoh buried the animals which Moses had made sacred, since he wished to conceal Moses' inventions. In Manetho's account, the Pharaoh sought refuge in Ethiopia from Moses and his allies. In Ar-

---

13. See especially Sterling, *Historiography and Self-Definition*, 182–83, and the literature cited there.

tapanus, Moses conducted a campaign against Ethiopia on behalf of the Pharaoh. Artapanus responds to the charge that Moses and his followers were lepers by claiming that an Egyptian, Chenephres, was the first to die of elephantiasis and by insisting that Moses was physically impressive. Gruen objects that "this was no somber contest for supremacy between Jewish and pagan intellectuals" and claims that the Jewish author "did not enlist in a deadly serious encounter to advance Jewish values against the claims of competing nations and cultures."[14] Artapanus was certainly not somber, whether he was "deadly serious" or not, but competitive historiography did not have to be somber. For all its exuberance, Artapanus's account served a serious purpose: to defend the ancestors of his people from Gentile slander and to extol them above the heroes of other peoples. The refutation of writers such as Manetho is only the negative side of his work. On the positive side he claimed for Moses the accomplishments of various heroes. The correspondences with Sesostris are especially striking. Sesostris was credited with being the first Egyptian to divide the country into nomes and to organize Egyptian religion. These accomplishments are claimed for Moses by Artapanus.[15] The motif of a campaign against Ethiopia was widespread. Semiramis was said to have subdued it. The Persian king Cambyses had tried and failed. Sesostris was said to have been the first man to conquer Ethiopia and the only Egyptian to rule over it. The Moses of Artapanus conquers it with a nonprofessional army. Moses even outshines the pagan gods. He is identified with Hermes, the supreme culture-bringer, and subordinates Isis, who is identified with the earth. He is also the teacher of Orpheus.[16]

The rationale underlying Artapanus's narrative, then, is clear enough, however unconventional the view of Judaism that it embodies. In this enterprise, the biblical account provided a starting point, but did not constrain the Hellenistic author to any significant degree. He draws freely on pagan legends, sometimes to borrow motifs, sometimes to invert and refute them. We may agree with Gruen that he shows wit and ingenuity, but this is not an exercise in humor or caprice.[17] It is a skirmish in the battle for the view of a people's origins that would have huge repercussions for their status and reputation in the Hellenistic age.

The Origin of Manetho's Account

But what of the account attributed to Manetho? Josephus presents this account as the fountainhead of a tradition of anti-Jewish slander, and some modern authors

---

14. Gruen, *Heritage and Hellenism*, 158, 160.
15. Sterling, *Historiography and Self-Definition*, 177.
16. See further, Collins, *Between Athens and Jerusalem*, chap. 1. For the exploits of Sesostris, Semiramis, and other legendary heroes of the Hellenistic Near East, see M. Braun, *History and Romance in Graeco-Oriental Literature* (Oxford: Blackwell, 1938).
17. Pace Gruen, *Heritage and Hellenism*, 160.

follow this assessment.[18] Similar accounts of Jewish origins, with increasingly vitri-olic variations, are found in such authors as Lysimachus, Chaeremon, and Apion, who, according to Josephus, carried on a vehement polemic against the Jews in Alexandria in the early Roman period. The bitter hostility of Jews and Alexan-drian Greeks in the first century C.E. is well-known. Manetho, however, wrote under Ptolemy I or Ptolemy II, in the first half of the third century B.C.E., and we have no evidence of such hostility at that early time.[19] Consequently, many schol-ars have argued that Manetho's account has suffered interpolation.[20] Specifically, the identification of Osarseph, leader of the lepers, with Moses in *Ag. Ap.* 1.250 seems to be added as a gloss, and is surely secondary, as there is no hint of it in the main narrative.[21] Nonetheless, the marauding invaders in the story come from Jerusalem, and are presumably the ancestors of the Jews.[22] It is often assumed that Manetho was giving an Egyptian rejoinder to the story of the exodus.[23]

It is also widely agreed, however, that the basic narrative reflects old Egyptian traditions, some of which related to the expulsion of the Hyksos in the sixteenth century B.C.E. and some of which derived from the upheaval caused by the reli-gious revolution of Akhenaten in the Amarna period.[24] The story of the lepers may reflect some historical memory of a plague that had swept the country in the second millennium, and was known as "the Asiatic illness."[25] The association with Avaris, city of Typhon, or with Seth, the mythical adversary of Osiris, represents the demonization of the Hyksos in Egyptian memory.[26] Gruen concludes that "the Manethonian tale does not derive from the Exodus or some garbled form of it.

---

18. Stern, *Greek and Latin Authors*, 64; P. Schäfer, *Judeophobia: Attitudes toward the Jews in the Ancient World* (Cambridge: Harvard University Press, 1997), 17–21. See especially J. W. van Henten and Ra'anan Abusch, "The Depiction of the Jews as Typhonians and Josephus' Strategy of Refutation in 'Contra Apionem'" in *Josephus' Contra Apionem*, ed. L. H. Feldman and J. R. Levison (Leiden: Brill, 1996), 272–309, who point out that both the Hyksos and the Jews are consistently associated with Seth-Typhon, the mythical enemy of the royal god Horus.

19. On Manetho, see G. P. Verbrugghe and J. M. Wickersham, *Berossos and Manetho, Introduced and Translated: Native Traditions in Ancient Mesopotamia and Egypt* (Ann Arbor: University of Michigan Press, 1996); Sterling, *Historiography and Self-Definition*, 117–36; P. Fraser, *Ptolemaic Alexandria* (3 vols.; Oxford: Clarendon, 1972), 1.505–11.

20. E. Meyer, *Aegyptische Chronologie* (Leipzig: Hinrichs, 1904), 71–79; J. G. Gager, *Moses in Greco-Roman Paganism* (SBLMS 16; Nashville: Abingdon, 1972), 118. See Verbrugghe and Wickersham, *Berossos and Manetho*, 116.

21. This is agreed even by Schäfer, *Judeophobia*, 20, who nonetheless insists that Manetho's original account was hostile to the Jews.

22. This was pointed out by V. Tcherikover, *Hellenistic Civilization and the Jews* (New York: Atheneum, 1970), 362; also Stern, *Greek and Latin Authors*, 64.

23. E.g., Tcherikover, *Hellenistic Civilization*, 363; Stern, *Greek and Latin Authors*, 64. A. Kasher, *The Jews in Hellenistic and Roman Egypt* (Tübingen: Mohr, 1985), 328, argues that the rejoinder was prompted by the translation of the Book of Exodus into Greek.

24. D. B. Redford, "The Hyksos Invasion in History and Tradition," *Orientalia* 39 (1970): 1–51; J. Assmann, *Moses the Egyptian* (Cambridge: Harvard University Press, 1997), 23–44.

25. Assmann, *Moses the Egyptian*, 27; H. Goedicke, "The 'Canaanite Illness,'" *Studien zur Altägyptischen Kultur* 11 (1984): 91–105.

26. Van Henten and Abusch, "Depiction of the Jews as Typhonians."

In its essentials, it has nothing whatever to do with Jews."[27] The question then is how it came to be applied to the Jews. Gruen has a novel suggestion, "that introduction of the Jews into Manetho's narrative...came from Jewish sources themselves." More specifically, "one can envision an earlier layer slanted to the benefit of the Jews."[28] There are two strands in Manetho's account, one the tale of the lepers and the other the story of Jerusalemites who invaded and pillaged Egypt. The latter strand, claims Gruen, "could easily derive from a Jewish construct." In support of this claim he argues that Jewish origin was a question of far greater importance to Jews than to Gentiles, that the destruction of pagan cults had a long and favorable history in Israel, and that Artapanus "provides direct testimony for a Jewish tradition of mobilization against Egypt."[29]

In order to assess the plausibility of this highly original suggestion we must take into account another Gentile narrative of Jewish origins, that of Hecataeus of Abdera who wrote under Ptolemy I and so was probably an older contemporary of Manetho.[30] Josephus claims that Hecataeus wrote a book entirely about the Jews, and cites it at length (*Ag. Ap.* 1.183–204), but this book has been shown decisively to be a Jewish forgery.[31] There is no doubt, however, about the authenticity of Hecataeus's excursus on the origin of the Jews in his *Aegyptiaka*, which is preserved in the *Bibliotheca* of Photius, who excerpted it from Diodorus Siculus.[32] According to Hecataeus:

When in ancient times a pestilence arose in Egypt, the common people ascribed their troubles to the workings of a divine agency; for indeed with many strangers of all sorts dwelling in their midst and practising different rites of religion and sacrifice, their own traditional observances in honor of the gods had fallen into disuse. Hence the natives of the land surmised that unless they removed the foreigners, their troubles would never be resolved. At once, therefore, the aliens were driven from the country, and the most outstanding and active among them banded together and, as some say, were cast ashore in Greece and certain other regions.... But the greater number were driven into what is now called Judea, which is not far distant from Egypt and was at that time utterly uninhabited. The colony was headed by a man called Moses, outstanding both for his wisdom and for his courage.

27. Gruen, *Heritage and Hellenism*, 61.
28. Ibid., 63.
29. Ibid., 65.
30. Stern, *Greek and Latin Authors*, 20–45; B. Bar-Kochva, *Pseudo-Hecataeus on the Jews: Legitimizing the Jewish Diaspora* (Berkeley: University of California Press, 1996), 7–43; Sterling, *Historiography and Self-Definition*, 55–91.
31. Bar-Kochva, *Pseudo-Hecataeus.*
32. Gager, *Moses*, 26–37; Schäfer, *Judeophobia*, 15–17.

On taking possession of the land he founded, besides other cities, one that is now the most renowned of all, called Jerusalem.[33]

Hecataeus goes on to give a remarkably positive account of Moses' legislation, including the prohibition of images. He notes, however, that "as a result of their own expulsion from Egypt he introduced a somewhat unsocial and intolerant mode of life" (*apanthrōpon tina kai misoxenon bion*). Hecataeus should not be regarded as either pro-or anti-Jewish. His interest in Judaism was incidental. Gruen has rightly noted that the account is a mixture of accurate and inaccurate information, and that Hecataeus probably had some Jewish informants to supplement his general reliance on Egyptian priests.[34] The more accurate information is found in his brief description of Mosaic legislation. The passage quoted above, however, about the expulsion of foreigners in response to a pestilence was presumably derived from Egyptian sources. This passage is a variant of the story in Manetho of the lepers. Hecataeus presents his account with the detachment of a neutral observer. Manetho makes no pretense of such detachment but reflects Egyptian tradition in all its animosity to the outcasts.

Hecataeus shows that, already at the dawn of the Hellenistic age — even before the work of Manetho — the ancestors of the Jews were identified with the expelled foreigners. His account of Jewish origins bears only superficial similarity to the biblical story of the exodus. The main point of resemblance is simply that the Jewish forebears were foreigners resident in Egypt, who migrated from Egypt to the land later known as Israel. The circumstances of the migration, however, are entirely different. Plagues figure in both accounts, but again they function in very different ways. It is not necessary to suppose that the account found in Hecataeus was dependent in any way on the story of Exodus. Egyptian tradition from the second millennium B.C.E. remembered the Hyksos as foreigners from Syria who were eventually expelled. The idea that Jerusalem had been founded by these people provided answers to two questions that would have been raised with no great urgency by the Egyptian tradition. Where did the Hyksos go, and who established the city and people in Judea, just beyond Egypt's borders? Given the negative portrayal of the Hyksos in Egyptian tradition, a derogatory view of the Jews was implied, but this was no more than the typical Egyptian contempt for "the vile Asiatics" that is well attested from the second millennium on.[35] Gruen, who recognizes that the impetus for this part of Hecataeus's account does not come from the Book of Exodus, objects that "it will not do to ascribe to Jewish informants only those details of Hecataeus' text that are accurate, while assigning the rest to malicious Egyptians, Hellenic formulas, or Hecataeus' own

---

33. Stern, *Greek and Latin Authors*, 27–28.
34. Gruen, *Heritage and Hellenism*, 53–54.
35. See Redford, "Hyksos Invasion in History and Tradition."

errors."[36] Hence his proposal that Diaspora Jews had a hand in fashioning the whole account. It is surely unlikely, however, that Jews would have invented a story that said that their ancestors had been driven from Egypt because they were blamed for a pestilence. We should have to suppose that Hecataeus had altered the hypothetical Jewish account considerably.

In fact, Hecataeus combines two motifs that appear separately in Manetho: the founding of Jerusalem by foreigners expelled from Egypt and the association of Moses and his followers with pestilence, identified in Manetho as leprosy. These motifs may have circulated independently in Egyptian tradition, deriving respectively from the expulsion of the Hyksos and the monotheistic revolution of Akhenaten.[37] Granted that no Jewish author is likely to have associated his forefathers with leprosy or pestilence, is it plausible that the identification with the Hyksos was a Jewish invention?

It is true that Josephus appears to endorse Manetho's initial account of the Hyksos, or Shepherds, who occupied Egypt but were subsequently expelled and founded Jerusalem in the land of Judea.[38] For Josephus, the claim that his ancestors had once ruled Egypt was a source of pride.[39] But Josephus is working from Manetho's account and trying to turn it to the advantage of the Jews. He cites no Jewish author in support of the claim. The only other Jewish author that Gruen can cite for a campaign by Moses against Egypt is Artapanus. But Artapanus is also responding to the account of Manetho, as we have seen, and he is ambivalent about the alleged attack on Egypt. He is at pains to make clear that Moses was opposed to attacking at first, and only did so in obedience to a divine voice. His conduct toward the Egyptian cults stands in direct contrast to that of the lepers in Manetho. Although it is true that "taking action against rival cults and abhorrent practices had a long tradition among Jews,"[40] there was no tradition of an invasion of Egypt among the Jews of the Diaspora. The Jewish settlers in Egypt in the Ptolemaic period sought the patronage of the Greek rulers, who in turn assumed much of the ideology of the Pharaohs.[41] While Jewish writers condemned idolatry, it is only in the Roman period, in the context of the great Diaspora

---

36. Gruen, *Heritage and Hellenism*, 54.

37. On the derivation of the story of the lepers from traditions about the Amarna age, see Redford, "Hyksos Invasion in History and Tradition," 49–50; Assmann, *Moses the Egyptian*, 29–44.

38. *Ag. Ap.* 1.73–91. Josephus concludes with the comment that the most remote ancestors of the Jews lived a nomadic life and were called "Shepherds." In *Ag. Ap.* 2.228 he says that this part of Manetho's account was in accordance with the chronicles.

39. Cf. *Ag. Ap.* 1.224, where he says that the Egyptians hated and envied the Jews because of "the domination of our ancestors over their country."

40. Gruen, *Heritage and Hellenism*, 64.

41. See Collins, *Between Athens and Jerusalem*, chaps. 1–2. On the appropriation of Pharaonic ideology by the Ptolemies, see especially L. Koenen, "Die Adaptation Ägyptischer Königsideologie am Ptolemäerhof," in *Egypt and the Hellenistic World* (ed. W. Peremans; Studia Hellenistica 27; Louvain: Louvain University Press, 1983), 174–90.

revolt under Trajan, that they exulted in the destruction of pagan shrines.[42] The Septuagint famously translated the phrase in Exod. 22:27 (LXX 22:28), *'elōhîm lō' t*ᵉ*qallēl*, "thou shalt not revile God," as "thou shalt not revile gods." Philo explained this text by saying that Moses commanded the Israelites not to "revile with unbridled tongue the gods whom others acknowledge, lest they on their part be moved to utter profane words against Him who truly is."[43] Josephus also says that "our legislator has expressly forbidden us to deride or blaspheme the gods recognized by others, out of respect for the very word 'God.' "[44] Artapanus is exceptional in claiming the Moses founded the animal cults, but he is typical of Hellenistic Jewish literature in presenting the Jewish forefathers as bringers of culture and benefactors of humankind.

Manetho's account of the Hyksos as marauding invaders drew on a long-standing tradition, which reverberated through Egyptian literature from the second millennium down to the Hellenistic age, reinforced by the more recent invasions of the Assyrians and Persians.[45] To be associated with the memory of the Hyksos was to invite execration in Egypt. At least some Jews were aware of the negative associations of Semitic invasion. *Sib. Or.* 3:611–14 prophesies that a great king will come from Asia and fill everything with evils and overthrow the kingdom of evil. This disaster will lead to the conversion of Egypt, but the Sibyl makes no suggestion that this king is Jewish. There were several prototypes for this figure, from the Hyksos to Cambyses and Antiochus Epiphanes. No Jewish author in Ptolemaic Egypt, however, would cast a Jewish king in such a hostile and aggressive role. The suggestion that the identification of the Jews with the expelled Hyksos was a Jewish invention remains unsupported and implausible.

Gruen is right, however, that Manetho's account was not a rejoinder to the biblical story of the exodus, a story that Manetho is unlikely to have known. There are, to be sure, a couple of details that might suggest otherwise. In Manetho's account, the lepers are forced to work in stone quarries. This is not an exact parallel to the forced labor of the Israelites, but it is somewhat reminiscent of the biblical story. Forced labor in ancient Egypt, however, was not reserved for the Hebrews. The similarity may be mere coincidence. More intriguing is the notice

---

42. E.g., *Sib. Or.* 5:484–88. J. M. G. Barclay, *Jews in the Mediterranean Diaspora: From Alexander to Trajan (323 B.C.E.–117 C.E.)* (Edinburgh: T. & T. Clark, 1996), argues for a tradition of "cultural antagonism" already in *Sib. Or.* 3, but this is a misreading of the rhetoric of the Sibyl, which culminates in an appeal for conversion. See the comments of Gruen, *Heritage and Hellenism*, 287, who notes the Sibyl's positive appeal to the Greeks.

43. Philo, *De specialibus legibus* 1.53. See also *Quaestiones et solutiones in Exodum* 2.5 and *De vita Mosis* 2.203–5. See P. W. van der Horst, " 'Thou shalt not revile the gods': The LXX Translation of Exod. 2:28(27), Its Background and Influence," in *Hellenism — Judaism — Christianity: Essays on Their Interaction* (Kampen: Kok Pharos, 1994), 112–21.

44. *Ag. Ap.* 2.237.

45. F. Dunand, "L'Oracle du Potier et la Formation de l'Apocalyptique en Égypte," in *L'Apocalyptique* (ed. F. Raphaël et al.; Paris: Geuthner, 1977), 47–67.

that Osarseph made a law for his followers that they should neither worship the gods nor refrain from sacred animals, and "should have intercourse with none save those of their own confederacy."[46] This notice recalls Hecataeus's reference to the "somewhat anti-social" laws of Moses. Peter Schäfer had argued that this is specifically an anti-Jewish charge, not grounded in the older Egyptian tradition about the Hyksos.[47] This is not necessarily so. The Hyksos had remained in Egypt a race apart, who preserved their Canaanite cult and were always regarded as foreigners, Asiatics.[48] Even if Manetho is alluding to Jewish customs, however, we need not conclude that he knew the Book of Exodus in any form. Jews who adhered to their traditional laws were notoriously reluctant to mingle with other races, and this social *amixia* underlies the comment of Hecataeus. Manetho required no knowledge of Jewish traditions to observe this reluctance. Manetho evidently identified the ancestors of the Jews with the Hyksos, even apart from the identification of Osarseph with Moses, which appears to be a secondary gloss. His portrayal of these people, however, was primarily an adaptation of Egyptian tradition that owed little or nothing to any Jewish source.

Conclusion

Most Hellenistic Jewish accounts of the origin of Israel follow the biblical story of the exodus, even if they embellish it in various ways.[49] But the Bible was not the only source of traditions about the origin of the Jews. Egyptian tradition associated the settling of Judea and the founding of Jerusalem with the expulsion of the Hyksos.[50] This association had unfortunate consequences for the Jews of Egypt, since it entailed negative stereotypes that were deeply entrenched in the Egyptian psyche. Both Artapanus and Josephus, in their very different ways, tried to adapt this tradition and turn it to their advantage. The blending and free adaptation of traditions finds its most colorful expression in Artapanus, but Manetho may have been just as creative in his reshaping of Egyptian traditions, quite independently of the biblical story. Both accounts, Egyptian and Jewish, were quite fantastic in their details, and not without entertainment value for their readers. But they were also profoundly serious in their implications for the nature of the Jewish people and the relations between Jew and Gentile in Hellenistic Egypt.

---

46. *Ag. Ap.* 1.239.
47. Schäfer, *Judeophobia*, 19.
48. Redford, "Hyksos Invasion in History and Tradition," 8.
49. See P. Enns, *Exodus Retold: Ancient Exegesis of the Departure from Egypt in Wis. 10:15–21 and 19:1–9* (HSM 57; Atlanta: Scholars Press, 1997); S. Cheong, *The Exodus Story in the Wisdom of Solomon: A Study in Biblical Interpretation* (JSPSup 23; Sheffield: Sheffield Academic Press, 1997).
50. It is quite unlikely that this tradition had any historical value as far as the origin of Israel was concerned, despite some modern suggestions to the contrary (e.g., B. Halpern, "The Exodus and the Israelite Historians," *Eretz Israel* 24 [1993]: 89–96).

7

The Testaments of the Twelve Patriarchs and Related Qumran Fragments

——— ◆ ———

Marinus de Jonge
University of Leiden

Introduction

In view of our common interest in the so-called pseudepigrapha of the Old Testament and a number of discussions about them in a period of over twenty-five years, it is fitting that my contribution to this volume in honor of my friend George Nickelsburg should be devoted to one of these writings. It will not come as a surprise to him that I have chosen the pseudepigraphon that has occupied me since the preparation of my dissertation: the *Testaments of the Twelve Patriarchs*.[1] Since my thesis appeared in 1953, many attempts have been made to shed light on the history and prehistory of that document with the help of fragments of related writings among the Dead Sea Scrolls, as those came to light.[2] For a considerable time, the fact that many fragments, although announced, remained unpublished made a proper assessment of the situation very difficult. Fortunately, we are now in a much better position.

As is well-known, the *Testaments* have been very popular among scholars; perhaps they have been studied more than any other single pseudepigraphon in the twentieth century. Though in their present form the *Testaments* are a Christian writing, many scholars have tried to remove the Christian elements as products of interpolation or redaction, and have tried to reconstruct earlier, Jewish stages

---

1. *The Testaments of the Twelve Patriarchs: A Study of Their Text, Composition, and Origin* (Assen: Van Gorcum, 1953; 2d ed., 1975).

2. In his study "Le Testament de Lévi (XVII–XVIII) et la secte juive de l'Alliance," *Sem* 4 (1952): 33–53, A. Dupont-Sommer connected *T. Levi* 18 with the Teacher of Righteousness, before any of the Aramaic Levi fragments from Qumran had been published. Already in 1950 he defended the origin of the *Testaments* (in their present state) in the Qumran sect. In this he was followed by M. Philonenko, *Les interpolations chrétiennes des Testaments des Douze Patriarches et les manuscrits de Qoumrân* (Paris: Presses universitaires de France, 1960), who minimizes the Christian influence in the *Testaments*. See also below, n. 23.

in the history of the work, going back to a *Grundschrift* to be dated somewhere in the second century B.C.E. (see particularly J. Becker, A. Hultgård, and J. H. Ulrichsen).[3] In this way the *Testaments* can be a source for our knowledge of the development of Jewish eschatological ideas from 200 B.C.E.–100 C.E., and for our insight into Jewish ethics during the period in which the early Christian movement originated. These more recent literary- and form-critical studies have, like earlier ones,[4] led to widely divergent results. I remain skeptical toward the possibility of applying modern standards of coherence and consistency to writings of this type. Many colleagues have simply tried to prove too much.

We know the *Testaments* through medieval manuscripts, but have evidence that they must have existed in some form in the beginning of the third century C.E. What happened between that date and the writing of the archetype of the available textual witnesses remains unknown. The reconstruction of the history of the *Testaments* before 200 C.E. is beset with even more difficulties. If a Jewish *Grundschrift* ever existed, it has been redacted so thoroughly that it cannot be reconstructed (let alone that we could still determine intermediate stages). A more likely alternative is to assume a Christian composition using a great deal of Jewish material of diverse provenance. Whatever option we prefer, however, comparison of elements in the *Testaments of the Twelve Patriarchs* with those in undisputed Jewish sources is of great importance. R. H. Charles took Cairo Genizah fragments of an Aramaic Levi document (with Greek parallels in an addition to an Athos manuscript of the *Testaments*) into account; he pointed to a medieval Hebrew *Testament of Naphtali* and the late *Midrash Wayissaʿu* as giving a parallel description of the wars mentioned in *T. Jud.* 3–7; 9 (see appendixes 1–3 in his edition). Comparison among this material (and among traditions common to the *Testaments* and *Jubilees*) formed, in my dissertation, an essential part of my analysis of the composition of the *Testaments*.[5]

The fragments related to the *Testaments*, discovered near Qumran, form a welcome addition to the previously available evidence. (1) First, the numerous fragments of an Aramaic Levi document link with fragments from the Cairo Genizah just mentioned. (2) In one fragment, Naphtali tells about his mother Bilhah. (3) A few more fragments have been connected with an Aramaic *Testament of Judah* and an Aramaic *Testament of Joseph*, but these ascriptions are far from certain. (4) Finally there are fragments connected to Levi's son Kohath and his grandson

---

3. J. Becker, *Untersuchungen zur Entstehungsgeschichte der Testamente der Zwölf Patriarchen* (AGJU 8; Leiden: Brill, 1970); A. Hultgård, *L'eschatologie des Testaments des Douze Patriarches*, vols. 1–2 (AUU, Hist. Rel. 6–7; Stockholm: Almqvist & Wiksell, 1977, 1982); and J. H. Ulrichsen, *Die Grundschrift der Testamente der Zwölf Patriarchen* (AUU, Hist. Rel. 10; Stockholm: Almqvist & Wiksell, 1991).

4. Friedrich Schnapp, *Die Testamente der Zwölf Patriarchen untersucht* (Halle: Max Niemeyer, 1884); R. H. Charles, *The Greek Versions of the Testaments of the Twelve Patriarchs* (Oxford: Clarendon, 1908); and idem, *The Testaments of the Twelve Patriarchs Translated from the Editor's Greek Text* (London: Black, 1908).

5. See esp. pp. 38–79.

'Amram. These fragments may be compared to the Aramaic Levi, as well as to other texts in one way or the other related to the patriarchs.

Fragments of an Aramaic Levi Document[6]

R. H. Charles rendered scholarship a great service by printing the text of Cairo Genizah fragments from the Cambridge University Library and the Bodleian Library in Oxford in appendix 3 (pp. 244–56) of his edition of the *Testaments of the Twelve Patriarchs*. He also provided the text of the partly overlapping addition found at *T. Levi* 18:2 in the eleventh-century Greek manuscript Athos Koutloumous 39 (= MS *e*) of the *Testaments* (plus that of a small Syriac fragment). Important in themselves,[7] these fragments drew comparatively little attention until nearly fifty years later, when J. T. Milik published a great number of small fragments under the siglum 1Q21[8] and a larger "Prayer of Levi" from a manuscript found in cave 4, corresponding to yet another addition in the same Greek manuscript, found at *T. Levi* 2:3.[9] These publications made clear that the fragments from the Cairo Genizah and those found at Qumran represented slightly different forms of one document. After 1955 not much happened until, finally, J. C. Greenfield and M. E. Stone published all available Qumran fragments in volume 22 of Discoveries in the Judaean Desert.[10] They assign the fragments to six different manuscripts: 4Q213, 4Q213a, 4Q213b, 4Q214, 4Q214a, 4Q214b, and call the writing under discussion "Aramaic Levi Document" (avoiding the word "testament"). A little earlier R. A. Kugler edited the same fragments but assigned them, like Milik before him, to two manuscripts, 4Q213 and 4Q214.[11] In his book Kugler also tries to reconstruct the entire document (which he calls

---

6. I have dealt with these fragments at some length in "Levi in Aramaic Levi and in the Testament of Levi," in *Pseudepigraphic Perspectives: The Apocrypha and Pseudepigrapha in Light of the Dead Sea Scrolls, Proceedings of the International Symposium of the Orion Center for the Study of the Dead Sea Scrolls and Related Literature* (ed. Esther G. Chazon, Michael Stone, and Avital Pinnick; STDJ 31; Leiden: Brill, 1999), 71–89. See also "The Testament of Levi and 'Aramaic Levi,'" *RevQ* 13, nos. 49–53 (1988): 367–85, reprinted in M. de Jonge, *Jewish Eschatology, Early Christian Christology, and the Testaments of the Twelve Patriarchs: Collected Essays* (ed. H. J. de Jonge; NovTSup 63; Leiden: Brill, 1991), 244–62.

7. They proved important in my analysis of the composition of the *Testament of Levi* in my dissertation, *Testaments of the Twelve Patriarchs*, 38–52.

8. D. Barthélemy and J. T. Milik, *Qumran Cave I* (Oxford: Clarendon, 1955), 87–92.

9. "Le Testament de Lévi en araméen: Fragment de la grotte 4 de Qumrân," *RB* 62 (1955): 398–406. Milik also published a small fragment in *The Books of Enoch: Aramaic Fragments of Qumrân Cave 4* (Oxford: Clarendon, 1976), 23–24. See n. 16 below.

10. *Qumran Cave 4. XVII. Parabiblical Texts, Part 3* (ed. G. J. Brooke et al.; DJD 22; Oxford: Clarendon, 1996), 1–72.

11. *From Patriarch to Priest: The Levi-Priestly Tradition from "Aramaic Levi" to "Testament of Levi"* (SBLEJL 9; Atlanta: Scholars Press, 1996). For a chart of corresponding identifications of the 4Q Levi-fragments by Greenfield/Stone and Kugler see A. Aschim in an appendix to his review of Kugler's book, *JBL* 117 (1998): 353–55.

"Aramaic Levi") on the basis of all available sources, and he compares the "Levi-priestly tradition" in it with that found in *Jub.* 30:1–32:9 and the *Testament of Levi*.[12]

However fragmentary the evidence (still) is, there is much more to compare in the case of the *Testament of Levi* than in the rest of the *Testaments of the Twelve Patriarchs*. It may be regarded as certain that *T. Levi* is directly or indirectly dependent on a written source identical or very similar to the Aramaic Levi Document (henceforth, "ALD"). This also explains why *T. Levi* differs so much from the other eleven testaments, in structure as well as in content. At the same time, comparing *T. Levi* with ALD brings out interesting Christian elements in the testament, which are structural rather than incidental and can, therefore, not be eliminated as later interpolations.

With regard to the reconstruction of ALD, many uncertainties remain. First is the matter of the exact wording of the earliest stage of the document. Where the Qumran fragments and the Cairo Genizah texts overlap, they often do not have an identical text; comparison with the Greek texts brings additional difficulties. The very existence of these Greek additions to an eleventh-century Greek manuscript of the *Testaments of the Twelve Patriarchs* raises many questions. How, and in what form, did this material reach the Christian scribe of the manuscript, or one of his predecessors? When was this text translated from Aramaic (or Hebrew), and by whom (a Jew or a Christian)? Because nothing is left of the beginning and the end of ALD we cannot determine its literary genre, and it is therefore better not to refer to it as a "testament." It is, however, in all likelihood related to 4QQahat and 4Q'Amram, which contain instructions (and visions) supposedly handed down in priestly circles through the generations; I return to these texts below.

The fragmentary nature of the evidence makes it sometimes difficult to determine the order of the fragments within ALD. As was already clear from Charles's appendix 3, there is a continuous text providing parallels from the end of *T. Levi* 8 to the end of *T. Levi* 13, excluding *T. Levi* 10. We find the end of a vision (chap. 8); a report of journeys to Bethel and to Isaac, and Isaac's instructions to Levi concerning his priestly duties (much longer than those found in *T. Levi* 9); a biographical account of Levi and his descendants (chaps. 11–12); and a long speech by Levi on the value of wisdom (chap. 13). New material, particularly in connection with the wisdom speech, has come to light, but as far as this section of ALD is concerned the picture has not changed.

Much more disputed is what preceded this section. *T. Levi* has two visions, one in chapters 2–5, one in chapter 8. In between we find the Shechem episode in

---

12. Or rather, a (Jewish) "Original Testament of Levi," which he thinks one can reconstruct. He does not discuss the present Christian testament. On this see my "Levi in Aramaic Levi and in the Testament of Levi," 85–89.

chapters 6–7. This episode follows Levi's appointment to the priesthood by the Most High (5:1–2) and the angel's command to execute vengeance on Shechem because of Dinah (5:3–7). The episode precedes the vision of Levi's investiture by seven angels (chap. 8). It has often been assumed that the "Prayer of Levi" (first edited by Milik, present in what is now called 4QLevi[b] ar 1–2 and the Greek addition to MS e at *T. Levi* 2:3), which ends with the introduction to a vision, pointed to the existence of two visions in ALD as well. Of a Shechem narrative only little remains (in columns a and b of the Cambridge Cairo Genizah fragment). Probably two new fragments (4QLevi[b] ar 3 and 4), dealing with a woman who has discredited the name of her father and adding a blessing for the pious of the Levitical line, should be added here (cf. *Jub.* 30:5–17). Greenfield and Stone raised doubts about the place of the "Prayer of Levi" in ALD but did not make a new suggestion.[13] Kugler, however, is of the opinion that there was only one vision in ALD, placed after the Shechem incident and before the journeys of Jacob and family to Bethel and to Isaac.[14] This solution, in my opinion, raises at least as many problems as it wants to solve.[15]

Can we say anything about what followed Levi's teaching on wisdom, corresponding to *T. Levi* 13? Some small fragments, now called 4QLevi[a] ar 3–5, announce the sins of the speaker's sons. Because of a supposed reference to Enoch, Milik suggested a parallel to the sin-exile-return passage in *T. Levi* 14.[16] The parallel is not close and the reading "Enoch" is far from certain.[17] The suggested place of these fragments consequently remains doubtful.

There is considerable doubt about the assignment of 4Q540 and 4Q541 to ALD, tentatively suggested by E. Puech,[18] but rejected by Greenfield and Stone, as well as by Kugler.[19] They would, in Puech's view, provide parallels to some clauses in *T. Levi* 17–18. Now it is likely that *T. Levi* (16:1), 17:1–11 extracts a source containing a story of the priesthood according to jubilees and weeks, but it is impossible to reconstruct the *Vorlage*.[20] Puech finds a parallel between 17:7–19

---

13. J. C. Greenfield and M. E. Stone, "The Prayer of Levi," *JBL* 112 (1993): 247–66.

14. Kugler, *From Patriarch to Priest*, 47–50, 68–87.

15. See de Jonge, "Levi in Aramaic Levi and the Testament of Levi," 81–83.

16. Milik, *Books of Enoch*, 23–24.

17. See Greenfield and Stone, *Qumran Cave 4. XVII*, 20–23.

18. E. Puech, "Fragments d'un apocryphe de Lévi et le personnage eschatologique: 4QTestLévi[cd](?) et 4QAJa," in *The Madrid Qumran Congress: Proceedings of the International Congress on the Dead Sea Scrolls, Madrid, 18–21 March 1991* (ed. J. Trebolle Barrera and L. Vegas Montaner; 2 vols.; STDJ 11; Leiden: Brill, 1992), 2.449–501. He also mentions J. T. Milik's suggestion to link 4Q548, commonly assigned to the 'Amram document, with *T. Levi* 19:1 (see p. 491, n. 48). Cf. also G. J. Brooke, "4Q Testament of Levi[d](?) and the Messianic Servant High Priest," in *From Jesus to John: Essays on Jesus and New Testament Christology in Honour of Marinus de Jonge* (ed. M. C. de Boer; JSNTSup 84; Sheffield: Sheffield Academic Press, 1993), 83–110.

19. Kugler, *From Patriarch to Priest*, 51–52.

20. See H. W. Hollander and M. de Jonge, *The Testaments of the Twelve Patriarchs: A Commentary* (SVTP 8; Leiden: Brill, 1985), 174–77.

and 4Q540. In this fragment we find the number "52," which Puech supposes to refer to a number of weeks; of the accompanying noun only a final *nun* is readable, however. This he connects with *T. Levi's* picture of seven jubilees, with a return to the land in the fifth week. *T. Levi* 17:10 also mentions a renewal of the house of the Lord, and this may, in Puech's view, correspond to "he will rebuild (?) [like] a servant of God [with] his g[oods], an[other] sanctuary w[hich] he will consecrate [for him (?)]" (line 5 of the fragment). The reconstruction of this line remains uncertain[21] and, apart from that, all this remains highly speculative.

The fragment 4Q541 9 i speaks of a priestly figure who will atone for all the children of his generation. Of him it is said: "His word is like the word of the heavens, and his teaching, according to the will of God. His eternal sun will shine and its fire will burn in all the ends of the earth; above the darkness it will shine. Then, darkness will vanish [fr]om the earth, and gloom from the dry land" (lines 3–5).[22] Puech points here to the description of the eschatological high priest in *T. Levi* 18:2–4, 9 (as well as to 4:3). M. Philonenko gladly hails this as another piece of evidence in favor of the Essene origin of the *Testaments*.[23] It is, however, not as simple as that.

The only thing we can say with certainty is that *T. Levi* 18 and the fragment under discussion give a similar description of an ideal priest. We may also compare 4QSb iv 27 (in the blessing of the priests): "... may he make you hol[y] among his people, like a luminary [...] for the world in knowledge, and to shine on the face of the many."[24] The coming priest will be like Levi himself, to whom the angel who accompanies him during his first vision says: "You will light up as a bright light of knowledge in Jacob, and you will be as the sun to all the seed of Israel" (4:3).[25] Exactly here, in *T. Levi* 18:2–4 and 4:4, the particular stance of the *Testaments* regarding the priesthood comes out.

Levi will be like the sun — a blessing will be given to him and to all his descendants — but only until the coming of God's Son, whom Levi's sons will kill (4:3–4). It is concerning God's Son that Levi should instruct his sons (4:5–6). Levi warns his descendants in no less than three sin-exile-return passages; the first in chapter 10; the second in chapters 14–15 (where the children of Levi are called "the lights of heaven," "darkened through ungodliness"; see 14:3–4);

---

21. F. García Martínez and Eibert J. C. Tigchelaar, *The Dead Sea Scrolls Study Edition* (2 vols.; Leiden: Brill, 1997–98), 2.1079, translate "[...] the sun [...] ... a sanctuary [...] he will consecrate [...]."

22. Translation in ibid., 2.1081.

23. M. Philonenko, "Son soleil éternel brillera (4QTestLévi^c–d[?] ii 9)," *RHPR* 73 (1993–94): 405–8, esp. 405–6: "Soulignons que la présence de ces précieux fragments ne confirme absolument pas le charactère chrétien des Testaments des Douze Patriarches, mais invite, tout au contraire, à reconnaître l'origine essénienne de ce pseudépigraphe."

24. Translation in García Martínez and Tigchelaar, *Dead Sea Scrolls Study Edition*, 1.157.

25. The imagery used here is, of course, also used with others than priests; see Hollander and de Jonge, *Commentary*, 142 (note on 4:3).

and in chapter 16. The section 17:8–11 again follows the sin-exile-return pattern in vv. 8–10. Return and renewal of the temple are, however, followed by the arrival, once again, of sinful priests (v. 11). After vengeance from the Lord and the priesthood's failure (18:1), the Lord will raise a new priest whose "star will rise in heaven as a king, lighting up the light of knowledge as by the sun of the day; he will be magnified in the world until his assumption" (v. 3). Nowhere do we find that the new priest will be from the tribe of Levi (contrast the king from Judah in *T. Judah* 24); it is clear that he cannot be a descendant of Levi, after what was said in 4:4, underlined by the word of the Most High in 5:2: "Levi, I have given you the blessings of the priesthood until I come and sojourn in the midst of Israel." In *T. Levi* 18 (and elsewhere), Jesus is meant, as is also clear from the reference in v. 7 to the story of his baptism (Mark 1:9–11 and parallels). One should respect these differences and resist the temptation to remove them as later interpolations in the *Testaments*, as many have done before knowing about 4Q541.

We should do all we can to reconstruct the Aramaic Levi Document, but we should be wary to assign to that writing every fragment with a parallel to *T. Levi*. It should also be noted that the other twenty-three fragments of 4Q541 cannot be connected with any text in *T. Levi*.[26] Moreover, it is not certain that it is Levi who announces the future priest in this fragment.[27] Puech opts for Levi as speaker, and mentions the possibility that 4Q540–41 belonged to a testament. 4Q541 fragment 24 ii, preserving what appears to be the conclusion of the document, gives final admonitions and promises to a son. Line 2 speaks of mourning, and M. A. Knibb has suggested that this may concern the death of the speaker, referred to as "your father" in line 5.[28]

4Q215: A Fragment of a *Testament of Naphtali?*

As long ago as 1956, J. T. Milik announced the discovery of parts of a *Testament of Naphtali* in Hebrew.[29] He said that it had no connection with the medieval *Testament of Naphtali*, but contained a genealogy of Bilhah in a larger form than that found in Greek *T. Naph.* 1:6–12. Much later, in 1976, he quoted in pass-

---

26. So also Kugler, *From Patriarch to Priest*, 51.

27. As Puech, "Fragments d'un apocryphe de Lévi," 485–91, reminds us, J. Starcky, "Les quatre étapes du messianisme à Qumrân," *RB* 70 (1963): 492, thought that the fragments under discussion belonged to a *Testament of Jacob*, addressed to Levi. See also A. Caquot, "Les testaments qoumrâniens des pères de sacerdoce," *RHPR* 78/2 (1998): 3–26, esp. p. 13.

28. See his "Messianism in the Pseudepigrapha in the Light of the Scrolls," *DSD* 2 (1995): 181–84.

29. See n. 1 on p. 407 of his "'Prière de Nabonide' et autres récits d'un cycle de Daniël: Fragments araméens de Qumrân 4," *RB* 63 (1956): 406–15. Compare p. 97 of his "Écrits préesséniens de Qumrân: d'Hénoch à 'Amram," in *Qumrân: Sa piété, sa théologie et son milieu* (ed. M. Delcor; BETL 46; Paris and Gembloux: Duculot; Louvain: Louvain University Press, 1978), 91–106.

ing only two lines, corresponding to *T. Naph.* 1:12.[30] Only recently the three fragments of the genealogy (4Q215) have been published, by M. E. Stone, in volume 22 of *Discoveries in the Judaean Desert*;[31] Stone also discovered that four other fragments with an apocalyptic text, commonly also assigned to the same testament, really belong to a different document, now labeled "4QTime of Righteousness" (4Q215ᵃ). Stone has also devoted an interesting article to 4Q215, "The Genealogy of Bilhah,"[32] in which he discusses the relationship among this document (which he continues to designate as *Testament of Naphtali*), the Greek testament belonging to the *Testaments of the Twelve Patriarchs,* and a passage in *Midrash Bereshit Rabbati* compiled by Rabbi Moses the Preacher in Narbonne in the eleventh century. He enters into a discussion with M. Himmelfarb, who already in 1984 had called attention to the parallels between the medieval midrash and the Greek testament.[33] She had, at that time, concluded that the parallels between the midrash and the testament were "not the result of independent Jewish transmission of these traditions, but of R. Moses' use of parts of the *Testaments* as a complete Christian document."[34] With 4Q215 in hand, Stone is able to show that the relationship between the midrash and 4Q215 is closer than that between the midrash and Greek *T. Naph.* 1:9–12, so that we may conclude that "one or another form of an apocryphal Hebrew or Aramaic Naphtali document which had existed in the period of the Second Temple was available to R. Moses the Preacher in Narbonne in the eleventh century."[35]

All three texts make Bilhah the daughter of a brother of Deborah, Rebekah's nurse mentioned in Gen. 35:8. In the Greek the brother is called Rotheus; in 4Q215, 'Achiyot; in *Bereshit Rabbati,* 'Achotay. Taken captive, he is bought free by Laban, who gives him his servant Aina (the Greek manuscripts differ here) as a wife; 4Q215 has "Channah," and this seems to be the original name behind the Chavah of *Bereshit Rabbati.* All three texts then relate how Channah first gives birth to Zilpah (who is named after the village/town in [or to which] Rotheus was taken captive) and to Bilhah. In all three sources the name "Bilhah" is explained

30. Milik, *Books of Enoch,* 198.

31. "215. 4QTestament of Naphtali," in *Qumran Cave 4. XVII. Parabiblical Texts, Part 3,* 73–82, now easily accessible in García Martínez and Tigchelaar, *Dead Sea Scrolls Study Edition,* 1.454–57. Preliminary edition in M. E. Stone, "The Hebrew *Testament of Naphtali,*" *JJS* 47 (1996): 311–21. See also R. H. Eisenman and M. Wise, *The Dead Sea Scrolls Uncovered* (Shaftesbury: Element, 1992), 156–60, and G. W. Nebe, "Qumranica I: Zu unveröffentlichten Handschriften aus Höhle 4 von Qumran," *ZAW* 106 (1994): 307–22, esp. 315–22.

32. *DSD* 3 (1996): 20–36.

33. M. Himmelfarb, "R. Moses the Preacher and the Testaments of the Twelve Patriarchs," *AJSR* 9 (1984): 55–78. The relevant passage is found on p. 119 of Ch. Albeck, ed., *Midrash Bereshit Rabbati* (Jerusalem, 1940).

34. Himmelfarb, "R. Moses the Preacher," 78.

35. Stone, "Genealogy of Bilhah," 36. The question how traditions found in the Pseudepigrapha reached authors and compilers of medieval midrashim is worthy of further investigation; the articles by Himmelfarb and Stone give some interesting considerations.

by a play of words on the root *bhl* (to hasten); immediately after her birth Bilhah is eager to suck.

After a blank of one line, 4Q215 tells how Laban gave Channah and her two daughters to Jacob after he had come from Esau. Zilpah was given to Leah and Bilhah to Rachel, and in due course Bilhah gave birth to "Dan [my] brother" — and to Naphtali himself, we may add, although the text breaks off at this crucial point. *Bereshit Rabbati* has a similar addition to the genealogy proper, but the Greek has no parallel here. The Greek attaches the genealogical remarks in 1:9–12 to the story of Naphtali's birth in 1:6–8 (cf. Gen. 30:1–3, 7–8).

In two respects, Greek *T. Naph.* 1:9–12 is more explicit than the related material. First it tells that Bilhah was born on the same day as Rachel (v. 9). Next it emphasizes that "Rotheus was of the family of Abraham, a Chaldean, god-fearing, freeborn and noble" (v. 10). It is apparently important to make clear that all sons of Jacob, also those born from slave women, are related to Abraham on their paternal as well as their maternal side.[36] This explains the interest in these particular genealogical details — although this sentence is absent in 4Q215 and *Bereshit Rabbati*. The details appear in the *Testaments* because their author(s) had access to this traditional material; yet it does not seem to be directly relevant for the purpose of the Greek *Testament of Naphtali*.

In 4Q215 the author repeatedly refers to Bilhah as "my mother," and because in the last readable line we meet "Dan [my] brother" the document must be ascribed to Naphtali. But was it a testament? Stone points to the Hebrew *Testament of Naphtali*, which in the section dealing with visions by Naphtali is more original than the Greek *Testament of Naphtali* (cf. *T. Naph.* 5–7). It must, therefore, go back to a much earlier document on which both the Greek and Hebrew *Testaments* draw independently. The Hebrew *Testament* we know does not have anything comparable to the genealogy of Bilhah under discussion, yet "it is possible that the Qumran fragment dealing with Bilhah's genealogy is derived from the same original document."[37] Hence Stone continues to speak of a Qumran TestNaphtali, and 4Q215 is (still) called 4QTNaph.

Here I tend to disagree with him, and I would suggest we drop the "T" and speak of 4QNaph. For one thing, not all Naphtali traditions need to come from one source, and for another, the common source of the Hebrew and Greek *Testaments* need not have been a testament. Indeed, the version of the two visions of Naphtali found in the Hebrew *Testament* has preserved a number of elements lacking in the Greek *Testament* that must have been present in the original document underlying both testaments. Stone rightly refers to Th. Korteweg's important essay of 1975, in which he argues this in great detail.[38] Korteweg, however, cau-

---

36. See Hollander and de Jonge, *Commentary*, 299, referring to some remarks by L. Ginzberg. See also this commentary for what immediately follows.

37. Stone, "Genealogy of Bilhah," 33.

38. See Korteweg, "The Meaning of Naphtali's Visions," in *Studies on the Testaments of the Twelve*

tiously speaks of "the haggadic tradition which underlies both, and which may or may not already have taken the form of a 'testament' itself"[39] — and rightly so. There is still another point to consider. The Hebrew text edited by Charles in appendix 2 (pp. 239–44) of his edition of the *Testaments*, and based on Oxford MS heb. d.11,[40] presents itself as *ṣww't nptly*; this is translated by Charles as "the *Testament of Naphtali*" and by E. Kautzsch as "der letzte Wille Naphtalis."[41] In his study of the testament as literary genre, E. von Nordheim classifies this writing as a "testament" only after some hesitation.[42] There is, in fact, also a second version of the Hebrew *Testament*, which bears the title "Haggadah on the Sons of Jacob." A. Hultgård has analyzed it at some length in an appendix to the second volume of his *L'eschatologie*.[43] Though this second version is generally shorter than the version printed by Charles, it gives essentially the same text — but it does not call it a "testament." This, again, raises the question whether the common tradition behind the *Testament of Naphtali* and the Hebrew document called "Testament" or "Haggadah" was a testament.[44]

Fragments Attributed to a *Testament of Judah* and to a *Testament of Joseph*

In 1978, J. T. Milik published some fragments which he thought he could ascribe to a *Testament of Judah* and a *Testament of Joseph*.[45] As in other cases, transcription,

---

Patriarchs: Text and Interpretation (ed. M. de Jonge; SVTP 3; Leiden: Brill, 1975), 261–90. See already pp. 52–57 in my *Testaments of the Twelve Patriarchs* of 1953. Becker, *Untersuchungen*, 105–13 (see n. 3 above for the following references), defends the priority of the Greek version; so also Hultgård, *L'eschatologie*, 2.128–35 (who, however, assumes that the Hebrew has kept some elements lost in the Greek). Ulrichsen, *Die Grundschrift*, 145–55, follows de Jonge and Korteweg.

39. Korteweg, "Meaning of Naphtali's Visions," 280.

40. He adds variants from two further manuscripts taken from an earlier edition by M. Gaster, "The Hebrew Text of One of the Testaments of the Twelve Patriarchs," *Proceedings of the Society of Biblical Archaeology* 16 (1893–94): 33–49, 109–17.

41. In E. Kautzsch, *Die Apokryphen und Pseudepigraphen des Alten Testaments* (Tübingen: Mohr, 1900), 2.489–92. The meaning "testament" for *ṣww'h* is post-Talmudic; M. Jastrow, *A Dictionary of the Targumim, the Talmud Babli and Yerushalmi, and the Midrashic Literature* (repr., New York: Pardes, 1950), 2.1265a, gives as meanings "command, order, verbal will."

42. E. von Nordheim, *Das Testament als Literaturgattung im Judentum der hellenistisch-römischen Zeit* (vol. 1 of *Die Lehre der Alten*; ALGHJ 13; Leiden: Brill, 1980), 108–14. It should be borne in mind that von Nordheim in his search for the characteristics of testaments assigns great importance to the testaments in the *Testaments of the Twelve Patriarchs*.

43. See pp. 288–96. This second version is found in MS Parma 563 De Rossi only; it was printed in S. A. Wertheimer, *Batei Midrashot* (2d ed. by A. J. Wertheimer; Jerusalem: Mosad Harav Cook, 1954), 1.199–203.

44. As in the case of *Midrash Bereshit Rabbati* — and that of *Midrash Wayissa'u* — one would like to know more about the history of the transmission of the Second Temple material down to the Middle Ages.

45. See his "Écrits préesséniens," 97–102.

reconstruction of lost words or clauses, and identification are interrelated, and his solutions have not gone unchallenged.

In the case of 4Q538, we have an episode in the story of Joseph and his brothers in Egypt, told by one of the brothers. Milik thinks that Judah is the speaker (cf. *T. Jud.* 12:11–12), but in view of the "... on my neck and hugged me" in line 6 of fragment a, which can be compared with Gen. 45:14, others have thought of Benjamin.[46] There is, however, nothing parallel in the *Testament of Benjamin*, nor in any other passage in the *Testaments*. Milik also connected 3Q7, fragments 6 and 5+3, with *T. Jud.* 25:1–2.[47] Here there is, again, very little to go on — only the name "Levi" and the mention of "the angel of the presence" can be used to establish a link with the passage in *T. Judah*; but the collocation of these words may just as well have to be explained differently.

The situation is only a little less controversial in the case of 4Q539, in which Milik finds parallels to *T. Jos.* 15:1–2, 16:4–5, and 17:1–2. In the tiny fragment 1, he connects the letters *mp* with the name Μέμφις found in *T. Jos.* 3:6; 12:1; 14:1–5; 16:1. Fragments 2 a–b (probably) refer to the Ishmaelites, and they mention a mourning of Jacob; this may be connected with the beginning of chapter 15 in the *Testament of Joseph*. Directly after this reference, "minas" are mentioned and the number "eighty"; to this may be compared the story in chapter 16 about complicated negotiations between eunuchs sent by the "Memphian (v. 1) [Egyptian (v. 5)] woman" and the Ishmaelites about Joseph. In v. 4, the woman is prepared to give as much as two minas of gold; in v. 5, her negotiator gives eighty pieces of gold (cheating his mistress by telling her that he had given a hundred). If these readings are right, the second parallel, in particular, is interesting.[48]

One of the striking features of the *Testament of Joseph* is that it has two paraenetical themes and illustrates them with two different stories, one about Joseph and the Egyptian woman (3:1–9:5) and the second about Joseph's slavery and imprisonment (11:2–16:6). It has always been likely that the author(s) of the *Testaments* used a special source for the second part of the *Testament of Joseph*.[49] Although there is no reason to assume that 4Q539 formed part of that particular

---

46. So K. Beyer, *Die aramäischen Texte vom Toten Meer* (Göttingen: Vandenhoeck & Ruprecht, 1984), 187, and F. García Martínez and A. S. van der Woude, *De rollen van de Dode Zee* (2 vols.; Kampen: Kok, 1994–95), 2.378–80, going back to F. García Martínez, "Estudios Qumranicos, 1975–85: Panorama Crítico (III)," *EstBib* 46 (1988): 325–74, esp. 326–30.

47. The 3Q fragments were published in M. Baillet, J. T. Milik, and R. de Vaux, O.P., *Les "Petites Grottes" de Qumrân* (DJD 3; Oxford: Clarendon, 1962), 99. Later M. Baillet tentatively added twenty very small fragments belonging to 4Q484; see *Qumrân Grotte 4. III* (DJD 7; Oxford: Clarendon, 1982), 3.

48. Beyer's transcription and reconstruction (*Aramäischen Texte*, 188) differs in many details from that by Milik. Compare also García Martínez and van der Woude, *De rollen van de Dode Zee*, 2.380–81, and especially García Martínez, "Estudios Qumranicos, 1975–1985 (III)," 330–32.

49. For details see Hollander and de Jonge, *Commentary*, esp. 362–65, 372–73, 393–94 and, in more detail, H. W. Hollander, *Joseph as an Ethical Model in the Testaments of the Twelve Patriarchs* (SVTP 6; Leiden: Brill, 1981).

source, it could point to the existence of a similar written tradition about the selling of Joseph.

Neither in 4Q538 nor in 4Q539 is there any indication that we are dealing with parts of a testament. In 4Q539, one may point to the fact that "my sons" and "my loved ones" are addressed in fragment 2, line 2 (cf. "my son[s]" in line 6), but such an address is fitting in other contexts than that of a testament.

Recently, T. Elgvin has drawn attention to 4Q474 and suggested that it may be part of a Joseph apocryphon or even a testament.[50] It is a poorly preserved text that mentions Rachel and refers a few times to a beloved son, which in Elgvin's eyes may be Joseph. He tentatively reconstructs line 2 as a rephrasing of Gen. 37:3–4 and 48:22 so as to read "she rejoi]ced(?) in a son loved by hi[s fath]er above all [his brothers(?)." Next he uses Gen. 30:24 to reconstruct line 4: "...to] ask the Lord that [He g]i[ve her another(?)] son[..." These lines, then, would reveal parallels with *T. Jos.* 1:2, 4; 10:5; 11:1; and *T. Benj.* 1:4–5 — not surprisingly, because they deal with the same subjects and depend on the same or similar Bible passages. There is no parallel with 4Q539 (nor with the so-called Apocryphon of Joseph preserved in 4Q371–73).

Elgvin then goes a step further by positing that lines 1–7 form a narrative introduction and that lines 8–14 are part of prophecies by Joseph to his descendants. If so, the fragment could be called a testament. His principal argument is the use of a verb in the second-person plural in line 4, translated as "you [as]ked(?)" (compared with "and there they cried out to the Lord" found only in the Armenian version of *T. Jos.* 19:4).

Elgvin's transcriptions and reconstructions are very ingenious, but remain extremely tentative as he himself admits time and again. This may be a text concerning Rachel and Joseph but there is no connection with the *Testaments of the Twelve Patriarchs.*

Fragments Connected with Kohath and 'Amram

Reviewing what has been said, I conclude that 4Q215 confirms the existence of a source from which the genealogical material in *T. Naph.* 1:9–12 was taken. Next, 4Q539 may provide evidence of a written tradition about the selling of Joseph that, in some form, was used in the composition of *T. Jos.* 11:2–16:6. In neither case is it clear that the author(s) of the *Testaments of the Twelve Patriarchs* knew and used a testament.

The (relatively) rich material belonging to an Aramaic Levi Document proved very important; it shows that the *Testament of Levi* is dependent on a source identical or similar to ALD. ALD has testamentary features, but is not a testament.[51]

---

50. T. Elgvin, "4Q474 — A Joseph Apocryphon?" *RevQ* 18, no. 69 (1997): 97–107.

51. At the end of the biographical section in ALD (v. 81, according to the numbering introduced

M. A. Knibb rightly calls it "an autobiographical narrative which includes significant passages of instruction."[52] He compares it with the first-person sections of the Genesis Apocryphon, the fragmentary "Apocryphon of Jacob" (4Q537),[53] and 4Q538 mentioned above. One may add, of course, 4Q215 and 4Q539.

On the other hand, 4Q540–41 may have belonged to a document giving final admonitions of Levi; this, however, cannot be proved beyond doubt.

At this point it may be helpful to look at 4QTQahat ar (=4Q542)[54] and 4Q'Amram ar (4Q543–48),[55] which give final instructions from Levi's son and grandson to their children. Both are mentioned in the biographical section of ALD, vv. 62–81 (see esp. vv. 67–68 and 74–77).[56] It is also remarkable that ALD not only mentions how Levi hands down general admonitions concerning true wisdom and righteous behavior (vv. 82–84; 88–99), but also reflects the notion that priestly instructions were handed down from generation to generation. In ALD vv. 12–13, Isaac instructs Levi, and in vv. 22, 50, this patriarch refers to the example and teaching of Abraham (cf. *Jub.* 21:10); in v. 57, he mentions the *Book of Noah* as the source for Abraham. We may compare *Jub.* 45:16, which states that Jacob gave all his books and the books of his fathers to Levi.[57]

Here 4Q542 frg. 1, ii 9–13, ties in with: "And now, to you, 'Amram, my son, I comma[nd . . .] and [to] your s[on]s and to their sons; I command [. . .] and they have given to Levi, my father, and which Levi, my father, has giv[en] to me [. . .] all my writings as witness that you should take care of them [. . .] for you; in them is great worth, in their being carried on with you." This may be compared to i 7–8: "Hold on to the word of Jacob, your father, and hold fast to the judgments of Abraham and to the righteous deeds of Levi and of me. . . ."[58]

---

by Charles), we find: "and all the days of my life were one hu[ndred and thir]ty seven years and I saw my th[ird]generation before I died." A strange remark, as it is not made by an author reporting the death of the patriarch, but by the patriarch himself. Moreover it is followed in v. 82 by an introduction to a speech given earlier by Levi, when his brother Joseph died. The text of this speech is given *in extenso* in the following verses. It exhibits a number of testamentary features, but is clearly not a farewell speech. Was this second speech added later? And how did the ending of ALD take up the information in v. 81 — compare *T. Levi* 12:6–7; 19:4? We simply do not know.

52. M. A. Knibb, "Perspectives on the Apocrypha and Pseudepigrapha: The Levi Traditions," in *Perspectives in the Study of the Old Testament and Early Judaism: A Symposium in Honour of Adam S. van der Woude on the Occasion of His 70th Birthday* (ed. Florentino García Martínez and Ed Noort; VTSup 73; Leiden: Brill, 1998), 197–213; quotation from p. 209.

53. García Martínez and van der Woude, *De rollen van de Dode Zee*, 2.376, write that although parallels point to Jacob as the central figure in this document, it cannot be excluded that Levi is the one who reports a vision.

54. See E. Puech, "Le Testament de Qahat en araméen de la Grotte 4 (4QTQah)," *RevQ* 15, nos. 57–58 (1991): 23–54.

55. Eisenman and Wise, *Dead Sea Scrolls Uncovered*, 151–56, and K. Beyer, *Die aramäischen Texte vom Toten Meer: Ergänzungsband* (Göttingen: Vandenhoeck & Ruprecht, 1994), 85–92.

56. Compare also 4Q559, frg. 2 and 3.

57. *Jub.* 7:38–39 mentions the succession from Enoch to Noah (cf. also *1 Enoch* 81:5–82:3) and 10:14 (cf. 17) that from Noah to Shem.

58. Translation in García Martínez and Tigchelaar, *Dead Sea Scrolls Study Edition*, 2.1083.

Of 4Q'Amram the beginning has been preserved, even twice, in 4Q543 frg. 1 as well as in 4Q545 frg. 1 col. i. Here we read how 'Amram addresses his sons and calls Aaron in particular. Especially important is that we possess the *incipit* of this writing: "Copy of the words of the visions of 'Amram, son of Kohath, son of Levi. All that he revealed to his sons and that he ordered them on the day of his death..." The writing is concerned with the final instructions of the patriarch before his death. The verb *pqd* is used here (as in 4QTQahat ii 9, 10, and in ALD vv. 82–84). It corresponds with Hebrew *ṣwh*, used in the Bible for instructions before death (e.g., in Gen. 49:33; 2 Sam. 17:23; and 2 Kings 20:1).[59] Next, the initial words resemble those in the beginning of the individual testaments in the *Testaments of the Twelve Patriarchs*, for example, *T. Levi* 1:1: "A copy of the words of Levi, which he enjoined on his sons before his death."

We should note that the initial words highlight 'Amram's visions (compare those of Levi). Interestingly, one of the visions took place when 'Amram was in Hebron, with his father Kohath, to build the tombs of their fathers, and had to stay there because of a war between Egypt and Canaan (4Q544 frg. 1 and 4Q545 frg. 1 col. ii). This is also mentioned in *Jub.* 46:9–11 and echoed in *T. Sim.* 8:2 and *T. Benj.* 12:3. Again we find a tradition known and used by the author(s) of the *Testaments*.[60]

4Q542 does not speak about visions but concentrates on exhortations to follow the instructions of the fathers; obedience to God will lead to eternal blessings, disobedience to divine punishment. A few times (frg. 1, i 4, 5, 12) the gift of Kohath and the fathers before him is called "inheritance" (*yrwtt'*). In lines i 11–13 we read: "...because you have kept and carried on [the] inheritan[ce] which your fathers gave you, truth, and justice, and uprightness, and perfection, and purit[y, and ho]liness and the priest[ho]od, according to a[l]l that I commanded you..."[61]

4QTQahat and 4Q'Amram deserve to be analyzed in greater detail, but what has been said above may suffice to establish a close link between these two documents and ALD (and possibly also with 4Q540–41). They represent a chain of priestly instructions, accompanied by promises of blessings and threats of divine punishment. Whether we call these instructions "testamentary" and these writings "testaments" (this remains dubious in the case of ALD) is, to a large extent, a matter of definition. Particularly since E. von Nordheim's study of 1980, mentioned above, it has become fashionable to speak of "testament" as a specific

---

59. And, of course, it corresponds to the word ἐντέλλομαι, frequently used in the *Testaments of the Twelve Patriarchs*.

60. For details see Hollander and de Jonge, *Commentary*, 127–28, note on *T. Sim.* 8:2.

61. Translation in García Martínez and Tigchelaar, *Dead Sea Scrolls Study Edition*, 2.1083. I note in passing, "and you will give me among you a good name," in line 10; cf. 4Q541 24 ii 5, and the announcement of future joy for Jacob, Isaac, and Abraham in line 11; cf. *T. Levi* 18:14.

literary genre.[62] Scholars have found it difficult, however, to agree on its characteristics. It should also be borne in mind that, on the one hand, a number of writings called διαθήκη are not farewell discourses spoken before dying, and that, on the other hand, such discourses are only seldom called "testaments"; strictly speaking only the *Testaments of the Twelve Patriarchs* and the Testament of Job qualify.

Conclusion:
No *Testaments of the Twelve Patriarchs* at Qumran

Three "testamentary" writings with priestly instructions by Levi, his son, and his grandson, handing down what their fathers told them, plus autobiographical narratives by Naphtali, Joseph, and perhaps Benjamin are all we have found. The Dead Sea Scrolls do not indicate the existence of a writing containing the final words of all sons of Jacob directed to their children. We do find references to the twelve sons of Jacob and the twelve tribes of Israel. In 4Q252–54 we have fragments of a "Commentary on Genesis," which deals, among other things, with the blessings of Jacob in Genesis 49. There is also the "Apocryphon of Joshua" (4Q378–79) that in 4Q379 frg. 1 speaks about the twelve sons of Jacob and their tribes, singling out Levi as "the beloved."[63] In general, however, the scrolls, in all their diversity, seem to focus their attention on Levi and his descendants.

---

62. See n. 42 and my forthcoming article, "Testamentenliteratur," in the *Theologische Realenzyklopädie.*

63. One should note that 11QTemple, cols. xxiii–xxv, describes the sacrifices of the twelve tribes (cf. 4Q365, frg. 25) and connects the names of the sons of Jacob with the gates of the temple in cols. xxxix–xli (cf. 4Q365 frg. 28 and also 4Q554 frg. 1, cols. i–ii).

8

The Metamorphosis of
Isaiah 13:2–14:27

───── ◆ ─────

Jonathan A. Goldstein
University of Iowa

The great Isaiah had foreseen the fall of Assyria. Could he have failed to foresee the events of the late seventh and early sixth centuries? There is reason to think that admirers of Isaiah, including Jeremiah, came to believe that Isaiah had indeed predicted both the rise and the still-future fall of Babylon. Those admirers were able to prove their point, it seems to me, by using an old manuscript of a real prophecy of Isaiah. They made only a few alterations at points where the manuscript may have been hard to read, to produce what we now have in Isa. 13:1–14:27. Let me explain why I think so. The words ascribed to Isaiah in those chapters have many strange features.

The content of the passage is as follows. In 13:2–22 is a description of the rising of merciless peoples from the distant mountains who will come upon "all the earth" on the "day of the Lord" to punish the proud and the wicked in a catastrophic invasion, which will be accompanied by eclipses of the heavenly bodies and by earthquakes. In 13:17 at least some of the inexorable invaders are identified as the Medes. The invaders (and perhaps the earthquakes, too) will destroy Babylon (13:18–22). According to 14:1–2, the aftermath will see the restoration of Israel, as Gentiles bring the Lord's people back from exile; the Israelites will possess their former captors as slaves. In 14:3–21 is a vigorous taunt song, which the liberated Israelites are to recite concerning the slain king of Babylon, contrasting his former arrogance with his humiliation in death. In 14:22–23, God promises to destroy Babylon completely. Strangely, in 14:24–27 comes an abrupt oath of the Lord to "break Assyria [not Babylon!] in My land" and to liberate the people.

───────────────

This article is taken from my forthcoming book, *Peoples of an Almighty God*, of which it constitutes chapter 4, section 3. The book will be published by Anchor-Doubleday-Dell.

The strange features of Isa. 13:2–14:27 go far beyond the mention of Assyria in 14:24–27. First, the prophecy bears the title, "The 'Babylon' Pronouncement, a Prophecy of Isaiah Son of Amoz." Both halves of this title are odd. Isaiah's own words let us know that he prophesied in the reigns of Uzziah, Ahaz, and Hezekiah, as does the editorial superscription to the book which bears his name. He certainly gave his predictions to Ahaz ca. 733 B.C.E. Babylon in Isa. 13:1–14:27 is portrayed as a cruel, great power, but from Isaiah's birth to the rise of King Nabopolassar in 626, Babylon could only with difficulty assert her independence and was more often the subject or victim of Assyria. Furthermore, in 13:19 Babylon is called "proud splendor of the Chaldeans." It is at least doubtful that Isaiah could have used that expression of Babylon. In the eighth century, Babylon had several kings of Chaldean stock, including Marduk-apla-iddina II, whose ambassadors came to Jerusalem in Isaiah's time. But during most of that century the Chaldean tribes were enemies of the city Babylon, and that hostility may have existed also in the opening years of the seventh century.[1] The Medes, too, are presented as a cruel, great power in Isa. 13:4–14, yet they were certainly no match for Assyria before the middle of the seventh century. Contrary to that passage, the Medes never overran the Near East, terrifying and slaughtering vast populations and destroying Babylon.

If Isaiah's prophetic vision really could penetrate the future, it should have been more accurate! And even if he did somehow predict the fall of a cruel Babylon to a cruel Media, what circle of Jews in the late eighth and early seventh centuries would have been interested enough to preserve a prediction that one distant power, then still small, would destroy another, also still small?

On the other hand, Jeremiah's generation bitterly resented the cruelty with which Nebuchadnezzar punished rebellious Judah, and they probably were impressed by his readiness to "kill his own people" (cf. Isa. 14:20) by accepting heavy casualties in his battle of 601 against Egypt and in the siege of Jerusalem.[2] Had not Babylon, like Assyria, exceeded her mandate as God's punishing instrument? Such Jews believed that Babylon in turn should be punished, and they looked to the Medes, the only great power bordering on Babylonia, to be the agents of God's retribution.[3] How, then, can Isa. 13:2–14:27 be the work of

---

1. See John Brinkman, *A Political History of Post-Kassite Babylonia* (AnOr 43; Rome: Pontificium Institutum Biblicum, 1968), 262–64; Sidney Smith, in *CAH* (ed. J. B. Bury, S. A. Cook, and F. E. Adcock, 1st ed., reprinted with corrections; Cambridge: Cambridge University Press, 1929), 3.47–50, 62–66.

2. For evidence of Nebuchadnezzar's cruelty, see Jer. 50:17; 51:34; Lam. 3:60–66. For information on the casualties incurred against Egypt, see my forthcoming *Peoples of an Almighty God*, chap. 2, sec. 2.

3. Jer. 51:11, 28. Cf. Georges Roux, *Ancient Iraq* (3d ed.; London: Penguin, 1992), 380. Herodotus ascribes to a Babylonian Queen Nitokris a system of defense works aimed against the danger from Media (i. 185). No such queen is otherwise attested, but the defense works were real. However, they may have been built in the reign of King Nabonidus as a defense against King Cyrus of Persia; cf. Raymond P. Dougherty, *Nabonidus and Belshazzar* (Yale Oriental Series: Researches 15; New Haven:

Isaiah? Rather, one would think, it must represent the ardent wishes of Jeremiah's generation, and somehow this later composition found its way into the collection of the works of Isaiah.

There is reason to think that the declaration of Isaiah's authorship in the second half of 13:1 (the verse which serves as the title of 13:2–14:27) reflects an editor's awareness of how incongruous the prophecy is as a work of Isaiah. The prophecies in the Book of Isaiah could have circulated separately before they were brought together into a collection, and they could have received titles either while separate or when placed in the collection. Still, Isa. 1:1 is a title for the whole book, "The Prophecies of Isaiah Son of Amoz..." Even if that verse is the title of only chapter 1, would not one assume, in the absence of statements to the contrary, that all pieces which followed were also by Isaiah? Yet the editor found reason to attach (or to leave in place) titles identifying Isaiah as the author not only of 13:2–14:27 but also of chapter 2.

One can guess why he did so. The glorious prophecy for Judah and Jerusalem in 2:1–5 follows somewhat incongruously on chapter 1, which is mostly an indictment of land and city, relieved somewhat by the promise that God will purge the dross and that the repentant will be redeemed. The title in 2:1 assures the reader that the author of 2:2–5 is indeed the same as the prophet of chapter 1. Similarly, the title of 13:2–14:27 may have been added or left in place because the editor wished to assure his reader that the same Isaiah who spoke to Ahaz also predicted the fall of Babylon, strange as it seems!

Even if we knew nothing of the history of the eighth and seventh centuries B.C.E., Isa. 13:2–14:27 would still be strange as a prophecy primarily concerned with Babylon. Babylon is not mentioned in the passage until 13:19. At least one scholar has suggested that, even in that verse, bbl ("Babylon") may be an interpolation.[4]

Despite the incongruities of Isa. 13:2–14:27, it is difficult simply to reject the information given in the title. The portrayal of the barbarians gathering to be the Lord's scourge on the Lord's day is in keeping with the teachings and diction of the prophecies which certainly belong to Isaiah. As in 13:5–18, the great prophet taught that God would purge the arrogant from the world and that God's wrath would occasion great slaughter and destruction. As in 14:5–6, he also taught that the wicked empire of his day would be punished for wronging many nations, not just for injuring Israel.[5]

Yale University Press, 1929), 38–62. Nabonidus reports how he feared the power of the Medes in the first year of his reign (556/5); see my forthcoming *Peoples*, chap. 5, sec. 3.

4. Rudolf Kittel in his note ad loc. in *BHK*[4]. There is no sign that Kittel believed (with me) that Isa. 13:2–14:27 was originally about Assyria, not Babylon. Did syntactical or metrical considerations lead him to his suggestion?

5. For parallels to Isa. 13:5–18, see Isa. 2:10–22 (although the prophet focuses on Judah, he means the entire human race; Bashan, the cedars of Lebanon, and the ships of Tarshish were all

One might try to explain away the anachronisms: "Babylon" in Isa. 13:2–14:27 might be a name for the Assyrian Empire — Assyrian kings on occasion called themselves "kings of Babylon," and elsewhere in the Bible a writer will use the name of one empire when he means another — and "Media" in our passage might be, not the name of an existing great power, but of a distant and barbaric people; the mention of the Chaldeans might be a later insertion.[6] Thus, Isaiah could have written most if not all of the passage.

Moreover, so effective is the taunt song in 14:3–21 that scholars have been reluctant to deny that Isaiah wrote it.[7] On the other hand, even defenders of 13:2–22 and 14:3–21 have held the Isaiah did not write 14:1–2, 22–23.[8]

The anachronisms, however, cannot be explained away so easily. Assyrian kings did on occasion take the title "King of Babylon," but the title was used only in Babylon, not by non-Babylonian subjects of the empire. At 2 Kings 15:19, "Pul," which may have been the Babylonian royal name of Tiglath-Pileser III, is used, but the writer still calls him "king of Assyria," not "king of Babylon." All biblical examples of anachronistic use of names for empires use the name of the earlier for the later, never the name of the later for the earlier.[9] Excellence of composition and agreement with the thought and diction of Isaiah in themselves do not guarantee that Isaiah was the author.[10]

The existing clues can point to a better way to solve the problems of Isa. 13:2–14:27, to show, first, that in most if not all of Isa. 13:2–14:27 we have words of Isaiah himself, written not against Babylon and her king, but against Assyria and her king and against Nineveh, her capital; and to show, second, that Jews of the sixth century B.C.E. who admired Isaiah and longed for retribution upon Babylon found it possible to read the passage as referring to her.[11]

The text itself makes Assyria the target of Isa. 14:25. The mark of Assyria

---

outside Judah); 6:11–13; 9:18–20; 10:22–23; 16:13; 17:1–6; 18:6; 19:2, 5–7; 23:11–12. For a parallel to Isa. 14:5–6, see Isa. 10:7.

6. Yechezkel Kaufmann, *Toledot ha-emunah ha-yisre 'elit*, vol. 3, pt. 1 (Tel-Aviv: Bialik Foundation and Dvir, 1938), 175–81, and idem, *The Religion of Israel from Its Beginnings to the Babylonian Exile* (translated and abridged by Moshe Greenberg; Chicago: University of Chicago Press, 1960), 382–83.

7. H. L. Ginsberg, *The Book of Isaiah: A New Translation* (Philadelphia: Jewish Publication Society, 1973), 14–15.

8. Ginsberg (ibid., 16–17) rejects 14:1–4a, 22–23; Kaufmann, only 14:1–2 (*Toledot*, vol. 3, pt. 1, 178–81).

9. Ezra 6:22; Neh. 13:6. Lam. 5:6 is probably not an anachronism but an allusion to history (cf. Ezek. 16:26–28; 23:3–12). Ezra 5:13 contains a correct designation of the date according to Cyrus's Babylonian regnal year, in which he indeed bore the title "King of Babylon." Long before, he had ascended the throne of Persia. Babylonians, Egyptians, and Greeks spoke of the Persian Empire as "the Medes."

10. Thus, Ginsberg rejects 13:2–22 (in *Book of Isaiah*, 11–12), despite Kaufmann's list of its parallels to the authentic Isaiah (*Toledot*, vol. 3, pt. 1, 179–80, n. 28).

11. The evidence I am about to present makes this a better solution than that proposed by Hermann Barth, *Die Jesaja-Worte in der Josiazeit* (Neukirchen-Vluyn: Neukirchener Verlag, 1977). On the shaky foundations of Barth's thesis, see the review by Wolfram Herrmann, *TLZ* 105 (1980): 828–30.

is on the rest of the verses, too. Although one passage in Jeremiah (50:31–32) denounces Babylon as the personification of "arrogance" (zdwn), the arrogance of the monarch in Isa. 14:13 was hardly characteristic of the kings of Babylon, even of the spectacularly successful Nebuchadnezzar II. The Books of Kings, Chronicles, and Ezekiel (who lived a quarter-century in exile under Nebuchadnezzar) do not accuse Babylon or her king of arrogance. Even in Habakkuk and Jeremiah (outside 50:31–32) the charges are only of wrongdoing and cruelty. Assyria, not Babylon, is the arrogant power in the histories and prophecies covering the age of the first temple and the Babylonian exile.[12]

Evidence from Mesopotamia, including the inscriptions of the Assyrian and Babylonian kings, confirms the impression given by the Bible. The Assyrian kings boastfully report their great military conquests; the kings of Babylon tell of their constructive and peaceful accomplishments, especially of the building and repair of temples.[13]

Though there are protests in Habakkuk and Jeremiah against the cruelty of Babylon, that trait as reflected in Isa. 14:3–6, 16–17, was characteristic rather of Assyria. Nebuchadnezzar's father, Nabopolassar, in an inscription boasts of having put an end to Assyrian cruelty.[14] The Books of Kings, Chronicles, and Ezekiel regard the Babylonian actions against Judah and her kings as just and make no accusations of cruelty. Even the Book of Lamentations complains only of the cruelty of war and siege and does not accuse the Babylonians.

The Assyrian kings, not the kings of Babylon, conspicuously "murdered their own people" (Isa. 14:20), grossly depleting the national manpower in war so that it is hard to find a trace of the Assyrians after the fall of their empire in 612.[15] By contrast, Babylonians survived for centuries as a subject nation after the fall of their kingdom in 539.[16]

The text of Isa. 13:2–14:27 contains one more valuable set of clues indicating

---

12. 2 Kings 18:19–35; 19:10–13, 21–24; Isa. 10:7–16; 36:4–20; 37:10–13, 22–25; Zeph. 2:15; 2 Chron. 32:10–19.

13. For inscriptions, see Ephraim A. Speiser, in The Idea of History in the Ancient Near East (ed. Robert C. Dentan; New Haven and London: Yale University Press, 1955), 64–65; A. K. Grayson, "History and Historians of the Ancient Near East," Or 49 (1980): 150–55, 160, 162–64, 170–71. Also noteworthy is the contrast between the position of the king of Assyria as high priest of the god Ashur and the humble position of the king of Babylon in religion and ritual; see Oppenheim, Ancient Mesopotamia (rev. ed., completed by Erica Reiner; Chicago and London: University of Chicago Press, 1977), 99, and Roux, Ancient Iraq, 399. Naturally, the kings of Assyria showed humility toward their own gods (Roux, Ancient Iraq, 341; Julian Reade, "Ideology and Propaganda in Assyrian Art," in Power and Propaganda [ed. Mogens Trolle Larsen; Mesopotamia: Copenhagen Studies in Assyriology 7; Copenhagen: Akademisk Forlag, 1979], 340).

14. For texts reflecting "cruel" Assyria, see Nah. 2:12–13; 3:1, 19. For the text of Nabopolassar's inscription, see Stephen H. Langdon, Die neubabylonischen Königsinschriften (Leipzig: Hinrichs, 1912), 61; English translation at Roux, Ancient Iraq, 377.

15. Roux, Ancient Iraq, 312–24 (through the reign of Sennacherib; can Isaiah have observed any later reign?); still heavier casualties came later (Roux, Ancient Iraq, 324–36).

16. Ibid., 387–88, 405–22.

that the passage originally dealt with Assyria rather than Babylon. Apart from the title in 13:1, only 13:19 and 14:22 connect the passage with Babylon. What happens to 14:22 if we remove the word "Babylon" and insert references to Assyria and her capital, Nineveh? The verse comes to contain a stunning double pun: "I will wipe out from Assyria ['aššūr] name and remnant [uš-'ār] and kith and [nīn wa-] kin from Nineveh [nīnua]."[17] It is likely that the author, at the end of 14:22, wrote not "declares the Lord" (n'm yhwh) but "from Nineveh" (mnynwh). The ease of the transition from one reading to the other is visible even in English transliteration. If a reader in the sixth century found "from Nineveh" inappropriate or somewhat illegible, he would immediately be led by the occurrences of "declares the Lord" in v. 23 and in the first half of v. 22 to read the same here at the end of v. 22. Our context is the only one in Isaiah 1–39 in which multiple occurrences of n'm yhwh come so close together.[18]

If "Nineveh" originally appeared in 14:22, we may be sure that it also stood in 13:2, where the text now has hr nšph ("bare[?] hill"). Nšph ("bare"?) is a word of unknown meaning which occurs nowhere else in the Hebrew Bible. If the correct reading is "Nineveh," the prophecy no longer has an inappropriate beginning. Rather, as one would expect, it comes to the point immediately: a standard is to be raised on the hill of Nineveh, capital of Assyria, to make it the target of the gathering barbarian hordes.[19] Nineveh stood on two hills, now called "Kuyunjik" and "Nebi Yunus." What the two were called in antiquity is unknown,[20] but there is no evidence to show that one of them was not called the "hill of Nineveh." Indeed, Isaiah need not have known anything about the geographical nomenclature of Nineveh; it was common knowledge that standards used as signals to assemble were raised on hills.[21]

Moreover, the enigmatic end of Isa. 13:2 can confirm that the verse originally contained references to Assyria or her capital city. No one has yet produced a satisfactory interpretation of pthy (the construct state of pthym, perhaps "openings" or "gates") in the last clause of that verse, wyb'w pthy ndybym ("Let them enter the gates[?] of nobles[?]"). Whatever pthym are, Mic. 5:5 contains good evidence that they are objects which Assyria was known to possess: "They shall waste the land of Assyria with the sword and the land of Nimrod in its pthym."

As for Isa. 13:19, "Babylon" may be an interpolation by those later Jews who wanted to find a prophecy by Isaiah predicting the fall of that city; on met-

---

17. Bezalel Porten has called to my attention that Isaiah elsewhere plays on the words 'ašer, 'aššūr, and the root š'r (11:11, 16). Nīnua, the ancient pronunciation of "Nineveh," is abundantly attested in cuneiform documents.

18. But see Jer. 3:12–14; 23:24, 28–29; 31:31–32, 36–37; 47:38–39; 51:24–25; Isa. 52:5.

19. Cf. Isa. 5:26–30; Jer. 4:6; 51:12, 27. In the old Hebrew letters used in Isaiah's time, nynwh, "Nineveh" (ᔓᔨ᙭᙭ᔍ), could look very much like nšph (ᔓ ᙭ᙎᔍ).

20. So I have been informed in a letter of March 14, 1984, from Prof. Erica Reiner, who consulted with the staff of the Chicago Assyrian Dictionary.

21. Isa. 30:17.

rical grounds alone one might suggest it is an interpolation.[22] And desires for retribution upon Babylon could have led such a Jew to misread (whether deliberately or unconsciously) "the pride of the arrogant" (g'wn zdym)[23] as "pride of the Chaldeans" (g'wn kśdym).

One can also easily explain the reference to the Medes in Isa. 13:17. The same sort of eye which misread nynwh ("Nineveh") as nśph could have misread gwy ("nation") as mdy ("the Medes"), and he or a later hand could have added the particle 't, which precedes the definite direct object.[24] The mention of an unnamed nation as God's punishing instrument is common.[25]

Sennacherib was the first king to make Nineveh the chief city of Assyria. Our reconstructed prophecy, too, treats Nineveh as the capital; therefore, it cannot have been written before the reign of Sennacherib (704–681).[26]

This reconstructed original of Isa. 13:2–14:27 is a cogent composition befitting Isaiah and his times and flows easily from clues in the extant text. There is more evidence in its favor: one later prophet can be shown to have read Isa. 13:2–14:27 when it still was directed at Assyria, when it still said nothing of Babylon; and another later prophetic composition just as clearly drew on Isa. 13:2–14:27 after it had been changed into a prophecy of the downfall of Babylon.

Zephaniah throughout his short book echoes the diction and ideas of Isaiah, and especially numerous are his borrowings from Isa. 13:2–14:27.[27] Zeph. 2:13–15 draws heavily upon that prophecy in the Book of Isaiah. In Zeph. 2:13, "He shall stretch his hand over the north and shall destroy Assyria and turn Nineveh into desolation, arid as the desert," we have the same parallelism of Assyria and

---

22. See my forthcoming Peoples, chap. 4, sec. 3.

23. The phrase occurs a few lines earlier, in Isa. 13:11.

24. In old Hebrew letters gwy is ᘐᖿᖾ, and mdy is ᖾ△ᒍ. Consider the parallels in Jeremiah 50–51. Jer. 50:9 is derived from Isa. 13:17, has the plural of gwy, and 't is absent, although one might expect it to be present. Jer. 51:11 is also derived from Isa. 13:17, has mdy, and ' t is present. Jer. 51:28 is also derived from Isa. 13:17 and has the plural of gwy without 't and has "the kings of mdy" with 't. Did the author of Jer. 50:9 and 51:28 know a text of Isa. 13:17 that did not have 't? Or do Jer. 50:9 and 51:11, 28 merely show how easily a later hand could add or omit the particle? On the omission of it in biblical poetry, see GKC 363, sec. 117b; Alfred M. Wilson, "The Particle 'et in Hebrew," Hebraica 6 (1889–90), 140, 219. On the tendency of later scribes to add it, see Isa. 14:4 with 1QIsaiah[a] 14:4, and E. Y. Kutscher, The Language and Linguistic Background of the Isaiah Scroll (1QIsa[a]) (STDJ 4; Leiden: Brill, 1974), 44.

25. Amos 6:14; Isa. 13:4; Jer. 5:15; 50:3; Deut. 28:36, 49–50.

26. On Sennacherib and Nineveh, see Roux, Ancient Iraq, 323–24. The ignominious details of the death of the tyrant in Isa. 14:18–20 may reflect the death of Sennacherib's father and predecessor, Sargon; see Hayim Tadmor, "The 'Sin of Sargon,'" Eretz-Israel 5 (1958): 157–58 (in Hebrew), and H. L. Ginsberg, "Reflexes of Sargon in Isaiah after 715 B.C.E.," JAOS 88 (1968): 49–53.

27. See H. L. Ginsberg, "Gleanings in First Isaiah," in Mordecai M. Kaplan Jubilee Volume, English section (New York: Jewish Theological Seminary of America, 1953), 258–59. Later (in Book of Isaiah, 11–12) he changed his mind and held that the author of Isaiah 13 borrowed from Zephaniah. Ginsberg's arguments can be refuted. With so great a number of borrowings in the Book of Zephanaiah from the Book of Isaiah, one would be surprised to find any passages showing borrowings in the reverse direction.

Nineveh as in our reconstruction of Isa. 14:22, and the same arid devastation as in Isa. 13:19–22. Both Zeph. 2:14 and Isa. 13:20 mention shepherds making their flocks lie down, although at Isa. 13:20, in contrast to Zeph. 3:14, the devastation is so great that the flocks will not lie down on the ruined site. According to both Zeph. 2:14 and Isa. 14:23, the qpwd ("bittern"?) will inhabit the ruins. In both Zeph. 2:15 and Isa. 13:21, wild beasts (or demons) will lie down on the site. If qpwd does indeed mean some kind of water bird, both at Zeph. 2:12–13 and at Isa. 13:19–22, 14:23, we have the incongruous prediction of both dry and watery devastation for the evil city. Where Isa. 13:21–22 mentions ruined mansions, Zeph. 2:14 mentions their windows, column capitals, thresholds, and cedar woodwork. Zeph. 2:15 contrasts the previous prosperity of arrogant Nineveh with her impending humiliation and destruction; Isa. 14:4–21 makes a similar contrast, about the king rather than about the city.

One must not be blind to the differences between Zeph. 2:13–15 and the parallels in Isa. 13:2–14:27. But so impressive is Zephaniah's debt throughout his book to that prophecy in the Book of Isaiah, that he must have known the text. He may have had his own reasons for somewhat changing its predictions in his own 2:13–15, but perhaps the departures there from the prophecy in Isaiah are due to nothing more than Zephaniah's faulty memory of his source. In any case, Zephaniah attests that the version of Isa. 13:2–14:27 that lay before him predicted the destruction of Assyria and Nineveh, not that of Babylon. Zephaniah also gives some attestation that in his time 14:1–2 stood in that prophecy, although perhaps not everyone will grant that the parallels between Zeph. 3:9, 19–20, and Isa. 14:1–2 are strong enough to justify that conclusion.[28]

Habakkuk prophesied at a time when Babylonian armies had begun to take spoils from Judah — at the earliest, well into the reign of Jehoiakim. His words may reflect a text of Isa. 13:2–14:27 wherein "Assyria" and "Nineveh" had been replaced by "Babylon." Just as Isa. 14:3–20 predicts the humiliating downfall of the arrogant, cruel, and destructive power, so Hab. 2:5–17 predicts the humiliating downfall of the greedy and destructive power. Both prophecies contain a taunt song (mšl) to be sung after the downfall of the tyrannical power (Hab. 1:6–17; Isa. 14:4–20). Both messages speak of the violence done to the Lebanon (Hab. 2:16; Isa. 14:8). Both complain of the tyrannical power's sins against plural nations, not just against the Lord's people (Hab. 2:5, 8, 13; Isa. 14:6, 16–17). In both, the tyrant is said to have sought to dwell on high (Hab. 2:9; Isa. 14:13). But even if Habakkuk read Isa. 13:2–14:27, we cannot tell whether he read it as a prophecy against Assyria and used it as a model for his message against Babylon, or whether already in his time someone had changed the text to make Babylon the target.

The parallels to Isa. 13:2–14:27 that run through Jer. 50:1–51:58 demonstrate

---

28. See Hab. 1:6–10, 15–17; 2 Kings 24:1–2.

conclusively that the author or authors of the latter knew Isa. 13:2–14:27.[29] He
(or they) also knew Habakkuk 1–2.[30] Did the version which lay before the later
writer or writers have Isaiah's original target, Assyria, or had it already been
turned into a prophecy against Babylon? Close examination of Jer. 50:1–51:58
gives an unequivocal answer.

Like Isa. 13:1, Jer. 50:1 both names the prophet who is supposed to be the
author and gives Babylon as his target. However, Jer. 50:2 does not have an
equivalent for the "bare[?] mountain" (*hr nšph*); the writer fails to specify the
place for raising the standard, unlike his or Jeremiah's practice elsewhere.[31] In
other verses, the writer seems embarrassed with his inability to read the word in
Isa. 13:2 designating the place for raising the standard. Though Nineveh stood on

---

29. I list, first, the passage in Jer. 50:1–51:58; second, the passage in Isa. 13:1–14:27 on which it
depends. I add any comments which I think necessary.
   Jer. 50:1; Isa. 13:1, 19 ("Babylon" paralleled to "Chaldeans"). Jer. 50:2; Isa. 13:2. Jer. 50:4–5; Isa.
14:1–2 (although Jeremiah believed that the Gentiles would give up idolatry, he did not have Isaiah's
enthusiasm for admitting them to the Lord's people). Jer. 50:6–9; Isa. 13:14, 14:2 (reference to the
flock and to the captors of the Lord's people; Jeremiah hopes that the captors will be despoiled and
annihilated [50:29, 35–37, 45], not that they will become slaves). Jer. 50:9; Isa. 13:4–5, 17.
   Jer. 50:10–13; Isa. 13:19–20. Jer. 50:14–16; Isa. 13:15–18. Jer. 50:16; Isa. 14:22. Jer. 50:16 (end);
Isa. 13:14 (end). Jer. 50:17–18 does not draw directly on Isa. 13:2–14:27, but Babylon there is paralleled to Assyria. Did the writer have some inkling that Isa. 13:2–14:27 was originally about the fall
of Assyria? Jer. 50:19–20; Isa. 14:1–3 (see above, on Jer. 50:6–9). Jer. 50:21, Isa. 14:22 (the writer
uses names from the Babylonian countryside, but the meaning of the passage is the same as that of
Isa. 14:22). Jer. 50:22; Isa. 13:4–5. Jer. 50:23; Isa. 14:4–6 (and 10:5). Jer. 50:24; Isa. 14:11–12. Jer.
50:25–27 (Media not named!); Isa. 13:17–19. Jer. 50:26; Isa. 14:22. Jer. 50:28; Isa. 13:14, 14:1–2. Jer.
50:29–30; Isa. 13:18. Jer. 50:33–34; Isa. 14:1–2 (however, for the writer in Jeremiah, only God, not
the Gentiles, will release the captives; see above, on Jer. 50:6–9).
   Jer. 50:35; Isa. 13:19 (the target is identified as Babylon and the Chaldeans). Jer. 50:35–37; Isa.
14:22 (the destruction of the enemy is essentially the same). Jer. 50:38–40; Isa. 13:19–22. Jer. 50:41–
42; Isa. 13:4, 9, 17–18. Jer. 50:44 (end); Isa. 14:27. Jer. 50:44–45; Isa. 14:24–25, 14:1–2 (the sheep
of the Lord's flock will drag off their Babylonian captors as prey, and Babylon will be destroyed; see
above, on Jer. 50:6–9). Jer. 50:46; Isa. 13:13.
   Jer. 51:1; Isa. 13:19. Jer. 51:2–4; Isa. 13:15–18. Jer. 51:6; Isa. 13:14. The metaphor of the cup of
drunkenness in Jer. 51:7 is Jeremiah's own (cf. 25:15–28), as is that of the balm in 51:8–9 (cf. 8:22;
46:11). Jer. 51:8 ("howl" [*hylylw*]); Isa. 13:6. Jer. 51:9 ("abandon her"); Isa. 13:14. Jer. 51:10; Isa.
14:1–2. Jer. 51:11; Isa. 13:17. Jer. 51:12; Isa. 13:2, 14:24 (and 21:8). Jer. 51:17–19; Isa. 21:9 (attack on
idols). Jer. 51:20–23; Isa. 14:5–6 (and 10:5). Jer. 51:24; Isa. 14:24–26. Jer. 51:25; Isa. 13:2 (mention
of a mountain). Jer. 51:27–28; Isa. 13:2–4 (raising a standard, nations, sanctification or purification
[Hebrew root: *qdš*], making sounds). Jer. 51:28; Isa. 13:17 (Media). Jer. 51:29; Isa. 13:13 (earthquake)
and 14:24–27 (God's plans). Jer. 51:31; Isa. 21:9. Jer. 51:34–35; Isa. 14:17 (and 10:7, 14). Jer. 51:37;
Isa. 13:21. Jer. 51:38–39; Nah. 2:12–14.
   Jer. 51:39 again has the metaphor of drunkenness; see above, on 51:7. Jer. 51:41; Isa. 14:12. Jer.
51:42; Isa. 14:23. Jer. 51:43; Isa. 13:19–22. Jer. 51:44; Isa. 21:9 (fall of Babylon and her god[s]). The
destroyer from the north in 51:48 is a motif of Jeremiah's own (1:14; 4:6; 6:1; etc.). Jer. 51:49; Isa.
13:14–15. Jer. 51:50; Isa. 13:14, 14:1. Jer. 51:52; Isa. 21:9. Jer. 51:53; Isa. 14:12–14. Jer. 51:57 again
has the metaphor of drunkenness (see above, on Jer. 51:7).
   Like Isa. 13:19–23 alongside Isa. 14:23, and like Zeph. 2:13 alongside Zeph. 2:14, the dry desolation
of Jer. 50:10–11, 38–40; 51:1; and 51:43 is incongruous alongside the flooding in Jer. 51:42.
   30. Jer. 51:58 contains an unmistakable allusion to Hab. 2:13.
   31. Contrast Jer. 4:6, 51:27; the location of the standard at Jer. 4:21 is clear from the context.

two hills, Babylon was flat. There was no reason to speak of the "hill of Babylon." A writer who had no model before him would have spoken rather of her tower, the famous ziggurat Etemenanki. Nevertheless, at Jer. 51:25 Babylon is called the "mountain of the destroyer" (*hr hmšḥyt*) and, for the future, a "mountain of burning" (*hr śrph*). Nowhere else in Jeremiah is the image of a volcano used, and it does not seem appropriate in Jer. 51:25. Let us rather note that *š* and *ś* (written identically in ancient Hebrew) occur in *nšph*, *mšḥyt*, and *śrph*, and that *nšph* and *śrph* both end in *ph*.

The conclusion seems inescapable: at some time before Jer. 50:1–51:58 was written, a version of Isa. 13:2–14:27 had puzzled a reader. Either that reader was unable to read "Nineveh" in 13:2 (because the writing was blurred), or he was unwilling to do so. It is hard to believe that all the original references to Nineveh and Assyria in Isa. 13:2 and 14:22 had become blurred. But believers in the great prophetic power of Isaiah could have had good reason to take advantage of any place in those verses that was hard to read or that merely looked something like what they wanted to see. Either way, they could (whether unconsciously or deliberately) alter the text without arousing too many suspicions among their contemporaries. Their beliefs could have driven them to remove legible or illegible references to Assyria and to replace them with references to Babylon. Why? Because otherwise the great Isaiah's prophecy in 13:2–14:27 contained too many falsehoods.

True, Nineveh and Assyria were destroyed, and the king was killed, fulfilling the prophecy. But the civilized world had not suffered a cruel and devastating invasion by barbarians from the mountains to extirpate sinners (contrary to Isa. 13:4–9). Contrary to Isa. 13:9, there were no noteworthy eclipses (eclipses of the moon are common). There were no quakes in heaven or earth (contrary to Isa. 13:13). Captive peoples did not return to their homelands, and certainly not the descendants of those deported from the northern kingdom of Israel, nor did the Lord's people possess their captors and oppressors as slaves (contrary to Isa. 13:14; 14:1–2). The powers which conquered Assyria did not perpetrate merciless massacres of children (contrary to Isa. 13:18). The final defeat of Assyria did not occur in the Holy Land (contrary to Isa. 14:25).

There was a prophecy by Isaiah of the fall of Assyria (10:5–27) which had been completely fulfilled by 609 B.C.E.; it seemed even to predict Josiah's moment of prosperity (10:27) and Assyria's turning in her last struggles to rely on Egypt (10:26). If Isa. 13:2–14:27 as a prophecy of Assyria's fall was not only superfluous but false, what could have been God's and Isaiah's purpose in revealing it? On the other hand, surely God and God's great prophet should have given some forewarning and comfort to Israel concerning Babylon. Thus there were good reasons for the faithful to read Isa. 13:2–14:27 as a prophecy against Babylon and even for them to alter the text deliberately. Whether innocently or deliberately, someone after the time of Zephaniah's prophecy did make that alteration. When?

Since 1878, most modern commentators have held that Jeremiah could not have written 50:1–51:58,[32] on insufficient grounds, in my view.[33] Many scholars who deny that Jer. 50:1–51:58 are by Jeremiah concede that the narrative at 51:59–64 truly transmits Jeremiah's deeds and words (except for implying that everything in 50:1–51:58 is his).[34] But Jer. 51:62 resembles Isa. 14:22–23 and 13:19–20 enough to justify the conclusion that Jeremiah himself drew on Isa. 13:2–14:27.[35] And the deeds and words in that narrative are dated (51:59) in the fourth year of Zedekiah, ca. 593 B.C.E. Even if, as most modern commentators hold, members of the generation after Jeremiah wrote all of Jer. 50:1–51:58 (and even Jer. 51:59–64), they must have written before Cyrus of Persia conquered the Medes in 550, for otherwise the name of the Persians would have been prominent among those of the peoples in Jer. 50:9; 51:11, 27–28.

Thus, at a time between Nebuchadnezzar's first harsh measures against the kingdom of rebellious Jehoiakim (ca. 599 B.C.E.) and 550 B.C.E., Isa. 13:2–14:27 (which Zephaniah in about 612 B.C.E. still knew as a prophecy of the fall of Assyria) was turned into a prophecy of the fall of Babylon to invaders, among whom were the Medes. The prophecy brought some small comfort to the Jews who suffered the fall of the kingdom and the exile, and it was to have important effects in the future.

32. Following K. Budde, "Über die Capitel l und li des Buches Jeremia," Jahrbücher für deutsche Theologie 23 (1878): 428–70; see Otto Eissfeldt, Old Testament: An Introduction (New York and Evanston, Ill.: Harper & Row, 1965), 362.

33. See Kaufmann, Toledot, vol. 3, pt. 2, 421–23, 467–69.

34. See John Bright, Jeremiah (AB 21; New York: Doubleday, 1965), 212, 259–60.

35. The verse from Jeremiah, like the passages in Isaiah, contains the verb hkryt ("wipe out," "cut off") and the removal of human and domestic animal inhabitants from the devastated site.

9

The Wisdom of the Scribe,
the Wisdom of the Priest,
and the Wisdom of the King
according to Ben Sira

◆

Martha Himmelfarb
Princeton University

In his account of the various occupations that make the world run, Ben Sira makes no secret of his view that the most exalted of all is that of the scribe:

> ...He who devotes himself
> to the study of the law of the Most High
> will seek out the wisdom of all the ancients,
> and will be concerned with prophecies;
> he will preserve the discourse of notable men
> and penetrate the subtleties of parables;
> he will seek out the hidden meanings of proverbs
> and be at home with the obscurities of parables.
> He will serve among great men and appear before rulers;
> he will travel through the lands of foreign nations,
> for he tests the good and the evil among men. (39:1–4)[1]

Ben Sira's term for this profession or calling is *swpr*[2] or γραμματεύς (38:24); the term appears only once in this passage, but at a prominent spot, the very

---

1. All translations of Ben Sira and the HB are taken from the RSV unless otherwise indicated. The RSV translates the Greek text of Ben Sira.

2. For the Hebrew of Ben Sira, I cite F. Vattioni, *Ecclesiastico* (vol. 1; Naples: Instituto Orientale di Napoli, 1968). Given the complex history of the text of Ben Sira, I consider both Greek and Hebrew wherever the Hebrew is extant. The differences between the Greek and Hebrew texts of Ben Sira on the subject of kingship and priesthood deserve further study. In the passages considered below, when the versions differ, it is usually because the Hebrew places greater emphasis on the royal qualities of the priestly covenants and does more to play down the covenant with David. But not all passages fit this pattern: for example, the Greek description of the covenant with Phinehas in 45:24 makes him

89

beginning of the account. The literal translation "scribe" seems hardly adequate for the activities Ben Sira describes. Thus the REB translates "scholar," while M. E. Stone uses "sage" and J. Marböck calls this figure "der schriftgelehrte Weise."[3] Although Ben Sira fails to mention Ezra in his praise of the fathers, his lofty understanding of the functions of the scribe surely reflects the career of the most famous biblical figure to bear the title "scribe."[4]

The Book of Ezra introduces its hero as "a scribe skilled in the law of Moses which the Lord the God of Israel had given" (Ezra 7:6). Like Ezra, Ben Sira's scribe is a skilled interpreter of the law of God, but the wisdom Ben Sira attributes to him goes beyond expertise in the Torah or in any of the great texts of the past. Indeed, Ben Sira's description of the scribe incorporates features usually associated with a somewhat different figure in biblical literature, the wise man, ḥkm. In the tradition of wisdom literature, to which Ben Sira belongs, wisdom is an ideal to which all should aspire. Elsewhere in biblical literature, however, wisdom is understood as belonging to a more limited group of people. Outside the Priestly document, which calls the skill of Bezalel and the craftsmen involved in making the sanctuary and its ornaments "wisdom" (Exod. 28:3; 31:6; 36:2) and the craftsmen, "wise-hearted" (Exod. 28:3; 31:6; 35:10; 36:2, 8),[5] the dominant association of wisdom is with wise advisers in the royal court. King Solomon himself, of course, is the greatest individual exemplar of wisdom in the Bible (1 Kings 3–4, 10), and I shall return to the significance of his wisdom for Ben Sira. Joshua, a leader if not a king, is granted the "spirit of wisdom" (Deut. 34:9). But beyond these two figures, the wise men of the Bible are wise advisers, whom the Bible understands as a standard feature of a royal court.

Joseph becomes second in command to Pharaoh by showing that he is even wiser than the resident advisers, "all the magicians of Egypt and its wise men" (Gen. 41:8). Elsewhere we read of the wise men of Pharaoh (Isa. 19:11), the wise men of Babylonia (Jer. 50:35; 51:57), and the wise men of the Persian court (Esther 1:13). Even Haman, a vizier like Joseph rather than a king, has his own wise men (Esther 6:13). The tales of Daniel assume a class of royal advisers who

---

"leader of the sanctuary and of his people," while the Hebrew mentions the sanctuary, but not the people.

3. M. E. Stone, "Ideal Figures and Social Context: Priest and Sage in the Early Second Temple Age," in *Ancient Israelite Religion* (ed. P. D. Miller, P. D. Hanson, and D. S. McBride; Philadelphia: Fortress, 1988), 575–86; J. Marböck, "Sir. 38,24–39,11: Der schriftgelehrte Weise. Eine Beitrag zu Gestalt und Werk ben Siras," in *La sagesse de l'ancien testament* (ed. M. Gilbert; 2d ed.; BETL 51; Louvain: Louvain University Press, 1990), 293–316. See also D. J. Harrington, "The Wisdom of the Scribe according to Ben Sira," in *Ideal Figures in Ancient Judaism: Profiles and Paradigms* (ed. G. W. E. Nickelsburg and J. J. Collins; SCS 12; Chico, Calif.: Scholars Press, 1980), 181–88.

4. So too Marböck, "Sir. 38,24–39,11," 297–99. See P. Höffken, "Warum schwieg Jesus Sirach über Esra?" ZAW 87 (1975): 184–201, for a very different position. Scribes appear in the Books of Samuel and Kings (and parallel material in Isaiah and Chronicles), and in the Books of Jeremiah, Ezra, Nehemiah, and Chronicles.

5. RSV translates "ability" and "able."

serve to interpret dreams and other portents for their king, although they are not called wise men.[6] The Book of Proverbs suggests the presence of such wise men in the Judean royal court: "These also are sayings of the wise" (24:23), and "These also are proverbs of Solomon which the men of Hezekiah king of Judah copied" (25:1).

When Ben Sira writes of the scribe, "He will serve among great men and appear before rulers" (39:4), he is attributing to him the functions of the wise man. Although the origins of the two professions are distinct, it is not difficult to see how the boundaries between scribe and wise man began to disappear. As an adviser in the royal court, the wise man offered practical advice to the king about the conduct of affairs. In the early days, there was no necessary relationship between wisdom and a written text. In addition to its wise men, the court of Hezekiah employed scribes and officials called recorders[7] (2 Kings 18:18). The work of these officials required technical skills not necessarily related to practical wisdom.

The promulgation of Deuteronomy naturally elevated the status of reading and writing, the skills of the scribe. Further, the scribe's role took on political dimensions, for society was now to be governed, at least ideally, on the basis of a text, which inevitably required interpretation. In the period between the appearance of Deuteronomy and the fall of the monarchy, the new power of the role of the scribe was not yet felt, for the king maintained control over the various aspects of life about which Deuteronomy legislated. But with the fall of the monarchy at the time of the Babylonian conquest, less than forty years after the "finding" of Deuteronomy, the importance of the scribe received a dramatic boost. Almost two centuries later, when the Persians wished to stabilize the situation in Judah, they called on the services of Ezra the scribe, an expert in interpretation of the Torah, which they understood, quite in keeping with Deuteronomy's intentions, as the constitution of the Jewish people.

With the Babylonian conquest, the Israelite wise man was out of work, at least on his home territory, for there was no longer a royal court in Jerusalem. The story of Joseph, it is true, provided a model for Jewish wise men serving foreign kings, a model developed in the Book of Daniel, but the fall of the monarchy was a severe blow to the profession of the wise man. Further, with the rise of the written text the understanding of wisdom inevitably underwent a certain redefinition. Daniel is not only an interpreter of dreams (chaps. 2, 4) as was his great predecessor Joseph, but also of the writing on the wall (chap. 5) and the recipient of an interpretation of a biblical text, the prophecy of Jeremiah that Israel's exile would endure for seventy years (chap. 9). Dreams are a medium of divine revelation, just

---

6. The term "wisdom" appears only in chap. 1 of the Book of Daniel, and it is restricted to Daniel and his friends.

7. Hebrew: *mzkyr* (the term appears in the singular).

as is the writing on the wall or indeed the Torah. But it is surely not accidental that the Book of Daniel includes the interpretation of written texts as the story of Joseph does not. Ben Sira, of course, claims that Wisdom is the Torah.

It is not surprising, then, that some of the functions once performed by wise men were taken over by scribes. Ezra the scribe serves as an official of the Persian crown. Nehemiah begins his career as the cupbearer of the Persian king, a position that suggests the role of court wise man, and while he is never called a scribe, he justified his reforms by reference to the "book of Moses" (Neh. 13:1), although his authority as Persian governor surely permitted him to impose his will as he saw fit. Ezra and Nehemiah are examples of the scribe who both studies the law and serves rulers.

In addition to the role of the wise man, there is another role Ben Sira associates with the scribe — the role of priest. The claim that being a scribe requires freedom from labor (38:24) may point in this direction.[8] Among the Greeks, leisure was the privilege of the gentleman; the most likely candidates for this role among the Jews were priests, since at least in theory their needs were provided for by the contributions of the people.[9] Further, the poem in praise of Wisdom at the center of Ben Sira's work (chap. 24) provides a powerful set of associations that point in this direction. In the poem Wisdom describes herself taking up residence among the people of Israel and serving in the Jerusalem temple (24:8–12). Ben Sira then identifies Wisdom with the Torah (24:23). Thus the poem equates the spheres of priest, wise man, and scribe, if not the roles themselves. The beginning of the integration of these roles can be discerned in the Book of Deuteronomy, although I think it is unlikely that Ben Sira had Deuteronomy in mind since later sources offer clearer models, such as the figure of Ezra.[10] Ezra, it should be remembered, was not only a scribe, but also a priest, as the Book of Ezra takes pains to show with its elaborate genealogy that goes all the way back to Aaron (7:1–5). But the dynamics of the development in Deuteronomy are worth considering because they have implications for Ben Sira's attitude toward the priestly commonwealth of his own time.

Deuteronomy is a revolutionary document, and its revolution had profound consequences for priests, although Deuteronomy does not devote a great deal

---

8. The claim is more emphatic in the Greek than in the Hebrew: "The wisdom of the scribe depends on the opportunity of leisure; and he who has little business may become wise" (Greek); "The wisdom of the scribe increases wisdom; he who lacks business will become wise" (Hebrew).

9. H. Stadelmann, *Ben Sira als Schriftgelehrter* (WUNT 2/6; Tübingen: Mohr [Siebeck], 1980), 13. Note also the saying of R. Simon ben Yohai, *Mek.* to Exod. 13:17, "The Torah was given to study only to those who eat manna, and those who eat the offering set apart for priests (*trwmh*) are equal to them."

10. Ben Sira's attitude toward Deuteronomy and the Deuteronomic History is the subject of some controversy. See, e.g., B. L. Mack, *Wisdom and the Hebrew Epic: Ben Sira's Hymn in Praise of the Fathers* (Chicago and London: University of Chicago Press, 1985), 119–20, and references there. Whatever Ben Sira's view toward the ideology of the Deuteronomic History, I hope my discussion here demonstrates his affinities to important aspects of the Book of Deuteronomy itself.

of attention to them. Priests had traditionally derived their authority from their role in the sacrificial cult, the purity laws associated with it, and certain mantic functions of the office. The centralization of the cult Deuteronomy demanded brought with it radical changes for priests accustomed to serving the Lord outside Jerusalem. But another aspect of the reform had implications even more revolutionary. For by placing a text at the center of Israel's communal life, Deuteronomy inevitably changed the nature of the priesthood both internally and externally. No longer could priests appeal to the traditional knowledge passed on by father to son through the generations in defending the way they conducted the affairs of the temple. The significance of this development may not have been immediately obvious. First of all, until the Babylonian conquest the temple remained under the control of the king. It is the power of the king that accounts both for idolatrous worship in the temple at the time of Manasseh and for the implementation of the Deuteronomic reform under Josiah. Only with the disappearance of the king in the Second Temple period do the full implications of the authority of the text become clear. Nehemiah was not a priest, and yet he dictates to priests about the management of the temple and the appropriateness of marriages they contract (Nehemiah 13). This is possible only because there was now a written document to which he could appeal over the priests' claim to traditional knowledge.

Although the full consequences of this aspect of the reform may not have been immediately apparent, it hardly escaped the notice of Deuteronomy's authors that they had undercut the traditional basis of priestly authority. The evidence for their realization lies in their effort to redefine the role of priests. One aspect of the redefinition of the priesthood associates priests with the book of the Torah; the other makes them judicial officials. As part of its program to establish itself as the constitution of the people of Israel, Deuteronomy prescribes that the king himself write a copy of the Torah, that is, Deuteronomy, with the limitations on his power that it specifies, *mlpny hkhnym hlwym* (17:18). The meaning of this phrase is not entirely clear;[11] what is clear is that Deuteronomy uses the phrase to associate the book of the Torah with the priests. The association of priests and text is also expressed in the teaching role Deuteronomy attributes to priests. Moses' blessing of the tribe of Levi juxtaposes teaching and sacrifice: "They shall teach (*ywrw*) Jacob thy ordinances, and Israel thy law; they shall put incense before thee, and whole burnt offerings upon thy altar" (33:10). Deuteronomy even transforms the role of priests in dealing with skin irruptions into teaching:

---

11. Translations differ considerably: "from that which is in charge of the Levitical priests" (RSV and NRSV), "at the dictation of the levitical priests" (REB, JB). The New Jewish Publication Society version resorts to implicit emendation: "When he is seated on his royal throne, he shall have a copy of this Teaching written for him on a scroll by the levitical priests"; a note to "by" reads, "Nuance of Heb. *milliphne* uncertain."

"Take heed, in an attack of leprosy, to be very careful to do according to all that the Levitical priests shall teach (*ywrw*) you" (24:8).[12]

While Deuteronomy associates priests with the book of the Torah, it never calls them scribes. The office Deuteronomy adds to the priestly repertoire is the office of judge. As part of its constitution for the Israelite polity, Deuteronomy calls for a judicial system in which cases too difficult to be resolved at the local level can be referred to a central court of appeal (17:8–13). Priests participate in the upper level of the judiciary system together with judges who are not priests, presumably lending some of the prestige of their traditional status to their new roles (17:9, 12). So, too, cases involving a malicious witness (19:16) are to be referred to the "the priests and the judges" (19:17). Deuteronomy even makes a parenthetical reference to the judicial function of priests in delineating their quite different role in the ceremony for ridding a city of guilt for a murder victim found outside the city (21:5).

Deuteronomy never directly associates priests with wisdom, but it does treat wisdom as a qualification for judges. In the opening chapter of Deuteronomy, Moses recalls how the people accepted his plan to relieve him of some of the burden of their affairs by choosing officials to serve as judges. These officials are described as "wise, understanding, and experienced men" (1:13) and as "wise and experienced men" (1:15); in contrast, when Moses takes a similar step at the suggestion of his father-in-law in the Book of Exodus, the men are described not as wise but as '*nšy-ḥyl*, "able men" (Exod. 18:21, 25). Deuteronomy's condemnation of bribery also associates wisdom with judges: "You shall not take a bribe, for a bribe blinds the eyes of the wise and subverts the cause of the righteous" (16:19).

A somewhat different set of associations for wisdom emerges in Moses' exhortation to Israel to observe the "statutes and ordinances" (4:5) that he has taught them, "for that will be your wisdom and your understanding in the sight of the peoples, who, when they hear all these statutes, will say, 'Surely this great nation is a wise and understanding people'" (4:6). Although Deuteronomy here refers to "statutes and ordinances" rather than the "book of the Torah," the association of wisdom with ordinances does suggest a connection between wisdom and text. This is a connection that we take for granted, but it is important to remember that the connection is possible only with the emergence of a text at the center of Israel's life.

Ben Sira wrote at the beginning of the second century, roughly four centuries after the last king sat on the throne in Jerusalem. In Ben Sira's day, the official head of the Jewish people in the eyes of its foreign ruler was the high priest. Despite the lack of a Davidic king, Ben Sira insists in his book that all is right with the world. To make his case, he offers the myth of Wisdom serving in the

---

12. I have modified the translation of RSV, which reads "direct" for "teach."

temple (chap. 24) and an account of Israel's history in which priests appear as almost royal figures (chaps. 44–50).[13]

The prominence of priests in Ben Sira's praise of the fathers has often been noted. Ben Sira devotes more lines (45:6–22) to Aaron than to any other figure from Israel's past; only Simon, who served as high priest while Ben Sira was a young man, is described at greater length (50:1–21). The most striking aspect of the passage about Aaron is the detailed description of his priestly garments, including a golden crown, *'trt pz* (46:12). The Priestly document of the Torah provides the high priest with a turban with a gold plate inscribed, "Holy to the Lord," (Exod. 28:37–38), but the crown is Ben Sira's own contribution. The phrase is drawn from Ps. 21:4[3]; there it describes the crown God has placed on the head of the king.

Further, Ben Sira notes that Aaron and his descendants are parties to a covenant that will endure "as the days of heaven," *kymy šmym* (45:15).[14] The source of the phrase is Psalm 89, a poem mourning the loss of the Davidic king: "I will establish his line for ever / and his throne as the days of the heavens (*kymy šmym*)" (89:30[29]).[15] Thus the phrase is drawn from a royal context, but of a peculiar kind: the psalm laments the failure of the promise of an eternal dynasty. This context makes Ben Sira's use of the phrase for Aaron's descendants all the more pointed.

After Aaron, Ben Sira turns to Phinehas. His focus is the covenant Phinehas receives rather than the nature of the zealous deed he performs (45:23–24). The eternity of this covenant, too, is noted (45:24). There follows a comparison of this covenant to the covenant with David (45:25). The details of the comparison are not clear, and the Greek and Hebrew differ significantly. But the import of the comparison is the superiority of the priestly covenant to the Davidic covenant.[16] The comparison concludes with an apostrophe to the descendants of Phinehas, praying that God grant them wisdom (45:25–26).[17] The Hebrew speaks also of God "who crowns (*hm'tr*) you with glory"; note that the verb "crown" has the

---

13. I am indebted for this understanding of the praise of the fathers particularly to Mack, *Wisdom and the Hebrew Epic*.

14. The Greek differs slightly: ἐν ἡμέραις οὐρανοῦ, "in the days of heaven" (RSV: "all the days of heaven").

15. I have modified the translation of RSV, which reads, "as the days of the heavens."

16. The Hebrew text of the first two-thirds of the verse reads *wgm brytw 'm dwd bn yšy lmth yhwdh* / *nhlt 'š lpne kbwdw nhlt 'hrn lkl zr'w*. Stadelmann translates thus: "Und auch Sein Bund mit David ... ist das Erbe eines Mannes vor dem Angesicht Seiner Herrlichkeit, das Erbe Aarons für alle seine Nachkommen"; the "man before the face of his glory" is Aaron, whose descendants have inherited the covenant with David (*Ben Sira*, 156–58; quotation, 157). I find the Hebrew extremely difficult to construe, and I am afraid that it will not bear the meaning Stadelmann assigns it. P. W. Skehan emends the Hebrew "in light of G and the parallelism," to *nahălat 'š libnô lĕbaddô*, which he translates, "was an individual heritage through one son alone" (P. W. Skehan and A. A. DiLella, *The Wisdom of Ben Sira* [AB 39; New York: Doubleday, 1987], 508, 510). The meaning of the comparison remains less than clear even after this emendation.

17. So in Hebrew; in Greek, only 45:26.

same root as the golden crown Ben Sira has already given Aaron (45:12). At the conclusion of the Hebrew version of the passage about Simon, which is also the conclusion of the praise of the fathers as a whole, the royal language applied earlier to Aaron's covenant appears again about the covenant with Phinehas:

> May his love abide upon Simon
> and may he keep in him the covenant of Phinehas;
> may one never be cut off from him;
> and as for his offspring, (may it be) as the days of heaven (*kymy šmym*).
> (51:24)[18]

Simon, too, is represented not only as the high priest but as a royal figure. His work projects (50:1–4) recall those of Hezekiah (48:17–22).[19] His glorious appearance as he emerges from the temple has a majestic quality that reminds us of the glorious garments of his ancestor Aaron, with their suggestion of a royal dimension to the high priest's role (45:7–13). The royal quality of Simon's high priesthood is reinforced in the climax of the passage, the account of the people bowing before him to receive the blessing he mediates (50:20–21).

As Ben Sira emphasizes the eternal covenants of priesthood made with Aaron and Phinehas, he downplays the covenant with David. It is only in the concluding verse of the passage about David that the Greek of Ben Sira mentions a covenant:

> The Lord took away his sins,
> and exalted his power for ever;
> he gave him the covenant of kings
> and a throne of glory in Israel. (47:11)

It is noteworthy that it is the power rather than the covenant that is called eternal.[20] The Hebrew does not even mention a covenant, and certainly not an eternal one; rather, God gave David *ḥq mmlkt*, the law of kingship.[21]

Not only does Ben Sira try to play down the Davidic covenant; he also insists that the institution of kingship was flawed. In the course of its entire history it produced only three pious kings:

> Except David and Hezekiah and Josiah
> they all sinned greatly,

---

18. The translation of the Hebrew is taken from the notes of the *Oxford Annotated Apocrypha, Expanded Edition* (ed. B. M. Metzger; New York, Oxford University Press, 1977), 196. The Greek reads, "May he entrust to us his mercy! / And let him deliver us in our days!"

19. Nehemiah, too, is credited with repairing walls and buildings (49:13), but the activities of Hezekiah are more clearly parallel to Simon's. Simon repaired and fortified the temple and laid foundations for retaining walls, dug a cistern, and fortified the city against siege. Hezekiah fortified the city, provided water, and withstood a siege. Simon does everything Hezekiah did, and in addition repairs the temple.

20. Stadelmann, *Ben Sira*, 160.

21. Compare the Hebrew of 45:24, the covenant with Phinehas, *ḥq bryt šlwm*; see ibid., 161.

> for they forsook the law of the Most High;
> the kings of Judah came to an end.... (49:4)

But it is Solomon, the only other king mentioned by name in the praise of the fathers, who poses the most difficult problem for Ben Sira, for Solomon is the most notable exemplar of wisdom in the Bible. If wisdom is intimately associated with kingship, it calls into question Ben Sira's claim that rule by high priest is preferable to rule by king. Unfortunately for Ben Sira, the biblical resources for associating priests with wisdom are limited, although, as we have seen, Deuteronomy contains such elements, even if they are not fully developed. Ben Sira's account of the career of Aaron mentions the teaching role of priests in language that echoes Deut. 33:10, but otherwise wisdom plays no role in it.[22] Rather, it is with the figure of Simon that Ben Sira takes his stand. At the climax of the praise of the fathers, Simon is described officiating in the temple (50:5–22) just as is Wisdom in chap. 24, and the similes comparing the magnificence of Simon's appearance to a series of natural phenomena including trees and other vegetation (50:5–11) recall the tree similes Wisdom applies to herself (24:13–17). Simon appears, then, almost as Wisdom's double.[23]

But in addition to making the case for the high priest as the great representative of wisdom, Ben Sira has to undercut Solomon's claim. He does not do so by ignoring it:

> How wise you became in your youth!
> You overflowed like a river with understanding....
> For your songs and proverbs and parables,
> and for your interpretations, the countries marveled at you. (47:14, 17)

Indeed, the river simile recalls the description of Wisdom/Torah in 24:25–27; the works Solomon wrote recall the subjects of the scribe's research in 39:2–3.

Rather Ben Sira attempts to disqualify Solomon by a severe judgment of his sins:

> ... You gathered gold like tin
> and amassed silver like lead.
> ... You laid your loins beside women,
> and through your body you were brought into subjection.
> You put a stain upon your honor,

---

22. Stone, "Ideal Figures," 580.

23. Mack argues that Ben Sira purposely excludes the "scholar-sage" from the praise of the fathers (*Wisdom and the Hebrew Epic*, 104–7). While he is correct that the office of scribe is not included, the parallels between the figure of Wisdom in chap. 24 and Simon in chap. 50 should not be overlooked. Mack's contention that the scribe of chap. 39 shows points of contact with the figure of Moses in the praise of the fathers is important (ibid.). In a more extended treatment of Ben Sira's view of scribe and sage, I hope to take this contention into account.

and defiled your posterity,
so that you brought wrath upon your children
and they were grieved at your folly,
so that the sovereignty was divided.... (47:18–21)

I have slightly modified the translation of the RSV following the suggestion of
P. C. Beentjes.[24] The RSV (so too REB) takes the end of v. 18, the accumulation of
silver and gold, as the last element of the praise of Solomon; it provides "but" to
connect the praise to the criticism: "But you laid your loins beside women.... "[25]
Against this view, Beentjes argues that Ben Sira measures Solomon by the standards of Deuteronomy's law of the king: "And he shall not multiply wives for
himself, lest his heart turn away; nor shall he greatly multiply for himself silver
and gold" (17:17).[26] Thus the negative side of the picture begins in the middle
of v. 18, with the amassing of gold and silver.

By appealing to the law of the king, Ben Sira suggests that Solomon's betrayal
of his wisdom was no accident. The stipulations of the law of the king reflect
an understanding of kingship as corrupting even as they attempt to check the
potential for corruption. Ben Sira exploits this understanding: if even the wisest
king in Israel's past fell victim to the temptations of his office, what hope was
there for the institution? Further, the invocation of the law of the king suggests
that Ben Sira did not understand his rejection of kingship as a radical break with
the traditions of Israel's past, but rather as a working out of the implications of
the Deuteronomic constitution and of the centrality of wisdom for the life of the
Jewish people. Thus Solomon is the crucial figure for Ben Sira's argument.

At the conclusion of the passage about Solomon, Ben Sira proclaims the con-
tinuation of David's line (47:22),[27] but the promise of a root of David's stock is
apparently seen as fulfilled in the past, for Ben Sira notes the continued existence

---

24. P. C. Beentjes, "'The Countries Marvelled at You': King Solomon in Ben Sira 47:12–22,"
Bijdragen: Tijdschrift voor filosofie en theologie 45 (1984): 9–11.

25. The Greek of v. 19 does not contain anything that could be construed as "but." The Hebrew
offers the connective *w*, which could mean "but" in the proper context, but can also mean "and."

26. Beentjes, "'The Countries,'" 9–11. I cannot agree with Beentjes's view that Ben Sira's under-
standing of Solomon's wrongdoing differs from that of the Deuteronomic History, which reports that
Solomon's foreign wives led him into idolatry in his old age (1 Kings 11:1–13). Beentjes notes the
absence in Ben Sira's account of reference to idolatry or to the foreignness of Solomon's wives ("'The
Countries,'" 8–9). But the law of the king itself associates the multiplication of wives with idolatry:
"And he shall not multiply wives for himself lest his heart turn away (*wl' yswr lbbw*)." Surely this
suggests that the wives are foreign, a likely circumstance for a king, since there is no reason why the
multiplication of Israelite wives would lead to idolatry. Compare 1 Kings 11:3, "And his wives turned
his heart away (*wytw nšyw 't-lbw*)."

27. "...He will never blot out the posterity of him who loved him; / so he gave a remnant to
Jacob, / and to David a root of his stock." The Hebrew of the verse is incomplete, and the last two
cola especially are severely damaged. They read, "...he gave to [ ], and to [ ]," but do not preserve
any traces of the name "David." Thus it is possible that the Hebrew concluded somewhat differently
from the Greek, although it should be noted that in this verse the extant Hebrew is quite close to
the Greek.

of Judah under a Davidic king after the fall of the northern kingdom (48:16).[28] Ben Sira even manages to play down the royal status of the two pious kings who follow David, Hezekiah and Josiah. The career of Hezekiah is intertwined with and largely subordinated to that of the prophet Isaiah, who gets credit for the failure of the Assyrian siege: "...They called upon the Lord who is merciful,...and the Holy One...delivered them by the hand of Isaiah" (48:17–25; quotation, v. 20). Josiah is praised highly, if briefly, for leading the people to repentance, but it is striking that some of the language of praise recalls the cult: "The memory of Josiah is like a blending of incense / prepared by the art of the perfumer..." (49:1). The use of cultic language for Josiah is the mirror image of the praise of Aaron and Simon in royal language.

Yet even a reader persuaded by Ben Sira's presentation might be forgiven for worrying that there were some ways in which things could be better: the high priest, after all, must report to a foreign ruler. The Greek version of the conclusion of the praise of the fathers hints at this, when after its description of Simon, it prays: "May he entrust to us his mercy! / And let him deliver us in our days" (50:24). The Hebrew, which was quoted above, makes no mention at all of deliverance, thus avoiding any dissonant note in its retelling of Israel's history. Outside the praise of the fathers, Ben Sira calls explicitly and in detail for the punishment of the nations (36:1–17), but the authenticity of this passage has been questioned.[29] Still, whether he committed his doubts to writing or not, Ben Sira could hardly have been untroubled by the condition of foreign rule in his own time.

It is different for the circumstance of rule by high priest, however. Here, it seems to me, Ben Sira is quite convinced, contrary to the dominant biblical view, that Israel has no need of a king. He has persuasively retold Israel's history so that there is no reason for nostalgia for kingship, and he has shown wisdom embodied not in the king, whose power corrupts, but in the person of the high priest, heir to the eternal covenants of Aaron and Phinehas.

---

28. Stadelmann, *Ben Sira*, 161–63.

29. T. Middendorp, *Die Stellung Jesu ben Siras zwischen Judentum und Hellenismus* (Leiden: Brill, 1973), 113, 125.

10

Social Relations and Social Conflict in the *Epistle of Enoch*

———— ◆ ————

Richard A. Horsley
University of Massachusetts Boston

George Nickelsburg was one of the first to focus on "social aspects" of Palestinian Jewish apocalyptic literature.[1] Now, roughly twenty years after he conducted a critical review of the discussion, one way to honor his important contribution to our understanding of such literature would be to continue the discussion of its social context and social location which he pioneered.

Nickelsburg's concise and critical survey enabled us to appreciate the inadequacies of previous constructions of the social context of apocalyptic literature and established some important procedural principles. For example, Plöger's theory that the Hasidim, already a "hard-and-fast group" prior to the Maccabean revolt, were not only the authors of Daniel but the ancestors of the Pharisees was simply far too simple an explanation for the complicated details of so much Second Temple history, particularly considering the serious lack of solid historical evidence.[2] Similarly, Hengel's extension of Plöger's thesis to explain the origins of the Essenes, who supposedly produced the Dead Sea Scrolls, resulted in a hypothesis too grand to be convincing about any particular document or community. While taking social factors into account, moreover, Hengel offered a mainly cultural explanation: the apocalyptic worldview was basically a negative response to Hellenistic forms of thinking that were perceived as a threat to the existence of

---

1. George W. E. Nickelsburg, "Social Aspects of Palestinian Jewish Apocalypticism," in *Apocalypticism in the Mediterranean World and the Near East: Proceedings of the International Colloquium on Apocalypticism, Uppsala, August 12–17, 1979* (ed. David Hellholm; Tübingen: Mohr [Siebeck], 1983), 641–54. Cf. subsequent critical surveys by Philip Davies, "The Social World of Apocalyptic Writings," in *The World of Ancient Israel: Social, Anthropological, and Political Perspectives* (ed. R. E. Clements; Cambridge: Cambridge University Press, 1989), 251–71; and Lester L. Grabbe, "The Social Setting of Early Jewish Apocalypticism," *JSP* 4 (1989): 27–47.

2. See Nickelsburg's ("Social Aspects," 641–43) evaluation of O. Plöger's *Theocracy and Eschatology* (translated from second German edition of 1962; Richmond: John Knox, 1968). Davies ("Social World," 256–57) offers a similar critique.

Judaism.[3] Nickelsburg rather pressed the case for addressing more genuinely sociological questions to the documents and stressed the importance of interrelating
a range of social factors. Most important perhaps, given the now-passing intellectual fad of constructing social-scientific "models," which tend to obscure rather
than illuminate particular social relations and dynamics, Nickelsburg insisted that
inquiry not only begin with but proceed by focusing on particular Jewish apocalyptic writings.[4] In pursuing the kind of agenda Nickelsburg outlined, this brief
study will focus on the same text he used as a "case study," the *Epistle of Enoch*
(*1 Enoch* 92–105).[5]

In the "Epistle of Enoch" appears "a bitter conflict between two groups generally called 'the righteous' and 'the sinners.'" Despite other vague designations
(*eusebeis* vs. *adikoi*), Nickelsburg finds evildoing of two kinds in the descriptions
of the sinners' behavior.

> First, the sinners are the rich and powerful, who persecute and oppress the
> righteous and lowly. They hoard wealth which they have obtained unrigh-
> teously, they banquet sumptuously... (96:5–6; 97:8–98:2). They impress
> others into their service to construct their lavish houses (99:13; cf. 94:6–
> 7). They are accused of robbing, torturing, and "devouring" the righteous, or
> treating them like beasts of burden, and of murdering them. They connive
> with the rulers, who support their oppressive deeds (103:9–15).[6]

Second, in a set of "*religious* charges" the sinners are described "as pagans or
apostates [who] practice idolatry (99:7), consume blood (98:11), and blaspheme
(94:9; 96:7)." Other sinners are blamed for disregarding and perverting Torah
(99:2, 14). They do not listen to the wise (98:9); they write lying and deceitful
words (98:15).

> Built into these latter passages is a sharp dichotomy between the members
> of the author's group, who are the protagonists of wisdom, and their op-
> ponents, who are false teachers and who can violate Torah while claiming
> that they are innocent. Although the Epistle discloses nothing about the
> structure or organization of the author's group or community, evidence in

3. See Nickelsburg's ("Social Aspects," 642–43) evaluation of Martin Hengel, *Judaism and Hellenism* (Philadelphia: Fortress, 1974), 174–247, 250–54. Cf. Davies, "Social World," 258–60.

4. Nickelsburg, "Social Aspects," 643–45; similarly, Davies, "Social World," 264. Grabbe ("Social Setting of Jewish Apocalypticism") reverts to the wide-ranging discussions of the 1960s and 1970s, borrowing from earlier social science and discussing a wide variety of materials from medieval Europe to modern California under the extremely broad and vague concepts of "apocalypticism" and "millennialism."

5. In addition to his "Social Aspects," Nickelsburg provides close analysis of the *Epistle of Enoch* in "The *Epistle of Enoch* and the Qumran Literature," *JJS* 33 (1982): 333–48; and in "Riches, The Rich, and God's Judgment in *1 Enoch* 92–105 and the Gospel according to Luke," *NTS* 25 (1979): 324–44.

6. Nickelsburg, "Social Aspects," 651.

the Apocalypse of Weeks (93:9–10 + 91:11–13) indicates that they understand themselves as the recipient of the revealed, eschatological gift of full
wisdom and knowledge . . . who will function as God's agents in the coming
judgment.[7]

It remained unclear twenty years ago just how to understand the *Epistle*'s kind
of rhetoric, such "loaded legal categories as 'robbery, injustice, and murder.' "[8]
Hesitating to press for further precision in their analysis of the historical situation
underlying such rhetoric, biblical scholars found some satisfaction in categories
borrowed from social science of the 1950s (which they had discovered in the
1970s). In language scarcely less vague than "the sinners" or "the righteous,"
those involved in ancient Palestinian Jewish apocalypticism, like those caught
up in millenarianism, were seen to have acquired a "sense of alienation" during
"times of social upheaval and turmoil." What mattered was their own sense of
relative deprivation.[9] This social-psychological explanation was sufficiently satisfying to interpreters that it seemed unimportant to determine more precisely the
social location of apocalyptic literature such as the *Epistle of Enoch* in historical political-economic structures and power relations. Cross-cultural studies of
"millenarianism," however, are so broadly conceived and couched in such vague
terms that they may obscure rather than illuminate the historical, political, economic, and religious dynamics from which Judean apocalyptic literature emerged.
Indeed, insofar as much of the cross-cultural material comes from societies without sharp class divisions and that are just now undergoing the impact of Western
colonization, studies of millenarianism may be misleading with regard to ancient
Judean society, which was sharply divided between rulers and ruled and had for
centuries been subject to imperial domination.

What study of ancient Judean apocalypses has not yet done, therefore, is
to consider more precisely the social location of such literature in the broader
political-economic-religious structure of Judea in the context of the Ptolemaic
and Seleucid (and later, the Roman) Empires.[10] The dominant conceptual appa-

---

7. Ibid., 652.

8. Ibid., 651.

9. Sheldon R. Isenberg, "Millenarianism in Greco-Roman Palestine," *Religion* 4 (1974): 35; Grabbe
("Social Setting," 30–31) is still convinced, despite the broad generalizations involved, that "millenarianism" provides an "important resource for building models to help with the social setting of Jewish
apocalypticism."

10. Davies ("Social World," 269) makes some suggestive passing observations that move in the
direction of the needed social-structural analysis but prescinds from pursuing it, apparently out of
his concern to "rescue" the term "apocalyptic" from "amateur sociology" as well as from theological
dogmatics. M. E. Stone, "Ideal Figures and Social Context: Priest and Sage in the Early Second
Temple Age," in *Ancient Israelite Religion: Essays in Honor of Frank Moore Cross* [ed. P. D. Miller,
P. D. Hanson, and S. D. McBride; Philadelphia: Fortress, 1987], 575–86) mentions the concept of
"social role," but offers no more precise delineation of the "particular context" of Ben Sira or of the
"group or tendency within Judaism" from which *Aramaic Levi* stems. John J. Collins ("Genre, Ideology,
and Social Movements in Jewish Apocalypticism," in *Mysteries and Revelations* [ed. J. J. Collins and

ratus of biblical studies has tended to block such questions. Insofar as we think of such literature as expressions of "Judaism" then the context is conceived of as an undifferentiated "-ism" without social structure and social dynamics. Strictly speaking, however, what scholars think of as "Judaism" did not yet exist in the Second Temple period. Rather, under the sponsorship of the Persian and then the Ptolemaic and Seleucid imperial regimes, the temple-state in Jerusalem dominated a number of village communities in a somewhat limited surrounding area. As historians, we are dealing not with a religion separable from other dimensions of life, but with a society in which the religious dimension was inseparable from political-economic relations. The temple stood at the center of a temple-state and its political economy, in which tithes and offerings were religiously motivated and legitimated taxes that supported the governing temple apparatus as well as the priesthood. Under the influence of European Protestant scholarship based in modern European religious and political history, biblical scholars and Jewish historians have projected the concept of "sect" onto vaguely defined movements or groups, such as the "Pharisees" and "Essenes." It is often assumed that some "group" or "community" constituted the source and/or addressees of each extant piece of literature, an assumption reinforced by the linking of the Dead Sea Scrolls with the "community" at Qumran.[11] Such an assumption is utterly unwarranted, however, as a consideration of the extremely low rate of literacy in ancient society should indicate. Virtually the only people who could read and write — and therefore produce and leave texts — were the scribes, who were usually dependent economically on the rulers (whether directly or indirectly). Thus very few movements among the ordinary people would have left literary remains (the movements focused on Jesus of Nazareth were significant exceptions!). And scribes who produced literary remains would not necessarily have been participants in some identifiable community or socially defined group. We should proceed rather in terms of the concrete historical political-economic-religious structures and dynamics identifiable in our sources.

Once we recognize that the rate of literacy was extremely limited, then it is possible to recognize also that, by definition, literature such as the *Epistle of Enoch* was produced by someone or some circle (as opposed to an identifiable "community" or "sect" on the model of Qumran) among the tiny educated elite that were literate. Indeed, evidence internal to the literature now combined into the collection called *1 Enoch* confirms that it was produced by "scribes" (*1 Enoch*

James H. Charlesworth; JSPSup 9; Sheffield: Sheffield Academic Press, 1991], 11–32) discusses mainly ideology and genre.

11. While objecting to the scholarly habit of assigning apocalypses and apocalypticism to "conventicles" or "small groups," Davies ("Social World," 257, 262, 267) still speaks in terms of undefined "social groups" and "sectarianism." Nickelsburg ("*Epistle of Enoch* and the Qumran Literature," 346) finds that there is little basis in the "Epistle" itself for concluding that the author represents a specific group or community or conventicle.

12:3–4; 15:1; 92:1) — to which Daniel the sage is compatible given his education in letters and his writing and reading activity (Dan. 1:3–7). Thus, whatever differences they may display, both "apocalyptic" literature such as that collected in *1 Enoch* and "wisdom" literature such as the Book of Sirach were produced by scribes or scribal circles. The first step toward defining more precisely where such literatures and their concerns fit in the wider society would appear to be to probe more carefully for information precisely in such literatures. The written sources are few. And in the case of apocalyptic literature, it has been difficult to identify clear indicators of the authors' social location and particularly the power relations in which they were involved, including social conflicts. In the case of wisdom literature, however, the indications are abundant indeed if we have eyes to see and ears to hear.[12]

Because they usually read Sirach without a sense of the particular social structure it presupposes, scholars have a rather vague impression of Ben Sira's audience, usually as "the broad sections of the population, sometimes... the wealthy."[13] The book contains so many comments critical of the wealthy and powerful that they or their children were almost certainly not the intended audience. Its focused reflection on the functions of the sage/scribe in relation to those in other positions in the social structure, particularly the long section in Sir. 38:24–39:11, indicates that the speaker's position is somewhere above the plowmen and artisans on whose labor a city depends but below and in service to those who rule. Ben Sira gives other indications that the addressees, like himself, stand beneath and somewhat vulnerable to the wealthy and powerful (8:1–2) and are learning "to serve princes" ("to stand in the presence of chiefs": 8:8).

Ben Sira refers to the rulers of the Jerusalem temple-state in what appear to be two (juxtaposed) sets of terms. He apparently uses several traditional Hebrew terms — especially *sr, mwsl,* and *swpt* — for rulers or officers of state almost interchangeably and synonymously. Of these only the last is translated consistently in the Greek as *kritēs.* Other positions are rendered with a variety of overlapping Greek terms, *sr* with *megistan, dynastēs,* and *hēgoumenos;* and *mwsl* with *hēgoumenos, dynastēs, kritēs,* and *kyrios.* In the following discussion, I will attempt to use the terms "chief," "ruler," and "judge," respectively, for *sr, mwsl,* and *swpt.* Most of these terms are used in construct (or other indications of relationship) with words such as "city," "people," and "assembly." In both Sir. 30:27 (33:19) and 39:4, "chiefs of the people" is paralleled by "rulers of the assembly." One also has the sense that there is some overlap or relationship between the "chiefs" and "rulers" among whom the scribes/sages serve in 39:4 and the *plethos presbuteron*

---

12. The following sketch of social relations in Judea evident in Sirach draws on a much longer study, Richard Horsley and Patrick Tiller, "Ben Sira and the Sociology of the Second Temple," in *Second Temple Studies* (Sheffield: Sheffield Academic Press, forthcoming).

13. Victor Tcherikover, *Hellenistic Civilization and the Jews* (trans. S. Applebaum; New York: Atheneum, 1959), 149.

among whom the sages stand and speak in 6:34 and 7:14. In 10:1–2 the "judge" of a people or city is parallel to the sagacious one who possesses "authority" and to "he who rules a city," and in 10:3 "king" is parallel to "chiefs." These interchangeable words thus appear not to be technical terms for specific offices of state. They are rather parallel, overlapping, almost synonymous terms for the ruling aristocracy, some but not all of whom may have had particular responsibilities and many of whom probably had similar or overlapping functions. Since Judean society was apparently headed by a temple-state, these terms all seem to have referred to members of the priestly aristocracy, as confirmed by Ben Sira's second set of terms.

Ben Sira's references to the high priest and his "brothers" indicate clearly that they were the rulers of the temple-state based in Jerusalem. Just as the high priest at the temple altar had "a garland of brothers around him ... the sons of Aaron in their splendor holding out the Lord's offerings" (50:5–13), so the high priest as head of state stood in the midst of a priestly aristocracy both in governing the people and in receiving their economic support. The Judean people are to serve "the Most High," who is understood as "the king of all." Since the (high) priests are the people's representatives to God, the latter bring their offerings to the priests. Since the (high) priests are God's representative to the people, established by everlasting covenant and given "authority and statutes and judgments" over the people, the people are to "honor the priest" with their tithes and offerings as the way of "fearing the Lord" (see esp. Sir. 7:29–31; 35:1–12; 45:20–22; and chap. 50). In this second set of terms referring to the rulers of the temple-state, it is clear that economics as well as politics is inseparable from and closely articulated with religion. The first fruits, guilt offerings, choice shoulder cuts from animal sacrifices, and so on were also tax revenues to "honor the priest," because in the eternal covenant bestowed on Aaron, these had been allotted to Aaron and his descendants as their "heritage" (see esp. 7:29–31; 45:20–21).

What then is the relationship between the people referred to by these two sets of terms? The "chiefs" and "rulers" and "judges" were apparently the ruling aristocracy among "the sons of Aaron." Not all priests, not even all of the Aaronides, would have belonged to the ruling aristocracy. Some individual high priests may have held a particular office (similar, e.g., to the "temple captain" in the first century C.E.). But we should not presume that all members of the dominant aristocracy held a particular "minister's portfolio," as in the cabinets of modern parliamentary governments. Although Ben Sira never explicitly mentions a *gerousia*, often presumed to have been the governing aristocracy in the temple-state, his "chiefs," "rulers," and "judges," would appear to match the *gerousia* mentioned in both Antiochus III's proclamation of restoration of the temple government in Jerusalem (Josephus, *Ant.* 142) and in the letter of the Hasmonean high priest Jonathan to Sparta a half-century later (1 Macc. 12:6).

A (the?) principal role of the scribes and sages such as himself, according to

Ben Sira, was to serve the "chiefs" (8:8). In the sustained discussion of the scribes' position and activities in 38:24–39:11, he portrays the scribes as advisers of the ruling councils, as members or advisers of courts who understood decisions and could expound judgments, and as members of embassies to foreign lands (cf. 4:9; 6:34; 7:14; 11:7–9; 15:5; 21:17; 34:12; 42:2). Their devotion to the study of the law and to the wisdom of the ancients was precisely for the purpose of their service to the ruling aristocracy. The teaching of the law, which had originated with Moses and been vested in the Aaronide priesthood (45:5, 17), had been delegated (perhaps gradually, over a period of generations) to the sages, both with regard to the people (37:23) and with regard to the aristocracy's exercise of its own governing authority (8:8; 9:17–10:5; 38:32–33; 38:34–39:4). The scribe stands behind "the wise judge" and "the government of the intelligent one" (9:17–10:5).

Insofar as they served the ruling aristocracy, scribes/sages must have been economically as well as politically dependent on patrons among the ruling families. Not surprisingly, Ben Sira advises aspiring sages to defer and to bow low to the ruler (4:7). He also offers extensive advice on the proper deferential behavior for the scribes when invited to dine with their patrons (13:9–11; 31:12–24). He also warns about the potential dangers involved in dealing with the powerful (13:9). Particularly dangerous, of course, would be "contending with the powerful" or "quarreling with the rich," lest the scribe "fall into their hands" (8:1–2, 14).

Yet the scribes/sages have a clear sense of their own authority independent of their dependence on the aristocracy. Their authority, at least in their own mind, came from their knowledge of wisdom and their faithful adherence to and teaching of the law of the Most High (which are the same thing for Ben Sira). Ben Sira refers repeatedly to the scribes' dedication to the covenantal laws and to divinely bestowed wisdom, from which they claim their own authority directly from God, independent of the high priesthood. Moreover, they also understood themselves as the successors of the prophets as well as their interpreters, speaking by divine inspiration (39:1–3, 6). They had their own sense of how the temple-state should operate — according to the law, the sacred traditions of the people, of which they themselves were the proper interpreters.

Thus, despite their dependence on and vulnerability to their patrons among the aristocracy, scribes such as Ben Sira speak both of criticizing the aristocracy and of attempting to mitigate oppression of the poor by the powerful. This is worth exploring in itself, but also because it may shed some light on woes against the rich sinners in the *Epistle of Enoch.*

The scribes/sages understood themselves as a cut above the peasant farmers and urban artisans politically and culturally. Such ordinary folk did not enjoy the leisure necessary to acquire and practice wisdom (38:24–34). Yet Ben Sira articulates an unmistakable sympathy and concern for the plight of the poor and urges his scribal protégés to assume responsibility to mitigate their exploitation by the wealthy and powerful. He explicitly mentions the "plowman" or other synonyms for the peasantry, which formed the economic base of any traditional agrarian society such as the ancient Judean temple community, more than he does artisans or household slaves. A survey of Ben Sira's use of terms often translated with "poor," however, suggests that they usually refer to a wide range of people. "Poor," "hungry," "needy," "desperate," and other synonymous terms refer apparently to a large proportion of the peasant producers. Like peasants in most agrarian societies, the Judean producers would have been economically marginal. They would therefore have been chronically in need of loans and even alms. They were thus vulnerable to the predatory practices of the wealthy and powerful.

Ben Sira articulates his concern for the poor in three ways. First, he urges his scribal protégés, in their own personal ethical behavior, to respond mercifully: "Stretch out your hand to the poor" with almsgiving, and do not "cheat the poor" or "reject the suppliant" (29:1–20, esp. 29:1–2, 8–12, 14–15). Second, Ben Sira offers some strikingly sharp criticism of those who take advantage of the desperate situation of the poor to enhance their own wealth.

> A rich person does wrong, and even adds insults;
> a poor person suffers wrong, and must add apologies.
> A rich person will exploit you if you can be of use to him,
> but if you are in need he will abandon you. . . .
> What peace is there between a hyena and a dog?
> And what peace between the rich and the poor?
> Wild asses in the wilderness are the prey of lions;
> likewise the poor are feeding grounds for the rich.
>
> (13:3–4, 18–19)

Such sayings may sound like matter-of-fact observations about the "natural" state of affairs, what life is like. Yet if heard from Ben Sira's own viewpoint, rooted in Mosaic covenantal concern for the Israelite people's continuing economic viability, such sayings have an edge. Although couched in traditional form and style of sapiential observations about life, they are in effect an indictment of the perpetual economic exploitation inherent in a political-economic-religious system in which the peasants are vulnerable to the power holders.

It goes almost without saying that the wealthy and powerful criticized in these passages were members of the priestly aristocracy. As in other pre-industrial agrarian societies, the productive forces in Second Temple Judea would not have been sufficiently developed to support a lay as well as a priestly aristocracy. The rise of the Tobiads to prominence in Jerusalem was based on their own economic base across the Jordan and on their maneuvering for position in the imperial mechanism of tribute collection from Palestine. To the extent that they exploited their wealth for further economic advantage within the Judean temple community, they may well have contributed to the crisis that emerged in the first quarter of the second century. Over against Tcherikover's and Hengel's earlier influential projections of Hellenistic Judea suddenly abuzz with commercial activity, it is simply not true that "Ben Sira frequently mentions merchants ... and that these passages reflect ... the money economy, the opportunity to invest one's means in profitable enterprises, and lively commercial traffic...."[14] Ben Sira mentions traders only at three points (26:29–27:2; 37:11; 42:5), where he articulates the negative view of merchants typical of traditional agrarian aristocratic societies. Otherwise Tcherikover and Hengel are projecting nascent capitalist mercantile relations onto Ben Sira's references to the acquisition/stockpiling/possession of "goods" (*chrēmeta*), wealth, and "gold" and to the use of other people's goods (Hengel focuses on 11:10–19; 13:24–25; 21:8; and 31:3–8). One of those passages ("Whoever builds his house with other people's goods ...," 21:8), in fact, indicates precisely the way that the wealthy and/or powerful exploited the poor in an agrarian society: by taking as tribute/tax/tithes what the peasant considered wrongfully taken or by charging interest on loans (which was prohibited in Israelite covenantal law; e.g., Exod. 22:25).

Ben Sira even gives some indications that it was the priestly aristocracy that was exploiting the peasants, even though he does not explicitly identify the high priests, the wealthy, and the chiefs, rulers, and judges, as mentioned above. In an unusually sustained section for Ben Sira (35:1–26), his discussion of sacrifices and offerings suddenly turns instead to a sustained declaration that the Most High will heed the supplication and appeal of the oppressed and do justice for the righteous, "breaking the scepters of the unrighteous." We notice also that several couplets at the opening of the passage relativize temple offerings by declaring that commandment-keeping and almsgiving are their equivalent. It seems that Ben Sira almost overshadows his exhortation to make sacrifices and offerings in the temple with an ominous warning to the "rulers" about exploiting the poor and humble. A shorter section (34:21–27) seems to be directed pointedly at the ruling priesthood.

> If one sacrifices ill-gotten goods, the offering is blemished....
> Like one who kills a son before his father's eyes
>   is the person who offers a sacrifice from the property of the poor....
> To take away a neighbor's living is to commit murder;
>   to deprive an employee of wages is to shed blood.

These are serious charges. The imagery used in this blunt warning is reminiscent of prophetic indictments in Amos. This passage approaches the severity of Amos 4:4–5 and 5:21–24, where God rejects sacrifices outright as sin, demanding justice instead. Even more important, this passage is reminiscent of Amos 2:6–8 in its suggestion that the wealthy and powerful, as creditors, were taking advan-

---

14. Ibid.

tage of the peasants who had fallen heavily into debt and were "foreclosing" on their goods.

Even more striking than Ben Sira's criticism of the wealthy and powerful priestly aristocracy, however, because of the potential "conflict of interest" involved, are some of Ben Sira's other exhortations to his scribal protégés/listeners. He urges them not simply to give alms and otherwise to attend to the needs of the poor themselves (4:1–4; cf. 29:8–9), but even to "rescue" the oppressed from the oppressor, and not to hesitate in giving a "verdict," presumably in their professional (or official) capacities (4:9). That would likely have entailed some form of opposition to the behavior of the ruling families on whom they themselves were politically and economically dependent. Yet he insists that his scribal listeners not "show partiality to a ruler" (4:17). Indeed, they should not aspire to a high office such as that of judge, or they would "be unable to root out injustice" and would be in situations where they would "be partial to the powerful, and so mar [their] integrity" (7:4–7).

What Ben Sira and his scribal colleagues were apparently facing was a recurrent problem in the history of Israel and Judah, as in other agrarian societies in which a small coterie of rulers held political or political-religious power over the peasant producers. They would have known such famous conflicts as Jeremiah's indictment of King Jehoiakim for rebuilding his royal palace with forced labor at a time of acute crisis for Judah (Jer. 22:13–19). Closer in time and in pattern to the exploitation Ben Sira complains about was the crisis Nehemiah had dealt with, when the rulers of the temple-state had taken advantage of the desperate economic plight of the Judean peasants in the mid–fourth century to get them into debt and to seize their lands:

> Now there was a great outcry of the people and of their wives against their Judean kin.... "We are having to pledge our fields, our vineyards, and our houses in order to get grain during the famine.... We are having to borrow money on our fields and vineyards to pay the king's tax. [They] are forcing our sons and daughters to be slaves, and some of our daughters have been ravished; we are powerless and our fields and vineyards now belong to others." (Neh. 5:1–5)

The ensuing account of Nehemiah's response also indicates precisely how the wealthy and powerful ruling aristocracy of the temple-state had been manipulating the desperate peasantry to aggrandize their own hold over the peasants' land and labor.

> I brought charges against the nobles and the officials; I said to them, "You are all taking interest from your own people.... Let us stop this taking of interest. Restore to them, this very day, their fields, their vineyards, their

olive orchards, and their houses, and the interest on money, grain, wine, and oil that you have been exacting from them." (Neh. 5:7–11)

This illustration from the mission of Nehemiah, the Persian governor for Judea, about how the ruling elite of the temple-state exploited their subjects, moreover, points to a determining aspect of the political-economic-religious structure of Second Temple Judea that is often ignored in treatments of Judean apocalyptic and wisdom literature. Contrary to the appearance from Ben Sira's ideology of Aaronide/Oniad rule grounded in the glorious Israelite tradition of officeholders, from Moses to Simon (chaps. 44–50), the Judean temple-state was not autonomous, not sovereign over its own affairs. From the outset the temple-state had been the creature of empire. Just prior to the time of Ben Sira, the high priestly regime in Jerusalem was dependent on its approval by the Ptolemies, and after about 200 B.C.E. was subject to the Seleucids.

This potentially determinative subjection of the temple-state to and dependence on imperial rule set up two interrelated structural conflicts that had a profound effect on events in Second Temple Judean history. First, it set up almost certain situations of conflict between the rulers of the temple-state and their scribal clients. The Judean priestly rulers depended on their imperial sponsors and were vulnerable to whatever influence and pressures they might receive in that connection. The scribes/sages such as Ben Sira, however, who functioned as the guardians and interpreters of sacred Israelite traditions, including Mosaic covenant principles, believed that the temple-state as well as Judean society should operate according to these sacred traditions. As can be seen in his paean of praise that climaxes in the exordium to the high priest Simon, Ben Sira had constructed a grand ideology of high priestly rule out of Israelite tradition.

Second, subjection of the temple-state set up potential conflict between rival cliques within the ruling aristocracy. Already under the Davidic monarchy, different factions within the royal family and their protégés competed for power. It is evident from the Books of Ezra and Nehemiah and other sources that priestly and other factions had been competing in early Second Temple times. The struggle between the Ptolemies and Seleucids for control of Palestine set up a situation in which rival factions in Jerusalem would make alliances with the opposing imperial regimes. The rise of the Tobiad family across the Jordan River, its intermarriage with the high priestly family, and its intrigue with the Ptolemaic regime further complicated the struggle for power in Jerusalem. Insofar as scribes and sages had no independent economic base, they would have associated with one of the rival factions among the ruling aristocracy. And insofar as scribes had varying ideas about policy and practice in the temple-state, they formed rival scribal circles, and their pursuit of their own political-religious agenda further complicated the struggle among rival factions among the aristocracy. Thus, although the structure of the temple-state under imperial rule was fairly simple, once the imperial situation and the cultural factor of the scribal commitment to indigenous Judean tradition are taken into account, this set up potential conflict between scribes and rulers, between rival ruling factions, and even between rival groups of scribes.

Read in this context, deduced largely from the near-contemporary Wisdom of Jesus ben Sira, the intense sets of woes pronounced against the rich sinners in the *Epistle of Enoch* appear to emerge from just such a conflict, between the rulers in Jerusalem and the scribal circle that produced the Enoch literature. Judging from other sections of the composite Book of 1 *Enoch*, the scribal circle from which the texts emerged viewed the Second Temple generally as illegitimate. In the "Animal Apocalypse," the rebuilt "tower" (temple) has polluted bread on its table and the shepherds (rulers) of the sheep are blind (1 *Enoch* 89:72–80). In the "Apocalypse of Weeks," a "perverse generation" whose deeds are all "perverse" arises in the seventh week (1 *Enoch* 93:9).

The simple fact that the *Epistle of Enoch* is literature means that it was produced by scribes. Despite the lack of obvious indications in the text, the author(s) left a few tracks here and there by which we can identify both author and addressees as scribes/sages. In a description of judgment, the Most High is expected to "set a guard of holy angels over all the righteous and holy" so that "the pious will sleep a sweet sleep" (100:5). "The wise among men" who "will see the truth" in the next verse appear to be more precisely the wise among the righteous and holy and pious. That is, the latter are a larger group among whom "the wise" have special knowledge and a special role. What Nickelsburg's text labels as "An Oath to the Wise" (98:1–3) appears to be an aside addressed directly to "the wise," who receive special knowledge. Further, the rich sinners are addressed as "fools" precisely because they "do not listen to the wise," that is, their scribal/sapiential opponents (98:9), whereas "all who listen to the words of the wise" are blessed (99:10). Apparently, the wise enjoyed the special role within the larger circles of the righteous. The *Epistle of Enoch* thus appears to be a scribe/sage addressing a circle of other scribes/sages, pronouncing woes of destruction in the divine judgment against the "rich/sinners" for oppressing the righteous/pious, who will be vindicated and rewarded in the divine judgment.

When we then examine the pronounced woes and blessings for a more precise determination of the relationship between the sinners and righteous, between the rich and those they oppress, there is no separation between what modern Westerners distinguish as "religious" and "political-economic" matters. As suggested by the above analysis of social relations and roles in Ben Sira's speeches, in an ancient society such as Judea, the wealthy were those who held political or political-religious power. The rulers used their positions to increase their wealth and thus to consolidate their power further. This is precisely what is found in the woes of the *Epistle of Enoch*. It is the "mighty" or powerful who gain great riches and an easy and luxurious lifestyle by their oppression and destruction of the righteous (96:8; 97:2). The political-economic-religious structure is similar to that evident in Amos 6:4–6, whose mockery of the idle rich "drinking wine from the krater/bowl" may be alluded to in 1 *Enoch* 96:5–6. That is, those who are indulging themselves in a luxurious lifestyle at the expense of the poor are the ruling families in Zion and Samaria (Amos 6:1).

In what ways have they oppressed the lowly righteous? Many of the indictments of the rich sinners are allusive and still vague. The hypothetical lament of the lowly over what has been done to them in 103:9–15, however, contains clearer indications of the oppressive relationship into which they were maneuvered.

> In the days of our tribulation, we toiled laboriously;
> We toiled and labored and were not masters of our labor;
> > we became the food of the sinners.
> And the lawless weighed down their yoke upon us;
> > our enemies were our masters,
> and they goaded and penned us in,
> > and to our enemies we bowed our necks,
> > and they had no mercy on us. (103:9, 11–12)

Following the pattern of how the future reward for the righteous matches their suffering in the present, they are reassured that they will receive much good "in the place of [their] labors" (103:3). Closely related is the assertion that "it was not ordained [for man] to be a slave [or] for a woman to be a handmaid" (98:4). These passages suggest clearly that, against the norms of the society (the Mosaic law), the righteous had been subjected to some equivalent of forced labor, perhaps debt-slavery or other labor for the wealthy, who had gained the power to determine how their labor would be deployed. In this connection, the repeated charge that the wealthy sinners "build their houses with sin" and "build their houses not with their own labors, [but] make the whole house of the stones and bricks of sin" (94:6–7; 99:13) suddenly makes sense. The wealthy rulers were unlikely to have manipulated the scribes into the physical labor of building; but they could easily have deployed those who came under their power in the building of their own houses. That this was contrary to traditional norms and expectations can be discerned by analogy to Jeremiah's objections to the way Jehoiakim rebuilt his palace with forced labor (and the objections by the Israelites to Solomon's forced labor to build the original temple [1 Kings 12]).

If the command that the powerful wealthy had over the labor of the lowly was rooted in the peasants' indebtedness or even debt-slavery, as in the crisis recounted by Nehemiah (Neh. 5:1–12), then some other accusations against the sinners also make sense. The rich sinners rejoice over the troubles of the righteous (98:13). They "lie awake to devise evil" (100:8). An indictment of the powerful wealthy of his time by the prophet Micah(2:1–2) may provide the key to these charges.

Woe to those who devise wickedness and evil deeds upon their beds!
When the morning dawns they perform it, because it is in their power.
They covet fields, and seize them; houses, and take them away;
they oppress the householder and house, people and their inheritance.

Peasants, who are always marginal economically — partly because of dues to the rulers in the form of taxes, tithes, and tribute — come easily into desperate circumstances, needing to borrow to feed their families (as in Neh. 5:1–5). The rulers and their officers, who have access to stores of staple goods such as grain and oil, are only too ready to makes loans — at high rates of interest. These rates were 25 percent and 100 percent on grain and oil, respectively, in the parable of Jesus (Luke 16:1–9), which matches figures from other traditional agrarian societies. Such exorbitant interest was contrary to the Mosaic covenantal tradition (Exod. 22:25; Lev. 25:36–38), but it was standard practice (again as in the account in Neh. 5:1–12). Rulers could thus take advantage of "the troubles of the righteous" by maneuvering them into indebtedness, and then by "foreclosing" on their ancestral inheritance, that is, their fields and houses, or by forcing family members into debt-slavery, or by forcing whole families effectively into the position of sharecroppers on their own land. Perhaps the "lying awake to devise evil" was a standing image, rooted in prophetic tradition since Micah, for the way the powerful and wealthy would scheme against vulnerable peasant families, in violation of the covenantal principle against "coveting the neighbor's house." When the powerful took action, they then also violated the covenantal principle against "stealing," as in the charge against them that by maneuvering peasants into debt they "plunder and sin and steal and get wealth" (102:9).

Another apparently typical means by which the wealthy exploited their desperate debtors was by manipulating the weights used to measure the grain or oil that they were borrowing. This is what Amos castigates in the charge that "they sell the righteous for silver" (2:6). The complaint against the rich sinners that they "weigh out injustice" (1 Enoch 95:6) may well be an allusion to this fraudulent practice. In this same connection, it is tempting to take the charge that they also "write lying words and words of error" as deceitful dealings in debt or labor contracts that they forced upon the vulnerable peasants.

Another standard indictment that the classical prophets made against the rulers and their officers was that they manipulated the courts. One could take several lines in the *Epistle of Enoch* precisely as allusions to such (ab)use of the courts: they "acquire gold and silver in judgment/unjustly" (94:7; 97:8; 97:10). Closely related to the way in which the wealthy and powerful could use the courts to their advantage is the lament of the righteous that when they had complained "to the rulers," to the high priest himself, or to the highest officers of the high priesthood (presumably the only court of appeal), the latter sided with their wealthy oppressors — others who were in the closed circle of the powerful and wealthy elite (103:14–15). All of these oppressive practices, of course, were blatant violations of Mosaic covenantal principles, which is pointedly articulated at several points in this section of 1 *Enoch* (e.g., 97:6; 98:4, 7–8, 12; 99:2).

The *Epistle of Enoch* may provide an important indication of the wider impe-rial dimension of the overall structure of political-economic-religious relations, depending on how the text of the key passage is reconstructed from the Ethiopic and Greek manuscripts. It has often been assumed that the wealthy sinners are accused of idolatry in 99:6–9. The Greek version (which Nickelsburg follows in his translation), however, apparently makes clearer than the Ethiopic version a distinction between "you sinners . . . who will be destroyed" in 99:6, 9, on the one hand, and "those who worship stones, and carve images of silver . . . and stone . . . " in 99:7, on the other. The latter are clearly the idolaters. Confirming the distinc-tion, the sinners are warned at the end of 99:7: "No help will you find from them," that is, the foreign idolaters. "Those who worship stones and demons" were presumably foreigners, and the warning that the sinners would receive "no help" from them suggests that they were the imperial patrons of the powerful and wealthy sinners. It is perhaps impossible to project just what the original (Ara-maic) text had in mind, but the Greek translator presents a subtle ironic play on words, comparing the sinners' exploitation of their people by building houses of stone and by gaining gold and silver (cf. 94:6–7; 97:8–9; 99:13) with their imperial patrons' idolatrous worship of images of stone, gold, and silver — false gods of power and wealth. If this reconstruction of the text and its meaning is reasonable, then it provides a window onto the determining imperial dimension of the overall structure of political-economic-religious power relations.

The social relations evident in the *Epistle of Enoch* thus appear parallel to those articulated by Ben Sira.[15] A scribal author (Ben Sira) addresses other scribes/sages and focuses, in part, on the relations between the powerful and wealthy (rulers) and the peasants that they rule, from whom they receive dues, and whom they op-press in various ways. The authors and their addressees see themselves as socially and/or culturally superior to the poor peasants. Yet the authors are concerned about the ways in which the poor are abused by the powerful and wealthy, as-suming that it is part of their responsibility to address or even to do something about such oppression. In both cases, this sense of responsibility is rooted in their personal commitment to the Mosaic covenantal tradition, the principles of which supposedly protected the rights of ordinary Israelites/Judeans. Particularly strik-ing is how Ben Sira and the woes of "Enoch" share the same rhetoric in charging the elite with "murder," with so oppressing the people that they are taking away the very life of their neighbors, in effect violating the covenantal commandment

---

15. For more general comparison of *1 Enoch* and Sirach on key themes, see Randal A. Argall, *1 Enoch and Sirach: A Comparative Literary and Conceptual Analysis of the Themes of Revelation, Creation, and Judgment* (SBLEJL 8; Atlanta: Scholars Press, 1995).

"you shall not kill" (99:15; 103:13; Sir. 34:25–27). The differences between this piece of apocalyptic literature and Ben Sira's book are also considerable. Ben Sira occasionally criticizes the wealthy and potentially oppressive rulers, whereas the *Epistle of Enoch* is completely devoted to a condemnation of them. While Ben Sira discusses the issues in a more detached and reflective manner, the *Epistle of Enoch* calls down divine judgment on the sinners in several series of prophetic woes. And while Ben Sira delivers his reflections and admonitions without much of a wider framing, the *Epistle of Enoch* finds considerable satisfaction in anticipating the future divine judgment in which the oppressive sinners will be destroyed and the righteous rewarded with what the sinners deprived them of; the wise themselves will be vindicated in their knowledge and commitment to the law.

We should not think that *1 Enoch* 92–105 is the product of a movement or group any more than we would understand the text of Sirach as testimony to Ben Sira heading a social movement. In both cases, they see themselves as having a role integral to the operation of the whole society. In both cases that role is situated between the rulers and the peasantry. Whereas Ben Sira is on such good terms with the incumbent high priest and his "brothers" that he proclaimed the glories of high priesthood and the incumbent high priest (Sirach 44–50), the producer and audience of the *Epistle of Enoch* were utterly opposed to both the incumbent rulers (and other wealthy) and the very institution of the high priesthood. They declared God's punitive judgment against the wealthy and powerful (94–105) and appear to have rejected the legitimacy of the temple-state itself (93:9). But in this section of *1 Enoch* we find indications neither of a separate community nor of alternative incumbents for the temple-state, as in some of the Dead Sea Scrolls, nor of a resistance movement, as in Daniel 11–12. At most, it would seem, we can imagine a relatively small scribal circle or clique, a circle of extremely dissident scribes. "The chosen ones . . . to whom will be given sevenfold wisdom and knowledge" and who "will uproot the foundations of violence" in the seventh week of the "Apocalypse of Weeks" (93:10 + 91:11) would appear to be a self-reference to this circle of scribes/sages. Also judging from the "Apocalypse of Weeks" (91:11–17), the scribes responsible for this literature envisaged, after the eighth week, in which the righteous would "execute righteous judgment on all the wicked" (presumably on the perverse, violent, and deceitful generation of the Second Temple period), a future age of righteousness under a "new heaven" in which "all humankind will look to the path of eternal righteousness." That is, they imagined, somewhat vaguely, a future societal life without sin, without oppression by the wealthy and powerful.

11

The Ironic End of Joash
in Chronicles

———— ◆ ————

Ralph W. Klein

Lutheran School of Theology at Chicago

In 842 B.C.E.,[1] the high priest Jehoiada engineered a *coup d'état* that installed the seven-year-old Joash[2] as king of Judah and expelled the only woman monarch, Athaliah (842/841–835), who for six years had ruled in succession of her slain son, Ahaziah (r. 843/842–842/841).[3] She had tried to wipe out the whole royal family when her son Ahaziah was killed, but was thwarted by Jehoshabeath, a sister of Ahaziah and, according to the Chronicler, the wife of Jehoiada (2 Chron. 22:11), who rescued Joash, an infant son of Ahaziah and hid him in the temple during Athaliah's reign. Athaliah was executed at the end of the coup, when the people of the land also executed Mattan, who presided as priest over a temple of Baal in Jerusalem.

Joash's rule lasted forty years (842/841–802/801) and is reported in both 2 Kings 12 and 2 Chronicles 24, with the latter chapter rewriting the text of Kings[4] and incorporating new information and a radical new theological inter-

---

1. The dates used for the Judean monarchy are taken from Gershon Galil, *The Chronology of the Kings of Israel and Judah* (Leiden: Brill, 1996), 147.

2. His name is spelled "Jehoash" in 2 Kings 12 (except for vv. 20, 21) and "Joash" in Chronicles. Since this article focuses on Chronicles, I will use the Chronicler's spelling of the king's name, as well as his spelling "Jehoshabeath" instead of "Jehosheba" for the name of the woman who saved the king, except in translations of the Kings text itself.

3. Galil (*Chronology*, 48) concludes that biblical chronologists later counted the beginning of Joash's reign from the time of the assassination of his father.

4. This has been the nearly unanimous assumption of scholars for the last two centuries. Recently, A. Graeme Auld has challenged this position in a forcefully written monograph (*Kings without Privilege: David and Moses in the Story of the Bible's Kings* [Edinburgh: T. & T. Clark, 1994]). Auld proposes that Kings and Chronicles independently supplemented a common inherited text that can be reconstructed from the texts they share in common. In his opinion, Chronicles did not omit the chapters narrating the questionable behavior of David and Solomon and the history of the northern kingdom. Rather, these materials were added by the Kings editor to the shared text. Since the shared text is itself

pretation of Joash's life. This study, offered in tribute to George W. E. Nickelsburg, a close friend and colleague for almost forty years, assesses the ways in which the Chronicler has rewritten the story of Joash that he found in Kings.

The account of Joash in Kings created theological problems for the Chronicler and his strict views on retribution, since he expected blessings or punishments to happen in just proportion and within a person's lifetime. He would have been surprised and even offended by the idea that Joash's successful efforts to repair the temple (2 Kings 12:4–16) were followed immediately by an invasion by Hazael of Aram, to whom Joash paid an enormous bribe (2 Kings 12:17–18), and also by a palace conspiracy that led to the assassination of Joash himself (2 Kings 12:19–21). The Chronicler used new information and a fresh interpretation of the materials inherited from Kings to provide a theologically coherent, if somewhat ironic,[5] account of the reign of Joash.

Introduction

2 Kings 12[6] [1]Jehoash was seven years old when he became king. [2]In the seventh year of Jehu, Jehoash became king, and he ruled forty years in Jerusalem. His mother's name was Zibiah of Beer-sheba.[7]

[3]Jehoash did what was upright in Yahweh's sight all his days because[8] Jehoiada the priest taught him.

[4]Only they did not remove the high places; the people were still sacrificing and burning incense on the high places.

2 Chron. 24 [1]Joash was seven years old when he became king, and he ruled forty years in Jerusalem. His mother's name was Zibiah of Beer-sheba.

[2]Joash did what was upright in Yahweh's sight all the days of Jehoiada the priest.

[3]Jehoiada secured two wives for him, and he engendered sons and daughters.

I call attention to the following significant changes introduced by the Chronicler:

---

postexilic, Auld attributes little historical credibility to the supplementary materials in Kings and Chronicles, saying, "I suspect in fact that this writer in Kings knew next to nothing about many of these ancient kings of the north" (139). For reasons set forth below in n. 9, I do not believe that Auld has successfully overturned the consensus.

5. For a discussion of irony in the text, see M. Patrick Graham, "Aspects of the Structure and Rhetoric of 2 Chronicles 25," in *History and Interpretation: Essays in Honour of John H. Hayes* (JSOTSup 173; Sheffield: Sheffield Academic Press, 1993), 78–89.

6. Second Kings 11:21 in English versions. English versification, therefore, is one less than the MT throughout this chapter.

7. The name of his mother is especially important, since there may have been some suspicion that the child brought forward by Jehoiada and Jehoshabeath was not really of the royal family. See even J. Maxwell Miller and John H. Hayes, *A History of Ancient Israel and Judah* (Philadelphia: Westminster, 1986), 303–5.

8. GKC 158b. Cf. Gen. 30:18; 31:49; 34:13; 1 Kings 8:33.

1. The Chronicler omits the synchronism with the northern kingdom as he does throughout his work.

2. The Deuteronomistic Historian had affirmed that Joash was faithful throughout his life, subject only to the limitation described in v. 4. The Chronicler, however, limited this fidelity to the lifetime of the priest Jehoiada and recorded the significant misdeeds of Joash in vv. 17–22. These faults provide a theological explanation for the Aramaean invasion (vv. 23–24) and the king's assassination (vv. 25–26).

3. The limitation placed on Joash's uprightness by 2 Kings 12:4 was omitted by the Chronicler, who has divided the life of Joash into two periods, in the first of which, before the death of Jehoiada, the king was completely upright.[9]

4. The additional information in Chronicles about Joash's wives and children[10] shows that Joash lived under God's blessing in the first period of his life and that his wives, since chosen by the high priest himself, were permissible. Since Jehoiada chose only two wives for the king, Joash in the Chronicler's eyes apparently did not transgress Deut. 17:17; two is hardly the "many wives" of which Deuteronomy warns. While some scholars would attribute this information on Joash's family to the source cited in v. 27,[11] it is important to note how general and vague this information is, revealing no detailed knowledge of the king's life.[12]

---

9. The limitation on a king's righteousness by referring to ongoing worship at high places is recorded for six kings in the Deuteronomic History. In two cases, the Chronicler repeats the information from Kings (2 Chron. 14:17 // 2 Kings 15:14 and 2 Chron. 20:33 // 2 Kings 22:43). The Chronicler's treatment of the other three passages, in addition to 2 Kings 12:4, seems also to be motivated by theological considerations. He omits the reference to high places under Amaziah (2 Kings 14:4; cf. 2 Chron. 25:2) since this king's life, like Joash's, was divided into good and bad periods, with the bad period beginning at 2 Chron. 25:14. The reference to high places in the account of Azariah/ Uzziah (2 Kings 15:4; cf. 2 Chron. 26:3) was also omitted because of the Chronicler dividing Uzziah's life into good and bad periods. In the reign of Jotham (2 Kings 15:35), the Chronicler rewrote the verse as he compared the king to his father Uzziah: "Only he did not invade the temple of Yahweh, and still the people acted corruptly" (2 Chron. 27:2). The latter clause is the Chronicler's recasting of the reference to the high places. Auld, *Kings without Privilege*, 86–88, interprets the four omissions by the Chronicler, in fact, as additions to the shared text by the author of Kings. I plan to publish in another context a complete discussion of Auld's interpretation of the references to the high places, which he considers a "crucial illustration" of his case.

10. For children as a sign of blessing see 1 Chron. 14:3–7 (David); 2 Chron. 11:18–23 (Rehoboam); and 2 Chron. 13:21 (Abijah).

11. Raymond B. Dillard, *2 Chronicles* (WBC 15; Waco, Tex.: Word Books, 1987), 188.

12. It is impossible to tell whether Jehoaddan of Jerusalem, the mother of Joash's son Amaziah (2 Chron. 25:1), was one of the two women picked by Jehoiada.

2 Kings 12	2 Chronicles 24

2 Kings 12

2 Chronicles 24

⁴Afterwards Joash decided to renew the house of Yahweh.

⁵And Jehoash said to the priests, "All the silver of the votive gifts, which is brought to the house of Yahweh — silver of the census tax, silver from the valuation of persons, or any silver that a person may voluntarily bring to the house of Yahweh — ¹³

⁵He gathered the priests and Levites and said to them, "Go out to the cities of Judah and gather from all Israel silver to repair the house of your God, year by year; and you shall act quickly in this matter." But the Levites did not act quickly.¹⁴

⁶let the priests take for themselves, each from his benefactors, and let them repair the damage to the house, wherever damage may be found."

⁷In the twenty-third year of King Jehoash, the priests had not repaired the damage to the house.

⁸So King Jehoash called to Jehoiada the priest and to the other priests, and he said to them, "Why have you not repaired the damage to the house? Now, do not take silver from your benefactors, but you shall give it for the damage to the house."

⁶So the king called to Jehoiada the chief,¹⁵ and he said to him, "Why have you not required the Levites to bring from Judah and Jerusalem the tax required by Moses the servant of Yahweh and by the congregation of Israel for the tent of testimony?"

⁹The priests agreed not to take silver from the people, and not to repair the damage to the house.

⁷"As for Athaliah, that wicked woman, her sons have broken into the house of God, and they have also given the votive gifts of the house of Yahweh to the Baals."

¹⁰Jehoiada the priest took a chest and bored a hole in its lid and put it on the south side of the altar, as one enters the house of Yahweh. The priests, the keepers of the threshold, would put there all the silver brought to the house of Yahweh.

⁸The king gave orders that they should make a chest and put it outside the gate of the house of Yahweh.

⁹They made a proclamation in Judah and Jerusalem to bring to Yahweh the tax required by Moses the servant of God for Israel in the desert.

---

13. The translation follows the suggestions of Mordechai Cogan and Hayim Tadmor, *II Kings* (AB 11; Garden City, N.Y.: Doubleday, 1988), 137.

14. H. G. M. Williamson (*1 and 2 Chronicles* [New Century Bible Commentary; Grand Rapids: Eerdmans, 1982], 320–21) proposes that vv. 5b–6 are secondary additions by a pro-priestly redactor. For counterarguments, see Dillard, *2 Chronicles*, 189–90, and Sara Japhet, *I and II Chronicles* (OTL; Louisville: Westminster/John Knox, 1993), 843. Japhet believes that the second occurrence of "Levites" in this verse refers to all members of the tribe, priests and Levites alike.

15. Normally the leading priest is called "chief priest" in Chronicles. See v. 11 and 2 Chron. 19:11 and 31:10.

Restoration of the Temple

2 Kings 12	2 Chronicles 24
	10And all the officials and all the people rejoiced, and they brought [the tax] and threw it into the chest until it was full.
11When they saw that there was much silver in the chest, the scribe of the king and the high priest would go up and bundle it up and count the money found in the house of Yahweh.	11Whenever someone brought the chest to the king's officers by the hand of the Levites, when they saw that there was much silver in it, the scribe of the king and the officer of the chief priest would come and empty the chest, take it, and return it to its place. So they did every day, and they gathered much silver.
12They would put the silver which had been weighed out into the hands of the workmen in charge of the house of Yahweh, and they paid it out to the carpenters and builders working in the house of Yahweh,	12And the king and Jehoiada gave it to those who did have charge of the work of the house of Yahweh, and they hired masons and carpenters to renew the house of Yahweh, and also workers in iron and bronze to repair the house of Yahweh.
13and to the masons and the stone cutters, to buy timber and quarry stone to repair the damage to the house of Yahweh, and for all the expenses of the temple to repair it.	13Those who were engaged in the project worked, and the repairing progressed in their hands. They restored the house of God to its proper condition, and they strengthened it.
14However, no silver basins, snuffers, sprinkling bowls or trumpets — any kind of vessel of gold and silver — were made from the silver which was brought into the house of Yahweh.	14When they had finished, they brought the rest of the silver before the king, and he made with it vessels for the house of Yahweh, both for the service and for the burnt offerings, and ladles, and vessels of gold and silver. And they offered burnt offerings in the house of Yahweh regularly all the days of Jehoiada.
15For they paid it to the workmen, and they repaired the house with it.	
16There was no accounting made with the people into whose hands they put the silver to pay the workmen, for they dealt honestly.	
17Silver from guilt offerings and sin offerings were not brought to the house of Yahweh, but it was for the priests.	

I call attention to the following significant changes:

1. The Chronicler adds a reference to the Levites in v. 5 and has Joash assign to them and to the priests the duty of actively collecting money for the repair of the temple. The Chronicler also changes the collection to an annual event, perhaps reflecting the customs of his time (see Neh. 10:33 [Eng. v. 32]). Joash criticized the Levites through Jehoiada for not collecting the funds rapidly enough. He also interpreted this collection as a tax legislated by Moses originally for the tabernacle (Exod. 30:11–16; 38:25–26) but now

due to the temple as well. The need for repairs is laid at the feet of Athaliah and her sons[16] in v. 7, who are accused of breaking into the temple and using its votive gifts for the Baals. The damage to the temple was *not* due to negligence by the clergy. In Kings, on the other hand, Joash had asked the priests to provide funds for repair of the temple from their own regular income, and he discovered that no repairs to the temple had been made after twenty-three years! He then reprimanded Jehoiada for not repairing the house and ruled that the priests would receive no more money directly, although they would not be required to finance repairs to the temple.

2. In Kings, Joash proposed that the contributions be deposited in a chest he placed in the temple, thus avoiding the priests as intermediaries. One of the king's officials and the high priest[17] would count the money and turn it over to those supervising the repairs in the temple. Cultic utensils did not have to be financed from these funds, and the priests were provided with restricted income from the guilt and sin offerings. The Chronicler moved the chest outside the gate of the temple where laypeople could deposit their money directly and not violate the holiness of the sanctuary. The proclamation reported in 2 Chron. 24:9 may reflect a communication strategy from the Persian period (cf. 2 Chron. 30:5; 36:22; Ezra 1:1; 10:7; Neh. 8:10).[18] In any case, the people joyfully paid this tax in great amounts, thus setting an example for the Chronicler's audience. Both the king and the high priest in Chronicles are represented by an official in the counting of the money, correcting an impression from Kings that the high priest and the scribe of the king were equal in rank. In Chronicles the high priest is roughly equal to the king himself. Excess funds gathered from the people were used to finance or provide raw material for cultic vessels — in direct contradiction to Kings. The existence of such surplus silver emphasizes the size of the people's gifts. Since there were no longer kings to provide these cultic vessels after the exile, the Chronicler may be providing an etiology for the provision of cultic vessels in his own time.[19]

---

16. Athaliah had attempted to wipe out the royal family (2 Chron. 22:10), and various members of the family had been killed in earlier incidents (2 Chron. 21:4; 22:1). Perhaps the term "sons" here should be understood as her "adherents."

17. This may indicate mutual suspicion between the king and the priesthood that could only be assuaged by their counting the funds together. On the other hand, there is no required accountability for those supervising the repair work. Cf. 2 Kings 22:7 // 2 Chron. 34:12. The contractors were trusted more than the priests!

18. See Michael Fishbane, *Biblical Interpretation in Ancient Israel* (Oxford: Clarendon Press, 1985), 159.

19. Wilhelm Rudolph, *Chronikbücher* (HAT 21; Tübingen: Mohr [Siebeck], 1955), 277.

Jehoiada's Death and Burial

15Jehoiada grew old and full of days, and he died. He was 130 years old at his death.

16They buried him in the city of David with the kings, for he had done good in Israel and toward God and his house.

The next three paragraphs, vv. 15–22, which are contained only in Chronicles, provide the theological rationale for the defeat and assassination of Joash. The Chronicler gives full honors to Jehoiada by crediting him with a life as long as Jacob's (Gen. 47:9) and similar to that of other patriarchs, matriarchs, and heroes of the faith.[20] Jehoiada had benefited Israel by restoring Joash to the throne, perhaps also serving as regent during his monarchy, and he had assisted God by repairing the house. This is the only time the Chronicler reports the death and burial of someone other than a king. Jehoiada's burial with the kings is a better fate than that of Joash (v. 25). With the death of Jehoiada, Joash's conduct and his fate turn from good to bad (cf. v. 2).

Transgression

17After the death of Jehoiada, the officials of Judah came and paid homage to the king. Then the king hearkened to them. 18They abandoned the house of Yahweh, the God of their ancestors, and worshiped the Asherim and the idols. Consequently the wrath of Yahweh was on Judah and Jerusalem on account of this guilt.

Joash listened to bad advisers, as had Rehoboam (2 Chron. 10:8–11), Ahab and Jehoshaphat (2 Chron. 18:4–11), and Ahaziah, whose mother Athaliah was his counselor (2 Chron. 22:3–4). King and people together turned from the worship of Yahweh to Asherim (cf. the apostasy of Asa's mother in 2 Chron. 15:16 and of Manasseh in 2 Chron. 33:3, 19) and idols (cf. the Philistines, who sent news of Saul's death to their idols [1 Chron. 10:9]). The divine wrath for these offenses was manifested in the invasion of the Arameans in vv. 23–24.

Prophetic Warnings and Royal Murder

19He sent prophets among them to bring them back to Yahweh. They warned them, but they did not give heed. 20Then the spirit of God clothed itself with Zechariah, the son of Jehoiada the priest. He stood above the people and said to them, "Thus says God: Why are you transgressing the commandments of Yahweh? You will not prosper. Since you have abandoned Yahweh, he has abandoned you." 21They con-

---

20. Sarah, 127; Aaron, 123; Moses, 120; Joseph and Joshua, 110. Historically, of course, Jehoiada's age seems unlikely because of general life expectancy and the age differential with his wife. Jehoshabeath was probably not much more than twenty at the death of her father Jehoram, who died when he was forty (2 Chron. 21:5). Ahaziah ruled for one year and Athaliah for six. Hence she would have been no more than twenty-seven at the time of the coup. Even if Jehoiada lived until two years before the death of Joash, he would have been sixty-five years older than his wife! Dillard (*2 Chronicles*, 192) is not willing to preclude 130 as an accurate figure.

spired against him and stoned him with stones, following the commandment of the king, in the court of the house of Yahweh. [22]Joash the king did not remember the loyalty that Jehoiada his father had shown to him, and so he killed his son. As he died, he said, "May Yahweh see and avenge!"

The guilt is shared by king and people alike; both refused to listen to prophets sent by God just as both had practiced idolatry. Zechariah was endowed with prophetic powers (1 Chron. 12:19; 2 Chron. 15:1) and delivered a speech which reflects the Chronicler's own theology through and through. Prospering (or lack of it) is a typical reward (punishment) for good conduct (misconduct) in Chronicles, and the Chronicler notes elsewhere that abandoning Yahweh leads to divine abandonment of the sinners (2 Chron. 12:5). A mob stoned Zechariah, on the king's orders. Thus, the son of the man who had made Joash king was executed at Joash's initiative, and the deed took place in the temple courts. At Joash's own coronation, his supporters had taken care to get Athaliah out of the temple and into the palace before they killed her. Zechariah's request for vengeance is answered in vv. 23–26.

While the report about the group of prophets and the speech of Zechariah may be the contribution of the Chronicler's own pen, the specific identity of Zechariah and his violent death may have come to the Chronicler from another source, perhaps the one mentioned in v. 27. A recent inscription may also attest to the historicity of Zechariah, the son of Jehoiada:[21] "Just as Ashyahu [Joash][22] commanded you to give by the hand of Zechariah silver of Tarshish to the house of Yahweh. Three sheqels." Though the name Zechariah is very common, his connection here with Joash and with fund-raising for the temple seems more than a coincidence.

The royal hostility toward Zechariah and the priests is anticipated in the Book of Kings, when Joash criticized Jehoiada and the priests for not repairing the temple and when Joash raided the temple to buy off Hazael.

The Aramaean Attack

2 Kings 12	2 Chronicles 24
[18]Then Hazael the king of Aram came up and fought against Gath and took it. And Hazael set his face to go up against Jerusalem.	[23]At the turn of the year,[23] an army host came up against him. They came to Judah and Jerusalem and destroyed all the officials of the people from among the people, and all their spoil he sent to the king of Damascus.

21. This was proposed by P. Kyle McCarter, Jr., at the Annual Meeting of the Society of Biblical Literature, San Francisco, November 1997.

22. Other names are attested in which the divine name appears in both the second and first position: Coniah and Jehoiachin.

23. The typical time for war (2 Sam. 11:1; 1 Kings 20:26; 1 Chron. 20:1).

[19]Jehoash king of Judah took all the votive
gifts, which Jehoshaphat, Jehoram, and
Ahaziah his fathers the kings of Judah had
dedicated, and his own votive gifts, and all
the gold which was found in the treasuries
of the house of God and the palace of the
king, and he sent them to Hazael king of
Aram so that he departed from Jerusalem.

[24]With a few men the army of Aram
had come, and Yahweh gave into their
hands an exceedingly great army, for
they had abandoned Yahweh the God of
their ancestors. On Joash they inflicted
punishment.

Kings and Chronicles both report an invasion by the Arameans, but the two
accounts vary in almost every detail. According to the Kings account, Hazael
(842–800 B.C.E.), a well-known king, captured Gath on the Mediterranean coast
and then threatened to attack Jerusalem. Joash raided the temple and also delved
into his own resources, and came up with a big enough bribe to send Hazael on
his way. In the Chronicler's telling, Hazael did not personally lead the attack and,
in fact, is not mentioned at all. Instead, the Aramaean army had a direct military
engagement with Judah and Jerusalem and inflicted punishment on the officers
of Judah who had led Joash astray. The booty taken by the army in its attack was
sent on to the king. These changes avoid the embarrassment of having Joash, the
restorer of the temple, undo his own repairs and impoverish the temple. In past
times God had given victory to small armies of his people when they were far
outnumbered (2 Chron. 13:3–18; 14:8–15). Now the same divine intervention
assisted the outmanned Arameans as they executed God's wrath on Judah. The
paragraph closes by repeating the people's offense of "forgetting Yahweh" and
indicating that this was punishment for the sins of Joash, even though he is not
mentioned in the battle account at all. Verse 25, however, indicates that he was
wounded in this battle.[24]

Joash's Death — Conclusion

2 Kings 12	2 Chronicles 24
[20]The rest of the acts of Joash and all that he did, are they not written in the Book of the Annals of the Kings of Judah?	
[21]His servants rose up and initiated a conspiracy against him, and they smote	[25]When they went away from him, leaving him severely wounded, his servants

---

24. Williamson (*1 and 2 Chronicles*, 325) believes that the Chronicler was dependent on an extrabiblical source for his version of the Aramaean War, but Japhet (*I and II Chronicles*, 851–52) argues
convincingly that the Chronicler modeled this account on his own narrative about Shishak's campaign
(2 Chron. 12:2–12).

Joash in the Beth Millo, which goes down to Silla.[25]

conspired against him because of the violence done to the son[26] of Jehoiada the priest, and they killed him on his bed. They buried him in the city of David, but they did not bury him with the kings.

[22]It was Jozabad[27] the son of Shimeath and Jehozabad son of Shomer, his servants, who struck him down so that he died. They buried him with his fathers in the city of David. Amaziah his son ruled in his stead.

[26]These are the ones who conspired against him: Zabad the son of Shimeath the Ammonitess and Jehozabad the son of Shimrith the Moabitess.

[27]As for his sons, the abundance of oracles against him, and the rebuilding of the house of God, behold they are written in the Midrash of the Book of Kings. Amaziah his son ruled in his stead.

The respective concluding summaries in vv. 20 and 27 of Kings and Chronicles are worded differently and have a divergent location, one before and one after the death of Joash.[28] It is unclear whether the Midrash of the Book of Kings (Chronicles) contained additional oracles about Joash or whether "the abundance of oracles" in v. 27 is only a reference back to v. 19. The assassination of Joash in Kings takes place without an adequate explanation; in Chronicles it follows his submission to the officials of Judah with the resultant turn to idolatry, his failure to listen to the prophets, his complicity in the execution of Zechariah, and his defeat by the Aramaean army. In fact, that defeat, according to Chronicles, left him wounded, and his servants conspired against him in response to his violence against Zechariah — the priest-prophet's final prayer for vengeance is granted. The conspiracy against Joash offers a kind of poetic justice since Joash had been involved in the conspiracy against Zechariah. The Chronicler gives a different location for the king's death (on his bed instead of in the Beth Millo), either

---

25. "Silla" may be a corrupt variant of Millo. Its inclusion in the text required the addition of "which goes down to."

26. LXX, Vulgate, MT use the plural form.

27. "Jozacar" is attested in many Hebrew manuscripts and may be original, although Chronicles was using a text with the Jozabad variant. The "Jo-" prefix is absent in Chronicles due to haplography (cf. the suffix on the preceding word).

28. In a discussion on the death of Josiah, H. G. M. Williamson ("Reliving the Death of Josiah," *VT* 37 [1987]: 12) argued that the Chronicler must have had a different edition of the Deuteronomic History, since he places the source citation at a different position than in Kings MT and the Chronicler is not known to move such citations from their position in his *Vorlage* (cf. 2 Chron. 35:26–27 and 2 Kings 23:28). He considers this the decisive argument in his discussion with Christopher Begg about whether Chronicles knew an alternate form of the Deuteronomic History. He mentions 2 Chron. 16:11; 2 Chron. 20:34; and 2 Chron. 25:26 as places where Chronicles follows the unusual placement of the formulae in Kings. Perhaps 2 Chron. 24:27 is a second case, in addition to Josiah, in which the Chronicler in fact moved the source citation found in his *Vorlage*.

because he did not understand the reference in Kings or because he was drawing a contrast with Joash's early life when he was hidden in a bedroom of the temple (see below). Both Kings and Chronicles report his burial in the city of David, but Chronicles adds that it was not with the other kings — in pointed contrast to the burial place of Jehoiada.[29]

Kings provides the names of the conspirators and the names of their fathers. Building on the feminine *taw* ending on Shimeath, and adding a *taw* to the parent of Jehozabad as well, the Chronicler interpreted both words as mothers' names and connected them to Ammon and Moab, respectively. Graham has noted the presence of two men named Jehozabad and three named Zabad in Ezra 10 and suggested that the hostility toward the Ammonites and Moabites in Ezra 9:1 may have led to the inclusion of these Gentiles in 2 Chron. 24:26 as well.[30] Ackroyd has remarked that those who had turned to alien deities were punished by alien instruments of divine wrath.[31]

The Irony of It All

The additional material and the theological interpretation introduced by the Chronicler lend a poignant tone to the account of Joash in Chronicles. These ironic items include:

1. Jehoiada and Jehoshabeath saved the life of Joash and put him on his throne, but Joash was implicated in the murder of their[32] son Zechariah. By the same token Zechariah was probably among the sons of Jehoiada who anointed Joash (2 Chron. 23:11).

2. At the command of the king,[33] people conspired against Zechariah and killed him (2 Chron. 24:21), but Joash's own servants conspired against him because of the violence done to the son(s) of Jehoiada. Both the bad Athaliah (2 Chron. 23:13) and the good Joash died by treason/conspiracy.

3. Zechariah was murdered in the same temple where Joash had been protected during the reign of Athaliah. Those who had crowned Joash carefully removed Athaliah from the temple before killing her.

---

29. Other kings to be given less than fully honorable burials in Chronicles are Asa (2 Chron. 16:14), Jehoram (2 Chron. 21:19–20), Uzziah (2 Chron. 26:23), and Ahaz (2 Chron. 28:27).

30. M. Patrick Graham, "A Connection Proposed Between II Chr 24,26 and Ezra 9–10," *ZAW* 97 (1985): 256–58. Japhet (*I and II Chronicles*, 854), on the other hand, believes that the information on the ethnic background of the assassins was found in the Chronicler's source and subsequently omitted in Kings.

31. Peter R. Ackroyd, *I & II Chronicles, Ezra, Nehemiah* (Torch Bible Commentaries; London: SCM, 1973), 161.

32. Jehoshabeath is never called the mother of Zechariah, but priests would not have had multiple wives.

33. These same people *transgressed* the commandments of Yahweh (24:20).

4. Jehoiada, the glorified high priest, is buried with the kings; Joash, the king whose life turned from good to bad, is not buried with the kings.

5. Worshipers turn from one deity to another. The sons of Athaliah used the votive gifts of the house of Yahweh for the Baals (2 Chron. 24:7). Subsequently, the people looted the Baal temple and killed Mattan, its priest. At the end, Joash himself and the people worshiped Asherim and idols (2 Chron. 24:28).

6. Jehoshabeath hid Joash and his nurse in a *bed*room of the temple (22:11); Joash's servants killed him on his own *bed* (24:25).

7. Joash *did not remember* the loyalty of Jehoiada and killed Zechariah his son; the name Zechariah means "Yahweh has remembered."

8. Joash *listened* to the officers of Judah and fell into sin, but he and the people *would not listen* to the warnings of the prophets.[34]

The net effect of these ironic twists is to show the ingratitude of Joash toward Jehoiada and his irresponsibility in leading the people. In several ways he even repeated the offenses of Athaliah. In recasting 2 Kings 12 the Chronicler provides a coherent theological and historiographical account of Joash and summons his readers to loyalty to Yahweh and to his temple.

---

34. The verbs are synonyms in Hebrew.

12

When Aseneth Met Joseph:
A Postscript

◆

Ross S. Kraemer
Brown University

Over the years, I have been fortunate to have had several mentors apart from my own teachers in college and graduate school, mentors who have encouraged and sustained me professionally and personally for the last quarter-century. Not surprisingly for a woman of my generation, all of these mentors have been men. Their early and abiding support for my scholarship on women and religion in antiquity seemed initially remarkable, and still seems so in retrospect. None has been kinder or more generous in spirit than George Nickelsburg, and none has had a better sense of humor.

Memory being what it is, I can no longer recall when I first met George Nickelsburg. It was without a doubt at an annual meeting of the Society of Biblical Literature in the mid-1970s, when George was already a well-respected scholar in the field, and I was very much a fledgling. It was almost certainly in one of two places: a session of the Pseudepigrapha Seminar, or, more probably, a late-night soirée at the Fortress Press suite conducted by the late John Hollar.

Whenever and wherever it was, the first memory of George I can clearly situate was on a Saturday afternoon, October 30, 1976, at the annual meeting in St. Louis, in a Pseudepigrapha session presided over by another of my mentors, Robert A. Kraft, devoted to the text virtually everyone else still calls *Joseph and Aseneth*. George and I sat together and exchanged notes and remarks during a paper by Gary Vikan on medieval woodcut illustrations of *Aseneth*.

Although at that time I had only the most cursory familiarity with *Aseneth*, in subsequent years the text came to fascinate me more and more. In 1998, Oxford University Press published my rather lengthy study, *When Aseneth Met Joseph: A Late Antique Tale of the Biblical Patriarch and His Egyptian Wife, Revisited*. George's gracious praise for the book adorns the dustcover.

When George wrote his kind words, he also sent me a detailed letter by email, raising a series of questions that were hardly appropriate for the back of a book. When the letter arrived, I was drowning in the details of the book's delayed production, and wrote him only a cursory reply, promising a more suitable response in the near future. Shortly thereafter, though, I received the invitation to contribute to this volume, and realized immediately that I could offer George no better tribute than to engage his thoughtful concerns in this public forum. What follows is my response to George's letter. I hope he will forgive me for taking so long to acknowledge the great care with which he read my work, and for seeming to have been terribly rude in postponing a response for so long.

George begins with kind praise for my deconstruction of the arguments that *Aseneth* is an Egyptian Jewish text written ca. 100 C.E. He says that I have made a "strong case" for placing the text instead in Syria ca. 400 C.E., and commends my willingness to waver between Jewish and Christian authorship. George then goes on to express some reservations, to which I will respond after summarizing them here.

George points out that in the book I often use expressions such as "could be construed," "seems quite plausible," and so forth. He suggests that while such phrasings reflect my view about the ambiguous nature of the text, they may, for example, in chapter 5, implicitly add force to arguments about an otherwise not-too-strong connection with mystical traditions.

My response is that I don't know how else to do this with any degree of intellectual honesty. My choice of these phrases was largely conscious, although I never counted them. They were certainly not intended to provide a rhetorical force for arguments that otherwise lack substance, but as we all know, authorial intentions often have little to do with rhetorical impact. Texts "say" things their authors didn't necessarily (consciously?) "intend," and my text is no exception.

George's second concern has to do with my parallels with adjurative and mystical texts. He mentions parallels with earlier apocalyptic and other texts, for example, with Tobit, Daniel, and *1 Enoch,* in which prayer leads to angelophany; and notes that Aseneth does not pray in order to invoke an ascent or descent. Finally, he wonders (1) whether including the "full array of earlier parallels" would affect how compelling my arguments are, and (2) whether the other evidence for a relatively late date makes the parallels more compelling.

Parallels are, by their nature, initially just that: comparable material that, by itself, demonstrates only similarity and not relationship. Certainly George is correct that angelic beings appear in response to (or at least following) prayer in Daniel, *1 Enoch,* and Tobit, and obviously all three are fairly early. (I confess, though, to having more doubts lately about the dating of Tobit. One of the consequences of having written this book is that I've become almost compulsively skeptical of arguments about dates for texts not securely attested in other ancient sources, or known in some material form that is itself securely datable. Certainly the Qumran fragments augur for a least a version of Tobit antedating *Aseneth*, at

least given my dates for *Aseneth!*) And of course I agree that the texts do not
say that Aseneth prays with the intention or expectation of initiating an angelic
descent. Nevertheless, that is precisely the sequence of events: Aseneth prays for
forgiveness, and an angel descends to her chamber.

As for whether a fuller array of earlier parallels would make the later material seem less compelling (2), I would offer several responses. First, I do discuss
the parallels with Daniel's visionary encounter in 10:6 (p. 35), in the context of
my larger argument that *Aseneth* is to some degree constructed out of traditional
materials. It is true, though, that I devoted much less consideration to the similarities with earlier material. By the time I was actually writing the book, I had
become convinced that the texts are much more likely to be late(r), and hence I
was simply less interested in going over material that is unlikely to postdate the
first century C.E. At the same time, by illustrating *Aseneth's* usage of traditional
material, I think I was "conceding" the presence of "earlier parallels" — I was just
also trying to refocus attention onto a different cultural matrix, as it were.

It is George's final suggestion (2) that I think is crucial. The cumulative nature of the other evidence for a relatively late date is certainly what ultimately
persuaded me. That is, the inherent flaws in the argument for an early date must
be considered in combination with the plethora of affinities with later materials;
and, in particular, the striking affinities with later representations of Helios, the
greater degree of cultural interest in Helios in the third and fourth centuries, the
peculiar commonalities with adjurative materials that extend beyond the general
patterns of prayer and angelophany to the specifics of clothing, gestures, and
elements such as the bizarre business about the bowls of food thrown out the
window, not to mention those neoplatonic bees. (I argue, on pp. 167–72, that the
mystical drama of the bees that encircle Aseneth, drop dead, revive, and fly off to
the courtyard of her family compound in 16.1–17.3 most resembles a neoplatonic
understanding of bees found in Porphyry's *On the Cave of the Nymphs*.)

Next, while George finds my parallel with the Helios material convincing,
he expresses reservations about the relationship between *Aseneth* and the Dinah
tradition, specifically referring to rabbinic traditions that suggest an inverse parallel between Pharaoh's son/Aseneth/Levi and Simeon (in *Aseneth*) and Shechem/
Dinah/Levi and Simeon (in Genesis).

Here is where we undoubtedly disagree. In the appendix on *Aseneth* and rabbinic traditions, I think I demonstrate the untenability of the arguments made by
V. Aptowitzer, which George cites several times in support of his own view that
a legend of Dinah as the mother of Aseneth undergirds the text(s). I think it
is not impossible that the author(s) knew such a legend, but then, as my book
shows, I am reluctant to make assertions about things I have no grounds to assess.
Nevertheless, I do not think that anything in the text itself supports the claim
that the author(s) knew such a legend. In my book I refute the argument that the
authorial claim that "Aseneth was in no way like the daughters of the Egyptians,

but was in all ways like the daughters of the Hebrews" (*Aseneth* 1.7) points to the Dinah legend. This story of Aseneth and Joseph is quite clear that Aseneth is the daughter of Pentephres and his unnamed (Egyptian, non-Israelite) wife.

Nevertheless, George's reading of *Aseneth* 22–29 as a recasting of the Dinah story, with Simeon and Levi reprising their original roles in Genesis 34, Pharaoh's son playing the part of Shechem, and Aseneth that of Dinah is an intriguing way to think about the final portion of the text(s), one which I did not consider. Perhaps my conclusion that the legend of Dinah as the mother of Aseneth does not underlie the present texts, and may not even have been formulated when *Aseneth* was composed,[1] deterred me from seeing this possible association. It would, in fact, have fit well with my discussion of *Aseneth*'s construction out of traditional "biblical" materials, and requires no recourse to rabbinic traditions for its possible usage here.

George next commends my discussion of the relationship between the short and long texts of *Aseneth* and says he has only one question: whether an explicit connection with a biblical text could be considered more original than a possible allusion or parallel in the short text, as he has argued about the two texts of *Testament of Abraham*.

I am enormously pleased to know that George found my arguments here compelling. Staking out a position in opposition to scholars whose work I respect tremendously, particularly Christoph Burchard, makes me quite nervous, so I am particularly gratified by George's response.

Assuming I have correctly understood his question, I think the answer is, I don't see why not, at least in theory. My argument that the longer text expands the shorter is not primarily based on my observations that the longer is more explicitly "biblical" than the shorter — or at least, I don't intend it as such. I think that other patterns of difference argue for the priority of the shorter text (at least in general), a pattern that then allows us to argue that in this particular case, the more explicit use of biblical materials and language is the result of expansion rather than abridgment.

George then compliments my book for putting the discussion of *Aseneth* on a different level, but remains convinced that Aseneth undergoes a religious conversion: the story takes her from idolatry to the worship of the true God, transforming her into a suitable bride for Joseph. He insists that it is a transformation from damnation to immortality, and not the transformation of a human into an angel.

Once again, it seems we disagree. We can probably debate ad nauseam whether it is either accurate or useful to say that Aseneth "converts." I am still convinced that the language and paradigm of conversion is more ours than that of the text(s)

---

1. See the appendix, particularly my critique of Aptowitzer's dating of the Dinah legend to the third century C.E. based on an (erroneous) association with R. Ammi (pp. 310–12).

and that if the author(s) meant to say this, there are probably more explicit ways to have done so.

On the one hand, obvious terminology like προσήλυτος and προσέρχομαι nowhere appears in the text. Μετανοέω occurs several times, but with the obvious meaning of repentance, which has no necessary connotation of conversion. It is perhaps instructive to compare the language of *Aseneth* with Josephus's narrative of the adoption of Judaism by Helene of Adiabene and her son, Izates (*Antiquities* 20§17ff.), if only because it is certainly the best and most detailed narrative in Greek of non-Jews who become Jews, and thus one of the few "controls" we have, despite what I consider a significant difference in dating. Although Louis Feldman, in the Loeb translation, renders the Greek of §17 as "Helena ... and her son, Izates, became converts to Judaism," what Josephus actually says is something closer to "they changed (μετέβαλον) their life to the customary practice of the Jews (τὰ Ἰουδαίων ἔθη)." In §34, Ananias teaches the king's wives to worship God (τὸν θεὸν σέβειν) according to the ancestral Jewish practices (ὡς Ἰουδαίοις πάτριον ἦν). The verb Josephus uses for what Izates desires to do in §35 is μετατίθημι. It is perhaps unsurprising that the language of Josephus that speaks of adopting the ancestral customs of the Jews is missing from *Aseneth,* since within the narrative framework of the story, these ancestral customs either do not yet exist (if what is meant is the Mosaic law) or barely exist, if the pre-Mosaic practices of the early patriarchs could be construed as part of these phrasings.

Part of my point, then, is that a known first-century Jewish writer construes becoming a Jew as primarily about the adoption of Jewish practices and a Jewish way of life, not about a moment of personal mystical transformation. If Josephus thought that any of these people had such experiences, they seem irrelevant to him, or at least to his purposes. I certainly do not wish to suggest that Josephus's representation conforms to some stereotype of Judaism as oriented to praxis as opposed to "belief" or "faith." I am simply observing that Josephus's description of the apparently historical Helena and Izates differs significantly from the language and paradigm of *Aseneth,* for which several explanations are possible, not the least of which is, as I would argue, that *Aseneth* is not about "conversion" to Judaism. But this is obviously far from a full consideration of the language and paradigms of "becoming a Jew" in Greco-Roman antiquity, and I realize this is a difficult issue to resolve.

Still, when I say that I am unconvinced that the text is fundamentally "about conversion," I mean that I am unconvinced that the framers of this tale were primarily interested in issues of the alteration and transference of religious identity and practice, particularly in their own communities (the precise set of assumptions by which many other scholars have read *Aseneth*). I do not think the authors (or early audiences) of *Aseneth* had *necessarily* to have *any* interest in conversion in their own times — contrary to George's assertion that "what the author says about idolatry and conversion applies to his own time."[2] I see no reason to think, following James Kugel's general methodology,[3] that a story of this type could not have its origins in speculation about the marriage of Joseph to the daughter of an Egyptian priest and that it had no inherent connection to contemporaneous social practices.

This is not to say that I think this is the only accounting for the text; on the contrary, as I think I demonstrate in the book, how one understands the emergence of this story depends a great deal on what one imagines as the context for that emergence. Samaritans, for instance, could easily have been interested in defending the legitimacy of the marriage and the purity of Joseph's lineage without having had any interest in contemporaneous conversion to Samaritan Judaism (or whatever the proper substantive is here). This, by the way, is an issue I only briefly sketched in the book proper — the appendix I had initially written made the book so long that Oxford balked. But I have been rescued by invitations for Festschriften twice in this regard: a revised version of the appendix, "Could *Aseneth* Be Samaritan?" will have already appeared in print by the time this article does.[4]

Apart from George's insistence on using the language of conversion, I essentially agree that the story takes us from Aseneth's idolatry through her transformation into a reverent follower of the God of Joseph, a suitable bride for the equally reverent Joseph. I continue to think that Aseneth *does* become an angel, although the precise meaning of that transformation requires an elaboration that the text alone may not facilitate. I would probably be inclined to see this transformation as a temporary experience of a state yet to come (a partially realized "eschatology" — to borrow from Christian theological terminology for a change!). In any case, I am not sure why George finds that the pairs "damnation/ immortality" and "human/angelic" seem mutually exclusive, rather than, at least in this text, if not in many other ancient imaginations, varied formulations of similar conceptions.

George then wonders whether my book leans much more toward analyzing *Aseneth* in relation to other texts rather than being an internal analysis of the text itself, perhaps because much of previous scholarship has focused on date, provenance, and authorship without attention to the external evidence I discuss.

Here I would have to agree, at least to some extent, that the book is particularly focused on the possible contexts of the text(s) rather than on a close reading of

---

2. "Stories of Biblical and Early Post-biblical Times," in *Jewish Writings of the Second Temple Period — Apocrypha, Pseudepigrapha, Qumran Sectarian Writings, Philo, Josephus* (ed. Michael Stone; vol. 2 of *The Literature of the Jewish People in the Period of the Second Temple and the Talmud*; CRINT; Philadelphia: Fortress, 1984), 69; the treatment of *Aseneth* runs from pp. 67–71.

3. Set forth especially in *In Potiphar's House: The Interpretative Life of Biblical Texts* (San Francisco: HarperCollins, 1990).

4. In *A Multiform Heritage: Studies in Early Judaism and Christianity in Honor of Robert A. Kraft* (ed. Benjamin Wright; SBL Honorarium Series; Atlanta: Scholars Press, 1999), 149–66.

the text(s) as a whole...although I thought I was often doing that, as well! Unquestionably, much of the book focuses on the relationship of the text(s) to the larger potential cultural matrix — not just to texts, unless ancient practice is also a text, and I don't want to get into those issues here. But I also think that a focus on internal analysis and one on relation to external texts are not as separable as George suggests.

Although I understand his point that "one can perceive [some of the internal evidence] with little or no appeal to external evidence," so much of this text has been read through filters of assumptions about (as George said) its date, authorship, provenance, and intentions that rereading it "on its own terms" is probably terra incognita. Then, too, his comment raises questions about how much of what seems to adhere in a text itself is really what we bring to it in the first place, even if we then think that we have merely seen what is already present. I learned to ask some of these questions before the vogue of postmodern literary criticism, but reading some of that literature has helped me to see even more how precarious claims about what is integral to a text may be.

George suggests that the questions he has raised could constitute another book, which would address the things he feels my book has left unexplained. I would consider such a book a great complement, and a great compliment, but I am also unlikely to be the one to write it. *Aseneth* and I have spent too much time together as it is in the last five years.

George concludes his letter by rightly taking me to task for failing to cite his own scholarship on *Aseneth*.[5] He wonders whether it is because I completely disagree with him on fundamental issues, or because his treatment is shorter than others, or because his focus (literary structure) differs from my intertextual, externally oriented treatment.

This is part of George's letter that I did apologetically and privately answer earlier, but I think I owe him a public explanation as well. The answers are several.

To the question about whether the reason is because I completely disagree with him, the answer is, not really. In some ways, of course, to the extent that his own work shared the prevailing (or, I hope, previously prevailing) consensus, I disagreed with that. Given George's (prior?) acceptance of the general consensus about *Aseneth*, what he had written is judicious, balanced, and articulate. Before I began this project, I regularly assigned or recommended George's treatments to my students, and I still routinely do so on many other texts.

In fact, my failure to cite George was not intentional. As I wrote in the preface (viii–ix), once I realized how different my own position was from that of most other scholars, I began to find it "unproductive to engage in the kinds of

---

5. In "Stories of Biblical and Early Post-biblical Times," above, and in his own earlier *Jewish Literature between the Bible and the Mishnah: A Historical and Literary Introduction* (Philadelphia: Fortress, 1981), 258–63.

traditional scholarly dialogue with earlier literature." That is, I decided that it was pointless to keep reading, and citing, every contribution to the literature on *Aseneth*, all the more so since I realized that I needed to be reading a lot of ancient sources and scholarship on later materials about which I knew relatively little, at least when I started. In general, I tried only to cite those works I thought crucial to the positions I wanted to challenge, or, far less frequently, to the new position I wanted to advocate.

Since I didn't really exclude his work deliberately, I suppose the answer to the second and third questions has to be "no." Even so, as I think further on it, I might still have responded little if at all to his analysis of the literary structure. To the extant that George's arguments seemed to me to rely so much on the old scholarly consensus, I would not have taken the time to ask whether, apart from that consensus, I might still agree with him. But in retrospect, I am truly sorry not to have noted his own thoughtful, responsible scholarship, most of all because failing to do so might give the erroneous impression that I have anything less than the utmost respect for him as a scholar, a colleague, and a wonderful friend. I hope this small piece is some minor restitution, and a public declaration of the inspiration and support he has been to me for many years.

Much love to you, George, and best wishes to your family as you begin the next stage of an admirable career!

13

Early Developments of the "Two-Ways Tradition(s)," in Retrospect

Robert A. Kraft

University of Pennsylvania

A strange thing happened to me on the way to submitting my contribution to this volume in honor of George W. E. Nickelsburg. On the evening of October 28, 1999, just as I was preparing to send off the final draft of this article, which I had presented to the Wisdom and Apocalypticism Group at the Society of Biblical Literature two years earlier[1] (largely at the invitation of George Nickelsburg and Ben Wright), a group of my colleagues and former students surprised me with a belated sixty-fifth-birthday party and presentation of a volume of essays in my honor,[2] which included George Nickelsburg's follow-up on the aforementioned SBL paper![3]

What to do now? If I had not been so (characteristically) late in submitting my piece for this volume in honor of George, bibliographers could have noted ironically that George's response to my efforts appeared in print prior to publication of my own essay.[4] They still will be able to do so, but with a twist. Given the situation, it seemed best that I include some comments on George's response, in hopes that our reciprocal attention to this "two-ways" material may help others to see the issues more clearly or at least to supplement and correct us as appropriate.

I have called this supplemented version of my 1997 SBL presentation a "retrospect." This is not only because of the situation described above, which permits me to take another look at the earlier material in the light of George's observations and suggestions. What is also clear from our respective articles is that

---

1. This material was circulated electronically on November 7, 1997, and presented for discussion in the group's session on November 24.

2. *A Multiform Heritage: Studies on Early Judaism and Christianity in Honor of Robert A. Kraft* (ed. Benjamin G. Wright; Homage Series 24; Atlanta: Scholars Press, 1999).

3. "Seeking the Origins of the Two Ways Tradition in Jewish and Christian Ethical Texts," 95–108.

4. Actually, the draft of the SBL paper had been (and the revised form remains) available electronically through my home page — http://ccat.sas.upenn.edu/rs/rak/kraft.html (follow the links to electronic publications, then to "Christianity," "Barnabas," and "Articles") — to those who knew how to use that increasingly important publication medium.

we both are operating in territory that, in somewhat different ways, is woven into our respective academic biographies. My Ph.D. dissertation, *The "Epistle of Barnabas" and Its Sources* (Harvard, 1961), and the follow-up translation and commentary, *Barnabas and the Didache* (Nelson, 1965),[5] forced me to explore some of the mysteries of the "two-ways tradition(s)," especially in their earliest Christian forms; George's Ph.D. dissertation, *Resurrection, Immortality, and Eternal Life in Intertestamental Judaism* (Harvard, 1967; published as HTS 26 in 1972), also drew him into contact with most of the relevant texts relating to the question of rewards and punishments, particularly resurrection.[6] This is quite obvious from our respective footnotes in our recent studies.

What follows is the 1997 article, with the text essentially as it was presented to the SBL group, but with notes added and/or fleshed out in this retrospective representation.

Two-Ways Forms

We have two explicit early Christian examples of this "basic binary" form of instruction for living:

Barnabas 18–21
Didache 1–6[7]

Barnabas describes the material as "another gnosis" (not explicitly as "wisdom") pertaining to teaching and authority, and uses the imagery of light/darkness as associated with angels of God/Satan and with eschatological continuity/temporality. The *Didache,* on the other hand, speaks simply of life/death — a binary lurking in the background in *Barnabas* (light leads to the appointed place; glory is due to the One who redeemed from death; the way of the Black One leads to eternal death), but not stated as such until the appended concluding words in *Barn.* 21.1–3:

The one who does these things will be glorified in God's kingdom;
The one who chooses those will perish with his works —

---

5. Ultimately, all of these materials will also be available electronically through my home page, where parts of them may already be found (e.g., the two-ways sections of *Barnabas* and the *Didache* in parallel alignment).

6. See especially chap. 6 (144–69), "The Qumran Scrolls and Two-Way Theology." In the conclusions (173f.), he sees an early "resurrection theology" that had been developed in connection with persecution and suffering coming to assume "the functions that previously belonged to the two-way theology" (with focus on eternal life and eternal death). "The two theologies mesh and complement each other."

7. For the texts in parallel, see my 1965 translation and commentary in the series edited by Robert M. Grant, The Apostolic Fathers: A New Translation and Commentary, vol. 3: *Barnabas and the Didache* (Nelson); this material is available electronically at gopher://ccat.sas.upenn.edu/ under "Electronic Publications and Resources" > "Kraft Publications" > "Christianity" > "Barnabas" > "Commentary"; the copyright is held by myself, and noncommercial use of the materials is freely permitted.

The day is near when all things will perish with the Wicked One!
But the Lord is near, and his reward.

Whether the short Latin document called the "Doctrina" actually constitutes a separate third witness to the two-ways tradition, as many have argued, or is to be understood as somehow derivative of both *Didache* (to which it stands very close overall) and *Barnabas* need not be argued here. What is especially interesting about "Doctrina's" presentation is that it includes both life/death (as in *Didache*) and light/darkness (as in *Barnabas*), followed by the mention of angels (see *Barnabas*) of righteousness/iniquity! At this point, the imagery of 1QS (*Community Rule* or *Manual of Discipline*; see esp. 3.13–4.26) also comes quickly to mind, on the one side, and of *Shepherd of Hermas* (esp. 33–36 = Mandates 5–6), on the other.

As the group of binary-minded sources enlarges, we find the following additional pairs: truth/error (1QS; *Testaments*); good/evil; law of the Lord/works of Belial; straight/crooked; and right hand/left hand.[8]

The apocalyptic connections in *Barnabas* and "Doctrina" are striking, and fit with other passages in the earlier portions of *Barnabas*. The lack of such apocalyptic tones in *Didache* is also striking, if also mitigated by the presence of the separate apocalyptic "appendix" at the end of the *Didache*. In my youth,[9] I argued that the evidence suggested that a two-ways "common source" lay somewhere in the shadowy background of *Barnabas* and the *Didache*, although neither probably used the source directly. I was undecided "whether, or to what extent, eschatology appeared in the source" (12), although I tended to suspect (and perhaps, wished to believe) that an eschatological connection was more likely than not, based on other clues in the two early Christian compilations.

This much was clearer to me: the two-ways materials in *Barnabas* must have been derived from an earlier form of this ever-growing two-ways tradition, which already was united with eschatological emphases in the school tradition on which *Barnabas* is dependent. The *Didache* form of the two ways (perhaps based upon an older "Doctrina," and developed further in various other Christian forms such as the *Apostolic Church Order, Life of Shenuti*, etc.) gave evidence of relatively more reworking (including expanding) and was almost completely free of eschatological connections or nuances (except in the "Doctrina" framework).

Two-Ways Contents

The materials common to these two streams of two-ways tradition, apart from the question of introductory or concluding frameworks, are almost exclusively

8. See Kraft, *Barnabas and the Didache*, 135 (to *Barn.* 18.1).
9. Ibid., 8f.

ethical — concerning duties toward God, neighbor, children, rulers, and slaves; vice lists; and the like. The materials tend toward parallelistic couplets strongly reminiscent of Jewish "wisdom" literature as represented in Proverbs and Sirach (and also reflected in some of the *Testaments of the Patriarchs*) — in synonymous, antithetical, and constructive (by steps) combinations. There are straightforward prohibitions as well as positive admonitions, and occasionally "theologically" tinged comments.[10]

Locating the Roots of the Two-Ways Approach

By definition, what is distinctive about the two-ways approach to ethical wisdom is the *form* in which it is presented — the binary framework. There seems to be nothing particularly characteristic about its ethical content that would help in tracing the background of the formulation(s), beyond the obvious "Jewish" context of some of the instructions — various references to God (including God's role as creator), warning against idolatry, prohibition of abortion, various echoes of laws and standards known from other Jewish sources (including biblical). That such contents are older than their occurrence in what come to be "Christian" sources is not difficult to demonstrate. But is it possible to determine significant details about the development and connections of this two-ways *form* prior to its incorporation into *Barnabas* and the *Didache* and their "Christian" predecessors?

Here we are reduced to assessing the various parallels. That two-ways imagery is very old in the Jewish biblical tradition, for example, is clear. Already in the pentateuchal materials, we find such words as "I have set before you life and good, death and evil..., life and death, blessing and curse; therefore choose life..." (Deut. 30:15–20). Whether this reflects the existence of such a *form* of teaching already in the period from which this section of Deuteronomy comes (Persian or earlier) cannot be determined, but is certainly possible. Was this a form that was known and used in other Near Eastern cultures? I should know the answer, but do not. In the Greek worlds, the image of Heracles at the crossroads (Xenophon, *Memorabilia* 2.1.21ff.) provides another sort of parallel, but brings us no closer to a concrete solution. We do not appear to be any better informed today than when I wrote three decades ago that "there is no reason to think that the form of the Two Ways tradition shared by *Barnabas* and the *Didache* had direct and immediate ties with Semitic Judaism. Rather it seems to have flourished in the Greek schools of Hellenistic Judaism for decades, if not centuries, before early Christian writers came to adopt it. Its ultimate origins are obscure and its family

---

10. E.g., *Barn.* 19.6c = *Did.* 3.9c (nothing happens without God); *Barn.* 19.7c = *Did.* 4.10 (references to trusting and fearing God who calls those in whom the Spirit is prepared); *Barn.* 19.8 = *Did.* 4.8 (sharers in what is imperishable/immortal).

tree in terms of Greek and Semitic (and even Egyptian) developments cannot be reconstructed with any assurance."[11]

The Dead Sea Scrolls are of some help, as I already knew then (see my commentary to *Barn.* 18.1b–2). But the parallels in the *Manual of Discipline* have less to do with establishing the presence of a two-ways *form* of ethical instruction than with casting light on the eschatological mood in which the form appears in *Barnabas* (see also the *Testaments* and *2 Enoch*). To warn about conflicting options, related to angels and rulers and spirits and inclinations, is not to arrange ethical or other instructions according to such a format. Perhaps 4Q392, a very fragmentary "liturgical work" that speaks about God creating darkness and light in relation to the "deeds of God" and the understanding of humans, would have given us something like our two-ways format, had more of it survived.[12] Similarly some of the "wisdom" texts presented by García Martínez on pp. 371–404 come closer to giving similar "ethical" instruction and lists (e.g., 4Q416–24, "sapiential works" dealing with the "mystery of existence," perhaps in contrast to the "mystery of sin/iniquity" in 1Q27; 4Q299–300), but, in general, what has survived in the Dead Sea Scrolls is not focused on "ethics" in the sense of the two-ways traditions. Even the copies of biblical Proverbs (two manuscripts from Cave 4) and Ben Sira (one manuscript from Cave 2) are rare among the Dead Sea Scrolls.

Directions, Hopes, and Suggestions

What can this all mean for those who wish to shed light on the development of "apocalyptic" and "wisdom" traditions in early Judaism? I am convinced, although the evidence is far from compelling in and of itself, that there were traditions of collecting and transmitting ethical instructions and exhortations governed by oral and written two-ways organizational devices (light/darkness, life/death, etc.) in Greek-speaking Judaism prior to the emergence of identifiable "Christian" literature. The contents thus transmitted focused on "ethical/practical wisdom" — how to live in a manner pleasing to the Creator God, with focus both on attitudes (e.g., don't be arrogant) and, more so, on specific actions that relate mostly to social situations (e.g., share things with neighbors, judge justly, avoid murder, etc.) — and almost never to cultic or ritual practices (unlike much of what has been preserved in the Dead Sea Scrolls; *Barn.* 19.12b–c = *Did.* 4.14a–b on confession of sins and appropriate prayer comes closest). God rewards right conduct and punishes its opposite, although this context is more assumed than explicated in the preserved materials. There is little that merits the label "apocalyptic" in the specific instructions contained in these two-ways materials.

---

11. Kraft, *Barnabas and the Didache*, 4.

12. For a translation, see Florentino García Martínez, *The Dead Sea Scrolls Translated: The Qumran Texts in English* (Leiden: Brill, 1994, 1997), 438.

The framework in which the two-ways section of *Barnabas* is cast, however, is explicitly "apocalyptic," with reference to angels of God and of Satan and with contrast between the present lawless time and the eternal age, and between eternal death and its opposite. This sounds very similar to some passages from the Dead Sea Scrolls, and especially the *Manual of Discipline*. Indeed, the idea that the two types of angels oversee the two ways could easily be associated with the traditions about the fall of the watchers and their harmful relation to humankind (e.g., in the first book of *1 Enoch*; compare Gen. 6:1–4), and with the ideas about the heavenly tablets, from which humans learn what ought to be done.[13] But I have no clear evidence for such associations.

That the nonapocalyptic framework of the *Didache* branch of the two-ways tradition can also be associated with Jewish "practical wisdom" traditions is also clear, when one considers the presentations in such works as Proverbs and Sirach.[14] Can anything be gained by attempting to determine whether the origins of the two-ways form was in an apocalyptic or a nonapocalyptic setting? Perhaps, as long as we keep in mind that both settings have strong and early rootings as well as complex developmental histories. Probably a stronger argument can be presented for the antiquity of pre-apocalyptic "ethical/practical wisdom" (as in Proverbs) than for the apocalyptic context. If we assume that the fairly obvious life/death binary, or even light/darkness (see Prov. 4:18f.), created an organizational format that came to be used in that sort of setting, it is a fairly easy step for emergent apocalyptic to adapt the tradition to its perspectives. This would help explain why the contents of the common two-ways tradition is so devoid of eschatological/apocalyptic language — it was never there in the first place!

On the other hand, it is possible to see apocalyptic contrasts and concerns as the magnet for creating the two-ways form as we know it, and subsequent discomfort with apocalypticism as the reason for the rise of the alternate approach. In this scenario, more attention would be paid to clues that survive in the *Barnabas* two-ways material suggesting apocalyptic connections that may have been deleted by an alternative tradition — for example, *Barn.* 19.10a, "remember the day of judgment night and day" (*Did.* 4.1a, "remember day and night the one who proclaims God's word to you"), or the virtual identity of *Barn.* 4.9b (not located in the two-ways section) and *Did.* 16.2b (in the apocalyptic appendix), which may well be fragments of an older two-ways stream exhorting endurance in the last times.[15]

I have no final wisdom at this point except to repeat the obvious. However these materials originated, or arrived at the forms in which we find them (asso-

---

13. Kraft, "Scripture and Canon in Jewish Apocrypha and Pseudepigrapha," in *Hebrew Bible/Old Testament: The History of Its Interpretation*, vol. 1, *From the Beginnings to the Middle Ages (until 1300)*, ed. Magne Saebo; part 1, "Antiquity" (Göttingen: Vandenhoeck & Ruprecht, 1996), 205f.
14. For specific passages, see Nickelsburg, "Seeking the Origins of the Two Ways Tradition."
15. Discussed in Kraft, *Barnabas and the Didache*, 6–7.

ciated with apocalyptic or not), both types of two-ways traditions have left their impact on early Christian literature, and probably both derive from variations already present in the Jewish roots from which Christianity emerged. More I cannot say on the basis of available evidence.

In his 1999 follow-up, Nickelsburg provides further evidence from Israelite and Jewish texts for the antiquity of the "two-ways construct" (binary polarities) without a clear two-ways literary framework, as well as support for the existence of the framework, both without and with eschatological/apocalyptic elements.[16] He argues that ideas of blessing and punishment for right and wrong deeds at some point became eschatologically charged, with the focus on eternal life and its opposite in death/destruction (108). He also sees strong evidence for a common Jewish instructional tradition that sometimes included reference to "the activity of two powers, i.e., good and evil angels, God and Satan" (108).

So, in retrospect — both short-term and long-term — where are we with respect to the origins and early development of two-ways traditions? George and I (and many others) agree that the concept of binary polarities with reference to human conduct is very old in Israelite and Jewish traditions. We agree that at some point — or points — in pre-Christian times a characteristic format was introduced or adopted in Jewish circles (George calls it the "two-ways catechism") that was used as a device for teaching, exhortation, and so on. We agree that this form of two-ways instruction was sometimes associated with concepts of eschatological rewards and punishments, and even with apocalyptic-type agencies (angelic powers, etc.), but sometimes did not have such connections — and all of this still within pre-Christian Jewish circles, and not limited to the Dead Sea Scrolls.

We do not seem to be in much disagreement (how dull!). Nevertheless, some of the issues that are not yet very clear, to me at least, include:

1. The situation outside of Israelite-Jewish-Christian circles. The Greek tradition of Heracles at the crossroads is well-known, but to what extent do other ancient cultures — especially in the Mediterranean and Near Eastern areas — produce similar "binary" approaches to desirable human conduct? Is it possible to identify similar traditions elsewhere, and to understand them as related or even unrelated to the Israelite/Jewish/Christian developments?[17]

2. What developments can be traced for alternative approaches, other than "binary polarities," to ethical exhortation and instruction in ancient Israel and early Judaism? How do the "two-ways" materials and forms relate

---

16. Nickelsburg, "Seeking the Origins of the Two Ways Tradition," 95f.

17. See Kurt Niederwimmer, *Die Didache* (Göttingen: Vandenhoeck & Ruprecht, 1989), 83ff., for a listing of some apparent Greek parallels, and the summary statement that "the parallels also reach as far as Islamic and even Buddhist tradition." What about Persia? Egypt? Syria?

to more casuistic/relativistic ideas for judging/evaluating conduct? Are different factors at work in the development of ancient law codes?

3. Are applications of "two-ways" standards and approaches affected by any other identifiable variables, such as insider/outsider considerations, or age, or gender,[18] or types of conduct (e.g., "ritual" rather than "ethical"; communal rather than individual)?

4. What considerations are significant, if not persuasive, for determining when and under what conditions transitions or transformations relating to Jewish and/or early Christian two-ways traditions might have taken place? For example, what led to the establishment of (an) instructional framework(s) or to the introduction (or removal) of eschatological ideas?

Of course, it is possible that the "two-ways" approach is ultimately so obvious and commonplace in human experience that it might have arisen spontaneously at various times and places in history. Parallels do not necessarily indicate influences. Nevertheless, there seem to be enough characteristic similarities among some of the sources to suggest some continuities, and while the efforts of past research, including our own, have made significant progress in exploring some of the roots and shoots of these traditions, clearly more remains to be done. Thank you, George Nickelsburg, for helping to open such doors for our successors to enter.

---

18. George's gender-aware statement that "the righteous can see where he or she is going" ("Seeking the Origins of the Two Ways Tradition," 96) set me to thinking whether there is conclusive evidence that women would be directly in view as recipients of two-ways instruction. The condemnation of procuring abortions (e.g., *Barn.* 19.5c and 20.2i = *Did.* 2.2b and 5.2i) might have only male interests in view. Even the non-"two-ways" exhortation in *Barn.* 10.8 that warns against "women who perform the lawless deed with the mouth" apparently is directed to men who are not to associate with such. Whether "Haustafel"-type instructions to wives (e.g., Eph. 5:22ff.) ever are found in the two-ways format is an interesting question.

14

Wisdom Psalms and the Shaping of the Hebrew Psalter

———— ◆ ————

J. Kenneth Kuntz
University of Iowa

In offering this essay on one small yet significant segment of biblical wisdom literature, I voice appreciation for my colleague, George Nickelsburg. During our thirty-year association at the University of Iowa, I have been enriched by many discussions with him on the themes and language of biblical and extrabiblical wisdom texts.

Introduction

Although individual psalms continue to evoke the attention of biblical scholars, in recent years much of their focus has been redirected to the Psalter as a whole. Accordingly, "Hymn Book of the Second Temple" is increasingly falling out of favor as a suitable subtitle for the Psalter. Since the postexilic era witnessed both the final shaping of the Psalter and its use in Jerusalem temple services, the subtitle seems warranted. Nevertheless, given the emergence of the synagogue during this era as the prime locus of communal prayer and scriptural study, "Prayer Book of the Synagogue" is being embraced as a more preferable Psalter subtitle. Whereas he finds both designations instructive, Bernhard Anderson registers his satisfaction with the second insofar as the Psalter opens with a poem reflecting "piety based on the study of the Torah."[1] Moreover, Anthony Ceresko cogently claims that "what we have in the Book of Psalms is exactly that, a *book*, not a collection of hymns."[2] In the hope of establishing a suitable angle of vision on our topic, I shall allude to a personal interaction with a venerable hymnal.

---

1. B. W. Anderson, *Out of the Depths: The Psalms Speak for Us Today* (rev. ed.; Philadelphia: Westminster, 1983), 23; see also his *Understanding the Old Testament* (4th ed.; Englewood Cliffs, N.J.: Prentice-Hall, 1986), 544.

2. A. R. Ceresko, "The Sage in the Psalms," in *The Sage in Israel and the Ancient Near East* (ed. J. G. Gammie and L. G. Perdue; Winona Lake, Ind.: Eisenbrauns, 1990), 227.

A few years ago, while visiting Wesley Chapel in London, I purchased *Hymns and Psalms,* the current hymnal of British Methodists. Its thoughtfully worded preface disclosed that the hymnal committee had operated at a high level of self-awareness. It was poised to assign this hymnal the best of all possible titles. And it took very seriously the task of *structuring* the diverse contents of the hymnal. With modesty it admitted that such structuring "had been modified during the committee's deliberations in the light of debate and criticism." And with pride it transmitted this statement from John Wesley's own preface to his 1780 hymnal: "The hymns are not carelessly jumbled together, but carefully ranged under proper heads, according to the experience of real Christians. So that this book is, in effect, a little body of experimental and practical divinity."[3] Indeed, in our own time, it is hard to imagine the publication of a hymnal that lacked a preface whose deliberate wording promised that order had emphatically triumphed over jumble.

Contemporary Psalms scholarship would assuredly be driven by different guidelines if the final editors of the Hebrew Psalter had also written a thoughtfully worded preface for the edification of their readers, one that transmitted statements from prefaces framed by previous editors. Since they did not, we must astutely resort to the limited means at our disposal in the hope that we might write that preface ourselves. Reflecting the perspective of a growing number of biblical scholars, I would maintain that both explicit and tacit indications of editorial activity show the Hebrew Psalter to be the end product of purposeful organization. Moreover, I share with such scholars a genuine concern that our quest for coherence be purged of any artificial factors (both the ingenious and not-so-ingenious) that might foster a skewed understanding of the text. Here I am constrained to admit that, not infrequently, inference seems to be the main avenue toward knowledge in this area.

Thus, in the name of balanced scholarship, Norman Whybray offers in a recent monograph his correction of what he perceives to be excessive scholarly claims currently entertained about the sequence of the Psalter and the intentions of its final editors.[4] Conceding that deliberately positioned wisdom and Torah psalms effect reinterpretations of adjacent compositions, he denies that such placement signals a concerted attempt by final editors to transform the long-evolving Psalter into a so-called wisdom book. In his case against editorial shaping, Whybray sometimes construes helpful suggestions advanced by those invested in this topic as if they are definitive conclusions. This new approach is still finding its way. Scholars keen about the shaping of the Psalter may not find Whybray's reflections inhibiting, but some might be swayed to approach this crucial topic with greater caution. Discussions about presumed macrostructures and microstructures in the

---

3. R. G. Jones, ed., *Hymns and Psalms* (London: Methodist Publishing House, 1983), x.
4. Norman Whybray, *Reading the Psalms as a Book* (JSOTSup 222; Sheffield: Sheffield Academic Press, 1996).

Psalter must be mounted in a disciplined manner. Even so, their legitimacy and promise cannot be gainsaid.

The issue I address is absent from an article written some years ago in which I reflected on the rhetorical, thematic, and formal dimensions of biblical Israel's wisdom psalms.[5] Yet today I am convinced that the placement of these psalms in the Hebrew Psalter is not the outcome of simple happenstance. Before setting forth my understanding of this matter, it seems fitting that I offer a brief statement of orientation to psalmic wisdom in biblical Israel. It will take account of three closely related concerns: the disputed nature of wisdom psalms as a form-critical category; major approaches and insights in twentieth-century scholarship bearing on our topic; and the identification of those canonical compositions which present themselves as our most promising wisdom psalm candidates.

Psalmic Wisdom in Biblical Israel

Several scholars have recognized that distinctive themes and language emanating from wisdom schools of biblical Israel have found their way into the Hebrew Psalter. Admittedly, the evidence has been variously interpreted. Based on a cultic perception of the Psalter in which he was heavily invested, Ivan Engnell held that "the Book of Psalms does not contain any 'wisdom psalms' at all."[6] In his essay on Psalm 73, J. Luyten avers that "a genre 'wisdom psalm' as such cannot be reconstructed."[7] And in his 1986 presidential address to the Society of Biblical Literature, James L. Mays claimed that "the classification 'wisdom psalms' is itself ambiguous."[8]

Nevertheless, I prefer to cast my lot with such scholars as Hermann Gunkel, Sigmund Mowinckel, Roland Murphy, and Leo Perdue, who embrace wisdom psalms as a viable, if not trouble-free, form-critical category. Gunkel affirms the existence of *Weisheitsdichtung* in the Psalter which he found yielding form-critical and thematic elements common to both biblical and extrabiblical sapiential texts.[9] He discerns in Psalms 127 and 133 the linking of pithy proverbs, and he regards Psalms 1, 37, 49, 73, 112, and 128 as more fully developed wisdom poems. Even

---

5. J. K. Kuntz, "The Canonical Wisdom Psalms of Ancient Israel: Their Rhetorical, Thematic, and Formal Dimensions," in *Rhetorical Criticism: Essays in Honor of James Muilenburg* (ed. J. J. Jackson and M. Kessler; Pittsburgh: Pickwick Press, 1974), 186–222.

6. Ivan Engnell, *A Rigid Scrutiny: Critical Essays on the Old Testament* (trans. J. T. Willis; Nashville: Vanderbilt University Press, 1969), 99.

7. J. Luyten, "Psalm 73 and Wisdom," in *La Sagesse de l'Ancien Testament* (ed. M. Gilbert; BETL 51; Louvain: Louvain University Press, 1979), 59, 63.

8. J. L. Mays, "The Place of the Torah-Psalms in the Psalter," *JBL* 106 (1987): 3.

9. Hermann Gunkel, *Einleitung in die Psalmen: Die Gattungen der religiösen Lyrik Israels* (Göttingen: Vandenhoeck & Ruprecht, 1933), 381–97; see also the recent English translation, *Introduction to Psalms: The Genres of the Religious Lyric of Israel* (trans. J. D. Nogalski; Macon, Ga.: Mercer University Press, 1998), 293–305.

so, Gunkel did not find wisdom psalms manifesting a distinctive *form* of their own. Also, he is not explicit about the number of psalms to be assigned to the *Weisheitsdichtung* category. Yet his acceptance of the presence of sapiential discourse and the existence of wisdom themes as important criteria for isolating wisdom psalms has remained a compelling methodological consideration.

Though Mowinckel chooses not to employ the designation "wisdom psalm" in his treatment of what he calls "learned psalmography," he does identify a corpus of psalms which he assesses as noncultic in origin and intention.[10] Here he adopts Gunkel's methodology of focusing on sapiential forms and themes. The ten psalms in question (1, 34, 37, 49, 78, 105, 106, 111, 112, and 127) are interpreted as private compositions that serve two fundamental purposes: praise of the deity and instruction of the young. Mowinckel finds the noncultic tenor of these compositions troublesome. Accordingly, he contends that since these sapiential psalms "had no more connection with the cultic life, the real 'Sitz im Leben' of the psalm poetry, they have failed to realize what a psalm really is."[11] Mowinckel's suggestions regarding the manner whereby learned psalmography was utilized in the context of school instruction that had no linkage with official acts of worship are effectively buttressed by H. L. Jansen, whose attention was more directed to intertestamental sapiential poems than to their biblical counterparts.[12]

In a perceptive form-critical essay, Roland Murphy argues that a uniformity of style and structure along with a recurrence of motifs and life-setting make it "feasible to speak of 'wisdom psalms' as a literary form parallel to the other psalm types."[13] He notes that several canonical psalms exhibit certain stylistic peculiarities that are indigenous to biblical wisdom literature. These include the *'ašrê* formula, the numerical saying, the "better" saying, the address of teacher to "son," the alphabetic acrostic, the simple comparison, and the admonition. Murphy also uncovers conventional wisdom motifs in various psalms. These include the contrast between wicked and righteous, the two ways, fixation on the problem of retribution, practical advice about everyday human behavior, and the fear of Yahweh. Identifying the *milieu sapientiel* as the appropriate background (but not exact *Sitz im Leben*), Murphy offers a restricted list of seven canonical wisdom psalms: 1, 32, 34, 37, 49, 112, and 128. In his monograph on biblical wisdom, *The Tree of Life*, Murphy concludes with characteristically sound counsel: "The reader is invited to form his or her own criteria for wisdom, and challenge the number

---

10. Sigmund Mowinckel, "Psalms and Wisdom," in *Wisdom in Israel and in the Ancient Near East* (ed. M. Noth and D. W. Thomas; VTSup 3; Leiden: Brill, 1960), 205–24; and idem, *The Psalms in Israel's Worship* (trans. D. R. Ap-Thomas; Oxford: Blackwell, 1962), 2.104–25.

11. Sigmund Mowinckel, "Traditionalism and Personality in the Psalms," *HUCA* 23/1 (1950–51): 226.

12. H. L. Jansen, *Die spätjüdische Psalmendichtung: Ihr Entstehungskreis und ihr "Sitz im Leben"* (Oslo: Norskevidenskaps-akademi, 1937).

13. R. E. Murphy, "A Consideration of the Classification, 'Wisdom Psalms'" in *Congress Volume, Bonn 1962* (VTSup 9; Leiden: Brill, 1963), 167.

of psalms that have been classified as 'wisdom.'"[14] Indeed, I have expanded the listing by two compositions (Psalms 127 and 133), and others have pressed for the inclusion of Psalms 73 and 119.

In my 1974 essay (see note 5) I summarized main advances in previous wisdom psalm research, named the rhetorical question as another stylistic feature of psalmic wisdom, and submitted that a focus on sapiential vocabulary enhances our understanding of wisdom psalms, but disappoints as a definitive criterion for identifying those compositions. Moreover, on the basis of their literary structure, I posited three subtypes of wisdom psalms: sentence, acrostic, and integrative. Shortly thereafter Leo Perdue's study *Wisdom and Cult* was published.[15] In his provocative chapter entitled "Didactic Poems and Wisdom Psalms," he inspects eleven texts which he embraces as "long didactic poems" attesting to the activity of both preexilic and postexilic Israelite sages. Discerning that one simple wisdom form plays a central role in each of these compositions, Perdue organizes them under three subcategories. Thus Psalms 1, 19B, 34, 37, 73, 112, and 127 are identified as "Proverb Poems," Psalms 32 and 119 as "'*Ashrê* Poems," and Psalms 19A and 49 as "Riddle Poems."

To say that some of these specimens fail to qualify as "long" poems is to voice an obviously minor objection. Of far greater import, sometimes Perdue appears rather arbitrary as he sets about isolating the central proverb, which yields the thesis of those poems belonging to the first subcategory. That is particularly the case with Ps. 34:23, where what I perceive as an appended element located outside the alphabetic acrostic framework is for Perdue the central proverb. (Throughout this essay I am following the Hebrew rather than the English versification.) Moreover, in light of Perdue's premise that a wisdom psalm worthy of the name must yield clues that it was originally "written by a sage for cultic service,"[16] it is understandable that "didactic poem" rather than "wisdom psalm" is often his preferred designation. Comparing Perdue's canon to Murphy's and my own, he upholds neither Murphy's inclusion of Psalm 128 nor mine of Psalm 133, and he introduces Psalms 19A, 19B, 73, and 119 as four additional didactic specimens.

On balance, psalmic wisdom is not a biblical topic that can be celebrated for its capacity to attract compelling scholarly consensus. Though it is reasonable to assume that biblical and other sages of the ancient Near East were familiar with and fashioned psalmic texts, we cannot as yet rest secure in our conjectures about where such literary activity transpired and what fundamental purposes it served. Perhaps some wisdom psalms originated in preexilic wisdom schools that were foremost dedicated to the proper training of youth. Perhaps others

---

14. R. E. Murphy, *The Tree of Life: An Exploration of Biblical Wisdom Literature* (Anchor Bible Reference Library; New York: Doubleday, 1990), 104.

15. L. G. Perdue, *Wisdom and Cult: A Critical Analysis of the Views of Cult in the Wisdom Literatures of Israel and the Ancient Near East* (SBLDS 30; Missoula, Mont.: Scholars Press, 1977), 261–343.

16. Ibid., 268.

originated in a postexilic temple context where the wise had a hand in the framing of cultic liturgies and in the gradual redaction of scripture itself. On the one hand, we may be drawn to Murphy's judgment that Luyten's denial of a wisdom psalm genre is "somewhat drastic."[17] On the other hand, we must honestly admit that, whereas it would be unfair to charge that the scholarship in question lies in a state of disarray, we have yet to meet any widespread agreement about a specific, well-defined corpus of canonical wisdom psalms. Recently Whybray lamented the lack of progress in this endeavor.[18] The task of establishing the exact parameters of psalmic wisdom is indeed difficult, for sages, prophets, and priests not only share some of the same formal elements of language, but they also focus on common concerns. Presumably, this latter consideration undergirds Murphy's cogent warning that "preoccupation with the problem of retribution does not define a wisdom psalm."[19]

As I proceed to focus more intently on various issues pertaining to the placement of wisdom psalms in the present form of the canonical Psalter, I shall affirm my earlier listing of nine candidates (Psalms 1, 32, 34, 37, 49, 112, 127, 128, and 133) and append to it one other, Psalm 73. Admittedly, the opening and closing cola of Psalm 73 lead one to infer that it is a thanksgiving song, and with some justification H.-J. Kraus states that "the identification of Psalm 73 as a 'didactic poem' obviously does not suffice."[20] Even so, the wisdom dimensions of this poem are of sufficient magnitude to warrant its inclusion here.[21] Then, on the assumption that the Psalter may once have concluded with Psalm 119, a composition whose wisdom status has been both affirmed and denied, we must venture some judgment about its relevance for the topic at hand.

Wisdom Psalms as a Component in the Final Hebrew Psalter

Taken in their totality, the ten compositions that I have isolated as wisdom psalms may be characterized in terms of their placement, superscriptions, and structure. Hosting a small number of poems, Book IV (Psalms 90–106) yields no wisdom psalm, although Psalms 92 and 94 contain easily recognized wisdom elements (92:7–8, 13–15; 94:8–11, 12–15). Book II (Psalms 42–72) and Book III (Psalms

---

17. Murphy, *The Tree of Life*, 103.

18. R. N. Whybray, "The Wisdom Psalms," in *Wisdom in Ancient Israel: Essays in Honour of J. A. Emerton* (ed. John Day, R. P. Gordon, and H. G. M. Williamson; New York: Cambridge University Press, 1995), 153.

19. Murphy, "A Consideration of the Classification, 'Wisdom Psalms,'" 164.

20. H-J. Kraus, *Psalms 60–150: A Commentary* (trans. H. C. Oswald; Minneapolis: Augsburg, 1989), 85.

21. In my essay, "The Canonical Wisdom Psalms of Ancient Israel," 207, I held that Psalm 73 "is not entirely void in sapiential nuance." Today that strikes me as a parade example of understatement.

73–89) each hosts one wisdom psalm offering the designation *mizmôr* ("psalm")
in its superscription. Psalm 49 is associated with the sons of Korah and Psalm 73
with Asaph.

To be sure, in Book I (Psalms 1–41) and Book V (Psalms 107–50) we encounter
substantial poetic collections. Each yields four wisdom psalms. It is noteworthy
that in both cases, three of the four are closely clustered (Psalms 32, 34, and 37, all
claimed as Davidic, in Book I; Psalms 127, 128, and 133, each a "song of ascents"
[*šîr hamma'ălôt*], in Book V). The other two wisdom compositions in question are
Psalm 1, which lacks a superscription, and Psalm 112, which is prefaced with the
words *hallĕlû yâ* ("Praise Yah!"). One Davidic wisdom psalm in Book I (Psalm 32)
is labeled a *maśkîl*, presumably to announce its artistic and didactic potential, and
another (Psalm 34) is one of the thirteen canonical psalms whose superscription
alludes to a specific historical incident directly bearing on David's personal life.
Of the four wisdom psalms in Book V, one (Psalm 133) names David in its superscription, another (Psalm 127) names Solomon, and two (Psalms 112 and 128)
mention no author. Moreover, several of the poems in Book I incorporate sapiential themes even if they cannot be perceived form-critically as wisdom psalms
(Pss. 25:8–10, 12–14; 31:24–25; 39:5–7; 40:5; 41:2). Then, given its conspicuous
alphabetic acrostic format and forthright use of wisdom vocabulary, Psalm 119 in
Book V makes some contribution to learned psalmography. Finally, despite their
diverse manner of pursuing the course, three widely accepted wisdom poems —
Psalms 34 and 37 in Book I and Psalm 112 in Book V — are alphabetic acrostics.

Wisdom Psalms in Book I

Book I of the Psalter is no stranger to wisdom. Indeed, the presence of four
readily identifiable wisdom psalms (1, 32, 34, and 37), the high incidence of
wisdom motifs in five other psalms (25, 31, 39, 40, and 41), and use of the
'ašrê formula as the opening component in Psalms 1 and 41, which serve as
its initial and terminating poems, all lead Murphy to infer that Book I "was
put together under particular influence of wisdom writers, from beginning to
end."[22] This astute assessment places Murphy in company with Mowinckel, who
submits that "while the earlier small collections [of psalms] came into existence
among the singers, the Psalter as a whole, and probably even the Davidic psalms
group I (Psalms 3–41), were collected by the learned, 'the scribes,' 'the wise.'"[23]
He claims that these scholar-sages of postexilic Israel created the larger Psalter
out of earlier collections of cultic psalms, to which they added specimens from
their own sapiential poetry. Such redactors closely identified wisdom with the
Torah and stipulated that the wise person is one whose "delight is in the law

---

22. Murphy, "A Consideration of the Classification, 'Wisdom Psalms,'" 162.
23. Mowinckel, *Psalms in Israel's Worship*, 2.204.

of Yahweh" (Ps. 1:2). Thus Joseph Reindl insists that the editing of the Psalter presupposes a thorough knowledge of the scriptures and a strong commitment to Torah piety, much in the spirit of Ben Sira's portrait of the ideal scholar and teacher (Sir. 39:1–11).[24] That the wisdom editors of the Hebrew Psalter and the poets who produced the wisdom psalms had the highest regard for Torah is clearly evident in Psalm 1, which presents itself as a deliberate preamble to all that follows in the Psalter. As noted by Perdue, its service to the Psalter parallels Prov. 1:1–7, which establishes the hermeneutical context for all of Proverbs.[25] This didactic poem, whose primary setting is not cultic but literary, commences with a crucial *'ašrê* formula (vv. 1–2). In Walther Zimmerli's opinion, such discourse stands midway between *Aussagewort* (assertion) and *Mahnwort* (admonition), two extensively employed modes of wisdom speech.[26] Without assuming the guise of direct address, the *'ašrê* formula functions as a most effective summons by declaring who, in fact, is fortunate. In this beatitude, it is the righteous individual (*ṣaddîq*), the one who is vigilant both in keeping distant from sinners and scoffers and in maintaining unbroken contact with the revelation of Yahweh's will. The two parabolic sayings (vv. 3–4) and the antithetical proverb with which the psalm comes to rest (v. 6) deftly contrast two conflicting ways of life. Clearly, the message of Psalm 1 is congenial with the sage's aphorism in Prov. 3:33, "The curse of Yahweh is on the house of the wicked, / but he blesses the abode of the righteous."

The *'ašrê* formula effectively sets the tone of Psalm 1. This means that the psalm does not turn merely on two opposing modes of human conduct. Rather, as Patrick Miller has insightfully remarked, here is "a celebration of a life that takes real pleasure in living according to God's will, that finds itself thus under the care and guidance of God and so is the object of true envy on the part of all who look upon it."[27] This wisdom psalm tenaciously asserts that the "way of the righteous," which is firmly grounded in the Torah of Yahweh, is truly the preferred way. And by contrasting these two lifestyles as sharply as possible, Psalm 1 equips the reader to receive the rest of the Psalter. This functional understanding of the Psalter's initial entry is forcefully articulated by Walter Brueggemann, who submits that as Psalm 1 summons the reader to a life centered on Yahweh's will, it "intends that all the Psalms should be read through the prism of torah-obedience."[28] Indeed, in the light of its strategic location at the head of the Psalter, Psalm 1 implies that this way will be spelled out at length in the poems that follow.

---

24. Joseph Reindl, "Weisheitliche Bearbeitung von Psalmen: Ein Beitrag zum Verständnis der Sammlung des Psalters," in *Congress Volume: Vienna 1980* (ed. J. A. Emerton; VTSup 32; Leiden: Brill, 1981), 340f.

25. Perdue, *Wisdom and Cult*, 330, n. 39.

26. Walther Zimmerli, "Zur Struktur der alttestamentlichen Weisheit," ZAW 51 (1933): 185.

27. P. D. Miller, Jr., *Interpreting the Psalms* (Philadelphia: Fortress, 1986), 82.

28. Walter Brueggemann, "Bounded by Obedience and Praise: The Psalms as Canon," *JSOT* 50 (1991): 64.

One such poem, of course, is its immediate neighbor, Psalm 2, a royal psalm, which terminates with the colon, "Happy are all who take refuge in him [Yahweh]" (2:12). Forming an artful inclusion with the *'ašrê* formula at the head of Psalm 1, the *'asrê* formula in Psalm 2 joins forces with other elements in the poem to dissuade the reader from perceiving Psalms 1 and 2 simply as disparate poems. Although W. H. Brownlee's notion that these two psalms together form a coronation liturgy is not compelling,[29] they hold several things in common. Both lack a superscription or attribution of authorship. They are linked by the catchword *hgh*, which is ordinarily rendered "meditate" in 1:2 and "plot" in 2:1. And as they reflect on contrasting righteous and unrighteous behavior, both use the verb *'bd* ("to perish") in forecasting the doom that awaits those who work at cross-purposes with the deity (1:6; 2:12). Perceiving Psalms 1 and 2 as a paired preface to the Psalter, Clinton McCann holds that once "Psalm 1 orients the reader to receive what follows as instruction, Psalm 2 introduces the essential content which the Psalter intends to teach — that the Lord reigns!"[30] Of course, the case for an in-tandem reading of Psalms 1 and 2 should not be overpressed. The individual integrity of these poems also merits notice. The international vistas of Psalm 2 far outdistance the range of Psalm 1 with its focus on the individual. Also, as John Willis aptly points out, Psalm 2 is "bound to time and circumstance" in ways that Psalm 1 is not.[31] Nevertheless, these introductory poems impart a uniform message about appropriate human conduct. Fully appreciating the impact of their joint witness, Joseph Brennan states:

> At the very beginning of the Psalter, the protagonists are introduced and the reader is invited to choose sides. On the one hand are "the just," whose activities are shaped by Yahweh's Torah, whose way is known to him, who are led by his anointed king, and whose happy lot is proclaimed in 1:1 and 2:12. On the other hand are "the wicked," "the sinners," and "the scorners," who, like the just, will appear under a variety of names throughout the rest of the book.[32]

Even so, if Psalm 2 joins Psalm 1 in properly introducing the entire Psalter, its function is mainly that of reinforcing what is already achieved by "timeless and didactic" Psalm 1.[33]

To summarize: the redactional position of Psalm 1 effectively reflects the belief of scholar-sages in postexilic Israel that if diligent meditation on Torah can bring blessings on Yahweh's people, it will be no less so with Israel's faithful reading of

---

29. W. H. Brownlee, "Psalms 1–2 as a Coronation Liturgy," *Biblica* 52 (1971): 321–36.

30. J. C. McCann, Jr., "The Psalms as Instruction," *Interpretation* 46 (1992): 123.

31. J. T. Willis, "Psalm 1 — An Entity," *ZAW* 91 (1979): 396.

32. J. P. Brennan, "Psalms 1–8: Some Hidden Harmonies," *BTB* 10 (1980): 25.

33. In agreement with G. H. Wilson, *The Editing of the Hebrew Psalter* (SBLDS 76; Chico, Calif.: Scholars Press, 1985), 206.

those sacred writings (Psalms 2–150) that follow Psalm 1. As Brevard Childs has persuasively argued, the sacred community is charged to study the psalms "not merely to find an illustration of how godly men prayed to God in the past, but to learn the 'way of righteousness' which comes from obeying the divine law and is now communicated through the prayers of Israel."[34] Unique in its lead position, and fervent in its support of Torah piety, the first of the canonical wisdom psalms forthrightly invites its readers to the task of theological reflection on the Psalter *as sacred literature*, which is central to Israelite well-being.

In the last quarter of Book I we meet three closely clustered wisdom poems: Psalms 32, 34, and 37. Since Book I almost exclusively hosts psalms of the individual, it is fitting that there be some contributions from Israelite sages, who had a proclivity for imparting their wisdom to individual persons. And since the most prominent *Gattung* in Book I is that of the individual lament, which reflects adverse life situations that require the sufferer to cope and that often yield unexpected opportunities for increasing in wisdom as well as in faith, it is all the more fitting that wisdom pitches her tent in this portion of the Hebrew Psalter.

As the first of the poems in question, Psalm 32 has as its immediate predecessor an individual lament rich in expressions of complaint, trust, and thanksgiving. At the end of Psalm 31, the petitioner addresses a group, no doubt an audience of the cultic community, to whom he bears witness. His testimony in vv. 24–25 has the ring of sapiential discourse. It reads in part, "Love Yahweh, all you his saints; / Yahweh preserves the faithful, / but pays back in full the one who acts arrogantly." Addressing this word to other human beings who may benefit from his testimony, the petitioner briefly reflects on the retribution motif in the manner of an Israelite sage. This wisdom element, with which Psalm 31 concludes, leads immediately to Psalm 32, a didactic piece (*maśkîl*) which appears to reflect a cultic setting, be it temple or synagogue.

In structure, Psalm 32 consists of a thankful testimony addressed to Yahweh (vv. 3–7), which is framed by obvious wisdom expressions. It is prefaced by two extensive *'ašrê* formulae celebrating the fortunate condition of the one who is forgiven (vv. 1–2). This pair of beatitudes might readily induce the reader to recall two others that are prominent at the outset of the Psalter (1:1; 2:12). The testimony is followed by strikingly varied discourse anchored in human experience. This includes a first-person promise of the sage that he will "instruct," "teach," and "counsel" his listeners (v. 8), a second-person admonition denouncing stubbornness which uses a vivid simile about "a senseless horse or mule" (v. 9), and a third-person antithetical saying (v. 10) declaring that "many are the torments of the wicked, / but steadfast love surrounds the one who trusts in Yahweh." It should be noted that Psalm 32 recalls the beginning of the Psalter in yet another way. Since the *'ašrê* formulae at the head of Psalm 32 interpret happiness as

---

34. B. S. Childs, *Introduction to the Old Testament as Scripture* (Philadelphia: Fortress, 1979), 514.

forgiveness, this helps to ensure that Psalm 1 will be read accurately. Psalm 32 instructs that the righteousness on which Psalm 1 reflects is characteristic not of sinless persons, but of forgiven persons now poised to take Yahweh's instructions seriously.

Psalm 32 closes with parallel vocatives inviting the "righteous" (*ṣaddîqîm*) and the "upright in heart" (*yišrê lēb*) to exult in Yahweh. Lacking a superscription (rare in Book I), Psalm 33 immediately opens with similar phraseology that reminds Gerald Wilson of "the Mesopotamian practice of providing successive tablets in a series with 'tag-lines' in the colophon which consisted of the incipit (opening line) of the next tablet in sequence."[35] The firm sequential relation resulting from the close verbal linkages of 32:11 and 33:1 is buttressed by the fact that the truth of the sage's statement in 32:10, namely, that "steadfast love surrounds the one who trusts in Yahweh," is reaffirmed in much of the hymnic discourse in 33:18–22.

That unit leads at once to another wisdom composition, Psalm 34, which resembles its predecessors in hosting an *'ašrê* formula, but deviates from them by placing it well into the body of its discourse (v. 9b, "happy is the man who takes refuge in him! [Yahweh]"). Like its immediate antecedent, Psalm 34 is a twenty-two-line poem, but it advances along its own course as an alphabetic acrostic. Following the pattern of Psalm 25, an individual lament containing two wisdom elements (vv. 8–10, 12–14), Psalm 34 lacks a *waw* line, and at its closure appends a *pe* line after *taw*.[36] This composition is the only canonical wisdom psalm to yield a superscription which recalls a concrete event affecting David's own pilgrimage as a struggling human being (here David is said to feign madness before Abimelech, who is confused with Achish of Gath [see 1 Sam. 21:12–15]). Psalm 34 is therefore lifted from any original cultic setting in order to avail itself for the edification of the reader who must cope with life's challenges. In the act of testimony, the psalmist says of himself, "This poor man called and Yahweh heard, / and from all his troubles he saved him" (v. 7). In the light of that disclosure, the superscription projects *backward* in recollection of David's plight and *forward* to the reader, who brings his or her own needs to the text. With its endorsement of prayerful devotion giving evidence of the proper fear of Yahweh (v. 10), its blend of realism and hope ("many may be the hardships of the righteous, / but from them all Yahweh delivers him," v. 20), and counsel about everyday attitudes and actions ("turn aside from evil, and do good; / seek peace, and pursue it," v. 15), this psalm is a classic manifestation of wisdom piety.

Above all, by virtue of its beatitude in v. 9b and its imperative, "Fear Yah-

---

35. Wilson, *The Editing of the Hebrew Psalter*, 175.

36. In *Studies in Israelite Poetry and Wisdom* ([CBQMS 1; Washington, D.C.: Catholic Biblical Association of America, 1971], 74), P. W. Skehan observes that as the final consonant in the acrostic, *pe* combines with *'alep* and *lamed* (the first and middle consonants of the Hebrew alphabet) to form *'lp*, thereby recalling the first consonant of the alphabet. Here the sage's preoccupation with order is readily apparent.

weh," which immediately follows (v. 10a), this wisdom psalm commends to the reader a reverential attitude toward the deity that fully meshes with the message projected by Psalms 1–2, which open the Psalter. In both contexts, taking refuge (*ḥsh*) in Yahweh (2:12c; 34:9b) and remaining receptive to his beneficent Torah for humanity (1:2; 34:9a) are persuasively advanced as the benchmarks of wisdom piety.

As the remaining wisdom poem in Book I, Psalm 37 joins Psalm 34 in presenting itself as an alphabetic acrostic, but it deviates from that composition in three respects: (1) it contains a *waw* component and appends no additional *pe* component; (2) it devotes a pair of lines to each Hebrew consonant, making it the longest of the canonical wisdom psalms; and (3) it lacks both a thought-sequence and a discernible variation in theme and mode of wisdom discourse that might yield helpful clues about strophic alignment.[37] Two individual laments (Psalms 35 and 36) separate Psalm 37 from its wisdom psalm antecedent (Psalm 34). Although the basis for its placement here is not readily knowable, two factors merit mention. First, complaint, hymnic, and even sapiential discourse all find their way into Psalm 36. Focusing on the behavior of the wicked, the opening strophe in Psalm 36 (vv. 2–5) has the ring of wisdom speech although it fails to qualify as a readily identifiable wisdom element. Second, as its lines unfold along an alphabetic axis of twenty-two consonants, Psalm 37 is immediately followed by an individual lament of twenty-two lines. As a poem that teems with positive and negative admonitions, Psalm 37 is replete with instruction that makes it an impressive specimen of wisdom poetry.

Despite its loose structure, Psalm 37 forcefully imparts its composer's stand on the traditional doctrine of retribution. On the one hand, the poet is quite mindful that the wicked regularly "prosper in their way" (v. 7) and that justice is slowly realized. On the other, he confidently declares that the good fortune of evildoers is insubstantial and fleeting (vv. 35–36). He anticipates that, ultimately in this life, Yahweh rewards and punishes. Once more, a wisdom psalm addresses that which is central to the Psalter's initial entry. Whereas Psalm 1 trenchantly exposes the polarity between the "righteous" (*ṣaddîq*) and the "wicked" (*rāšāʿ*) and succinctly announces their contrasting fates, Psalm 37 tarries with that polarity. Given the poet's frequent enlistment of the same two nouns in his protracted reflections, the contrast is appreciably intensified. Moreover, if Psalm 37 confronts the inequities of this life with greater realism than does Psalm 1, the discourse of Psalm 37 truly reinforces its antecedent. It is not improbable that as Book I of the Psalter was being drawn together, its editors were saying among themselves, "Let Psalm 37 be read through the prism of Psalm 1."

---

37. By contrast, the strophic structure of Psalm 34 can be discerned with relative ease (hymnic declaration, vv. 2–4; thankful testimony and ensuing instruction, vv. 5–11; instruction via sapiential *admonitions*, vv. 12–15; instruction via sapiential *sayings*, vv. 16–22; appended element, v. 23). However, a strophic analysis of Psalm 37 is attempted by Perdue, *Wisdom and Cult*, 280–83.

Finally, the three psalms with which Book I concludes all contain a brief wisdom element (39:5–7; 40:5; 41:2), and the 'ašrê formula is attested in the last two. Surely ample evidence is at hand to support our thesis that as they sought to honor their commitment to wisdom piety, the scholar-sages of postexilic Israel exerted a significant impact on the shaping of the Hebrew Psalter's first book.

Wisdom Psalms in Books II and III

Only in Book V does wisdom psalmody resurface as a dominant element in the Psalter. Nevertheless, in Psalm 49 of Book II and Psalm 73 of Book III we have two further specimens of wisdom poetry. Both deal with the thorny issue of theodicy, that is, the apparent silence of God to the hell of human suffering. This puts them in league with their most immediate wisdom psalm predecessor, Psalm 37, whose poet also ruminated about the ways of divine justice.

What can be surmised about the immediate context of Psalm 49? Book II (Psalms 42–72) opens with a series of Korahite psalms of which this is the last. A substantial Davidic collection of psalms opens with Psalm 51, and four more Korahite poems begin with Psalm 84 in Book III. When we consider the most proximate neighbors of Psalm 49 in form-critical categories, we discover a remarkable variety. Psalm 47 is an enthronement hymn, Psalm 48 a song of Zion, Psalm 50 a covenant renewal liturgy, and Psalm 51 an individual lament. Of course, the two compositions which precede Psalm 49 bear an attribution to the sons of Korah. The superscriptions in the two which follow name Asaph and David, respectively, as their authors. Wilson has argued with reference to Psalms 47–51 that ancient editors sometimes use so-called genre designations in order to "bind together, to 'soften' transition between groups of psalms."[38] In this instance, each of the five poems in question yields a superscription containing the noun *mizmôr* ("psalm"). In the center of this corpus stands our wisdom psalm, which is more than a little preoccupied with the idea of retribution.

A helpful insight about the placement of Psalm 49 is offered by McCann. Having mounted a strong case that Psalms 46–48 constitute "a coherent sequence" which resolutely proclaims the deity's *universal* sovereignty, McCann calls attention to the vocative, "all you peoples" (v. 2a), in the first member of the opening bicolon of Psalm 49.[39] Though he is silent on the matter, that vocative is enhanced by another, "all inhabitants of the world" (v. 2b), in its second member. Inviting *all people* to acquire wisdom (v. 4), and, more specifically, to avail themselves of the knowledge which he has acquired from having pondered life's inequities, the psalmist forecasts the demise of the rich and powerful, who vaunt their own

38. Wilson, *The Editing of the Hebrew Psalter*, 163.
39. J. C. McCann, Jr., "The Book of Psalms: Introduction, Commentary, and Reflections," in *The New Interpreter's Bible* (ed. L. E. Keck; Nashville: Abingdon, 1996), 4.876.

resources and threaten the well-being of others. By anchoring this poem in his conviction that human redemption lies in God alone, who rules over all, the lesson of this wisdom poet accords well with the message projected by the poetry of Psalms 46–48 to which it has been affixed.

Admittedly, the wisdom status of Psalm 73 is more tenuous than that of Psalm 49. Nevertheless, the sapiential vocabulary that Psalm 73 employs, its intense concern about the problem of theodicy, and its affinities to the Book of Job, as these have been thoughtfully delineated by Luyten, demand that it be considered in this essay.[40] In addition to standing at the head of the main body of the Asaphite psalms (73–83), Psalm 73 also has the distinct honor of introducing Book III of the Hebrew Psalter. It follows on the heels of the editorial colophon with which Book II terminates: "Finished are the prayers of David, the son of Jesse" (Ps. 72:20).[41] Whereas most of the Psalter's communal laments are centered in Book III (Psalms 74, 79, 80, 83, and 85), Psalm 73 voices the complaint of the individual who wonders how he can reconcile his belief in God's justice with apparent inequities in God's government of the world. Nevertheless, the problem of theodicy that so fully engages the individual in Psalm 73 invades the opening cola of Psalm 74, the communal lament which immediately follows. In no way is the juxtaposition of Psalms 73 and 74 inept.

It is indeed noteworthy that Books I and III both commence with sapiential discourse which unmasks the ways of the wicked. The exuberant opening statement of the poet in Psalm 73, "Truly God is good to the upright, / to those whose heart is pure," freely endorses the orthodoxy of Psalm 1 with its confident assurance that the righteous experience blessing and the wicked disaster.[42] Yet as Psalm 73 unfolds, the inadequacy of this *schwarz-weiss Technik* of doing theology is thoroughly exposed. As it takes the floor, critical wisdom calls into serious question the fundamental presupposition of Psalm 1. Very early in Psalm 73 the poet admits to his doubt: "my feet almost stumbled" (v. 2). That doubt is triggered by the prosperity of the wicked, whose arrogant and oppressive activity is described at length (vv. 4–12). In contrast to the wicked, who are "not afflicted" (v. 5), the psalmist is "constantly afflicted" (v. 14). Nevertheless, Psalm 73, like its successor, Psalm 74, does not surrender the faith, for new insight is acquired which centers on God's assuring nearness (73:23, 28). Thus, in both its negative and positive articulations, Psalm 73 speaks in a more penetrating way about the realities under discussion in Psalm 1. In so doing, it does not end up masking a fundamental piety that occupies the center of psalmic wisdom. Rather, as it ably

---

40. Luyten, "Psalm 73 and Wisdom," 71–80.

41. See Walter Brueggemann and P. D. Miller, "Psalm 73 as a Canonical Marker," *JSOT* 72 (1996): 50, who hold that as Psalm 73 positions itself at the head of Book III, it "appears to stand in a curious and surely intentional relation to Psalm 72."

42. Here we follow the widespread practice of emending the MT from reading "to Israel" to reading "to the upright," which entails only the deletion of an *'alep* and modest repointing.

reports the poet's change of perspective on life about him, Psalm 73 moves toward solace and solution in its articulation that what is truly good is the experience of divine presence.

Brueggemann makes a compelling case that Psalm 73 initiates a new phase in the Psalter: "It does so by reiterating the theological assumption of Psalm 1, but then it moves abruptly against that assumption in its own argument, only to arrive at an affirmative theological conclusion which would evoke and permit praise."[43] As the reader encounters Psalm 73 at very nearly the midpoint within the completed collection of canonical psalms, a glance backward seems highly appropriate, not only in terms of what is articulated in Psalm 1, but also in subsequent psalms as they reflect on the weal and woe of human existence and celebrate God's assuring presence. At the same time, Psalm 73 invites the reader to move forward in the Psalter. This wisdom poem may well constitute the lens through which the sages intended that the remainder of Psalter be read. If we are correct in our assumption that the psalms in the Psalter are the product of purposeful arrangement, this may not be too great a claim to make.

Wisdom Psalms in Book V

How, then, are we to interpret the placement of the four wisdom psalms of Book V (Psalms 107–50)? The first of these compositions, Psalm 112, stands early in the collection; two others, Psalms 127 and 128, appear consecutively at approximately the midpoint; and after an interval of four psalms, the last specimen, Psalm 133, finds its place.

Appearing second among three consecutive Hallelujah psalms, Psalm 112, like its immediate predecessor, is a tightly framed acrostic poem. It is so structured that the initial consonants of its twenty-two cola range flawlessly through the entirety of the Hebrew alphabet. Details about the extensive common terminology that Psalms 111 and 112 employ need not detain us here.[44] Nevertheless, two especially noteworthy unifying factors invite mention. First, at a late juncture in Psalm 111, namely, the *reš* colon (v. 10a), we read, "the beginning [*rē'šît*] of wisdom is the fear of Yahweh," and at its first opportunity, in its *'alep* colon (v. 1b), Psalm 112 declares by means of an *'ašrê* formula, "Happy is the man who fears Yahweh." A shared motif draws neighboring psalms into intimate juxtaposition. Second, within the didactic listing of Yahweh's attributes that signal his positive interaction with humankind is mention in Ps. 111:4 that he is *ḥannûn wĕraḥûm* ("gracious and compassionate"). Those same qualities are predicated to the active God-fearing person in Ps. 112:4. This pair of Hebrew adjectives spans two-thirds of the *het*

---

43. Brueggemann, "Bounded by Obedience and Praise," 83.
44. A useful listing may be consulted in L. C. Allen, *Psalms 101–150* (WBC; Waco, Tex.: Word Books, 1983), 95.

colon in both compositions. The two poems, one a hymn and the other a wisdom psalm, are well paired. Indeed, Kraus's suggestion that "they could have been written by the same poet or in a common circle of writers" is entirely reasonable.[45] Finally, since Psalm 112 replicates Psalm 1 in its choice of opening and closing words, linking the opening word, "happy" (*'ašrê*), with the righteous God-fearing person and the closing word, "perish" (*tō'bēd*), with the wicked, the editors must have been mindful of the initial entry of the Psalter as they invited Psalm 112 into the canon. Though it is a poem in its own right, Psalm 112 is also dedicated to the task of recapitulation as it endorses the truth of Psalm 1.

Our remaining wisdom psalms find their locus in the "Songs of Ascents" (Psalms 120–34). And whether played out in the family (Psalms 127 and 128) or in the larger context of fraternal harmony (Psalm 133), all three manifest a strong communal interest. Focusing on the "ruling and working of Yahweh in the life of human beings," Psalm 127 consists of two extended wisdom sayings.[46] The first (vv. 1–2) exposes the vanity of constructing a house, protecting a city, and general human toil apart from the deity. The second (vv. 3–5) emphasizes the blessing of many children as a divine gift, and in so doing makes use of an *'ašrê* formula: "Happy is the man who fills his quiver with them" (v. 5). It is precisely that mechanism which establishes the linkage between Psalms 127 and 128, for the opening colon of Psalm 128 is likewise an *'ašrê* formula which affirms, "Happy are all who fear Yahweh" (v. 1). The blessings that ensue, including pleasure in one's work and an enviable family life, are not interpreted as an automatic playing-out of a cosmic system of retribution. Rather, they are affirmed as evidence of Yahweh's gracious dealings in Israel's behalf. Finally, this pair of wisdom psalms stands out from its immediate context insofar as it is framed by two communal laments (Psalms 126 and 129).

Our last wisdom poem, Psalm 133, in its conspicuous brevity, rigorously reinforces the celebration of God-fearing and harmonious human existence to which Psalms 127 and 128 are also dedicated. Consisting of one expanded picturesque proverb, Psalm 133 provides in its ejaculatory phrase, "how good and pleasant," an impressive counterpart to the *'ašrê* formula to which psalmic wisdom has so often availed itself. Whereas Psalm 133 is situated between Psalms 141:5–10 and 144:1–7 on column XXIII of the Qumran Psalms Scroll (11QPs^a), as it finds its place in the Masoretic Text it is framed by two liturgical compositions, Psalm 132, commemorating Yahweh's choice of Zion and the Davidic dynasty, and Psalm 134, invoking priestly blessing on the nocturnal congregation assembled in the Jerusalem sanctuary.[47]

Finally, if it can be argued that Psalm 119 makes some contribution to learned

---

45. Kraus, *Psalms 60–150*, 362.
46. Ibid., 455.
47. J. A. Sanders, *The Dead Sea Psalms Scroll* (Ithaca, N.Y.: Cornell University Press, 1967), 78.

psalmography, this is not the occasion to subject that stellar alphabetic acrostic to a close reading. Suffice it to say that I applaud the efforts of Will Soll to pare down its alleged wisdom vocabulary and to call its viability as an authentic wisdom psalm into question.[48] Moreover, Westermann's thesis that the Psalter once opened with Psalm 1 and ended with Psalm 119 makes sense.[49] In such a psalmic collection, Psalm 119 had a crucial role to play in presenting the Psalms as God's own word that summoned the faithful to careful reading and study. Here it parallels the wisdom tag with which the Book of Hosea concludes: "Whoever is wise, let him understand these things" (Hos. 14:9). As the Hebrew Psalter presently exists, Psalm 119 no longer plays that role. Yet there is no place in Book V for its massive presence to hide. Fervently dedicated to the cause of Torah piety, its linkage with the message and function of Psalm 1, whose status as a wisdom psalm is widely affirmed, should not go unnoticed.

Conclusion

Since merely one out of fifteen compositions in the Hebrew Psalter appears to be a wisdom psalm, it is safe to say that many other psalm types can be celebrated as more pervasive and perhaps even more compelling. Yet these wisdom compositions effectively attest to the marked impact that wisdom and Torah teachers in the postexilic Israelite community played in establishing the Psalter in its final form as a collection of sacred texts. Moreover, by virtue of both their presence and strategic location, these psalms accomplish much in affecting the shift whereby Israel's former words to God in its praise, supplication, and thanksgiving were transformed into becoming God's own word to Israel, the revelation of God's nature and will, on which the faithful were invited to fix their attention intently.

---

48. Will Soll, *Psalm 119: Matrix, Form, and Setting* (CBQMS 23; Washington, D.C.: Catholic Biblical Association of America, 1991), 115–25.

49. Claus Westermann, *Praise and Lament in the Psalms* (trans. K. R. Crim and R. N. Soulen; Atlanta: John Knox Press, 1981), 253.

15

The Ending of Luke and the Ending of the *Odyssey*

——— ◆ ———

Dennis R. MacDonald
Claremont School of Theology and Claremont Graduate University

Luke's most obvious and dramatic alteration of the ending of Mark's Gospel is his addition of two appearances of Jesus to his disciples.[1] In the first, Jesus appears to Cleopas and an unnamed disciple as they walk to the village of Emmaus (24:13–35). In the second, he appears to "the eleven and their companions," including Cleopas and the unnamed disciple (24:36–51). Scholars long have sought to identify the origins of these stories.[2]

If Luke inherited these stories from tradition, he surely transformed them to serve his own theological ends, insofar as the embedded discourses clearly develop themes characteristic of his redaction of Mark's empty-tomb narrative.[3] These speeches are Lukan, but what about the narrative framework around them, namely the Emmaus story (24:13–18 and 24:28–35) and the assembly story (24:36–43 and 24:50–51)? Scholars usually ascribe these narratives to traditional legends about the appearances of Jesus or occasionally to an antecedent

---

1. Other changes, too, are significant. In Luke, Mark's young man at the tomb becomes two men, later identified as two angels (24:4 and 24:23). Whereas Mark's women failed to tell the disciples to go to Galilee to see the risen Jesus, Luke's women reported what they had been told: not that Jesus had gone before them to Galilee, as in Mark, but that "the Son of Man must be delivered into the hands of sinful men, and be crucified, and on the third day rise" (24:7–11).

2. Joachim Wanke, including material prior to 1973, provides a thorough discussion of research on the Emmaus story (*Die Emmauserzählung: Eine redaktionsgeschictliche Untersuchung zu Lk 24.13–35* [Erfurter theologische Studien 31; Leipzig: St. Benno-Verlag, 1973], 3–19).

3. See Joseph A. Fitzmyer, *The Gospel according to Luke* (AB 28A; New York: Doubleday, 1985), 2.1555–56. Wanke discusses the parallels between Luke 23:55–24:9 and 24:19b–27 and shows that Luke's redaction of Mark's empty-tomb narrative directly informed the speech of Jesus in the Emmaus story (*Emmauserzählung*, 73–91). He also concludes that the story was a Lukan creation, based on a tradition concerning a postresurrection appearance of Jesus to the disciples at a meal similar to the scene in Luke 24:36–49 (126).

written source.[4] It is more likely that Luke himself created these stories;[5] as I hope to show, he modeled them after the appearance of Odysseus to Laertes in the last book of the *Odyssey*.[6] The author of Luke-Acts displays an intimate knowledge of Greek rhetoric, historiography, philosophy, and literature.[7] Luke's literary aware-ness and competence leave little doubt that he, like all well-educated Greeks, had been exposed to the Homeric epics.[8]

After slaying the suitors and revealing his identity to Penelope, Odysseus sought to reveal himself to his father, Laertes, who no longer lived in the city but by himself in a modest farm "far from the city" (24.212). Odysseus told him-self he would go to the farm to "see whether he [Laertes] will recognize me and know me by sight, or whether he will fail to know me, since I have been gone so long a time" (217–18). He went to his father's home and found him working in his vineyard, "nursing his sorrow," sorrow for his long-lost son and the devastation of his estate by Penelope's suitors (231; cf. 233). Instead of disclosing his identity to Laertes immediately, Odysseus thought he might "test him with taunting words"

---

4. G. J. Goldberg has observed similarities between the Emmaus story and the so-called *Testa-monium Flavianum*, a Christian redaction of a passage about Jesus in Josephus ("The Coincidence of the Emmaus Narrative of Luke and the Testamonium of Josephus," *JSP* 13 [1995]: 59–77). Goldberg suggests the existence of a common source behind both accounts (76–77). It is more likely that the Christian redactor of Josephus was influenced by the famous story in Luke 24.

5. Udo Borse has analyzed the Emmaus story in detail and concluded, if somewhat tentatively, that Luke himself composed it under the influence of Genesis, the Book of Judges, and the Book of Tobit ("Der Evangelist als Verfasser der Emmauserzählung," *SNTU* 12 [1987]: 35–67). This conclusion confirms that of Wanke.

6. Frederick Williams argues that the Emmaus story is a variant on a popular ancient tale of meeting a deity in disguise ("Archilochus and the Eunuch: The Persistence of a Narrative Pattern," *Classics Ireland* 1 [1994]: 96–112, esp. 107–9). The similarities Williams identifies are interesting but too general to account for many of Luke's details. Furthermore, every element shared between this "narrative pattern" and the Emmaus story appears also in the appearances of Odysseus to Laertes in *Odyssey* book 24, obviating any dependence on a folktale. Long before Luke, Euripides had imitated Laertes' recognition of Odysseus in Electra's recognition of Orestes (Joachim Dingel, "Der 24: Gesang der Odyssee und die Elektra des Euripides," *Rheinisches Museum* 112 [1969]: 103–9).

7. More than any other writings of the New Testament, Luke-Acts quotes from Greek literature: from Aratus's *Phaenomena* in Acts 17:28, and from Euripides' *Bacchae* in 26:14. For discussions of Luke's knowledge of Greek literature and compositional education see especially Eckhard Plümacher, *Lukas als hellenisticher Schriftsteller: Studien zue Apostelgeschichte* (SUNT 9; Göttingen: Vandenhoeck & Ruprecht, 1972); Richard I. Pervo, *Profit with Delight: The Literary Genre of the Acts of the Apostles* (Philadelphia: Fortress, 1987); and Robert Morgenthaler, *Lukas und Quintilian: Rhetorik als Erzählkunst* (Zurich: Gotthelf Verlag, 1993). Wilhelm Nestle has argued for the direct influence of Euripides on Acts in "Anklänge an Euripides in der Apostelgeschichte," in his *Griechische Studien: Untersuchungen zur Religion, Dichtung und Philosophie der Griechen* (Aalen, Germany: Scientia Verlag, 1968), 226–39. Recently K. O. Sandnes has reargued, as others have before him, the case of Socratic influence in Paul's speech in Athens ("Paul and Socrates: The Aim of Paul's Areopagus Speech," *JSNT* 50 [1993]: 13–26).

8. See, for example, Peter Hofrichter, "Parallele zum 24: Gesang der Ilias in der Engeler-scheinungen des lukanischen Doppelwerkes," *Protokolle zur Bibel* 1 (1993): 60–76, who argues for direct literary influence from the *Ilias*.

(240). He thus asked his father why he was so sad, who he was, and if he knew anything concerning his friend Odysseus, "whether perchance he still lives, or is now dead and in the house of Hades" (263–64).

Laertes answered that he himself was Odysseus's father and that "wanton and reckless men now possess" his estate. He was certain that his son had died on his return journey, prey to fish, beasts, or birds, bereft of a fitting burial (289–96). Laertes then sought to know the identity of the inquisitive stranger.

In response, Odysseus told one of his famous lies, stating, among other things, that he and Odysseus had met years ago and hoped that they would meet again someday. At the utterance of Odysseus's name, "a black cloud of grief enfolded Laertes, and with both his hands he took the sooty dust and poured it over his gray head, groaning without pause" (315–17).

No longer able to restrain himself, the hero embraced his father and said, "That man am I, father, myself, standing here, of whom you ask, come back in the twentieth year to the land of my fathers" (321–22). Laertes, long convinced that his son had died, said he needed "some clear sign, that I may be sure" (329).

Odysseus told him, "first take a look with your eyes at this scar," a boyhood scar on his leg from the tusk of a wild boar. This was the same scar that the nurse Eurycleia saw when washing Odysseus's feet, allowing her to recognize him.[9] In addition, Odysseus gave detailed information about the trees he and his father had planted many years ago. "So he spoke, and his father's knees were loosened where he stood, and his heart melted, as he recognized (ἀναγνόντος) the signs that Odysseus showed him without error. About his dear son he flung both his arms, and the much-enduring noble Odysseus caught him, fainting, to himself" (345–48). Together they went to Laertes' home for a meal with Telemachus and Laertes' faithful servants, who were astonished when they saw their lord. Odysseus told them, "Forget your wonder" (394); it was time to eat. One of the servants ran up to him, clasped and kissed his hands, and expressed his joy at seeing once again the master he thought was dead. "[T]he gods themselves have brought you — hail to you and all welcome, and may the gods grant you happiness" (401–2).

The parallels with Luke 24:13–43 are obvious, although apparently never previously analyzed. Like Odysseus, who went to his father's farm far from the city, Jesus approached two of his disciples outside the city on their journey to Emmaus; the disciples, prevented from recognizing him, played roles similar to Laertes.

---

9. *Od.* 19.386–507; see also 21.217–20 and 23.73–77.

Odyssey 24.216–18	Luke 24:16
[Odysseus speaks:] "I will make trial of my father and see whether he will **recognize me** (μ' ἐπιγνώῃ) and take heed of me with **his eyes** (ὀφθαλμοῖσιν) or whether he will **fail to recognize me.**" [Laertes failed to recognize his son.]	**[T]heir eyes** (ὀφθαλμοί) were kept from **recognizing him** (ἐπιγνῶναι).

Odysseus asked Laertes who he was and why he looked so sad; Jesus asked the disciples what they had been discussing as they walked along. Laertes, "weep-ing," answered the stranger (*Od.* 24.280); the disciples "stopped momentarily, full of gloom" (Luke 24:17).[10] Laertes and Cleopas each explained the situation to the "stranger" (ξεῖν) or "sojourner" (παροικεῖς) by recounting past events (*Od.* 24.281 and Luke 24:18). They both lamented the presumed deaths of the very people to whom they were speaking, laying the blame for their situations on wicked men: "wanton and reckless men," namely, the suitors; "our chief priests and leaders," who "handed him [Jesus] over to be condemned to death and cru-cified him" (*Od.* 24:282 and Luke 24:20).[11] Although both Laertes and Cleopas failed to recognize the person before them, they demonstrated their faithfulness to the one they presumed was dead.

In the *Odyssey* a meal follows the recognition by Laertes, but in Luke the recognition occurs at the meal itself.

Odyssey 24.358–61	Luke 24:29
[Odysseus speaks to Laertes:] "But **let us go to the house** which lies near the orchard, for there I sent Telemachus and the cowherd and the swineherd that with all speed they might prepare our meal." So spoke the two, and **went their way to the handsome house.** [A meal follows.]	[The disciples speak to Jesus:] **"Stay with us,** because it is almost evening and the day is now nearly over." So he **went to stay with them.** [A meal follows.]

In these parallels, the role of Odysseus applies not to Jesus, as one might have expected, but to the disciples. Odysseus was able to invite Laertes to his father's own little house because the hero earlier had made arrangements for such a meal (*Od.* 24.214–18). Jesus could hardly have played host, so Luke momentarily reversed the roles by having the disciples extend the invitation to Jesus.

---

10. Several manuscripts read ἐστε for ἐστάθησαν. If one adopts this reading, Jesus would have asked the disciples "why are you so gloomy?" For a defense of this reading, see L. Ramaroson, "La Première question posée aux disciples d'Emmaüs en Lc 24.17," *Science et Esprit* 47 (1995): 299–303.

11. Compare also Luke 24:20–21 ("we had hoped [ἠλπίζομεν] that he was the one to redeem Israel") and *Od.* 24.313–15 ("And our hearts hoped [ἐώλπει] that we should you meet").

Jesus "took the bread, blessed and broke it, and gave it to them. Then their eyes (ὀφθαλμοί) were opened, and they recognized him (ἐπέγνωσαν αὐτόν)" (Luke 24:30–31; cf. *Od.* 24.216–18 and 346). The signs of Odysseus's identity to Laertes were the scar and memory of planting trees; the sign of Jesus' identity was the breaking of bread.[12] When Laertes recognized Odysseus, his heart melted; when the disciples recognized Jesus, they said, "Were not our hearts burning within us while he was talking to us on the road?" (Luke 24:32).

Even though this recognition ends the story of the Road to Emmaus, another recognition scene follows, and it too echoes the end of the *Odyssey*. Odysseus went with his father to his humble home for a meal; the two disciples returned to the others, who had convened to eat.

Odyssey 24.361–64	Luke 24:33
[T]he two...went their way to the handsome house. And **when they had come to the** stately **house, they found** (εὖρον) Telemachus and the swineherd carving meat in abundance.	[T]hey got up and returned to Jerusalem, and **they found** (εὖρον) the eleven and their companions gathered together.[13]

The two disciples told what had happened to them, and "[w]hile they were talking about this, Jesus himself stood among them" (Luke 24:36). What follows in Luke resembles Odysseus's appearance to Laertes' slaves.

Odyssey 24.391–94	Luke 24:37–38
And **they**, when they saw Odysseus, and recognized him in their minds, **stood in the halls lost in wonder.** **But Odysseus addressed them** with winning words, and said: "Old man, sit down to dinner, and the rest of you wholly **forget your fright.**"	[When Jesus stood in their midst:] **They were startled and terrified, and** thought they were seeing a ghost. **He said to them, "Why are you so frightened, and why do doubts arise in** your hearts?"

To demonstrate that he was not a ghost, Jesus told them to look at his hands and feet, presumably because they displayed the wounds of the crucifixion, although Luke earlier had said nothing about nails in Jesus' hands or feet. Jesus' wounds play

---

12. Luke is not clear what about the bread was revealing: the ingesting of it (which Luke does not even mention, although it may be inferred), or the similarity of the breaking of the loaf to Jesus' last meal with the disciples (although Cleopas apparently was not present for that meal), or to a divine act of opening their eyes only coincidentally related to the breaking of the bread. It is possible that they saw the wounds on Jesus' hands as he broke the bread, but if so, one might have expected Luke to have made a point of it. Furthermore, Luke's reader could not have taken it that way: Luke never before mentioned the nailing of Jesus to the cross.

13. The disciples seem to have been eating; see 24:41–42.

the same role as Odysseus's scar by which Laertes (like Eurycleia and Penelope earlier) was able to recognize him.

Odyssey 24.331–32	Luke 24:39
First take a **look with your eyes at this scar** [on the thigh], which a boar gave me. [Cf. 24.321: "**That man am I**, father, **myself** (αὐτὸς ἐγώ).]	**Look at my hands and my feet;** see that **it is I myself** (ἐγώ εἰμι αὐτός).

Odysseus gave Laertes a second sign: information about the planting of trees together in Odysseus's youth. Jesus gave his disciples a second sign: he ate a piece of broiled fish to prove he was no ghost (Luke 24:41–43). The result of the recognitions in both stories was joy (*Od.* 24.345–47 and 397–43; Luke 42:41 and 42:52–53). One might summarize the parallels like this:

Odyssey 24.216–394	Luke 24:13–43
Odysseus, thought dead, returned alive.	Jesus died but returned alive.
Odysseus went to his father's farm, outside the city, to see if he would "recognize" him "with his eyes."	Jesus met the disciples on the road, outside Jerusalem, but "their eyes were kept from recognizing him."
Laertes was sad as he worked his garden.	The disciples were sad as they walked and talked.
The "stranger" initiated conversation with questions.	The "sojourner" initiated conversation with a question.
Laertes expressed his sadness over the death of his son and the violence of the suitors.	Cleopas expressed sadness over Jesus' death and the violence of the Jewish authorities.
Odysseus spoke with Laertes about himself in the third person, but the old man still did not recognize him.	Jesus spoke with the disciples about himself in the third person, but the disciples still did not recognize him.
Odysseus revealed himself by means of his scar and memory of the planting of trees, and there was a meal at another venue.	Jesus revealed himself by breaking and distributing bread at a meal at another venue.
Odysseus had told Laertes to look at the scar on his leg for proof. ["I am that man (αὐτὸς ἐγώ)."]	Jesus told the disciples to look at the wounds on his hands and feet: "It is I (ἐγώ εἰμι αὐτός)."
Those who recognized Odysseus were astonished, and he comforted them.	On recognizing Jesus, the disciples were terrified, and he comforted them.

One might attribute these parallels merely to the garden-variety recognition scene, but Luke retains distinctive features from Homer's account not displayed in the typical recognition. For example, both recognitions take place outside cities; both narrators comment on the sadness of the addressees; both heroes thought dead give speeches without revealing their identities; both heroes use body scars as signs for recognitions; both heroes also reveal themselves in a second location, at a meal. Luke's dependence on Homer also explains a peculiarity in the text. Commentators often note the unarticulated motivation for the blindness of the disciples: Why were they prevented from recognizing Jesus? The nonrecognition by Laertes presents no such problem. Laertes had not seen Odysseus in twenty years.[14] The disciples, however, had seen Jesus just three days earlier and should have recognized him at once. Luke needed to delay the recognition until the breaking of the bread, and to this end he used the ambiguous passive voice, "their eyes were kept from recognizing him."

One of the most difficult questions to answer about ancient literary imitations is this: Did the author want his readers to detect the influence of the model? Many examples of mimesis are disguised, concealing the antecedent. Such apparently is the case with Luke's use of Mark and Q. On the other hand, imitations often revealed their models by various kinds of markers or flags, such as direct allusions, distinctive details, or significant names. The *Acts of Andrew*, for example, used proper nouns to alert the reader to compare his stories with those of classical mythology, Homer above all.[15] I have argued elsewhere that Luke, too, used significant names in Acts to point to a popular Greek myth.[16]

Two proper nouns appear in Luke 24 that long have baffled interpreters. Luke states that the two disciples were on their way to the village Emmaus, sixty stadia, or about seven miles, from Jerusalem. No archaeological site matches this description. Early on, the village came to be identified with ancient Emmaus/Nicopolis, modern Khirbet Imwas, some eighteen miles west of Jerusalem. This identification almost certainly generated the textual variant "one hundred and sixty stadia."[17] In any case, Luke seems to have been uncertain of the location, and, if so, why did he mention the village at all?[18]

---

14. *Od.* 24.218: "Since I have been gone so long a time." Reliance on the epic might also explain an awkwardness in Luke's use of the stigmata. Luke had said nothing about the manner of Jesus' affixing to his cross (nor had Mark, his source for the death of Jesus), namely the use of nails in his hands and feet (cf. John 20:24–29). Had Luke himself been responsible for the revelation of Jesus to his disciples by means of his wounds, one might have expected him to have prepared the reader for the wounds by having mentioned the nails earlier.

15. Dennis R. MacDonald, *Christianizing Homer: "The Odyssey," Plato, and "The Acts of Andrew"* (New York: Oxford University Press, 1994).

16. "Luke's Eutychus and Homer's Elpenor: Acts 20:7–12 and *Odyssey* 10–12," *Journal of Higher Criticism* 1 (1994): 5–24.

17. *ABD*, s.v. "Emmaus," 2.497–98.

18. Fitzmyer suggests the evangelist retained the name from tradition because it conformed to his insistence that Jesus appeared to the disciples exclusively in Judea (*Gospel according to Luke*, 2.1562).

Unusual, too, is the naming of one disciple Cleopas, a name otherwise unat-
tested in the New Testament and exceedingly rare in antiquity. The very fact that
it was so rare has prompted many interpreters to ascribe it to pre-Lukan tradition,
even to authentic historical memory.[19]

But the similarities between Luke 24 and *Odyssey* 24 suggest another solution.
Odysseus's two most faithful servants were Eurycleia and Eumaeus. The nurse
Eurycleia recognized Odysseus from the scar on his leg. Her name, as ancient
commentators were quick to note, was a compound of ευρυ, "far and wide," and
κλεος, "renown." The name Cleopas trades on the same word and means "all
renown" (Κλεοπᾶς). I suggest it is no accident that Far-flung-fame (Eurycleia)
recognized the identity of Odysseus and that Fame-galore (Cleopas) recognized
the identity of Jesus.

Significant, too, is the place-name Emmaus (Ἐμμαοῦς). Odysseus revealed
his identity to Eumaeus (Εὔμαιος) by showing him the scar on his leg.[20] In other
words, the two unusual proper nouns in Luke's tale, Cleopas and Emmaus, may
be flags to read Luke's story against the recognition of Odysseus by Eurycleia and
Eumaeus, both of whom, like Laertes, recognized Odysseus, long thought dead,
by his wound.

If Luke's readers picked up these clues and compared the last chapter of the
Gospel with the last book of the epic, they should have seen significance to the
story invisible on the surface. Odysseus visited Hades, but he never actually died.
Jesus did. Odysseus's wound came from a hunting accident; Jesus' wounds came
from his unjust execution. The recognition of Odysseus by Laertes demonstrated
merely that the hero had returned home after twenty years. The recognition of
Jesus by the disciples demonstrated his status as the Messiah who conquered
death. That is, Luke did not merely imitate Homeric epic, he emulated it by
exalting Jesus at the expense of Odysseus.

19. Ibid., 2.1564.
20. *Od.* 21.217–31.

16

Augustine and the Strange Career of Romans 9:10–29

——— ◆ ———

James F. McCue
University of Iowa

Romans 9:10ff. is a text with a long and complex history in the Latin tradition. It is the predestination text par excellence. Although the Greek church did not read it this way, and though initially Augustine did not read it this way, by the time he became a bishop, Augustine did read it this way. However, a funny thing happened to the text at that point: for the next fifteen years, Augustine continued to preach and teach as though he had never heard of predestination, and then, when it was forced back on his agenda, he only slowly came out clearly in favor of predestination. This article shows how Augustine first developed his predestinarian views, establishes that they disappear for fifteen years, shows how they finally emerged in a form considerably different from their initial form, and finally hazards an explanation of how and why the great doctor of predestination could, for fifteen years, teach the doctrine that he had rejected in favor of predestination.

I shall not offer an elaborate account of Romans. Suffice it simply to begin with a standard English translation of Rom. 9:10–29. We will have to look more closely, at certain points, at the Latin which lay before Augustine, but it would be a waste to try to establish his entire Latin text. It was not exactly the Vulgate; and, indeed, he seems to have worked from a different text in the *Expositio quarumdam quaestionum ex epistula ad Romanos* (394 C.E.) and the *De diversis quaestionibus ad Simplicianum* (397).

> Nor is that all; something similar happened to Rebecca when she had conceived children by one husband, our ancestor Isaac. Even before they had been born or had done anything good or bad (so that God's purpose of election might continue, not by works but by his call) she was told, "The elder shall serve the younger." As it is written, "I have loved Jacob, but I have hated Esau." What then are we to say? Is there injustice on God's

169

part? By no means! For he says to Moses, "I will have mercy on whom I have mercy, and I will have compassion on whom I have compassion." So it depends not on human will or exertion, but on God who shows mercy. For the scripture says to Pharaoh, "I have raised you up for the very purpose of showing my power in you, so that my name may be proclaimed in all the earth." So then he has mercy on whomever he chooses, and he hardens the heart of whomever he chooses. . . .

This text does not seem to have been particularly troublesome up until this time. It seems to have been a fairly common solution to the apparent injustice to Esau, that God's hatred for him was based on God's foreknowledge of how Esau would live. Predestination, as in Rom. 8:29–30, seems to follow from God's foreknowledge: "those he foreknew he also predestined . . . " — *quos praescivit, et praedestinavit* . . . The advantage of such a reading — available to all who held that God possessed perfect knowledge of future contingencies and possibilities[1] — was that it took care of the problem of God's justice, so emphatically insisted on at this juncture in Romans.

However, although Augustine picked up early on this interpretation, he modified it in one important respect. Across the early 390s he was changing his mind about the nature of human freedom. In the earliest anti-Manichaean writings, and in the chronologically early parts of *De libero arbitrio*, Augustine maintained a simple and straightforward conception of human freedom and its relation to sin. We are free to do good or evil. Absent such freedom, there can be no conception of sin. Late in his career, when he wrote his *Reconsiderations* (*Retractationes*), he would be at pains to explain that when he spoke so extravagantly about freedom in these early works he was really talking about the condition of Adam — *his* freedom, before the fall. This explanation may have persuaded some of Augustine's contemporaries, but it has not persuaded anyone recently.

One can trace a change from the early to the late parts of *De libero arbitrio*. The first and part of the second books were written in 388, shortly after his conversion. The second was completed and the third written in 395. One sees in the latter parts many more references to scripture and a much greater emphasis on the burden inherited from Adam: in addition to the loss of the gift of immortality, Augustine writes, our clouded intellects have difficulty *knowing* the good which we are to do, and our weakened wills have difficulty in the actual *willing* and *doing*. There is no notion of impossibilities here, only of increased difficulty. Faith and turning to God in prayer still lie in our power.

In this transitional moment Augustine begins to address certain problems

---

1. I use a scholastic language here as a kind of shorthand; fourth- and fifth-century writers did not speak this way. See, for example, John Chrysostom, *Homilies on Romans*, Homily XVI, especially his comments on chapter 9, verse 10; text in *Select Library of Nicene and Post-Nicene Fathers*, first series, 11:466.

posed by the text of Romans. Why this interest? It seems to have had little to do with an internal crisis, after the Lutheran manner, but seems to have been a function of maturing fourth-century church institutions and of the challenge of Manichaeanism. Commentaries on Paul, Romans, and on scripture generally abounded in the second half of the century.[2] A large Christian literature was being created under the peace following the Constantinian settlement, and interpretation of the inherited scripture was a central undertaking. As a presbyter in 391, Augustine had petitioned his bishop for additional time for the study of scripture, which he felt he had previously neglected.[3] Whether or not the permission was granted, scriptural texts play an increasingly important role in Augustine's work in the 390s.

Moreover, the challenge of the Manichaean interpretation of the Scriptures drew attention particularly to Paul[4] and Genesis. In his *Confessions*, Augustine says that he was much occupied with Paul even prior to his conversion, but his earliest writings do not support this statement. It may have been true, but one could not prove it on the basis of what he wrote between 387 and 392/3.

In 394, Augustine wrote *Expositio quarumdam quaestionum in epistula ad Romanos*. He describes its genesis:

> While I was still a presbyter, it happened that those of us who were together at Carthage were reading the Apostle's Epistle to the Romans. The brethren asked me certain questions and I answered as best I could. They wanted my answers in writing rather than in unwritten form, and so a single book was added to my previous writings.[5]

One of the texts discussed was Rom. 9:10ff. In his *Retractationes*, Augustine observes that he had vigorously investigated the matter, and had not yet discovered the nature of election: "Nondum diligentius quesiveram, nec adhuc inveneram qualis sit electio gratiae."[6] He explained God's love for Jacob and hatred for Esau in the following way:

> It is written that "I have loved Jacob, but I have hated Esau." This has led some (*nonnullos*) to think that the Apostle Paul has taken away free choice of the will (*liberum arbitrium voluntatis*), by means of which we please God

---

2. A quick glance at Johannes Quasten, *Patrology*, 1960, 3:ix–xvi, will confirm this.

3. *Ep.* 21.3.

4. Note that in *Contra Fortunatum* (392), it is Fortunatus who is presented as using Pauline texts in support of his position.

5. *Retract.* 1.23. At approximately the same time, Augustine wrote two works on Romans, one on Galatians. *Diversis quaestionibus ad Simplicianum 83* dealt with a number of Pauline texts (including Rom. 9:10ff.), and *De libero arbitrio 3* reverses the direction of that work while citing texts from Romans.

6. *Retract.* 1.23.2: "I had not yet sought very assiduously, nor had I yet discovered what is the election of grace."

by the good of piety or offend God by the evil of impiety. For they say that
before there were any works, good or evil, of the two who were not yet
born, God loved the one and hated the other. *But we reply that this was
done by means of God's foreknowledge, by which God knew of the yet unborn
of what sort each was going to be.*[7]

However, this is not all. Augustine was already developing a more complex
view of the interaction of grace and works, and he is sensitive to the Pauline
insistence that it is through faith rather than works that we are saved.

One might say that therefore it is works that God chooses in the one whom
he loves, even though the works do not yet exist, because God foresees
them. But if it is works that God chooses, how is it that the Apostle says
that election is not by works? Accordingly we must understand that good
works are done out of love, but that love is in us through the giving of
the Holy Spirit, as the same Apostle says: "The love of God (*charitas dei*) is
poured out in our hearts through the Holy Spirit, which [Spirit] is given us"
[Rom. 5.5]. Therefore no one ought to glory in their works as though they
were their own; they have them through the gift of God, since it is that love
that works good in them. What is it then that God chooses (*elegit*)? If God
gives the Holy Spirit (through whom love works good) to whom he wills,
how does he choose to whom he will make the gift? Absent merit, there is
no election. (*Si enim nullo merito, non est electio.*) Apart from (*ante*) merit
all are equal, and between absolute equals one cannot speak of "election"
(*nec potest in rebus omnino aequalibus electio nominari*). But since it is only
to believers that the Holy Spirit is given, it is not works that God chooses,
which he then rewards by giving the Holy Spirit so that we might work
good through charity; God chooses faith. For if one does not believe in him
and continue in the will to receive him (*in accipiendi voluntate permaneat*),
one does not receive God's gift, the Holy Spirit, through which one is
able to work good by the love that is poured out. Accordingly, God does
not elect the works of someone in his foreknowledge, works which God
himself is going to give. On the contrary, it is faith which God elects in
his foreknowledge: who God foreknows will believe in him, to that one he
elects to give the Holy Spirit that he might do good works and thereby attain
life eternal.... Therefore that we believe is our doing (*quod ergo credimus,
nostrum est*); but that we do good works is of him who gives the Holy Spirit
to those who believe in him.[8]

---

7. *Exp. quaest. Rom.* 60. Emphasis added.

8. *Exp. quaest. Rom.* 60. I have not tried consistently for inclusive language. I am, after all,
translating, and Augustine uses male pronouns quite unselfconsciously.

He adds, apropos Rom. 9:16, "So it depends not on human will or exertion, but on God who shows mercy":

> Paul does not deny (*tollit*) the free choice of the will; but he says that our will does not suffice unless God assists it by making our good intentions effective of good through the gift of the Holy Spirit.... God's mercy is given to the antecedent merit of faith, his hardening [of Pharaoh] to the antecedent impiety.[9]

Augustine covers much the same ground in *Diversis quaestionibus ad Simplicianum* 83, q. 68, except that he expresses more puzzlement over Jacob and Esau:

> Nor can this be understood, except perhaps by those who love the Lord their God with all their hearts.[10]

In attributing predestination to foreknowledge Augustine is hardly breaking new ground. Ambrosiaster had interpreted this text in this fashion prior to 384.[11] We find much the same thing in Chrysostom's sixteenth homily on Romans. Moreover, prior to Augustine, Ambrosiaster and Ambrose had developed a full account of the Adamic heritage, roughly comparable to what we find in the later books of *De libero arbitrio*; we have all fallen in Adam in the sense that we inherit a condition of proneness to sin. But, like the Augustine of *De libero arbitrio* 3.19–20, although this may be *called* sin, it is not something for which the individual has to answer to God. Guilt and condemnation apply only to our actual unrighteous deeds.[12] Augustine does not seem to have adopted this tradition on first becoming a Christian, but by 394, with his insistence on faith rather than works as the object of foreknowledge, he seems to have been edging beyond it.

This brings us to the crucial text, *Diversis quaestionibus ad Simplicianum* 1.2. Shortly after Augustine became a bishop,[13] he received from Simplicianus,[14] an old friend and Ambrose's successor at Milan, a request that he clarify several obscure texts: Rom. 7:7–25; Rom. 9:10–29; and six texts from the first three Books of Kings (= 1 and 2 Samuel and 1 Kings).

---

9. *Exp. quaest. Rom.* 62. The text could also be translated as "making us merciful so as to do good works," etc. The Latin is "misericordes nos efficiendo ad bene operandum per donum Spiritus sancti."

10. *Div. quaest. Simpl.* 68.6.

11. CSEL 81, pt. 1, xv.

12. See J. N. D. Kelly, *Early Christian Doctrines*, 2d ed. (San Francisco: Harper & Row, 1978), 353ff., for texts. In his handling of the issue of original sin, Kelly, like many others, attributes too much importance to the Vulgate's misconstrual of Rom. 5:12.

13. Augustine gives us the details in *Retract.* 2.1.

14. We know of this Simplicianus that he had for at least a decade prior to this time been concerned with Paul, and very much aware of the difficulties which he presented. (On this see Ambrose, *Corpus Christianum*, vol. 44, xxiii, n. 2.) Moreover, he had been revered by Augustine since about that time as Ambrose's "father" (*Conf.* 8.1), and Augustine had discussed the Christian faith with Simplicianus prior to Augustine's conversion.

Now I think it is time to turn to the second question you have posed: that
I explain the entire passage [Rom. 9:10–29] . . .

Before examining the text in detail, Augustine observes that the letter's purpose is "that no one should glory in the merits of works" (*de operum meritis nemo
glorietur*). He then proceeds, quite perfunctorily, to put aside the opinion that
election is based on works. The position to which he devotes far greater attention
is the one that had most recently been his own.

> Is it "according to election" because God who knows all things in advance
> sees the faith that is to be in Jacob, sees this even before his birth; so that
> though no one merits being justified by his or her works, since God justifies
> the Gentiles by faith and no one has faith except by free will, did not God
> by foreknowledge choose whom he would justify, foreseeing the future will
> to believe? (1.2.5)

The position put forth in this cumbersome question is rejected.

> Shall we say that there would have been no election unless there had been
> some differentiation in the mother's womb, either of faith or works or of
> some sort of merits? (1.2.6)

This was precisely what he had said in *Exp. quaest. Rom.* 60, but now his
position has changed. The question now is whether faith itself is to be considered
one of the gifts of God's grace. Augustine's answer is that faith is as much a
consequence of God's grace as are works. He answers this way, first because
it is a simpler and more straightforward way of reading this and a number of
other Pauline texts, especially 1 Cor. 4:7 ("What do you have that you have not
received?"), which plays an important role throughout the argument. Second,
the answer fits better with the overall theme of the letter: that we have no
basis for glorifying ourselves. But third, this more straightforward reading of the
text is now opened to Augustine because he has found a way to address his
theodicy concerns. Augustine is merely quoting Paul when he insists that there
is no injustice on God's part. But the sentence has a different ring in Augustine's
text. In Paul, the sentence ends discussion; for the Platonizing Augustine, it is an
invitation to further investigation.

Three things are clear to Augustine: first, that God, had God so chosen, *could*
have made a believer of Esau: "Who would say that means were lacking even to
the Almighty to persuade Esau to believe?" (1.2.14). Second, God did *not* choose
to do this. And third, "Let this be fixed and immovable in a mind sober in its
piety and firm in faith, that there is no injustice (*iniquitas*) in God" (1.2.16). The
tension among these three certainties generates the doctrine of original sin in its
"Augustinian" form. The argument is somewhat convoluted.

We must firmly and tenaciously believe that God has mercy and hardens as he will, and that this is in accord with a justice that is hidden (*occultae*) and unsearchable (*investigabilis*).[15] This justice is to be observed in human and earthly business. Unless we possessed (*teneremus*) certain traces of this heavenly justice impressed here, our infirm minds would never attain to the holy sanctum of the spiritual commands. . . . In this desert of our mortal life and condition, if some slightest drop of the divine dew did not sprinkle us, we would burn up even more quickly than we would die of thirst. Accordingly, since human society is held together by giving and receiving . . . it is clear that no one could claim injustice if a creditor demanded what was owed him, and certainly not if a creditor wished to forgive a debt. And this would not be for the debtors to decide but for the creditors. No one can be accused of injustice who demands something that is owed him, nor can he be accused of injustice who wishes to give up what is owed him: this is for the creditor, not the debtors to decide. . . . Now all human beings are a kind of single mass of sin (*una quaedam massa peccati*). As the Apostle says, "All die in Adam" (1 Cor 15.22), from whom the entire human race derives the origin of the offense against God. Humankind owes to the divine and supreme justice a debt of punishment (*supplicium*), *and whether this is collected or remitted there is no injustice.* (1.2.16)

The change in the understanding of what we may call "original sin" (Augustine does not use the expression here) is as follows. According to *De libero arbitrio* 3, we are subject to death, ignorance, and difficulty because of Adam's sin. We inherit a damaged nature. But we do not owe a debt of punishment. We are punished only for those sins which we commit as individuals. We may call the Adamic inheritance "sin," but it is not such in the strictest sense. The phrase "massa peccati" appears earlier in Augustine's *De diversis quaestionibus* 83, q. 68.3, but there it is used to speak of the universality of the consequences (death, ignorance, etc.) of the Adamic inheritance.

Because *all, even before they are born, are deserving of condemnation,* that some are condemned antecedent to and independent of any particular act is no injustice. Universal damnation would be just; that some are rescued from this desperate condition is simply an act of God's unfathomable mercy.

Here is the root of Augustine's doctrine of original sin: Pauline predestination coupled with a quasi-platonic concern with theodicy. Augustine's personal expe-

---

15. In view of the fact that Augustine immediately speaks of the *uestigia* of the divine justice impressed upon human affairs, it is tempting to read *inuestigabilis* in a sense opposite to the one given here. Indeed, at least one manuscript reads *ininuestigabilis*, suggesting that the word could have this reverse meaning. I believe, however, that the translation given is the more plausible one, reflecting Rom. 11:33: "quam incomprehensibilia sunt iudicia eius et investigabiles viae eius."

rience of sin seems not to have created problems for his earlier theologies, and it is a mistake to try to read him here as a kind of Luther *avant la lettre*.

Very late in Augustine's career, when the issues of grace and predestination had become focal in his polemic against Pelagianism and, more particularly, against those who sided with him against Pelagius on original sin but who were appalled at his doctrine of predestination, Augustine looked back to this question in *Diversis quaestionibus ad Simplicianum* as evidence that predestination was no novelty in his teaching. This claim may be true, but it is seriously misleading. A reader who had somehow missed that particular question could have read virtually everything Augustine had written during the fifteen years between *Diversis quaestionibus ad Simplicianum* and the opening of the Pelagian controversy and not found treatment of predestination. The same reader, moreover, would have found Augustine teaching or at least implying the more common doctrine of foreknowledge, which in *Diversis quaestionibus ad Simplicianum* he had rejected. In what follows I will first show this pattern and then try to make sense of it.

It is difficult to establish the *absence* of something from a body of writing as extensive, complex, and difficult to date as Augustine's.[16] I can at most, therefore, illustrate my claim that predestination virtually[17] disappears from Augustine's production in 397–412. I propose to do this by comparing three works that are all compendious statements of the Christian faith: *De fide et symbolo* (393); *De catechizandis rudibus* (400); and *Enchiridion*. None is particularly polemical in intent.[18] The striking observation that results from such a comparison is that, relative to predestination, grace, and original sin, *De catechizandis rudibus* is much closer to *De fide et symbolo* than to *Enchiridion*. The crucial work is *De catechizandis rudibus*.[19] So far as I can see, although several passages in *Catechizandis* go well beyond Augustine's earliest theology, none teaches or necessarily presupposes the theology of *Diversis quaestionibus ad Simplicianum*. Consider the following:

> Neither did the devil in any manner harm God, whether in falling himself, or in seducing man to death; nor did man himself in any degree impair the truth or power or blessedness of his maker, in that, when his partner was seduced by the devil, he of his own deliberate inclination consented unto her in the doing of that which God had forbidden. For by the most righteous laws of God all were condemned, God himself being glorious in

---

16. Augustine's writings are among the easiest to date with respect to completion or publication. However, since he worked for many years on individual works, it is often difficult to say when a particular *part* of a work was written.

17. "Virtually" — I add this word not simply out of scholarly caution but because there is an interesting exception to my general claim, to which I shall subsequently return.

18. See *Enchir.* 6.

19. One might argue that precisely because it is meant for *rudibus* ("the uninstructed"), predestination might appropriately be omitted. But this would be telling only if there were other works — for the more advanced, let us say — that *did* contain this theology. However, as far as I can determine there are no such works.

the equity of retribution, while they were shamed through the degradation of punishment: to the end that man, when he turned away from his Creator, should be overcome by the devil and made his subject, and that the devil might be set before man as an enemy to be conquered, when he turned again to his Creator; so that whosoever should consent unto the devil even to the end, might go with him into eternal punishments; whereas those who should humble themselves to God, and by his grace overcome the devil, might be counted worthy of eternal rewards. (*Catech.* 18.30)[20]

One gets no hint that it is God who effects the turning. The theology presupposed is rather the view before *Diversis quaestionibus ad Simplicianum* 1.2 that the turning to God lies in our power, that grace is God's responsive gift, and that by grace we work good.

Another text touches more directly on the issue of predestination:

He would have spared them [those lost in the flood], as at a later period he spared the city of Nineveh when it repented, after he had announced to it, by means of a prophet, the destruction that was about to overtake it. Thus, moreover, God acts, granting a space for repentance even to those who he knows will persist in wickedness, in order that he may exercise and instruct our patience by his own example. (*Catech.* 19.32)

There is not a hint of Augustine's belief that those lost in the flood could not have repented without God's grace, *and that God chose not to grant them that mercy.*

Enchiridion, on the other hand, although also intended as a general compendium of Christian belief, is clear and explicit with respect both to the doctrines of grace and predestination.[21]

The first book of *De doctrina christiana* was written shortly after *Diversis quaestionibus ad Simplicianum*,[22] yet there is not a hint of the recently achieved theological breakthrough. The brief mention of the consequences of the fall (13.14) and of the obstacles created by the guilt of our previous individual sins (16.17) could have been written much earlier.

There is an interesting passage in Augustine's 102nd letter (409) that at least hints at the doctrine of predestination, but that does so in a way that may help explain why such discussion is absent elsewhere. The letter replies to a series of questions sent by a presbyter, Deogratias, setting forth objections from a common acquaintance who is not a Christian. One of the questions is why God waited so long before sending Christ, since, according to the Christians, only through him

---

20. Except where otherwise indicated, I use the translation from *NPNF.*

21. Regarding grace, see c. 32; for predestination, c. 98. Predestination is here closely tied to Romans 9.

22. See *Retract.* 2.4.

is salvation possible. Augustine first replies that even those who, before Christ's coming, "believed in him both as dwelling with the Father and as destined to come in the flesh" (*Ep.* 102.12) would be saved; but then he continues:

> What answer... could they make, if, leaving out of view that depth of the wisdom and knowledge of God within which it may be that some other divine purpose lies much more deeply hidden, and without prejudging the other reasons possibly existing, which are fit subjects for patient study by the wise (*ubi fortassis aliud divinum consilium large secretius latet, sine praeiudicio etiam aliarum forte causarum, quae a prudentius investigari quaeunt...*), we confine ourselves, for the sake of brevity in this discussion, to the statement of this one position, that it pleased Christ to appoint the time in which he would appear and the persons among whom his doctrine was to be proclaimed, according to his knowledge of the times and places in which men would believe on him? For he foreknew, regarding those ages and places in which his gospel has not been preached, that in them the gospel, if preached, would meet with such treatment from all, without exception, as it met with, not indeed from all, but from many, at the time of his personal presence on earth, who would not believe in him.... (*Ep.* 102.14)

In *De praedestinatione* 9.17–18, Augustine explains that in this letter he did not deem it necessary to discuss predestination rather than foreknowledge in writing to pagans; but in fact he is not writing directly to pagans but to a fellow bishop.[23]

Augustine sets forth his long since rejected view of predestination as foreknowledge, even as he suggests that there might be something deeper involved, something that might reveal itself to "the patient study of the wise." Predestination and original sin are thus alluded to as esoteric doctrine. Moreover, he is willing not merely to *tolerate* a doctrine of predestination as foreknowledge (which he had explicitly rejected in *Diversis quaestionibus ad Simplicianum*); he is willing to *teach* it.

I return subsequently to one clear exception to the generalization which I am proposing, to one passage in which Augustine, in the years immediately preceding controversy with the Pelagians, clearly teaches original sin and predestination in their full "Augustinian" sense. However, because this passage sheds light on why in 412/413 Augustine suddenly returned to these issues with such vigor, I defer consideration of this passage for the moment.

If we ask what Pelagius might have objected to in Augustine's writings before 412, the answer would seem to be relatively little. A. J. Smith has convincingly

---

23. The *NPNF* translation of *De predestinatione* 9.17 could make it appear that Augustine is quoting himself in a sense opposite from his original meaning. The problem would seem to lie in the two opposed meanings that *investigare* could have in fourth-century Christian/North African Latin.

shown that Pelagius made use of Augustine's *Expositio quarumdam quaestionum*,[24] and that, like the Augustine of that work, he interprets predestination as fore-knowledge: "I will have mercy on him whom I know to be able to merit mercy."[25] Much of Rom. 9:14–19 he puts in the mouth of Paul's opponents. On neither of these points is Pelagius original or outside the tradition. Foreknowledge he could have found in the earlier Augustine, as noted, in Ambrosiaster, or in the Rufinus translation of Origen.[26] There is no reason to suppose that there is any anti-Augustinian polemic here.

Pelagius also knew a number of Augustine's earlier writings, and Augustine often expressed his impatience with the way in which he was quoted in support of Pelagian positions. But this does not warrant the conclusion that Pelagius cited Augustine as a means of polemicizing against the Augustine of the first decade of the new century. It is at least conceivable that Pelagius may have been unaware of deep or fundamental differences between himself and Augustine.

We have Augustine's testimony that Pelagius had objected to a passage from *Confessions*, which Pelagius is alleged to have heard while he was still in Rome (i.e., before 409). The passage was, "Give what you command, and command what you will."[27] This may require that I modify slightly the suggestion that Pelagius, prior to the outbreak of the controversy in 412, was unaware of his disagreement with Augustine. But three points should be noted: (1) The testimony comes from the very last years of Augustine's life, long after the alleged events; (2) at best Augustine knows of Pelagius's objection only secondhand; and (3) it is not altogether clear what happened. Consider the text of *De dono perseverantiae* (c. 53):

> And which of my smaller works has been able to be more generally and more agreeably known than the books of my *Confessions*? And although I published them before the Pelagian heresy had come into existence, certainly in them I said to my God, and said it frequently, "Give what Thou commandest, and command what Thou willest." Which words of mine, Pelagius at Rome, when they were mentioned in his presence by a certain brother and fellow bishop of mine, could not bear; and contradicting somewhat too excitedly, nearly came to a quarrel with him who had mentioned them.

Pelagius objected to the expression and *almost* got into an argument over it: "contradicens aliquanto commotius, pene cum eo . . . litigavit." Whatever this twenty-five-year-old near-argument might have been, it did not take place in writing, and Augustine was not present. Since it is not mentioned until a very late

---

24. A. J. Smith, "The Latin Sources of the Commentary of Pelagius on the Epistle of St. Paul to the Romans," *JTS* 19 (1917–18): 162–230; 20 (1918–19): 55–65, 127–77.

25. Alexander Souter, *Pelagius' Expositions of Thirteen Epistles of Paul* (2 vols.; Cambridge: Cambridge University Press, 1922, 1926); quote from 2.75.

26. Ibid., 1.191–92.

27. *De dono perseverantiae* 20.53; from *Conf.* 8.40.60.

date, it seems unlikely that Augustine even heard of it until a long time after the event. Was there a Pelagian polemic against Augustine prior to Augustine's first anti-Pelagian writings? Perhaps,[28] but it is striking that the only specific attack to which Augustine refers is a prayer which bears some resemblance to Wisdom 8:21.

Consequently, although Augustine is correct in claiming that he came to understand predestination and grace in Augustinian fashion long before he had ever heard of Pelagius, this claim is seriously misleading. Only if we recognize this can we make sense of the last phase of controversy with Pelagianism, the so-called semi-Pelagian controversy.

Augustine writes *De praedestinatione sanctorum* in 428 or 429 in response to letters from Prosper and Hilarius, who have described some semi-Augustinians[29] who are having difficulty with predestination:

> I am greatly amazed that they say that there was no need to trouble the hearts of so many simpler people (*minus intelligentium*) with the uncertainty of this kind of disputation; that the catholic faith had been no less usefully defended for years without this definition of predestination by so many other catholic writers and by our earlier writings ... especially against the Pelagians. (*Praed.* 20.52; my translation)

> Those brethren of ours, on whose behalf your pious love is solicitous, have attained with Christ's Church to the belief that the human race is born injured by the sin of the first man (*credunt cum ecclesia Christi peccato primi hominis obnoxium nasci genus humanum*), and that none can be delivered from that evil save by the righteousness of the Second Man. Moreover, they have attained to the confession that men's wills are anticipated by God's grace; and to the agreement that no one can suffice to himself either for beginning or for completing any good work. (*Praed.* 1.2; *NPNF*, slightly modified)

These statements suggest that semi-Augustinians had followed Augustine's lead on issues which had until then been salient over against Pelagius, but they only gradually seemed to realize that predestination was part of the package. This is inconceivable had they known *Diversis quaestionibus ad Simplicianum*, in which predestination is central, with grace and original sin the subordinate themes.

But this observation puts before us the question of why in 412 Augustine so drastically changes, if not his mind, at least his theology. If in 409 he was still willing to teach a version of predestination on the basis of foreseen faith

---

28. R. F. Evans, *Pelagius: Inquiries and Reappraisals* (New York: Seabury Press, 1968), sees Jerome as the principal object of Pelagius's polemic; T. Bohlin, *Die Theologie des Pelagius und ihre Genesis* (Uppsala: Lundequistska bokhandeln, 1957), 10–15, sees the polemic aimed at Arian and Manichaean writers.

29. If they are to have a label this seems more appropriate than the more familiar "semi-Pelagian." They were followers of Augustine.

(*Ep.* 102), reserving for the patient study of the wise the quite different opinion which he harbored for some twelve years, why does this piece of esoterica now become a matter of life and death for the church and the focus of his theology? Since Augustine never acknowledges that his writing of 412 represents other than what he had been teaching since 397, we can hardly expect him to provide an explanation. I believe, however, that he does provide material for an answer.

Augustine's first anti-Pelagian[30] writing was *De peccatorum meritis et remissione et de baptismo parvulorum ad Marcellinum libri tres.* (*NPNF* translates the title, "On the Merits and Forgiveness of Sins, and on the Baptism of Infants.") As Augustine writes in *Retractationes:*

> I accordingly wrote first of all three books under the title, "On the Merits and Forgiveness of Sins," in which I mainly discussed the baptism of infants because of original sin.... (2.23)

Like so much of Augustine's work, *Peccatorum meritis* was written in response to a request for a friend, Marcellinus:

> So strongly has this impulse led and attracted me to solve, to the best of my humble ability, the questions which you have submitted to me in writing, that this issue has little by little become more important than any others in my mind (*ut ea causa in animo meo paulisper vinceret alias*). (1.1; my translation)

The "little by little" — *paulisper* — is enough to indicate that the importance of the Pelagian issue was not immediately evident; Augustine did not explode immediately into a theological fury at the outrageousness of the Pelagians. What brought about the change?

We have, I believe, a clue in one of the rare texts before 412 that echoes the theology of *Diversis quaestionibus ad Simplicianum*, Epistle 98, written in 408 in response to a set of questions posed by his fellow bishop Boniface. The relevant question is whether parents harm baptized infant children if they sacrifice on their behalf to false gods. To answer this question, Augustine first discusses the presuppositions and consequences of infant baptism. He speaks quite straightforwardly of the guilt (*culpa*) and the inherited debt (*obligatio contracta*) (*Ep.* 98.2) which we inherit from Adam's fall. It is only through baptism that the child is freed "from that condemnation which by one man entered the world. He who does not believe this...is an unbeliever" (*Ep.* 98.10.)

Augustine enters the controversy with the Pelagians first because Pelagius's ideas seem to undercut the church's practice of infant baptism. But this concern

---

30. It has often been observed that Augustine is first drawn into controversy with the followers of Pelagius rather than with Pelagius himself, and that he only gradually turns his attention to Pelagius. It did not seem important to mark this differentiation in this text.

is broadened by Augustine's conviction that, in addition, a major tradition in the church's prayer would be damaged if Pelagian views prevailed. Throughout the anti-Pelagian writings he returns to the pattern of prayer in which we ask that God give us the spirit we need. A single example must suffice, but the briefest survey of these writings will turn up scores of parallels:

> When we turn to him...God helps us; when we turn away from him he forsakes us. But then he helps us even to turn to him.... When, therefore, he commands us in the words, "Turn ye unto me, and I will turn unto you," ...we say to him, "Turn us, O God of our salvation," and again, "Turn us O God of hosts," what else do we say than, "Give what thou commandest?" (*Pecc. merit.* 2.5.6)

Here the case is made on the basis of scriptural examples of prayer, but Augustine just as commonly makes his point with reference to the petitionary prayers so common in the Latin tradition.[31]

In the process, Rom. 9:10ff. loses salience. Eventually Augustine will return to it when he claims that he has been teaching the same thing since *Diversis quaestionibus ad Simplicianum*, but the text makes only the most perfunctory appearance in *Peccatorum meritis*, with no hint there of its predestinarian implications. Here and in the works of the next several years, Romans 9 functions principally to remind us that "there is no unrighteousness with God," a view that is neither uniquely nor characteristically Augustinian.

---

31. By way of example, see *De dono perseverantiae* 13.33.

17

The Sabbath Halakhah in the Context of Rabbinic Judaism's Theological System

—— ◆ ——

Jacob Neusner
Bard College

No scholar of his generation has made a more formidable contribution to the study of the history of Judaism, with special reference to Second Temple times, than George W. E. Nickelsburg. And among my contemporaries, none has more consistently, loyally, or ably contributed to projects that I have organized over many decades than has he. Companion, friend, often teacher, always guide and collaborator, he has ornamented his, and my generation: *Er trat an meiner Seiten, einen bessern findst du nicht.*

In his honor let me call attention to how the hermeneutics of a systematic theology, such as is put forth in the rabbinic writings of late antiquity, govern the reading of scripture by the same rabbis who produced those documents. But this reading moves from the Hebrew Scriptures of ancient Israel forward and outward. If, as Brevard Childs states, "The Evangelists read from the New [Testament] backward to the Old,"[1] we may say very simply, the sages read from the Written Torah forward to the oral one. I propose to show what that means through a specific case.

The Mishnah and related compilations make the opening statement of a large and coherent theological structure, which animates the entirety of the rabbinic writings of late antiquity in all its parts and imparts cogency to the message of each with the messages of all the others. The theological system built on the Mishnah, Tosefta, and *Baraita* corpus rests on four propositions, all of them variations on the authorized history of scripture from Genesis through Kings, a reworking of scripture along lines set forth by scripture.

1. God formed creation in accord with a plan, which the Torah reveals. By the facts of nature and society set forth in that plan, world order can be shown

---

1. See his brilliant work, *Biblical Theology of the Old and New Testaments: Theological Reflection on the Christian Bible* (Minneapolis: Fortress, 1993), 720.

to conform to a pattern of reason based on justice. Those who possess the Torah — Israel — know God; those who do not — the Gentiles — reject God in favor of idols. What happens to each of the two sectors of humanity corresponds to its relationship with God. Israel in the present age is subordinate to the nations because God has designated the Gentiles as the medium for penalizing Israel's rebellion. Throughout Israel's subordination and exile the Gentiles' role is to provoke Israel to repent. Private life as much as the public order conforms to the principle that God rules justly in a creation of perfection and stasis.

2. The perfection of creation, realized in the rule of exact justice, is signified by the timelessness of the world of human affairs, their conformity to a few enduring paradigms that transcend change (theology of history). No present, past, or future marks time, but only the recapitulation of those patterns. Perfection is further embodied in the unchanging relationships of the social commonwealth (theology of political economy), which assure that scarce resources, once allocated, remain in stasis. A further indication of perfection lies in the complementarity of the components of creation, on the one side, and, finally, in the correspondence between God and man, in God's image (theological anthropology), on the other.

3. Israel's condition, public and personal, marks flaws in creation. What disrupts perfection is the sole power capable of standing on its own against God's power, that is, man's will. What man controls and God cannot coerce is man's capacity to form intention, and, therefore, to choose either arrogantly to defy, or humbly to love, God. Because man defies God, the sin that results from man's rebellion flaws creation and disrupts world order. The paradigm of the rebellion of Adam in Eden governs the acts of arrogant rebellion leading to exile from Eden, thus accounting for the condition of humanity. But, as in the original transaction of alienation and consequent exile, God retains the power to encourage repentance through punishing man's arrogance. In mercy, moreover, God exercises the power to respond to repentance with forgiveness, that is, with a change of attitude evoking a counterpart change. Since, commanding his own will, man also has the power to initiate the process of reconciliation with God through repentance, an act of humility, man may restore the perfection of that order that through arrogance he has marred.

4. God ultimately will restore that perfection that embodied God's plan for creation. In the work of restoration, death that comes about by reason of sin will die, the dead will be raised and judged for their deeds in this life, and most of them, having been justified, will go on to eternal life in the world to come. The paradigm of man restored to Eden is realized in Israel's

return to the Land of Israel. In that world or age to come, however, that sector of humanity that through the Torah knows God will encompass all of humanity. Idolaters will perish, and humanity that comprises Israel at the end will know the one, true God and spend eternity in God's light.[2]

Now, recorded in this way, the story told by the Mishnah proves remarkably familiar to the ancient scripture of Israel, with its stress on God's justice (to which God's mercy is integral), man's correspondence with God in having the power of will, man's sin and God's response. But the Mishnah and the other halakhic compilations do not tell their story through narrative but through law. The story that the law means to translate into normative rules of conduct turns out to account for the condition of the world and also to adumbrate the restoration of humanity to Eden through the embodiment of Israel in the Land of Israel.

Sages call the Mishnah "the oral Torah," and it is therefore correct to ask the following: Is the purpose of the literature congruent with the message of the Hebrew Scriptures, also known as the Written Torah? If we translate into the narrative of Israel, from the beginning to the calamity of the destruction of the (first) temple, what is set forth in both abstract and concrete ways in the Oral Torah, we reprise the story laid out in Genesis through Kings and amplified by the principal prophets.

These form the paramount motifs of the law, and they recapitulate the story of humanity. First comes Adam and Eve and their fall from Eden, then Israel and its fall from the Land of Israel. But Israel has what Adam lacked, which is the Torah, and by realizing its norms in the life of the community, Israel has the power to restore itself to the Land of Israel, and, standing for humanity, to bring Adam and Eve back to Eden. Eden is represented by the law of the Mishnah as life eternal, Israel being defined there as those who will rise from the dead, stand in judgment, and enter into immortality:

A. All Israelites have a share in the world to come, as it is said, "Your people also shall be all righteous, they shall inherit the land forever; the branch of my planting, the work of my hands, that I may be glorified" (Isa. 60:21).

B. And these are the ones who have no portion in the world to come:

C. (1) He who says that the resurrection of the dead is a teaching which does not derive from the Torah, (2) or that the Torah does not come from heaven, or (3) an Epicurean (*m. Sanh.* 10:1).

That well-crafted system explains why each of the four parts of the theology of the Mishnah within the encompassing Oral Torah — (1) the perfectly just character

---

2. I have shown that these four propositions encompass the entire system of rabbinic Judaism in my *Theology of the Oral Torah: Revealing the Justice of God* (Kingston, Ontario: McGill-Queen's University Press, 1998).

of world order; (2) indications of its perfection; (3) sources of its imperfection; (4) media for the restoration of world order and their results — belongs in its place, and why set in any other sequence the four units become incomprehensible.

The sages of the halakhah have hermeneutics on their side. In their reading of the Written Torah as a whole, in canonical context, as a record of life with God, they are right to say their story recapitulates the Written Torah's story. But in the Mishnah, they design the story of the restoration of Israel to the land, of Adam to Eden. Start to finish, creation through Sinai to the fall of Jerusalem, all perceived in the light of the prophets' rebuke, consolation, and hope for restoration, scripture's account is rehearsed in the Oral Torah. All is in proportion and balance. Viewed as a systematic hermeneutic, the sages' theology accurately sets forth the principal possibility of the theology that is implicit in the written part of the Torah — to be sure, in a more systematic and cogent manner than does scripture. So it is entirely within the imaginative capacity of the Oral Torah to raise the question: What came before in relationship to what we have in hand? To state the matter more directly, are the rabbis of the Oral Torah right in maintaining that they have provided the originally oral part of the one whole Torah of Moses our rabbi? To answer that question in the affirmative, sages would have only to point to their theology in the setting of scripture's as they grasped it. The theology of the Oral Torah embodied in the halakhah of the Mishnah and associated compilation tells a simple, sublime story.

1. God created a perfect, just world and in it made man in God's image, equal to God in the power of will.

2. Man in his arrogance sinned and was expelled from the perfect world and given over to death. God gave man the Torah to purify his heart of sin.

3. Man educated by the Torah in humility can repent, accepting God's will of his own free will. When he does repent, man will be restored to Eden and eternal life.

In our terms, we should call it a story with a beginning, middle, and end. In sages' framework, we realize, the story embodies an enduring and timeless paradigm of humanity in the encounter with God: man's powerful will, God's powerful world, in conflict, and the resolution thereof. The task of the law of the Mishnah and related writings was to spell out the requirements of that community that would restore Adam and Eve to Eden, through Israel to the Land of Israel.

Now that we have dealt with the hermeneutics, we may reasonably translate the result into exegetics. I take as my specific case the theology that emerges from a reading of the halakhah of the Sabbath as set forth in the Mishnah, Tosefta, Talmud of the Land of Israel, and Talmud of Babylonia. The Written Torah represents the Sabbath as the climax of creation. The theology of the Sabbath put forth in the Oral Torah's halakhah derives from a systematization of definitions implicit in the myth of Eden that envelops the Sabbath. Sages' thinking about the Sabbath invokes in the formation of the normative law defining the matter the model of the first Sabbath, the one of Eden. The two paramount points of concern — (1) the systematic definition of private domain, where ordinary activity is permitted, and (2) the rather particular definition of what constitutes a prohibited act of labor on the Sabbath — precipitate deep thought and animate the handful of principles brought to concrete realization in the two tractates. "Thou shalt not labor" of the commandments refers in a generic sense to all manner of work; but in the halakhah of *Shabbat*, "labor" bears very particular meanings and is defined in a quite specific, and somewhat odd, manner. We can make sense of the halakhah of *Shabbat-Erubin* only by appeal to the story of creation and the governing metaphor derived therefrom — the sages' philosophical reflections that transform into principles of a general and universal character the case at hand.

Given the broad range of possible points of halakhic emphasis that the Written Torah sustains: the dual formulation of matters in the Ten Commandments that make remarkably slight impact here; rest for animals and slaves playing no role in the articulation of the law; the focus, for the Day of Atonement, on the rite of the day, so too for Passover — we realize that sages made choices. Why the stress on space and activity? When approaching the theme and problem of the Sabbath, they chose to answer two questions: What does it mean to remain "in his place," and what constitutes the theory of forbidden activity, the principles that shape the innumerable rules and facts of the prohibition? Accordingly, we must ask a basic question: What is it about the Sabbath of creation that captures sages' attention?

We work back from the large structures of the halakhah to the generative thought — how sages thought, and about what did they think — that gives definition to those structures. And, among available formulations, clearly they gave priority to the creation story of Gen. 1:1–2:3, which accounts for the origin of the Sabbath. The foci of their thinking are located in what is implicit and subject to generalization in that story. The halakhah realizes in detailed, concrete terms generalizations that sages locate in and derive from the story of creation. And what they find is a metaphor for themselves and their Israel, on the one side, and the foundation for generalization, out of the metaphor — in abstract terms susceptible to acute concretization — on the other. That is, the Sabbath of Eden forms the model — like this Sabbath, so all else. And sages, with their remarkable power to think in general terms but to convey thought in examples and details, found it possible to derive from the model the principles that would accomplish their goal: linking Israel to Eden through the Sabbath, the climax of their way of life, the soul of their theological system.

Our task, then, is first to identify the halakhah that best states in detail some of the principles that sages derived from their reading of the story of the Genesis of Eden. Building on the definition supplied by that halakhah, which supplies to the

Sabbath its program of legislation — the things subjected to acute exegesis, the things treated as other than generative — we may then undertake to construct an encompassing theory to find a position, within a single framework, for all of the principal halakhic constrictions at hand. Clearly, the halakhah of *Erubin* is not the place, since that body of halakhah takes for granted layers of profound thought and speculation that have already supplied the matter's foundations. Nor, for the same reason, will the halakhah of *Shabbat* help, for its framers know as established principles a set of conceptions, for example, about the definition of forbidden activity, that presuppose much but articulate, in this context, remarkably little. Accordingly, when it comes to decoding sages' reading of the story of creation culminating in the Sabbath of Eden, there is no reading the halakhah of *Shabbat* or of *Erubin* out of the context of the Sabbath as sages defined that context.

If in the halakhah of *Shabbat* sages know that the division of the world, on the Sabbath, into public and private domains precipitates the massive exegetical task undertaken both there and in *Erubin,* and they further have in mind a powerful definition of the meaning of an act of labor — of what labor consists — those facts on their own give little direction. For neither *Shabbat* nor *Erubin* defines its context; both presuppose analogies and metaphors that are not articulated but constantly present. Only when we know what is supposed to take place on the Sabbath — in particular the model of the Sabbath that originally celebrated creation — to the exclusion of the model of the Sabbath that would focus the halakhah upon the liberation of slaves from Egypt (Deuteronomy's version) or the cessation of labor of the household, encompassing animals and slaves (Exodus's version) — only then shall we find the key to the entire matter of the Sabbath of the halakhah of the Oral Torah. Then we may identify the setting in which the rules before us take on meaning and embody profound religious thinking.

I find the halakhah that presents the model of how sages think about the Sabbath and accounts for the topical program of their thought — the fully articulated source of the governing metaphor — is *Shebi'it.* That tractate describes the observance of the Sabbath that is provided every seventh year for the Land of Israel itself. The Land celebrates the Sabbath, and then Israel, in its model. The Land is holy, as Israel is holy, and the Priestly Code leaves no doubt that for both, the Sabbath defines the rhythm of life with God: the seventh day for Israel, the seventh year for the land. For both, moreover, to keep the Sabbath is to be like God. Specifically, that is when God had completed the work of creation, pronounced it good, sanctified it — imposed closure and permanence, the creation having reached its conclusion. God observed the Sabbath, which itself finds its definition as the celebration and commemoration of God's own action. This is what God did, this is what we now do. What God did concerned creation, what we do concerns creation. And all else follows. The Sabbath then precipitates the imitation of God on a very particular occasion and for a very distinctive purpose. And given what we have identified as sages' governing theology — the systematic account of God's perfect justice in creation, yielding an account and explanation of all else — we find ourselves at the very center of the system. The meeting of time and space on the seventh day of creation — God having formed space and marked time — finds its counterpart in the ordering of Israelite space at the advent of time, the ordering of that space through the action and inaction of the Israelites themselves.

To state matters very simply, *Erubin*, with its sustained exercise of thought on the commingling of ownership of private property for the purpose of Sabbath observance and on the commingling of meals to signify shared ownership, accomplished for Israel's Sabbath what *Shebi'it* achieves for the land's. On the Sabbath inaugurated by the Sabbatical Year the land, so far as it is otherwise private property, no longer is possessed exclusively by the householder. So, too, the produce of the land consequently belongs to everybody. It follows that the halakhah of *Erubin* realizes for the ordinary Sabbath of Israel the very same principles that are embodied in the halakhah of *Shebi'it*. That halakhah defines the Sabbath of the land in exactly the same terms: the land is now no longer private, and the land's produce belongs to everybody. The Sabbath that the land enjoys marks the advent of shared ownership of the land and its fruit. Sharing is so total that hoarding is explicitly forbidden, and what has been hoarded has now to be removed from the household and moved to public domain, where anyone may come and take it.

Here we find the Sabbath of creation overspreading the Sabbath of the land, as the Priestly Code at Genesis 1 and at Leviticus 25:1–8 defines matters. The latter states,

> When you enter the land that I am giving you, the land shall observe a Sabbath of the Lord. Six years you may sow your field and six years you may prune your vineyard and gather in the yield. But in the seventh year the land shall have a Sabbath of complete rest, a Sabbath of the Lord; you shall not sow your field or prune your vineyard. You shall not reap the aftergrowth of your harvest or gather the grapes of your untrimmed vines; it shall be a year of complete rest for the land. But you may eat whatever the land during its Sabbath will produce — you, your male and female slaves, the hired hand and bound laborers who live with you, and your cattle and the beasts in your land may eat all its yield. (Lev. 25:2–7)

The Sabbatical Year bears the message, therefore, that on the Sabbath, established arrangements as to ownership and possession are set aside, and a different conception of private property takes over. What on ordinary days is deemed to belong to the householder and to be subject to his exclusive will on the Sabbath falls into a more complex web of possession. The householder continues to utilize his property but not as a proprietor does. He gives up exclusive access thereto, and gains in exchange rights of access to other people's property. Private property is commingled; everybody shares in everybody's. The result is, private property takes on a new meaning, different from the secular one. So far as the householder proposes to utilize his private property, he must share it with others, who do the same for him. To own, then, is to abridge ownership in favor of commingling rights thereto; to possess is to share. And that explains why the produce of the land belongs to everyone as well, a corollary to the fundamental postulate of the Sabbath of the Land.

Now the halakhah of *Shebi'it* appeals to the metaphor of Eden, and, along those same lines, if we wish to understand how sages thought about the Sabbath, we have here to follow suit. But that is hardly to transgress the character of the evidence in hand, the story of the first Sabbath as the celebration of the conclusion and perfection of creation itself. Since, accordingly, the Sabbath commemorates the sanctification of creation, we cannot contemplate Sabbath observance outside of the framework of its generative model, which is Eden. What sages add in the halakhah of the Oral Torah becomes self-evident: Eden provides the metaphor for imagining the Land of Israel, and the Sabbath, the occasion for the act of metaphorization.

Then, the hermeneutics in hand, the exegesis of the halakhah becomes possible. Specifically, we have found the governing question to which the details of the law respond; specifically, what about Eden on the Sabbath defines the governing metaphor out of which the principles of the halakhah work themselves out in the articulation of acute details that yields our halakhah? Working back from the details to the organizing topics, and from the topics to the principles that govern, we find ourselves able to frame the right question.

It is: What qualities of Eden impress sages? With the halakhah as the vast corpus of facts, we focus upon two matters: (1) time and space, (2) time and activity. How is space demarcated at the specified time, how is activity classified at that same time? The former works itself out in a discussion of where people may move on the Sabbath and how they may conduct themselves (carry things as they move). The latter finds its definition in the model of labor that is prohibited. With Eden as the model and metaphor, we take a simple sighting on the matter. First, Adam and Eve are free to move in Eden where they wish, possessing all that they contemplate. God has given it to them to enjoy. If Eden then belongs to God, God freely shares ownership with Adam and Eve. And — all the more so — the produce of Eden is ownerless. With the well-known exception, all the fruit is theirs for the taking. So we find ourselves deep within the halakhah of *Shebi'it*.

For the halakhah of *Shebi'it* sets forth in concrete terms what is implicit in the character of Eden. In the Sabbatical Year the land returns to the condition characteristic of Eden at the outset: shared and therefore accessible, its produce available to all. The Sabbatical Year recovers that perfect time of Eden when the world was at rest, all things in place. Before the rebellion, man did not have to labor on the land; he picked and ate his meals freely. In the nature of things, everything belonged to everybody; private ownership in response to individual labor did not exist, because man did not have to work anyhow. Reverting to that perfect time, the Torah maintains that the land will provide adequate food to everyone, including the flocks and herds, even if people do not work the land. But that is on condition that all claim of ownership lapses; the food is left in the fields, to be picked by anyone who wishes, but it may not be hoarded by the landowner in particular. Avery-Peck states this matter as follows:

> Scripture thus understands the Sabbatical year to represent a return to a perfected order of reality, in which all share equally in the bounty of a holy land that yields its food without human labor. The Sabbatical year provides a model through which, once every seven years, Israelites living in the here-and-now may enjoy the perfected order in which God always intended the world to exist and toward which, in the Israelite world view, history indeed is moving.... The release of debts accomplishes for Israelites' economic relationships just what the agricultural Sabbatical accomplishes for the relationship between the people and the land. Eradicating debt allows the Israelite economy to return to the state of equilibrium that existed at the time of creation, when all shared equally in the bounty of the Land.[3]

The Priestly Code expresses that same concept when it arranges for the return, at the Jubilee Year, of inherited property to the ownership of the original family: "You shall count off seven weeks of years, so that the period of seven weeks of years gives you a total for forty-nine years.... You shall proclaim release throughout the land for all its inhabitants. It shall be a jubilee for you; each of you shall return to his holding and each of you shall return to his family" (Lev. 25:8–10). The Jubilee Year is observed as is the Sabbatical Year, meaning that for two successive years the land is not to be worked. The halakhah moreover establishes that when land is sold, it is for the span of time remaining to the next Jubilee Year. Then it reverts to the original owner. That then marks the reordering of landholding to its original pattern, when Israel inherited the land to begin with and commenced to enjoy its produce. Just as the Sabbatical Year commemorates the completion of creation, the perfection of world order, so does the Sabbath.

So, too, the Jubilee Year brings about the restoration of real property to the original division. In both instances, Israelites act so as to indicate that they are not absolute owners of the land, which belongs to God and which is divided in the manner that God arranged in perpetuity. Avery-Peck states the matter in the following way:

---

3. Alan J. Avery-Peck, *Yerushalmi Shebi'it* (translation), in *The Talmud of the Land of Israel: A Preliminary Translation and Explanation: Shebi'it* (ed. Jacob Neusner; Chicago: University of Chicago Press, 1991), 3.

On the Sabbath of creation, during the Sabbatical year, and in the Jubilee
year, diverse aspects of Israelite life are to return to the way that they were at
the time of creation. Israelites thus acknowledge that, in the beginning, God
created a perfect world, and they assure that the world of the here-and-now
does not overly shift from its perfect character. By providing opportunities
for Israelites to model their contemporary existence upon a perfected order
of things, these commemorations further prepare the people for messianic
times, when, under God's rule, the world will permanently revert to the
ideal character of the time of creation.[4]

Here we find the halakhic counterpart to the restorationist theology that the Oral
Torah sets forth in the haggadah. Israel matches Adam, the Land of Israel, Eden,
and, we now see, the Sabbatical Year commemorates the perfection of creation
and replicates it. If the perfection of creation is the well-ordered condition of the
natural world, then the Land of Israel, counterpart to Eden, must be formed into
the model of the initial perfection, restored to that initial condition.

It is in this context that we return to the halakhah of *Shabbat-Erubin,* with
special reference to the division of the world into private and public domain, the
former the realm of permitted activity on the Sabbath, the latter not. If we may
deal with an ʿerub-fence or an ʿerub-meal, how are we to interpret what is at stake
in these matters? In both instances, private domain is rendered public through the
sharing of ownership. The ʿerub-fence for its part renders public domain private,
but only in the same sense that private domain owned by diverse owners is shared,
ownership being commingled. The ʿerub-fence signals the formation of private
domain for the sanctification of time — but with the ownership commingled. So
what is "private" about "private domain" is different on the Sabbath from secular
time. By definition, for property to be private in the setting of the Sabbath, it must
be shared among householders. On the Sabbath, domain that is totally private, its
ownership not commingled for the occasion, becomes a prison, the householder
unable to conduct himself in the normal manner in the courtyard beyond his door,
let alone in the other courtyards in the same alleyway, or in other alleyways that
debouch onto the same street. And the halakhah makes provision for those —
whether Israelite or Gentile — who do not offer proprietorship of their households
for commingling for the Sabbath.

What happens, therefore, through the ʿerub-fence or ʿerub-meal is the redefinition of proprietorship: what is private is no longer personal, and no one totally
owns what is his, but then everyone (who wishes to participate, himself and his
household together) owns a share everywhere. So much for the "in his place"
part of "each man in his place." His place constitutes an area in which ordinary

4. Ibid., 4.

life goes on, but it is no longer "his" in the way in which the land is subject to his will and activity in ordinary time.

If constructing a fence, or constructing the gateway, of the alleyway and its courtyards, signifies joint ownership of the village, now turned into private domain, what about the meal? The 'erub-meal signifies the shared character of what is eaten. It is food that belongs to all who wish to share it. But it is the provision of a personal meal, also, that allows an individual to designate for himself a place of Sabbath residence other than the household to which he belongs.

So the Sabbath loosens bonds, those of the householder to his property, those of the individual to the household. It forms communities, the householders of a courtyard into a community of shared ownership of the entire courtyard, the individual into a community other than that formed by the household to which he belongs — now the community of disciples of a given sage, the community of a family other than that in residence in the household, to use two of the examples common in the halakhah. Just as the Sabbath redefines ownership of the land and its produce, turning all Israelites into a single social entity, "all Israel," which, all together, possesses the land in common ownership, so the Sabbath redefines the social relationships of the household, allowing persons to separate themselves from the residence of the household and to designate some other, some personal, point of residence instead.

The main point of the law of private domain in *Shabbat* and *Erubin*, as seen in the model of *Shebi'it*, is to redefine the meaning of "private domain," in which each man is to remain in "his" place. The law aims to define the meaning of "his," and to remove the ownership of the land and its produce from the domain of a householder, rendering ownership public and collective. Taking as our model the halakhah of the Sabbatical Year in tractate *Shebi'it*, we note that in the year that is a Sabbath, the land is to be owned by nobody and everybody, and the produce of the land belongs to everyone and no one, so that one may take and eat but thank only God. It is no one's, so everyone may take; it is everyone's, so everyone may eat, and God alone is to be acknowledged. Since, on the Sabbath, people are supposed to remain within their own domain, the counterpart to *Shebi'it* will provide for the sharing of ownership, thus for extending the meaning of "private domain" to encompass all the partners in a shared locus. "Private domain," his place, now bears a quite different meaning from the one that pertains in profane time. The Sabbath recapitulates the condition of Eden, when Adam and Eve could go where they wished and eat what they wanted, masters of all they contemplated, along with God. Israel on the Sabbath in the land, like Adam on the Sabbath of Eden that celebrated creation, shares private domain and its produce.

Israel on the Sabbath in the land, like God on the Sabbath of Eden, rests from the labor of creation. And that brings us to the question, What about that other principle of the Sabbath, the one set forth by the halakhah of *Shabbat*? The richly detailed halakhah of *Shabbat* defines the matter in a prolix, yet simple way. On the Sabbath it is prohibited deliberately to carry out in a normal way a completed act of constructive labor, one that produces enduring results, one that carries out one's entire intention: the whole of what one planned and that one has accomplished in exactly the proper manner. That definition takes into account the shank of the halakhah of *Shabbat* as set forth in the Mishnah tractate, and the amplification and extension of matters in the Tosefta and the two Talmuds in no way revises the basic principles. Here there is a curious, if obvious, fact: it is not an act of labor that itself is prohibited (as the Ten Commandments in Exodus and Deuteronomy would have it), but an act of labor of a very particular definition.

No prohibition impedes performing an act of labor in an other-than-normal way. In theory, one may go out into the fields and plough, if he does so in some odd manner. He may build an entire house, so long as it collapses promptly. The issue of activity on the Sabbath therefore is removed from the obvious context of work, conventionally defined. Now the activity that is forbidden is of a very particular sort, modeled in its indicative traits after a specific paradigm. A person is not forbidden to carry out an act of destruction, or an act of labor that has no lasting consequences. He may start an act of labor if he does not complete it. He may accomplish an act of labor in some extraordinary manner. None of these acts of labor is forbidden, even though, done properly and with consequence, they represent massive violations of the halakhah. Nor is part of an act of labor that is not brought to completion prohibited. Nor is it forbidden to perform part of an act of labor in partnership with another person who carries out the other requisite part. Nor does one incur culpability for performing an act of labor in several distinct parts, for example, over a protracted, differentiated period of time. A person may not willingly carry out the entirety of an act of constructive labor, start to finish. The issue is not why not, since we know the answer: God has said not to do so. The question is, Whence the particular definition at hand?

Clearly, a definition of the act of labor that is prohibited on the Sabbath has taken over and recast the commonsense meaning of the commandment not to labor on the Sabbath. Considerations enter that recast matters from an absolute to a relative definition. One may tie a knot — but not one that stands. One may carry a package, but not in the usual manner. One may build a wall, only if it falls down. And one may do pretty much anything without penalty — if he did not intend matters as they actually happened. The metaphor of God in Eden, as sages have reflected on the story of God in creation, yields the governing principles that define forbidden labor. What God did in the six days of creation provides the model.

The details of the halakhah then emerge out of a process in which two distinct sources contribute. One is the model of the tabernacle. What man may do for God's house he may not do for his own — God is always God; the Israelite aspires only to be "like God," to imitate God, and that is a different thing. The other is the model of the creation of the world and of Eden. Hence to act like God on the Sabbath, the Israelite rests; he does not do what God did in creation. The former source supplies generative metaphors, the like of which may not be done; thus acts like sowing, like harvesting, like lifting boards from public to private domain, and the like are forbidden. The latter source supplies the generative principles, the abstract definitions involving the qualities of perfection and causation: intentionality, completion, the normality of the conduct of the action, and the like. The mode of analogical thinking governs, but, as we see, a double metaphor pertains, the metaphor of God's activity in creation, the metaphor of the priests' and Levites' activity in the tabernacle. Creation yields those large principles that we have identified: the traits of an act of labor for God in creation define the prohibited conditions of an act of labor on the Sabbath. By appeal to those two metaphors, we can account for every detail of the halakhah.

What then takes place inside the walls of the Israelite household when time takes over space and revises the conduct of ordinary affairs? Israel goes home to Eden. How best to make the statement that the land is Israel's Eden, that Israel imitates God by keeping the Sabbath — meaning not doing the things that God did in creating the world but ceased to do on the Sabbath — and that to restore its Eden, Israel must sustain its life — nourish itself — where it belongs? To set forth those most basic convictions about God in relationship to man and about Israel in relationship to God, I can imagine no more eloquent, no more compelling and appropriate, medium of expression than the densely detailed halakhah of *Shebi'it, Shabbat,* and *Erubin.* Indeed, outside of the setting of the household, its ownership, utilization, and maintenance, I cannot think of any other way of fully making that statement stick. In theory implausible for its very simplicity (as much as for its dense instantiation!), in halakhic fact, compelling, the Oral Torah's statement accounts for the human condition. Israel's Eden takes place in the household open to others, on the Sabbath, in acts that maintain life, share wealth, and desist from creation.

The key words, therefore, are in the shift from the here and now of time in which one works like God, to the *then* and *there* when one desists from working, just as God did at the moment the world was finished, perfected, and sanctified. Israel gives up the situation of man in ordinary time and space, destructive, selfish, dissatisfied, and doing. Then, on the Sabbath, and there, in the household, with each one in place, Israel enters the situation of God in that initial, that perfected and sanctified then and there of creation: the activity that consists in sustaining life, sharing dominion, and perfecting repose through acts of restraint and sufficiency. The Sabbath forms the perpetual occasion for the restoration of Israel to Eden — just as I said at the outset — and forms the heart and soul of scripture's account of Israel viewed from God's perspective: the New and the Last Adam.

18

Exegesis of Genesis 1 in the Gospels of Thomas and John

◆

Elaine H. Pagels

Princeton University

Just as the Gospels of Thomas and John, for all their similarities, nevertheless articulate somewhat conflicting traditions about Jesus, so also these two Gospels articulate conflicting traditions about creation. Several scholars recently have investigated the former; this article primarily explores the latter.[1] In his recent monograph, Greg Riley, for example, depicts the "communities of John and Thomas" living "in close . . . proximity" with one another, sharing both agreements and disagreements.[2] Riley concludes that John's author writes in response to earlier traditions that survive in Thomas, intending his teaching on bodily resurrection to refute the view of spiritual resurrection expressed in the *Gospel of Thomas*. April De Conick, in her recent monograph and subsequent article, disagrees with Riley's characterization of the conflict, but agrees with the premise, suggesting instead that John's author is arguing against a Thomas tradition encouraging the disciples to seek visions through ecstatic ascent.[3] Helmut Koester and Stephen Patterson have set forth a comparative analysis of sayings involving,

This is a revision of a paper read at a session of the Thomas Group of the AAR/SBL Annual Meeting in San Francisco, November 1997. I am very grateful to colleagues and friends from whom I learned much while discussing the work in progress, especially Helmut Koester and Karen King; and to those who generously offered comments and criticisms that much improved earlier written drafts: Robert McL. Wilson, Birger Pearson, John Turner, April De Conick, Ismo Dunderberg, and Louis Painchaud. A version of this article appeared in *JBL* 118 (1999): 477–96.

1. As we might expect, however, the interpretation of creation articulated in Thomas bears implications for Thomas's view of Jesus, as we shall see.
2. Gregory J. Riley, *Resurrection Reconsidered: Thomas and John in Controversy* (Minneapolis: Fortress, 1995), 177.
3. April De Conick, *Seek to See Him: Ascent and Vision Mysticism in the "Gospel of Thomas"* (Leiden: Brill, 1996); "'Blessed are those who have not seen' (John 20:29): Johannine Dramatization of an Early Christian Discourse," in *The Nag Hammadi Library after Fifty Years* (ed. John D. Turner and Anne McGuire; Leiden: Brill, 1997), 381–400.

for example, Christology and anthropology, that points toward the same conclusion: that the Johannine author polemicizes against certain traditions about
Jesus and his message that we find in the *Gospel of Thomas*.[4] Without accepting
all their conclusions (since this research, like Michael Williams's recent book,[5]
raises questions concerning the category "gnostic," which Koester and Patterson
sometimes apply to Thomas's logia),[6] I adopt, here, a similar method, comparing
patterns of Genesis exegesis in these two respective gospels.

In order to relate what happened "in the beginning" to bring about the present
human condition, each Gospel author invokes and interprets Genesis 1 — John
in his remarkable prologue (which may, of course, predate the Gospel itself), and
Thomas in a cluster of sayings that occur throughout his gospel.[7] Steven Davies,
in his incisive recent article, points out that both John and Thomas, in contrast
with the Synoptic Gospels, speak of the kingdom of God not eschatologically but
protologically — that is, by comparing ordinary life in the present not with that
of the coming kingdom, but with that of the primordial creation.[8] Davies persuasively demonstrates that "Jesus, as Thomas portrays him, insists that the world
ought to be considered to be in the condition of Gen. 1:1–2:4 and, accordingly,
that people should restore themselves to the condition of the image of God."[9]

Davies focuses primarily on similarities between Thomas and John; but what
I find even more striking are the differences. When we compare their respective
Genesis exegeses, we find a clash of exegetical traditions.

We do not know, of course, whether or not John actually read the text we call
the *Gospel of Thomas;* but comparison of the Johannine prologue with the above-
mentioned cluster of Thomas sayings suggests that he knew — and thoroughly
disagreed with — the type of exegesis offered in Thomas. As we shall see, John's

---

4. Helmut Koester and Stephen Patterson, *Ancient Christian Gospels: Their History and Development*
(Philadelphia: Trinity Press International, 1991), 75–124; see also Stephen J. Patterson, *The Gospel of
Thomas and Jesus* (Sonoma, Calif.: Polebridge, 1993).

5. Michael Williams, *Rethinking Gnosticism: An Argument for Dismantling A Dubious Category*
(Princeton: Princeton University Press, 1996). On defining the terms, see the excellent article
by R. McL. Wilson, "Gnosis and Gnosticism: The Messina Definition," in Ἀγαθὴ ἐλπις: *Studi
Storico-Religiosi in Onore di Ugo Bianchi* (Rome: "L'Erma" di Bretschneider, 1994), 539–51. See now
A. Marjanen, "Is Thomas a Gnostic Gospel,"in *Thomas at the Crossroads* (ed. R. Uro; Edinburgh:
T. & T. Clark, 1998), 107–39.

6. See, for example, Koester and Patterson, *Ancient Christian Gospels,* 83; 118–25; Stephen Patterson repeatedly invokes "Thomas's gnosticizing proclivity," for example on pages 135, 155, and 157 of
The "Gospel of Thomas" and Jesus. Further, Ismo Dunderberg's incisive analysis has demonstrated the
complexity of making such comparison, and rightly warns against "generalizing about the relationship
of the *Gospel of Thomas* to the Johannine writings," considering that "their relationship may vary
from one saying to another" ("John and Thomas in Conflict?" in Turner and McGuire, *Nag Hammadi
Library after Fifty Years,* 361–80).

7. Use of these names is not meant to denote actual authorship, but to follow a conventional
terminology, without presuming that we know the identity of either author.

8. Steven Davies, "The Christology and Protology of the Gospel of John," *JBL* 111 (1992): 663–
83.

9. Ibid., 664.

author not only was aware of this clash of traditions, but actively engaged in polemic against specific patterns of Genesis exegesis he intends his prologue to refute.

This is not to say that Thomas's Genesis exegesis was original or unique. Even a glance at the cultural environment indicates the opposite: namely, that the basic pattern of Thomas's Genesis exegesis was widely known and shared among various groups of Genesis readers, ranging from Jews living in Egypt who read the Septuagint in the light of Greek philosophic reflection (of whom Philo is, of course, the most obvious example) to people engaged with Hermetic practice (whether Jews, Gentiles, or both).[10] Nor is Thomas's theology so characteristically "gnostic" as earlier interpreters often have assumed (and certain contemporary interpreters still seem to assume; see, for example, n. 6 above.) Instead, Thomas's Genesis exegesis articulates a conviction commonplace, in generalized form, in Jewish exegesis — one that Paul shares, and articulates in Romans 1:19:

> What is knowable of God is clear to them (ἀνθρώπων, human beings); for God himself revealed it to them. For the invisible things of God — namely, his eternal power and deity — have been seen, intelligible since the creation of the universe, in the things that are made.

But besides such generalized correlations as these between cosmology and anthropology, Thomas's Genesis exegesis goes much farther, back to the time before cosmic creation. Furthermore, as we shall see, it apparently follows an exegetical pattern articulated in a range of extant sources.

Briefly summarized, Thomas takes Gen. 1:3 to mean that when the primordial light appeared on the "first day," prior to the world's creation, there appeared in that light the form of a primordial *anthrōpos* — whom log. 77 implicitly identifies with Jesus — through whom all things are to come into being. As Hans-Martin Schenke has shown, much of Thomas's theology (and that of other "gnostic" ex- egesis) is based on interpretation of Gen. 1:26–27, which describes the creation of "humankind according to the image of God."[11] According to log. 83, Jesus declares that his disciples will come to see "your images which came into being before you" (*anetnhikōn ntahšōpe hi tetne*) — that is, before the creation of the

---

10. C. H. Dodd, *The Interpretation of the Fourth Gospel* (Cambridge: Cambridge University Press, 1953), 54–73; see the important contributions of Birger A. Pearson, including *Gnosticism, Judaism, and Egyptian Christianity* (Minneapolis: Fortress, 1990), and his article "Pre-Valentinian Gnosticism in Alexandria," in *The Future of Early Christianity: Essays in Honor of Helmut Koester* (ed. B. A. Pearson; Minneapolis: Fortress, 1991), 455–66.

11. Hans-Martin Schenke, *Der Gott "Mensch" in der Gnosis: Ein religionsgeschichtlicher Beitrag zur Diskussion über die paulinische Anschauung von der Kirche als Leib Christi* (Göttingen: Vandenhoeck & Ruprecht, 1962). On patristic exegesis of this verse, see R. McL. Wilson, "The Early History of the Exegesis of Gen. 1.26," in *Papers Presented to the Second International Conference on Patristic Studies Held at Christ Church, Oxford, 1955* (ed. K. Aland and F. L. Cross; vol. 1 of *Studia Patristica*; TU 63; Berlin: Akademie-Verlag, 1957), 420–37; see also Jarl Fossum, "Gen. 1,26 and 2,7 in Judaism, Samaritanism, and Gnosticism," *JSJ* 16 (1985): 202–39.

world, in the primordial light/*anthrōpos*.[12] Such logia as 22 and 61 suggest that Gen. 1:27b ("male and female he created them") depicts humanity's subsequent loss of its original, singular condition, and its devolution into a "divided" condition, deprived of the divine image. But those who succeed in overcoming division (exemplified especially by sexual division; cf. log. 11 and 61) recover their original identity with the "undivided" (*petšēš*) — the singular primal *anthrōpos* (cf. log. 114) — and thereby find access to recognize themselves as "sons of the living Father" (*nšēre mpeiōt*, log. 50). Such exegesis articulates Thomas's conviction that whoever "seeks and finds" (cf. log. 2) must — and can — find access to God through the divine "image" given in creation.

All this may sound familiar — and with good reason; Hellenistic and rabbinic Jewish exegesis, as well as Philo and the Poimandres tractate, offer, as we shall see, many affinities with this sketch of Thomas's Genesis exegesis. But as Schenke has shown in his masterful monograph, we find the closest parallels in certain of the Nag Hammadi texts and related sources, namely, in *The Writing without Title, Eugnostos*, the *Apocryphon of John*, and Irenaeus's account of "Ophite and Sethian" Genesis exegesis (*Haer.* 1.30.1). Such evidence indicates that the exegetical pattern Thomas sets forth was well-known and diversely interpreted, perhaps especially among Jewish circles in Egypt.[13]

Tracing this exegetical pattern in the Thomas logia and in parallel texts and placing these in their cultural environment offer new insights into the Johannine prologue. Seen from this perspective, John's author aims the polemic in his prologue not only, as commentators long have noted (see n. 35), against Jewish, pagan, and "gnostic" readers of Genesis (whatever we mean by "gnostic"; see n. 5), but also against those Christians who (like Thomas's author) follow such an exegetical pattern. Against such views, as we shall see, John, interpreting Gen. 1:1-3, insists that the primordial divine light — far from being accessible through the "image of God" implicitly present in human nature — resides exclusively in the *logos* (see John 1:3), and becomes perceptible to humankind exclusively through the *logos* incarnate. For his polemical purpose, John builds into his prologue what I call the "three negations." First, John declares, when the primordial light shone forth, that it shone into what John regards as utter darkness, "and the darkness did not understand [or: overcome, κατέλαβεν] it" (John 1:5). Second, when it came into the cosmos, human beings failed to recognize ("know"; ἔγνω, 1:10)

---

12. Schenke notes affinity between such a view and, for example, Heb. 1:3: ὃς ὢν ἀπαύγασμα τῆς δόξης καὶ χαρακτὴρ τῆς ὑποστάσεως αὐτοῦ; cf. also Col. 1:15; Wis. 7:26. Schenke sees such exegesis also standing behind such passages as Phil. 2:6, which characterizes the son as ὃς ἐν μορφῇ θεοῦ ὑπάρχων; see Schenke, *Der Gott "Mensch" in der Gnosis*, 134.

13. Besides the influential work of Birger Pearson, cited in n. 10 above, see, for example, the conclusions to M. Waldstein, "The Primal Triad in the *Apocryphon of John*," in Turner and McGuire, *Nag Hammadi Library after Fifty Years*, 154–87. See also the work of J. E. Fossum, *The Image of the Invisible God: Essays on the Influence of Jewish Mysticism on Early Christology* (NTOA 30; Göttingen: Vandenhoeck & Ruprecht, 1995).

that light; and third, that even when it came to "its own," its own rejected it (1:11).

Let us look first, then, at the *Gospel of Thomas.* Logia that refer to the creation account (or to its themes, such as "the beginning") include, for example, log. 4, 11, 18, 19, 37, 49, 50, 77, 83, 84, and 85. Those implicitly related to it include such logia as 22, 24, 61, and 70.[14] Many of these sayings relate, too, to Thomas's understanding of baptismal ritual, which, as Jonathan Smith persuasively argues, was understood to restore the initiate to the situation of Adam in paradise.[15] Reflecting on the work of Davies, Smith, De Conick, and of other scholars, the following section sketches the widespread pattern of Genesis exegesis that underlies these passages — the pattern which became the target of polemical counterexegesis in the Johannine prologue.

Let us begin from the opening of Thomas's *Gospel,* adopting the hypothesis that the sayings are not randomly arranged, but carefully ordered to lead one through a process of seeing and finding "the interpretation of these sayings" (log. 1). This is not to suggest, however, that the author follows an obvious or syllogistic rationale. Instead, as Louis Painchaud has shown in the case of two other texts discovered at Nag Hammadi,[16] the author of Thomas sets forth a complex, riddling composition that requires the reader to "continue seeking until he finds," experiencing in the process (as the "living Jesus" explains in log. 2) both distress and astonishment while struggling to intuit its hidden truth.

According to the very first logion, Jesus promises great reward: whoever succeeds may overcome the power of death (log. 1), the power which felled Adam, and, by implication, all his descendants (log. 85). Logion 2 adds that whoever persists in the painful and startling process of "seeking" will recover the birthright of Adam — will "rule over all things," which Gen. 1:26–28 characterizes as the appropriate role given to the human species at creation. Continuing the contrast with Adam, log. 3, echoing Gen. 1:26–28 (... ἀρχέτωσαν τῶν ἰχθύων τῆς θαλάσσης καὶ τῶν πετεινῶν τοῦ οὐρανοῦ ... καὶ πάσης τῆς γῆς ...), warns that those who miss the divine kingdom will fall behind the "birds of the sky" and the "fish of the sea" instead of ruling over them, according to divine command. For those who fail to "know (themselves)," failing to recognize themselves as "sons of the living Father," Jesus declares, "dwell in poverty," indeed, "are poverty" — their situation contrasting sharply with that of Adam, who "came into

---

14. We need to keep in mind Ismo Dunderberg's warning to base our analyses on specific sayings, not upon whole (and so, of course, composite) texts. Also, De Conick, *Seek to See Him,* has contributed much to our understanding, especially of Jewish and Hermetic sources that may relate to these sayings.

15. J. Z. Smith, "The Garments of Shame," *HR* 5 (1966): 217–38; for De Conick and Fossum's reply, see "Stripped before God: A New Interpretation of Logion 37 in the *Gospel of Thomas,*" *VC* 45 (1991): 123–50.

16. *The Writing without Title* and the *Gospel of Philip;* see Louis Painchaud, *L'écrit sans titre: Traite sur l'origine du monde* (Louvain: Peeters, 1995), and his essay "The Composition of the Gospel of Philip (CGII,3): Rhetorical Analysis," presented at the annual meeting of the SBL in 1996.

being from a great power and a great wealth" (*adam šōpe ebol ... mn ounoč mmnt-rmmao*, log. 85). Logion 4 continues to point toward the situation of Adam: the "small child, seven days old" dwells in the "place of life" at the beginning of time, that is, as Davies points out, on the sixth "day" of creation.[17] As those who are old must become reborn (cf. John 3:5f.) so those who are many "shall become one and the same" (*oua ouōt*, log. 4; literally, "one alone"), recovering the singular image of God originally bestowed in creation (cf. Gen. 1:27a). Underlying logion 4 (and related logia, including 22 and 61, as we shall see) is the inference that its author shares with Philo, Poimandres, and certain rabbinical exegetes, such as R. Samuel bar Nachman — that Gen. 1:27 describes human creation occurring in two stages.[18] When "God created *adam* in his image," he first created a singular being ("in the image of God he created him"). Yet immediately after that, humankind devolved into a dual species, divided into male and female ("male and female he created them"; 1:27b).[19] Logion 11 describes the dilemma this devolution has caused: "On the day you were one, you became two. When you become two, what will you do?" The central theme that connects the cluster of sayings here discussed is the disciple's hope of being restored from his present, divided existence back into the image of the original "single one" — the unity with the primordial *anthrōpos* enjoyed in the "place of light."

In the previous sentence I use the masculine pronoun deliberately, since, although several logia indicate the author's awareness of women among Jesus' disciples, Thomas apparently regards gender — especially feminine gender — as an obstacle to recovering the original divine image.[20] Apparently assuming that Gen. 1:27 (like Genesis 2) describes a two-stage process, log. 61 instructs the disciples to reverse that process — to go back and undo the damage. Beginning from a well-attested Q saying, log. 61 relates a dialogue in which Salome challenges Jesus, questioning his identity in sexually charged language: "Who are you, man,

---

17. Davies, "Christology and Protology," 668.

18. For discussion, see, for example, the monograph by R. Baer, *Male and Female in Philo of Alexandria*, and W. A. Meeks, "The Image of the Androgyne: Some Uses of a Symbol in Earliest Christianity," *HR* 13 (1974): 165–208.

19. As J. Jacobsen Buckley and other scholars have shown, this devolution agrees, as well, with the account of Eve's creation in Genesis 2; see her "An Interpretation of Logion 114 in the *Gospel of Thomas*," in *Female Fault and Fulfillment in Gnosticism* (Chapel Hill and London: University of North Carolina Press, 1986), 84–104; G. Quispel, *Makarius, Das Thomasevangelium und das Lied von der Perle* (Leiden: Brill, 1967), 65–113; S. Arai, " 'To Make Her Male': An Interpretation of Logion 114 in the *Gospel of Thomas*," in *Studia Patristica* 24 (ed. E. A. Livingstone; Louvain: Peeters, 1993).

20. Unlike, for example, Poimandres, Thomas, in conformity with the great majority of Jewish tradition, seems to envision that image in masculine form. See, for example, Elliot R. Wolfson, *Through a Speculum That Shines: Vision and Imagination in Medieval Jewish Mysticism* (Princeton: Princeton University Press, 1994). Much as I might like to agree with scholars like Steven Davies, who excises log. 114 from the genuine Thomas collection [see *The "Gospel of Thomas" and Christian Wisdom* (New York: Seabury, 1983), 153], on this point I agree with Marvin Meyer [see "Making Mary Male: The Categories 'Male' and 'Female' in the *Gospel of Thomas*," *NTS* 31 (1985): 554–70], who accepts the final saying and interprets it symbolically.

that you have come up on my couch, and eaten from my table?" Jesus' response shows that he rejects the divisive categories of sexual identity (cf. Gen. 1:27b), and he declares instead that "I am he who is from the undivided" (*petšeš* — that is, from the singular one of Gen. 1:27a). When Salome responds, "I am your disciple," Jesus warns her that whoever is divided "will be filled with darkness," and implies that whoever identifies with the "undivided" — apparently the ἄνθρωπος κατ᾽ εἰκόνα θεοῦ — will be "filled with light."

Logia 16–19 pick up this theme of restoration. According to log. 16, Jesus rebukes those who look for the kingdom of God eschatologically. Instead, he directs them toward "the beginning" — the place where one may "stand," "know the end," and "not taste death," restored to the dawn of creation, before Adam became mortal. Then, in log. 17, Jesus promises to give his disciples what is impossible to perceive in the ordinary world. According to logion 19, Jesus pronounces blessing as follows: "Blessed is the one who came into being before he came into being." Going back to the beginning, then, requires not only that one go back to the beginning of time, but back even before the Genesis account of human creation.

But how can one accomplish this paradox? What *was* there before human creation — or even before the creation of the universe? Logion 77 suggests the answer. Before human creation — indeed, before "all things" (*ptērou*) — there was the primordial light, the light that appeared on the first "day" (Gen. 1:3). Davies notes from log. 77 that the primordial light pervades all creation, "is evident, for example, within logs and under stones."[21] Yet even *before* creation that light appeared, manifesting itself as well in human form. Logion 77 personifies the divine light, which here speaks in the first person, with a human voice:

> anok pe pouoein paei ethijōou tērou
> anok pe ptērf nta ptērf ei ebol nhēt
> auō nta ptērf pōh šaroei

> I am the light which is above them all.
> I am the all. From me did the all come forth,
> and to me did the all extend.

This exegesis, which envisions the light, so to speak, as an anthropomorphic being, surely echoes, as many scholars have noted, a pun on φῶς and φώς with an acute accent,[22] apparently read into the Septuagint translation of Gen. 1:3. Yet if log. 77 follows Jewish tradition by anthropomorphizing the primordial light, it simultaneously diverges from such tradition by depicting "the living Jesus" speaking with that divine voice. Predictably, extant parallels most often identify the one

---

21. Davies, "Christology and Protology," 664; see also the excellent discussion on 664–74.
22. G. Quispel, "Der Gnostische *Anthropos* und die jüdische Tradition," *ErJb* 22 (1953): 195–234; idem, "Ezekiel 1:26 in Jewish Mysticism and Gnosis," *VC* 34 (1980): 1–13.

who appears in the light as the "first man." Some mean by this not the "first man" of Gen. 1:26, but rather his predecessor (cf. Gen. 1:3), a being of radiant light. *The Writing without Title* (NHC II,5 and XIII,2), for example, explains that "there is an immortal man, a man of light" (*oun ourōme nathanatos rrmouoein*, 103.19; 107.26–27), who exists before all things, manifested in that light "in which a human being appeared, very wonderful" (108.9–10). The text goes on to explain that "the first Adam, he who is of the light, is spiritual (*pšorp če nadam nte pouoein oupneumatikos*). He appeared on the first day. The second Adam is psychic. He appeared on the sixth day" (117.28–32). The same text goes on to say that a third Adam is "earthly" (*oukhoikos*) who appeared "on the eighth day"—the latter referring, apparently, to Gen. 2:7, read through the lens of 1 Cor. 15:43ff., as Louis Painchaud has shown.[23]

A similar pattern apparently underlies *Eugnostos*, which associates an "immortal man" with "the beginning of the light" (3.76.21–23; 81.12). Irenaeus attests that certain heretics, whom the Greek text identifies as "Sethians, whom some call Ophianoi, or Ophites," call *anthrōpos* the God of all things, also calling him "light, and blessed, and immortal" (*Haer.* 1.30.1). According to the Latin text, such people say there is "a certain first light in the power of Bythos, blessed and incorruptible and infinite, who also is called first man" (ibid.). *Apocryphon of John* 2.14.16–20 includes language similar to Thomas's log. 77, speaking of "the one through whom everything came into being, the first man," who is "father of all, the image of the invisible one," who reveals himself "in a male form" (*hn outupos nandreacs* or, according to BG 48.19, in a human form, *mpesmot nourōme*).

Is this being who appears in the primordial light divine or human? Logion 50, which also refers to Gen. 1:3, explains that the "place of light" is "where the light came into being on its own accord." The latter phrase, difficult to translate and to understand, reads literally, "where the light came into being by its own hand" (*pma enta pouoein šōpe nmau ebol hitootf ouaatf*). April De Conick, reflecting on this passage, concludes that "this is not a Jewish concept. Rather, it is rooted in the Hermetic construction of a 'self-begotten' god."[24] I am less confident about discriminating, in this ancient and complex text (and one translated, of course, from Greek into Coptic), between a "Jewish concept" and a Hermetic one, especially given the confluence of Jewish and Egyptian tradition in the Hermetic corpus. How could we discriminate between the two in, for example, Poimandres, which interprets Gen. 1:3 as referring to the "voice of light," which declared itself to be "*nous*, your God"?

What "Poimandres" points out here is simply that, according to Gen. 1:3, it is God who calls himself (or an emanation of himself) into being. The Septuagint translation of the passage reads simply, καὶ εἶπεν ὁ θεός γενηθήτω φῶς · καὶ

---

23. Painchaud, *L'écrit sans titre*, esp. 423–29.
24. De Conick, *Seek to See Him*, 67.

ἐγένετο φῶς. Anyone who read this passage and could identify God as light —
and Philo, of course, could do this as well as any pagan Egyptian — could read the
passage similarly. The *Apocryphon of John*, for example, which Michael Waldstein
ascribes to "Hellenistic Jewish intellectuals,"[25] similarly identifies the light with
both the "first man" (*pehoueit nrōme*) and Barbelo, the divine being "through
whom all things came into being" (BG 29.6.14). Hans Martin Schenke brilliantly
has traced the *Apocryphon of John*'s account of the divine *anthrōpos* to exegesis of
Gen. 1:26. Now, I suggest, we can see that it implicitly involves exegesis of Gen.
1:3 as well. The author of the *Apocryphon of John* twice mentions Gen. 1:2 in order
to correct one interpretation of the verse and to offer an alternative one (BG
44.19–45.1; 45.20–46.14): "'Moses'" saying that a "spirit of God" moved over
the waters refers to the agitation of the divine "mother." Continuing to narrate
what happened to "the mother," the author goes on to Gen. 1:3, explaining that
"a voice came to her" — apparently the voice that says, "Let there be light" —
and that voice reveals "the man and the son of man" (*prōme auō pšēre mprōme*).
Both man and son of man, as Schenke notes, are prototypes of the *anthrōpos*
whose subsequent creation is narrated in Gen. 1:26. Thus at least one version of
the *Apocryphon of John* implicitly identifies the appearance of the divine *anthrōpos*
with that of the primordial light. The second manuscript of the *Apocryphon of John*
makes this identification explicit by repeatedly identifying the divine *anthrōpos*, in
its various manifestations (including its human antitype) as light (NHC II 14.33;
15.4).

The parallel sources I have cited, then, like log. 77, similarly identify the being
who appears in the primordial light as both *anthrōpos* and *theos*, in ways that
their authors leave (and, no doubt, understand to be) mysterious. And while
Thomas has the "living Jesus" speak from that light, he says that this divine light
simultaneously pervades the universe, shining forth from beneath the nearest
rock, and from within any rough-hewn log. What God calls into being in Gen. 1:3,
then, is an emanation of God's own being — light that simultaneously manifests
the divine, the prototype of the human, and the energy manifested throughout
"all things."

Readers who adopt such exegeses of Gen. 1:3 would, of course, be asking the
obvious question: how does the primordial light relate to that *anthrōpos* whose
creation is told in Gen. 1:26–27? As Schenke has shown,[26] most of the sources
cited assume that the medium of that relationship is the divine image. Several
present complex scenarios of celestial sabotage, some involving discrepancy between the "image and likeness" (Gen. 1:27). *The Writing without Title*, for example,
tells how the archons plotted to create humankind "according to the image of

---

25. See Waldstein, "Primal Triad," 185.
26. Schenke, *Der Gott "Mensch,"* esp. 95–156.

their body, and the likeness of the Adam of Light" (12.33–35). *The Hypostasis of the Archons* describes how the archons made a human being "wholly *choikos*" (cf. 1 Cor 15:47)[27] for the purpose of luring the luminous image down from above (87.12–88.10). The *Apocryphon of John* sets forth an elaborate tripartite scheme of interpreting Gen. 1:26 (and Gen. 5:3, which narrates the birth of Seth in Adam's image; see n. 13 above).

Exegetical strategies like these, involving conflict between the Father and lower cosmic powers, are, however, entirely absent from the *Gospel of Thomas*. Instead, Thomas's author sets forth a simpler exegesis, and one far more appropriate to the context of traditional Jewish monism. As we have seen, Poimandres interprets Gen. 1:3 similarly, attributing to the "voice of light" these words: "I am *nous*, your God," and goes on to say that:

> ... the *nous*, father of all, being life and light, brought forth a human being equal to himself, whom he loved as his own offspring, for he was very beautiful, having the image of his father.

Thomas's log. 50 interprets the relationship between the primordial light and its manifestation among human beings, explaining that the light "manifests itself in their image." The unexplained appearance of the plural refers, as De Conick observes, to the plural of Gen. 1:26, "since it states that the light was manifested through a collective image."[28]

Davies concurs: the plural "presumably refers to unmanifest images of God (i.e., actualized people) who perceive the primal light, and so manifest the light to themselves."[29] Logion 50 proceeds as "Jesus" instructs his disciples, when asked their identity (literally, "you — who?"), to answer, "We are his sons, and we are the elect of the living father." Asked for "the sign of your father in you," they are

---

27. See Painchaud, *L'écrit sans titre*, 192, 424–26. For Pauline influence in related texts, see E. Pagels, "Exegesis and Exposition of the Genesis Creation Accounts in Selected Texts from Nag Hammadi," in *Nag Hammadi, Gnosticism, and Early Christianity* (ed. C. Hedrick and R. Hodgson; Peabody, Mass.: Hendrickson, 1968), 257–86.

28. De Conick, *Seek to See Him*, 69. Karen King has persuasively shown that the author of Thomas has a community in mind: see "Kingdom in the *Gospel of Thomas*," *Forum* 3 (1987): 48–97.

29. Davies, "Christology and Protology," 669–70. April De Conick, who elsewhere interprets the passage in the context of Jewish ascent literature, suggests that the use of the plural in log. 50 (*touhikōn*) indicates that the passage refers to the images of angels, whom she takes to be the envisioned interlocutors; see De Conick, *Seek to See Him*, 68–70. In support of this contention, she cites two midrashim (*Exod. Rab.* 30:16 and *Num. Rab.* 16:24), the *Samaritan Targum* on Gen. 9:6, and the theology of Simon Magus, which Moses Gaster has identified as related to Jewish mystical literature. Yet the *Gospel of Thomas* never mentions angels, and the passages she adduces, although difficult to date, are generally considered to be much later than Thomas. The Marcosian passage, which probably dates from the mid- to late second century, seems to me to have nothing significant in common with Thomas. Other teachers, like Valentinus, *Adv. haer.* 1.11.1ff., would suggest that the divine being in whose image humanity is made is dyadic, "masculofeminine," in the phrase of *Ap. John* II; but such an idea remains alien, and, I think, repugnant to the author of Thomas, who insists throughout, as I note below, on the singular, monistic nature of the *anthrōpos* and of the divine reality he reflects.

to answer that it is "movement and rest" — an answer that again recalls Gen. 1:3–2:2, which begins with the spirit's movement over the waters, continues through the six days of creation, and concludes with divine "rest" (2:2).[30]

Thus the cluster of logia that interpret Genesis 1 direct those who seek access to God toward the divine image given in creation. According to log. 24, Jesus himself rebukes those who seek access to God elsewhere — even, or perhaps especially, those who seek it by trying to follow Jesus himself. The disciples who ask Jesus to "show us the place where you are, since it is necessary for us to seek it" (log. 24), do not even merit a direct reply for so misguided a request. Instead, Jesus' answer sounds like a non sequitur. He directs the disciple not toward himself (as does the Jesus of John 14:6) but toward the light hidden within: "There is light within a man of light, and he lights up the whole world; if he does not shine, there is [or: he is] darkness"; that is, one must discover, through the divine image, the light that illuminates "the whole world," or else live in darkness, within and without.

Logion 83 explains that "the images are revealed to man, but the light in them remains concealed in the image of the light of the father" (hn thikōn mpouoein mpeiōt). This difficult saying seems to suggest that although one may glimpse the divine image, one may not see its full radiance, nor that of its prototype. The following saying (log. 84) contrasts the pleasurable experience of seeing one's face in a mirror with the nearly unbearable experience of "seeing your images which came into being before you."

Helmut Koester has taken such statements in Thomas as evincing a kind of "gnostic understanding," which takes as its premise "the discovery of one's own divine origin."[31] Hence, he explains, "for the gnostic understanding it is crucial to know that one's own origin lies before the beginning of earthly existence."[32] Now we can further specify this statement by observing that what Thomas directs the disciple to seek is not "divine origin" in the sense inferred from an underlying "gnostic myth," according to which humanity — or some part of it — is naturally divine. Instead, the disciple is to recover the form of the original creation κατ' εἰκόνα θεοῦ.

What effects that transformation, as I read Thomas's *Gospel*, is baptism. For when the disciples ask when they shall "see" Jesus, he replies in words that call them back to the state of Adam in paradise: "When you take off your clothes without being ashamed" (log. 37). As Jonathan Smith has shown, this statement, coupled with the injunction to put one's garments underfoot and to "tread upon them, like little children," suggests a baptismal context. Logion 50, which De Conick interprets in the context of Jewish ascent literature, also fits plausibly

---

30. Davies, "Christology and Protology," 670.
31. Koester, *Ancient Christian Gospels*, 120.
32. Ibid., 118.

into the context of baptismal instruction; thus the questions and responses may be intended for use either — or both — in catechetical instruction and in baptismal liturgy.

Our evidence suggests, then, that Thomas's theology and anthropology do not depend on some presupposed, generic "gnostic myth." Instead, as Schenke previously suggested and subsequent research has confirmed,[33] the source of this religious conviction is, quite simply, exegesis of Genesis 1 — and, as we have seen, exegesis that follows a pattern both widely known and varied in the ancient world. Such exegesis connects the *eikōn* of Gen. 1:26–27 with the primordial light (or the light/*anthrōpos* of Gen. 1:3) to show that the divine image implanted at creation enables humankind to find — by means of baptism — the way back to its origin in the mystery of the primordial creation.

The Johannine Gospel, of course, also opens with reflection on Genesis 1. But the Johannine prologue and the Thomas logia emphasize very different "moments" in that first creation account. Subsequently, each draws from the account very different — even, in many respects, opposing — conclusions. Thomas privileges the appearance of the primordial light (1:3) as "Act 1" of the drama, and moves quickly to "Act 2," the creation of humankind in its image (Gen. 1:26). "Act one," then, shows how the divine manifests itself "in the beginning"; "Act 2" shows how it manifests itself to humankind. John's author, too, apparently has Gen. 1:3 in mind as he describes what he takes to be "Act 1" — the divine *logos* effecting all creation (John 1:3–5). But according to John, "Act 2" occurs only long ages *after* creation — when the logos becomes incarnate (1:14). Here John differs not only from Thomas, but from all other exegesis that derives from mainstream Jewish speculation on Genesis, evinced in sources ranging from Philo and Poimandres to the *Odes of Solomon* or *The Writing without Title.*

For John, then, "Act 1" includes the whole revelation of the *logos* from creation of the primordial light, the universe, and humankind, through the Torah to the time of John the Baptist — all these only setting the stage, so to speak, for the culmination of the divine drama. As noted, John envisions "Act 2" — the successful revelation of the divine — occurring only when the *logos*, previously manifest as light (1:3–4), finally appears in the world in human form. John insists that whenever the light previously had appeared — in three scenes preceding "Act 2" — it met with stunning failure. First, John declares, the light encountered opposition and incomprehension (1:5); second, lack of recognition (1:10); and, finally, outright rejection (1:11).

By interpreting Genesis in this way, John implicitly refutes the premise that, as we have seen, Thomas shares with many other Genesis exegetes — that throughout the ages since creation, the divine light has manifested itself — successfully — in the cosmos and in humanity. Philo, for example, sometimes takes light as the

---

33. Davies, "Christology and Protology"; De Conick, *Seek to See Him.*

symbol of God or as the knowledge of God revealed to humanity and to the cosmos (*Somn.* 1.75). Alternatively, Philo explains that the river gushing forth from
Eden symbolizes the wisdom of God, or, alternatively phrased, the *logos* of God
(*Leg.* 1.65). Philo elsewhere takes these expressions to refer to the embodiment
of the primordial light, or, as he calls it, τοῦ νοῦ τοῦ φωτός.

But John's author, as we have seen, disagrees. What happened when the divine light first appeared? To this question John responds with the three negations
that mark his prologue. First, John declares, the divine light "shines in the darkness, and the darkness has not understood" — or overcome — "it" (the verb
καταλαμβάνειν, which can be translated either way, is a well-known double
entendre).[34] Many commentators, from Bultmann to Tobin,[35] have pointed out
the note of resistance, opposition, and even hostility that characterize the initial
response of "the darkness" to the light. Second, even though John defines the
light as "the light of humanity" (1:4), and as "the true light which enlightens
everyone" (1:9), his account emphasizes the universal human failure to recognize
it. When it came into the world (1:9) and, indeed, already "was in the world, and
the world came into being through it" (δι'αὐτοῦ, the light, or *logos*), still "the
world did not know it" (αὐτόν, the light/*logos*) (1:10). Third, even when the light
(or *logos*) came to its own, it was rejected by those to whom it is most akin.

The difficulty in translation indicated in vv. 10 and 11 derives, of course,
from well-known grammatical inconsistencies. John switches the pronoun from
the expected neuter to masculine, having chosen, apparently, to privilege the
presence of the divine *logos* rather than the light; here light is only an aspect of
logos. So, Dodd notes:

> In verse four a transition is made to φῶς, and φῶς, not λόγος, is formally
> the subject of the propositions made in verses 9–12. While, however, φῶς
> is formally the subject, the corresponding pronoun, referring to the subject
> of the sentence, is in the masculine, αὐτόν, not agreeing with φῶς, which
> is neuter.

Dodd concludes that "the propositions in question really refer to the masculine λόγος, here considered in its aspect as light"; yet he also acknowledges the
possibility that "the thought of incarnation is already in the evangelist's mind, and
the propositions of verses 9–12 refer to Christ as incarnate."[36] I agree with both
suggestions, against those interpreters who have made the latter the centerpiece

---

34. See, for example, the discussion in Ben Witherington, *Jesus the Sage: The Pilgrimage of Wisdom*
(Philadelphia: Fortress, 1994), 288; J. Painter, *The Quest for the Messiah: The History, Literature, and
Theology of the Johannine Community* (Edinburgh: T. & T. Clark, 1991), 470.

35. R. Bultmann, *The Gospel of John: A Commentary* (trans. G. R. Beasley-Murray; Philadelphia:
Westminster, 1971), 46ff.; Dodd, *Interpretation of the Fourth Gospel*, 201–12; D. Tobin, "The Prologue
of John and Hellenistic-Jewish Speculation," *CBQ* 52 (1990): 252–69.

36. Dodd, *Interpretation of the Fourth Gospel*, 268.

of their exegesis. Raymond Brown, for example, is one of many who interpret the "three negations" as foreshadowing the rejection of the incarnate *logos*.[37] As I read the prologue, however, both its intellectual and cultural context (see the appendix, for example, for a brief review of recent studies comparing it with the *Odes of Solomon*, on the one hand, and with *Trimorphic Protennoia*, on the other) and its dramatic structure indicate the opposite. What the prologue shows is that the "word of the Lord," having first acted to create and sustain the universe, and then having manifested itself to Israel, nevertheless, despite all of this, failed to penetrate the deep darkness in which John sees the world plunged. Finally, then, the word "became flesh and dwelt among us," incarnate — so that some people now could declare triumphantly, with John's author, *"We saw his glory, glory as of the only begotten of the Father!"* (1:14).

Even writing nearly fifty years ago, without knowledge of the Nag Hammadi library, C. H. Dodd suggested that both Hellenized Jews like Philo and other Egyptians (whether Jews, Gentiles, or both, he does not specify) engaged with Hermetic traditions that set forth, as their basic premise, the exegetical pattern we have found in the Thomas logia, which proclaims the *syngennea* between the *anthrōpos kat'eikona*, created within humankind, and its divine prototype, characterized variously as *anthrōpos*, *logos*, *nous*, and *phōs*. Investigating the relationship between the Johannine prologue and these other sources, Dodd attempts to delineate both its affinities with them and its differences from them, as well as from rabbinic Judaism and "gnosticism" (he uses the term as synonymous with dualism and docetism).[38] Such scholars long have recognized that the prologue includes a "clearly polemical purpose."[39] Rudolf Bultmann, who wrote those words in 1941, finds polemic against followers of John the Baptist, against Jewish exegesis, and against "gnosticism." In agreement with Bultmann, both Dodd and Brown read the Johannine prologue as "strongly antignostic." (Whatever we may speculate about its author's intent, however, the Gospel of John remains so evocative that followers of Valentinus would read it — even, or especially, its prologue — as a source of their theology).[40]

The present investigation suggests, however, that John directs his polemic not only against Jewish and pagan readers of Genesis, and not only against "gnostics" — whatever one takes that to mean — but against a pattern of Genesis exegesis adopted as well by such Christians as Thomas's author. For John, indeed,

---

37. Raymond E. Brown, S.S., *The Gospel according to John* (AB 29; Garden City, N.Y.: Doubleday, 1966), 26–31.

38. Dodd, *Interpretation of the Fourth Gospel*, 97–114, 250–85.

39. Bultmann, *Gospel of John*, 15.

40. See, for example, E. Pagels, *The Johannine Gospel in Gnostic Exegesis* (Nashville: Abingdon, 1973); S. Petrement, *Le Dieu séparé: Les origines du gnosticisme* (Paris: Cerf, 1984); A. H. B. Logan, *Gnostic Truth and Christian Heresy: A Study in the History of Gnosticism* (Edinburgh: T. & T. Clark, 1996).

"cosmology is not ... a path to knowledge of God and eternal life."[41] But many of his predecessors and contemporaries, Christian as well as Jewish and pagan — including Paul, for example — did understand cosmology to offer such a path. I noted above Rom. 1:19, in which Paul declares the conviction (received, no doubt, from his own religious education) that "what of God is invisible" has been revealed to human beings by God himself, "intelligible since the creation in the things that are made."

Although John seems not to challenge this Pauline view — if, indeed, he knew it — he apparently does intend to take on all whose Genesis exegesis differs markedly from his own. Dodd incisively compares the prologue with a wide range of non-Christian Genesis exegesis, and goes on to conclude that the "decisive difference" marking John as a Christian text is that "the evangelist conceives of the *Logos* as incarnate, and of the *alēthinos anthrōpos* as not merely dwelling as *nous* in all men, but as actually living and dying on earth as a man." The recent discoveries have shown, however, that not all of John's fellow Christians would agree with this statement. What Dodd regards as the glory of John's gospel message — that of the *logos* "who actually lives and dies on earth as a man" — is never mentioned in Thomas's *Gospel*. Its author may assume, of course, that the "living Jesus" once lived and died "on earth as a man," but does not suggest that he finds this significant. Conversely, what Dodd regards as religiously inadequate — the conviction that the divine *anthrōpos* "merely dwells as *nous* (or, as Thomas would say, *phōs*) in all men" — is, as we have seen, closely analogous to the hidden "good news" that Thomas's *Gospel* proclaims.

We cannot fault Dodd, writing before the publication of the Nag Hammadi texts, for labeling such views "docetic," then "gnostic." Now, however, we can see that John apparently directs polemics against a type of Genesis exegesis used by a wide range of readers, both Jewish and Christian, and perhaps even pagan as well. In one sense, these observations validate the insights earlier expressed by Bultmann, Dodd, and Brown — namely, that John opposes convictions traditionally identified as "gnostic." Yet we now see that what scholars traditionally identified as "gnostic tendencies" instead sometimes turn out to be forms of Jewish and Christian teaching relatively unfamiliar to us — unfamiliar precisely, in all probability, because of the active and successful opposition of such writers as the author of John. Finally, my analysis suggests that Thomas's author understood his message to be based not on some presupposed "gnostic myth," but, like John's prologue, on exegesis of Genesis 1.

---

41. Dodd, *Interpretation of the Fourth Gospel*, 285.

Appendix

Gesine Schenke, John Turner, and Carsten Colpe, among others, have partici-
pated in the complex discussion of the prologue's relationship to religious poetry
with which it shares a common provenance — especially *Trimorphic Protennoia*
(CG XIII, 1) and the *Odes of Solomon*. Schenke, in her pioneering edition of *Trimorphic Protennoia*,[42] has noted many parallels to the Johannine prologue; Carsten
Colpe, too, itemizes what he characterizes as "stupendous parallels" between the
two.[43] John Turner, in the introduction to his edition, suggests that a later editor
inserted Johannine language for the purposes of polemicizing against orthodox
Christian Christology "in favor of a higher (Sethian) one."[44] Such analysis allows
us to locate the religious milieu from which the prologue emerged more precisely
than, as suggested by Dodd, within a range of "Jewish wisdom tradition."

For our purpose, I focus on only one aspect of such comparison: namely, how
each poem characterizes the modes of divine revelation. Certain passages from
Trimorphic Protennoia suggest that its author, like the Johannine author, may have
in mind — and probably does — the opening verses of Genesis 1. Consider, for
example, *Trim. Prot.* 46.10–13: "[The speech/*sm̄ē*] exists from the beginning, in
the foundations of the all. For there is light that exists hidden in silence, and
it was the first to come forth" (cf. Gen. 1:3). Does *Trimorphic Protennoia* presuppose the exegetical pattern that we have seen in the *Gospel of Thomas* and related
sources? This passage's references to the "speech existing from the beginning" and
to "light . . . [that] was the first to come forth" clearly echo Gen. 1:3. Furthermore,
according to 36.6–8, the divine presence manifested in the forms of *protennoia*,
voice (*sm̄ē*), and *logos* is depicted as light pouring down upon darkness, and within
the primordial water: "I came down to the underworld and I shone [down upon
the] darkness. It is I who poured forth the water. It is I who am hidden within
[radiant] waters." Besides these apparent allusions to Gen. 1:2–3, *Trimorphic Protennoia* celebrates divine revelation given "from the beginning," from creation,
which manifests itself within "everyone": "I move in every creature . . . I move in
everyone, and I delve into them all. . . . I exist before the all, and I am the all,
since I exist in everyone." Thus the poem emphasizes that the divine presence
manifests itself through a kind of genetic affinity, so to speak with all beings,
indwelling them. ·

---

42. See Gesine Schenke, " 'Die dreigestaltige Protennoia': Eine gnostische Offenbarungsrede in
koptischer Sprache aus dem Fund von Nag Hammadi," *TLZ* 99 (1974): 731–46, and the incisive article
by G. Robinson, "The *Trimorphic Protennoia* and the Prologue of the Fourth Gospel," in *Gnosticism and
the Early Christian World: In Honor of James M. Robinson* (ed. J. Goehring, C. Hedrick, and J. Sanders;
Sonoma, Calif.: Polebridge, 1990), 37–50.

43. Carsten Colpe, "Heidnische, jüdische und christliche Überlieferung in den Schriften aus Nag
Hammadi III," *JAC* 17 (1974): 109–25.

44. John Turner, "Introduction: NHC XIII,1, *Trimorphic Protennoia*," in *Nag Hammadi Codices XI,
XII, XIII* (ed. C. W. Hedrick; Leiden: Brill, 1990), 400.

Trimorphic Protennoia, like John 1:5, goes on to tell how the divine light "shone down upon the darkness," but sees the opposite result from the one John describes. Instead of encountering only hostility and resistance (cf. the "first negation" of John 1:5), here the light illuminates the darkness, so that the divine presence is recognized:

> I shone down upon the darkness. It is I who poured forth the water. It is I who am hidden within [radiant] waters.... I am the real voice; I cry out in everyone, and they recognize me, since a seed indwells them.... I revealed myself — yes, I — among all those who recognized me, for I am joined with everyone by virtue of the hidden thought. (36.5–27)

What allows for such recognition, then, is the repeatedly affirmed connection between the divine and the things below. *Trimorphic Protennoia* makes no explicit mention of the divine "image" indwelling humanity, however, and no apparent reference to Gen 1:26.

The conviction that *protennoia* descends in three successive manifestations, however, appearing finally as *logos*, clearly does presuppose some difficulty in communication between *protennoia* and human beings. Because of hostile forces opposed to the light, the *logos* tells how he hid from his adversaries in order to reach "his own." As soon as he slipped off his disguise to reveal himself, however, "his own" recognized him immediately and received him with joy. The author of *Trimorphic Protennoia* never envisions the possibility — stated in the Johannine prologue — that those who belong to the *logos*, "his own," might reject their divine brother. Contrary to the "third negation" of the Johannine prologue ("he came unto his own, and his own did not receive him," 1:11), *Trimorphic Protennoia* describes the *logos*'s reunion with those who were longing for him: "I hid myself in everyone, and I revealed myself within them, and every mind seeking me longed for me, for it is I who gave shape to the all ... and it is I who put the breath into my own" (45.21–29). "I hid myself within them all until I revealed myself among my members, which are mine, and I taught them about the ineffable ordinances, and about the brethren" (49.20–23).

While the Johannine prologue, then, first proclaims that the light shines down into hostile and uncomprehending darkness, then enters the world it brought into being, yet remains unrecognized, rebuffed, and finally is rejected even by "its own," *Trimorphic Protennoia* agrees, against the prologue, with those traditional exegeses of Genesis mentioned above in seeing a continuing process of revelation occurring since the beginning of time. According to the latter pattern, light first illuminates the primordial darkness, then is recognized by those who perceive their essential affinity with the indwelling *protennoia*, and the *logos* finally manifests itself in human form to reveal itself within "its own."

When we compare the Johannine prologue with a different collection of religious poetry — the *Odes of Solomon* — we find a similar result. According to the

Odes — again by contrast with the Johannine prologue — the *logos*, the primordial light, first shines in the darkness, then is recognized by those he created, and, third, revealing himself to his own, is received with hymns of praise. Here again, as in *Trimorphic Protennoia* (as well as in the wide range of Jewish sources I have surveyed), the divine presence is continually revealing itself to humankind, "from the beginning" to the present time. James Charlesworth and Jack Sanders have analyzed the literary relationship between the *Odes* and the prologue, Sanders concluding that "the *Odes Sol.* and the *Trim Prot.* are kindred documents, in that they help show what sort of speculation existed in the intellectual milieu out of which the prologue arose."[45] Comparison with both sources similarly indicates how the prologue's author breaks with a more inclusive Jewish understanding of theology, anthropology, and cosmology, in favor of the exclusive teaching of the Johannine Gospel.

Like certain passages of *Trimorphic Protennoia*, certain elements of the *Odes of Solomon* suggest that its author may be alluding to Gen. 1:3, and may envision a human form manifest in the primordial light: "The spirit brought me before the face of the Lord, and because I was the son of man, I was named the light, the Son of God." Sanders notes verbal similarities between passages he selects from various *Odes* and the Johannine prologue. For each of the passages central to our current discussion — John 1:4–5, 1:10, and 1:11 — Sanders cites parallels he draws from various sections of the *Odes*. Opposite John 1:5, for example, he places *Odes Sol.* 18.6; opposite John 1:10, *Odes Sol.* 24.12; opposite 1:11, *Odes Sol.* 7.12; 41.11; and 8.12. Such parallels may demonstrate literary relationship, as Sanders intends to suggest.

More striking, however, is that the *Odes of Solomon*, like *Trimorphic Protennoia*, communicate through similar language a message diametrically opposed to that of the prologue. Where John declares that "the light shone into darkness, and the darkness has not grasped [or overcome] it," the author of *Odes Sol.* 18 instead envisions the possibility that the light may vanquish darkness, or, conversely, that darkness may vanquish light; but the outcome of this conflict is far from decided, nor is it perceived as a singular cosmological event. Instead, the odist entreats the Lord to resolve the (apparently continual) conflict in favor of light and truth: "Let not light be conquered by darkness, nor let truth flee from falsehood." Second, I have noted that the prologue insists that "the true light that enlightens everyone was coming into the world, and the world did not recognize it" (1:10). But what Sanders places as a parallel to this verse actually states the opposite: "The dwelling place of the word is humankind, and his truth is love." The same ode goes on to praise the word's presence and activity in humankind from the dawn of creation:

---

45. See James H. Charlesworth, *The Odes of Solomon* (Missoula, Mont.: Scholars Press, 1977), and Jack T. Sanders, "Nag Hammadi, *Odes of Solomon*, and NT Christological Hymns," in Goehring, Hedrick, and Sanders, *Gnosticism and the Early Christian World*, 51–66; quote from p. 59.

"He is the light and the dawning of thought; and by him the generations spoke to one another; ... from him came love and equality, and they spoke one to another what was theirs." Not only did the divine *logos* enable "the generations" to communicate with one another and to recognize one another, but it also enables human beings to recognize itself: "[T]hey were inspired by the word, and they recognized him who made them." In agreement with John 1:2, then, the odist praises the *logos* as the one through whom all beings are brought into being, but — contrary to John 1:10 — sees as a natural consequence that those created by the divine word recognize that word within them. Further, by contrast with John 1:11, the seventh ode declares that "his own" do recognize the divine word — and the odist takes for granted that, recognizing him, they receive him with joy:

> The Father of knowledge is the word of knowledge ... the created one ... he has allowed him to appear to those who are his own, in order that they may recognize him that made them, and not suppose that they had come into being on their own.

Sanders, seeking parallels to the "negations" of the Johannine prologue, cites, as if parallel to 1:10 ("the world did not receive him"), *Odes Sol.* 24.12: "They were rejected, because the truth was not within them" — but the latter phrase refers not to human failure to receive the divine word, but, as the context shows, to the Lord's rejection of foolish arrogant people who contrive lies (24.9–13) — a statement very much in the mode of the psalmist. And lest anyone conclude from such human wickedness that the divine revelation was obscure, the odist concludes by proclaiming the widespread availability of divine truth: " ... for the Lord revealed his way, and spread widely his grace. And those who recognized [his way] knew his holiness." Again, seeking parallels to the "third negation" of the Johannine prologue ("he came unto his own, and his own did not receive him," 1:11) and finding one parallel in content, Sanders places three passages that include verbal parallels, but that state rather the opposite of John 1:11. The first is *Odes Sol.* 7.12, cited above: "[The Father] has allowed [the word] to appear to those who are his own, in order that they may recognize him who made them"; the second is 8.12: "I turn not my face from my own, because I know them." Both of these hymns suggest that the Lord's "own" are the Lord's from the beginning of time (see *Odes Sol.* 7.13–14); 8.13 seems to suggest, like *the Gospel of Thomas*, that the Lord's "own" images existed before their actual creation ("and before they had existed, I recognized them, and imprinted a seal on their faces").

The diversity of our sources and the enormous hermeneutical inventiveness we find in ancient exegesis of Gen. 1:1–2:5 should warn us not to attempt to hammer all of our sources into a single mold. Nor should we imagine that we can find a single key to unlock the hermeneutical difficulties of such a great range of texts. But, having glanced at two sources central to discussion of the provenance of the Johannine prologue — *Trimorphic Protennoia* and the *Odes of Solomon* — we can see that they reflect the basic theological premises that we find in the *Gospel of Thomas* and its parallels — that divine "light" existing from the beginning is available to humanity from the time of creation, and ever since. As we have seen, the authors of *Trimorphic Protennoia* and the *Odes of Solomon* may have had in mind exegesis of Gen. 1:3 that identifies the "first light" with the "son of man" or, equally, the "Son of God." But neither text, so far as I can see, links the divine light's access to humanity specifically with the "image and likeness" of Gen. 1:26 as does the *Gospel of Thomas* and its parallels. Yet both *Trimorphic Protennoia* and the *Odes of Solomon* seem to agree with the more generalized theme widespread in Jewish theology, that (in Paul's words) "what can be known of God was visible through the things that were made" (Rom. 1:19), through creation as a whole, often connected more specifically with the creation of humankind in a kind of implicit relationship with God (or God's divine word).

19

Enoch in Egypt

———— ◆ ————

Birger A. Pearson
University of California, Santa Barbara

In one of his many articles on Enochic texts and traditions, our jubilarian made the following comment: "The Christian preservation and transmission of Enochic texts in Egypt needs to be studied further."[1] This observation I take to be justification for the subject of my contribution to his Festschrift, which will deal not only with Enochic texts in Egypt but also Egyptian Christian traditions relating to the figure of Enoch. My task is made easier because I have dealt with such matters before, and most notably in association with my old friend.[2] And, in general, I have a long-standing interest in the early history of Christianity in Egypt.[3] So what follows is only an update on, and complement to, previous research that I have done and in which I am still engaged. I am glad for the opportunity to do this on Enoch and Enochic traditions, for one need only mention the name "Enoch," and an association with George W. E. Nickelsburg comes immediately to mind.

In what follows I take up, first, the various Enochic books that circulated or were composed in Egypt and the extent of their influence. Observations on the figure of Enoch as represented in Coptic texts and in Coptic archaeology follow. Conclusions on the groups in which the Enochic traditions flourished can then be drawn.

---

1. George W. E. Nickelsburg, "Two Enochic Manuscripts: Unstudied Evidence for Egyptian Christianity," in *Of Scribes and Scrolls: Studies on the Hebrew Bible, Intertestamental Judaism, and Christian Origins Presented to John Strugnell on the Occasion of His Sixtieth Birthday* (ed. H. W. Attridge, J. J. Collins, and T. H. Tobin; College Theology Society Resources in Religion 5; Lanham, Md.: University Press of America, 1990), 251–60.

2. B. A. Pearson, "The Pierpont Morgan Fragments of a Coptic Enoch Apocryphon," in *Studies on the Testament of Abraham* (ed. G. W. E. Nickelsburg, Jr.; SBLSCS 6; Missoula, Mont.: Scholars Press, 1976), 227–83.

3. See esp. Birger A. Pearson and James E. Goehring, eds., *The Roots of Egyptian Christianity* (SAC 1; Philadelphia: Fortress, 1986); and Pearson, *Gnosticism, Judaism, and Egyptian Christianity* (SAC 5; Minneapolis: Fortress, 1990).

Books of Enoch in Egypt

We begin at the beginning, with *1 Enoch*. As is well-known, *1* ("Ethiopic") *Enoch* is a composite work made up of five main sections. They are, in the chronological order usually given to them in contemporary scholarship:[4] (1) the Astronomical Book (*1 Enoch* 72–82, third century B.C.E.); (2) the Book of Watchers (chaps. 1–36, third century B.C.E.); (3) the Epistle of Enoch (chaps. 91–108, second century B.C.E.); (4) the Book of Dreams (chaps. 83–90, second century B.C.E.); and (5) the Book of Parables (or Similitudes, chaps. 37–71; first century B.C.E./C.E.). What is not so well-known, however, is when and how *1 Enoch* achieved its final shape as this is reflected in the Ethiopic manuscripts.[5] Another question, more directly related to our task, is: Are all five of these sections attested in Egypt? What about the latest section of the work, the Book of Parables? As will be seen shortly, it does appear that the Book of Parables was known to Origen of Alexandria. It was also known to the compiler of the biography of Mani attested in the Cologne Mani Codex.[6] And one might expect that the Ethiopic version of *1 Enoch* as a whole was translated from a Greek version brought from Egypt.[7] As to the Book of Giants, attested at Qumran[8] and appropriated by the prophet Mani and his followers, there is to my knowledge no certain evidence that that work was known in Egypt.[9]

There is still another question, to which I have found no satisfactory answer: When and how were the Aramaic Enoch books translated into Greek? Where this occurred is a matter of surmise: it probably happened in Egypt, presumably in the Jewish community of Alexandria. If *2 Enoch* is allowed as evidence,[10] at least some of the Enochic books comprising *1 Enoch* were already extant in Greek versions in first-century Alexandrian Jewish circles, for, as Nickelsburg has shown,[11] *2 Enoch*

---

4. See, most recently, James C. VanderKam, "*1 Enoch*, Enochic Motifs, and Enoch in Early Christian Literature," in *The Jewish Apocalyptic Heritage in Early Christianity* (ed. J. C. VanderKam and W. Adler; CRINT 3/4; Assen: Van Gorcum; Minneapolis: Fortress, 1996), 33–101.

5. On the various stages in the literary development of *1 Enoch*, see G. W. E. Nickelsburg, *Jewish Literature between the Bible and the Mishnah: A Historical and Literary Introduction* (Philadelphia: Fortress, 1981), 150–51.

6. See below, on the Manichaean "apocalypse of Enoch."

7. On the relationship between the Ethiopic version and the Greek versions, see *APOT* 2.167.

8. For the Qumran Aramaic fragments of the Book of Giants, see J. T. Milik, *The Books of Enoch: Aramaic Fragments of Qumran Cave 4* (Oxford: Clarendon, 1976), 57–58; 298–339. The Book of Parables is not attested in the Qumran manuscripts.

9. Milik (ibid., 319) argues that the Book of Giants was known to George Syncellus, the chronographer, who presumably got his knowledge of the Enochic writings through the works of the Alexandrians Panodorus and Annianus (ca. 400 C.E.). The evidence he cites is ambiguous. It would appear that the Book of Giants was transmitted eastward rather than westward, as can be seen especially in the Middle Persian Manichaean fragments. See Milik, *Books of Enoch*, 298–310.

10. On *2 Enoch* see below.

11. Nickelsburg, *Jewish Literature*, 185–88.

shows clear dependence on *1 Enoch*. Moreover, the parallels cited by Nickelsburg come from four of the five main sections of *1 Enoch* (all except the Parables).[12]

It would appear that the earliest attestation, in Christian sources, of *1 Enoch* in Egypt is in the *Epistle of Barnabas*, presumably written in Alexandria in the early second century or maybe even earlier.[13] In *Barnabas* 4.3, reference is made to the "final scandal," and this is accompanied by the phrase "as Enoch says." While no corresponding passage in *1 Enoch* has been identified, the phrase may indicate a general reference to eschatological sections in *1 Enoch* known to the author of *Barnabas*.[14] In chapter 16 there is apparent use of passages from the Epistle of Enoch, that is, from the Apocalypse of Weeks embedded in that section, introduced by the phrase, "For the Scripture says..."[15] It is noteworthy that *1 Enoch*, or at least parts of it, is counted as "Scripture" by the author of *Barnabas*.

The next attestation of *1 Enoch* in Alexandria would be Athenagoras's *Embassy for the Christians* (176–80), if indeed that obscure Christian apologist was an Alexandrian.[16] In chapter 24 of his work Athenagoras refers to the fallen angels who brought forth the giants, in language that suggests dependence on the Book of Watchers. He discusses the myth as something that "the prophets have declared."[17] The Book of Watchers is also used by Clement of Alexandria twice in his *Selections from the Prophets* (*Eklogai*), with explicit attestation to Enoch, and once in his *Stromateis* without attestation. For Clement, too, Enoch was clearly one of the prophets.[18]

The text of *1 Enoch* is used several times by Origen, and with him we begin to see evolution in the status of the "Book(s) of Enoch." In his early treatise *On First Principles,* he argues for the noncreated, divine status of the Holy Spirit, and in his discussion he refers to authoritative sources that state that God created everything; there he cites unspecified statements made "in the Book of Enoch" (1.3.3). Subsequently, in the same treatise, he quotes *1 Enoch* 21.1 and 19.3, introduced respectively by the words "Enoch speaks thus in his book," and "in

---

12. Ibid., esp. 185.

13. Second half of the first century, according to VanderKam, "*1 Enoch*," 36. On the possible relationship between *Barnabas* and first-century Judaism in Alexandria, see B. A. Pearson, "Christians and Jews in First-Century Alexandria," in *Christians among Jews and Gentiles: Essays in Honor of Krister Stendahl on His Sixty-fifth Birthday* (ed. G. W. E. Nickelsburg and G. W. MacRae; Philadelphia: Fortress, 1986), 206–16, esp. 211–14.

14. See the discussion in VanderKam, "*1 Enoch*," 36–38.

15. Ibid., 38–40.

16. So ibid., 40. A tenth-century manuscript of the apology reads, "A Plea Regarding Christians by Athenagoras, the Athenian, a Philosopher and a Christian," which leads Cyril Richardson to conclude that Athenagoras was "a Christian philosopher of Athens." Richardson gives no weight to the fourteenth-century Byzantine writer Nicephorus Callistus's claim that Athenagoras was the first head of the catechetical school of Alexandria, and teacher of Clement. See C. C. Richardson, *Early Christian Fathers* (repr., New York: Macmillan, 1970), 290–91, 297, 300.

17. For a good discussion see VanderKam, "*1 Enoch*," 40–42, 65–66.

18. For detailed discussion see ibid., 44–47.

the same book, Enoch himself being the speaker."[19] Later, but presumably still in his Alexandrian phase, in his *Commentary on John*, Origen gives the etymology of "Jordan" ("going down" — *yrd*) and adds that "Jared was born to Maleleel, as it is written in the Book of Enoch — if anyone cares to accept that book as sacred — in the days when the sons of God came down to the daughters of men."[20] Origen's reference to the "Book of Enoch" is to a passage in the Parables, *1 Enoch* 37.1. But here Origen is acknowledging that the canonical status of the "Book of Enoch" is questionable. Later, in his Caesarean period, in his twenty-eighth *Homily on Numbers*, Origen refers to "booklets called 'Enoch,'" which "do not appear to be regarded as authoritative among the Jews."[21] Finally, in his treatise *Against Celsus*, Origen says that "the books entitled Enoch are not generally held to be divine by the churches."[22] Thus, the final position of Origen on the collection of "books" of Enoch, which he can also call the "Book of Enoch," is that it has no canonical authority in the church.

This negative view of *1 Enoch* becomes standard in Alexandrian Catholic Christianity (and elsewhere, of course), and is stated with presumed finality in Athanasius's famous paschal letter of 367. In his discussion of "apocryphal" books, allegedly used by the heretical "Melitians," Athanasius asks rhetorically: "Who has made the simple folk believe that those books belong to Enoch even though no Scriptures existed before Moses?"[23] As we shall see, the "finality" of the great patriarch's pronouncement was not everywhere recognized, certainly not by the "heretics" but also not by the presumably "orthodox" monks of Upper Egypt, at least not for a long time.

But before we take up the monastic reception of *1 Enoch* and other Enochic books, we should note that the myth of the fallen angels (in the Book of Watchers) played a considerable role in gnostic and Hermetic traditions in Egypt. The most notable example is found in the Nag Hammadi tractate *Apocryphon of John* (NHC II,*1*) 29,16–30,11, wherein the roles of the wicked Shemihazah and his angels are assumed by the biblical creator and his archons.[24] Similar use of the myth is found in the untitled treatise, *On the Origin of the World* (NHC II,*5*) 118,17–121,35, and in the gnostic *Pistis Sophia*, book 1, chaps. 15 and 18. A somewhat different use

---

19. Ibid., 54–55.

20. 6.25; ANF 10.371.

21. Quoted in VanderKam, "1 Enoch," 57.

22. *Cels.* 5.54; *Origen: Contra Celsum* (trans. Chadwick; Cambridge: Cambridge University Press, 1965), 306. For discussion see VanderKam, "1 Enoch," 57–59.

23. Translation by David Brakke, in *Athanasius and the Politics of Asceticism* (Oxford: Oxford University Press, 1995), 330, quoted and discussed by David Frankfurter, "The Legacy of Jewish Apocalypses in Early Christianity: Regional Trajectories," in VanderKam and Adler, *Jewish Apocalyptic Heritage*, 129–200, esp. 170–71.

24. For a detailed discussion, see my article, "1 Enoch in the *Apocryphon of John*," in *Texts and Contexts: Biblical Texts in Their Textual and Situational Contexts, Essays in Honor of Lars Hartman* (ed. T. Fornberg and D. Hellholm; Oslo: Scandinavian University Press, 1995), 355–67.

appears in the *Valentinian Exposition* (NHC XI,2) 38,27–38, wherein the leading role is played by the devil rather than the demiurge.[25]

As noted, the Enochic literature played a major role in the development of Manichaeism. In Egyptian Manichaeism, use of the myth of the Watchers in *1 Enoch* is attested in the *Kephalaia of the Teacher*. In chapter 38 of that work reference is made to "the watchers of heaven who came down to the earth" and who "revealed crafts in the world" with destructive results, and who were bound by four angels "with an eternal chain." In chapter 39, reference is made to their prison "in the depths of the earth," and to their progeny, the giants.[26]

Enochic literature may also have been known to some of the authors of the various treatises that circulated in Egypt under the name Hermes Trismegistus. The alchemist Zosimus of Panopolis, in one of his treatises addressed to one Theosebeia, mentions the myth of the fallen angels and attributes this to Hermes; but the ultimate source is probably *1 Enoch*.[27] In the Hermetic treatise *Asclepius*, chapter 25, a reference to angels mingling with humans may reflect knowledge of the same myth. The passage in question is included in the fragment preserved in Coptic in Nag Hammadi Codex VI.[28]

Turning to manuscript evidence of *1 Enoch* in Egypt, we note first that fragments of two different manuscripts, probably of the fourth century, have been found at Oxyrhynchus (P. Oxy. 2069), three fragments of the Book of Dreams and two of the Astronomical Book in the Epistle of Enoch.[29] The manuscripts in question could have come from elsewhere (Alexandria?). However that may be, they undoubtedly served the purposes of the Christian community at Oxyrhynchus, where so many Christian (including biblical) manuscripts have been found.

The two other manuscripts of the Greek version of *1 Enoch* found in Egypt, discussed by Nickelsburg,[30] probably reflect a monastic provenience. They are Cairo 10759, part of a parchment codex (fifth to sixth centuries) found a century

---

25. For discussion see VanderKam, "*1 Enoch*," 73–76. On the "Books of Jeu" ascribed in *Pistis Sophia* to Enoch, see below.

26. See now the translation by Iain Gardner, *The "Kephalaia of the Teacher": The Edited Coptic Manichaean Texts in Translation with Commentary* (NHMS 37; Leiden: Brill, 1995). On the alleged "apocalypse of Enoch," see below.

27. For discussion, see VanderKam, "*1 Enoch*," 83–84. For a possible use of *2 Enoch* by Zosimus, see below.

28. NHC VI,8: 73,3–12. See esp. Jean-Pierre Mahé, *Hermes en Haute-Égypte* (BCNH "Textes" 7; Laval, Quebec: Université Laval, 1982), 2.83, and his comments, 2.88–89, 239. For a recent English translation of the Hermetica see Brian P. Copenhaver, *Hermetica: The Greek "Corpus Hermeticum" and the Latin "Asclepius" in a New English Translation with Notes and Introduction* (Cambridge: Cambridge University Press, 1992), esp. 82, 242.

29. J. T. Milik, "Fragments grecs du livre d'Hénoch (P. Oxy. XVII 2069)," *Chronique d'Égypte* 46 (1971): 321–43; Milik, *Books of Enoch*, 75–76; cf. also Frankfurter, "Legacy of Jewish Apocalypses," 189.

30. Nickelsburg, "Two Enochic Manuscripts."

ago in a Christian grave at Akhmim, ancient Panopolis; and P. Chester Beatty 12 (fourth century). The first contains a substantial portion of the Book of Watchers. The second contains a substantial portion of the Epistle of Enoch. The burial place in which the first was found was probably that of a monk.[31] The monastic provenience of the Chester Beatty Codex is probable.[32]

The text of 1 *Enoch*, or at least parts thereof, circulated in Upper Egypt in Coptic, as can be seen from a fragment discovered in a cemetery near Antinoopolis. It comes from a parchment codex of the fifth or sixth century and contains parts of 1 *Enoch* 93, that is, part of the Apocalypse of Weeks.[33] How much more of 1 *Enoch* was preserved in that manuscript cannot be known,[34] but we can surmise that the codex came originally from one of the nearby Coptic monasteries.

Thus we see that 1 *Enoch*, or at least parts thereof, circulated widely in Egypt, first in Alexandria and then in the Chora. After the fourth century its circulation seems to have been confined largely to the Coptic monasteries.

We turn to 2 ("Slavonic") *Enoch*, a book that was probably composed in Egypt, although its attestation there is much slighter than is the case for 1 *Enoch*. Probably composed in Greek in the Jewish community of first-century Alexandria,[35] 2 *Enoch* evidently achieved only a limited circulation among Christians in Egypt. It may have been known to Origen,[36] but otherwise its circulation seems to have been limited mainly to gnostic and Hermetic circles. Madeleine Scopello has made a very good case for the use of 2 *Enoch* by the author of the gnostic apocalypse *Zostrianos* (NHC VIII,1). Specifically, she argues that passages at the beginning (5,15–17) and end (128,15–18) of *Zostrianos* are dependent respectively on 2 *Enoch* 22.10 [J] and 24.3 [J].[37] And I have argued elsewhere for the probable influence of 2 *Enoch* on the author of the Hermetic *Poimandres* (*Corpus Hermeticum* 1).[38] Finally, it may be that Zosimus of Panopolis's reference to the

---

31. So Frankfurter, "Legacy of Jewish Apocalypses," 188.

32. Albert Pietersma, "Chester Beatty Papyri," *ABD* 1.901–3.

33. Sergio Donadoni, "Un Frammento della versione copta del 'Libro di Enoch,'" *Acta Orientalia* 25 (1960): 197–202.

34. Donadoni (ibid., 202) surmises that it contained only the Epistle of Enoch and cites the subscript title of the Beatty papyrus in support: Ἐπιστολὴ Ἐνώχ.

35. See F. I. Andersen's translation of the Slavonic version and his introduction in *OTP* 1.91–213, esp. 94–97. Milik's view that 2 *Enoch* was written by a Byzantine monk in the ninth or tenth century (*Books of Enoch*, 107–16) has not gained wide acceptance.

36. Influence from 2 *Enoch* 21 and 22 has been detected in the *Homily on Numbers* already cited. See VanderKam, "1 *Enoch*," 58, who cites H. J. Lawlor, "Early Citations from the Book of Enoch," *Journal of Philology* 25 (1897): 164–225, esp. 203.

37. M. Scopello, "The Apocalypse of Zostrianos (Nag Hammadi VIII.1) and the Book of the Secrets of Enoch," *VC* 34 (1980): 376–85. See also my discussion in "From Jewish Apocalypticism to Gnosis," forthcoming in a report on the Copenhagen International Conference on the Nag Hammadi Texts in the History of Religions, held in Copenhagen in September 1995.

38. B. A. Pearson, "Jewish Elements in *Corpus Hermeticum* 1 (*Poimandres*)," chap. 9 in idem, *Gnosticism, Judaism, and Egyptian Christianity*, 136–47, esp. 138–39.

222 Birger A. Pearson

first man Adam as constructed of four elements, East (ἀνατολή), West (δύσις), North (ἄρκτος), and South (μεσημβρία), is dependent on 2 Enoch 30 [JJ].[39]

In addition to 2 Enoch, there are other books attributed to Enoch in texts and traditions in Egypt. In book 2 of the gnostic Pistis Sophia, chapter 99, Jesus tells Maria of "mysteries" that are written "in the two Books of Jeu which Enoch has written as I spoke with him out of the Tree of Knowledge and out of the Tree of Life in the paradise of Adam." A similar reference to "Books of Jeu," written by Enoch in paradise and deposited on Mount Ararat, occurs in book 3, chapter 134.[40] "Books of Jeu" do, indeed, exist in Coptic,[41] and were probably known to the authors of Pistis Sophia (Askew Codex), but unfortunately the extant portions of 1–2 Jeu reveal no connection with Enoch.[42]

An "apocalypse of Enoch" is referred to in the Cologne Mani Codex, a late-fourth- or early-fifth-century miniature parchment codex discovered somewhere in Upper Egypt.[43] Presumably translated into Greek in Egypt from an original East Aramaic version sometime in the mid–fourth century,[44] it contains alleged quotations from "apocalypses" attributed to Adam, Sethel, Enosh, Shem, and Enoch, biblical precursors of the prophet Mani. These "apocalypses" have been thoroughly studied by John C. Reeves,[45] who considers them to be Manichaean creations based on available Jewish and Christian lore associated with the respective patriarchs. What is noteworthy about the supposed "apocalypse of Enoch" is that it clearly demonstrates a dependence on 1 Enoch (as well as other sources), including the Book of Parables.[46]

There does exist, in fragmentary form, one Enoch apocryphon that was clearly

---

39. For the text see Walter Scott, Testimonia (vol. 4 of Hermetica: The Ancient Greek and Latin Writings Which Contain Religious or Philosophic Teachings Ascribed to Hermes Trismegistus; Oxford: Clarendon, 1936; repr., London: Dawsons of Pall Mall, 1968), 106–7. The same tradition relating to Adam is found in the Sibylline Oracles 3.26. On the Coptic Enoch apocryphon, which may reflect influence from 2 Enoch, see below.

40. For the text and translation see Carl Schmidt, ed., and Violet MacDermot, trans., Pistis Sophia (NHS 9; Leiden: Brill, 1978), 247, 349. For discussion see VanderKam, "1 Enoch," 74–76.

41. See Carl Schmidt, ed., and Violet MacDermot, trans., The Books of Jeu and the Untitled Text in the Bruce Codex (NHS 13; Leiden: Brill, 1978).

42. Could it be that the author of books 1–3 of Pistis Sophia was familiar with a tradition according to which Enoch was identified with Jeu, the "true God" of the Books of Jeu (1 Jeu 5 et passim)? We recall that Enoch came to be identified with Metatron, "Little Yahweh," in 3 (Hebrew) Enoch (chaps. 3–12). The name "Jeu" (Coptic ΙΕΟΥ) is clearly a variant of YHWH.

43. See now the critical edition prepared by Ludwig Koenen and Cornelia Römer, Der Kölner Mani-Kodex: Über das Werden seines Leibes (Papyrologica Coloniensia 14; Opladen, Germany: Westdeutscher Verlag, 1988). For an English translation of pp. 1–99 see Ron Cameron and Arthur Dewey, The Cologne Mani Codex: "Concerning the Origin of His Body" (SBLTT 15; Early Christian Literature Series 3; Missoula, Mont.: Scholars Press, 1979). The material after p. 99 (100–192) is fragmentary.

44. Koener and Römer, Mani-Kodex, xv.

45. J. C. Reeves, Heralds of That Good Realm: Syro-Mesopotamian Gnosis and Jewish Traditions (NHMS 49; Leiden: Brill, 1996).

46. Chapter 7 of Reeves's book (pp. 183–206) is devoted to the "apocalypse of Enoch," and contains the Greek text, an English translation, and detailed commentary.

composed in Egypt, probably in a monastic setting. That apocryphon was edited, translated, and commented upon by me in the article referred to at the beginning of this essay.[47] The extant material, now preserved in the Pierpont Morgan Library in New York (C3),[48] consists of fragments of nine folios from a papyrus codex inscribed in Sahidic Coptic. Considerations of space prevent me from discussing this apocryphon in detail. Suffice it to say that the surviving material features revelations received by Enoch pertaining to his future role as "scribe of righteousness" in the judgment of humankind. In one passage, Enoch's sister Sibyl[49] counsels him not to write down people's sins too hastily.[50] I would assign the composition of this apocryphon, whether in Coptic or originally in Greek,[51] to the fifth or sixth century.

In the aforementioned article I made reference to fragments from a parchment codex of another Enoch apocryphon found at Aswan, preserved in Cairo (Cairo MS 48085) and edited by H. Munier.[52] These fragments were briefly discussed by J. T. Milik, together with the Pierpont Morgan fragments,[53] and he expressed the view, which I shared, that the two sets of fragments were probably not of the same work. He commented that, except for fragment 3, recto, the rest of the material "seems rather to belong to a homily."[54] This insight has turned out to be correct, for I can now identify the homily in question. Study of the fragments has convinced me that they come from the recently published *Encomium on the Four Bodiless Living Creatures*, attributed to John Chrysostom,[55] and extant in Sahidic Coptic in a ninth-century parchment codex now in the Pierpont Morgan Library (M612).[56] While there are some divergences between the fragments and the homily, I have found that much of the material in the fragments can be restored based on the text of the homily, that is, chapters 25–27. In this material,

---

47. See n. 2.

48. See L. Depuydt, *Catalogue of Coptic Manuscripts in the Pierpont Morgan Library* (Corpus of Illuminated Manuscripts 4 [text], 5 [plates]; Louvain: Peeters, 1993), no. 97 (p. 188).

49. That the (pagan) Sibyl was sister of Enoch is unique to the Coptic tradition. See Pearson, "Coptic Apocryphon," 239–40. In Jewish tradition, Sibyl was a daughter (or daughter-in-law) of Noah. See J. J. Collins's introduction to the *Sibylline Oracles* in OTP 1.317–26, esp. 322.

50. See below for further discussion.

51. In a brief review of my article ("Studi Copti, n. 1," *Vetera Christianorum* 15 [1978]: 122), Tito Orlandi disagrees with my view that the text is an original Coptic composition.

52. Henri Munier, "Mélanges de littérature copte, III: Manuscrits coptes sa'idiques d'Assouan," *Annales du Service des Antiquités de l'Égypte* 23 (1923): 210–28, esp. 212–18 (3: "livre d'Énoch [?]"). Munier (210, n. 1) expresses the view that the fragments in question came from the Monastery of Saint Simeon near Aswan. No date for the fragments is given.

53. Milik, *Books of Enoch*, 100–104.

54. Ibid., 104. It should be noted that Milik and I worked independently of each other at approximately the same time.

55. Leo Depuydt, general editor, *Homiletica from the Pierpont Morgan Library* (CSCO 524, Scriptores Coptici 43 [Coptic text]; 525, Scriptores Coptici 44 [English translations]; Louvain: Peeters, 1991). The *Encomium* is edited and translated by Craig S. Wansink (CSCO 524.27–46; 525.27–47).

56. Depuydt, *Catalogue*, no. 96 (pp. 185–87). As Depuydt notes, part of this manuscript is now in Berlin.

Enoch, "scribe of righteousness," is associated with the creature with the human face (Rev. 4:7). Thus, it now appears that there were at least two, slightly different, versions of the *Encomium,* the one found in the Monastery of St. Michael near Hamouli in the Fayum (M12), and the one from a monastery near Aswan (Cairo 48085). The role played by Enoch in this homily and in related material in Coptic will be discussed in what follows.

The Figure of Enoch in Coptic Tradition

Of the antediluvian patriarch Enoch, seventh from Adam, the scripture says simply: "Enoch walked with God; then he was no more, because God took him" (Gen. 5:24). So complete was his disappearance, so it would seem, that Enoch is never again mentioned in the Hebrew Bible. But, as is well-known, he had a fabulous career outside the Bible, as the various books of Enoch and other traditions inform us. Beginning as a son of Adam, he eventually became a "second God."[57] To be sure, his virtual deification as Metatron is mainly confined to Jewish sources, notably *3 Enoch.*[58] That this tradition would not appeal to Christians[59] is understandable enough, since for Christians it is Jesus who began as a "son of Adam" and who eventually became not only a "second God" but the Second Person of the Holy Trinity.[60]

Some years ago William Adler prepared a short paper for the Pseudepigrapha Seminar of the Society of Biblical Literature on "Enoch in Early Christian Literature."[61] In that paper he identifies seven "functions or characteristics," as found in early Christian texts:

a. Enoch's translation (Heb. 11:5; *1 Clem.* 9; Justin, *Dial.* 19; Irenaeus, *Haer.* 5.5; *Asc. Isa.* 9.6; Tertullian, *De resurrectione carnis* 58; *De anima* 50; Eusebius, *Praep. ev.* 7.7; *Gospel of Nicodemus* 9 (25); *Ps.-Clem. Rec.* 4.12; Augustine, *Civ.* 15.19)

b. Enoch's repentance (Clem. Alex., *Strom.* 2.15)

---

57. See now Philip S. Alexander, "From Son of Adam to Second God: Transformations of the Biblical Enoch," in *Biblical Figures outside the Bible* (ed. Michael E. Stone and Theodore S. Bergren; Harrisburg, Pa.: Trinity Press International, 1998), 87–122.

58. See also the *Jerusalem Targum,* Gen. 5:24.

59. But see n. 42, above. There may be a hint of this tradition in one of the fragments of the Pierpont Morgan apocryphon; see Pearson, "Coptic Apocryphon," 237–38.

60. I do not doubt that early Christian development of Christology, perhaps beginning with the apostle Paul (Phil. 2:9), took place under the influence of, or at least in tandem with, Jewish traditions relating to the exaltation of Enoch. Alexander ("Transformations," 114) refers more guardedly to "dialectic between the two traditions."

61. W. Adler, "Enoch in Early Christian Literature," in *SBLSP 1978* (Missoula, Mont.: Scholars Press, 1978), 1:271–75.

c. Enoch's uncircumcision (Justin, *Dial.* 19.92; Aphrahat, *Demonstrations* 11.3)

d. Enoch as priest (*Apos. Con.* 8.5.3)

e. Enoch as discoverer of astrology (Eusebius, *Praep. ev.* 9.18)

f. Enoch as "scribe of righteousness" (*Apoc. Paul* 20; *Gospel of Bartholomew* 17; *Ps.-Titus Ep.* 2.153; *T. Ab.* [short recension] 11)

g. Enoch as opponent of antichrist (*Gospel of Nicodemus* 9 [25]; *Apocalypse of Elijah; Tertullian, De anima* 50; *Apoc. Pet.* [Eth.] 2: Hippolytus, *De antichristo* 43; *History of Joseph the Carpenter* 31–32)

h. Significance of the name "Enoch" ("grace of God": Eusebius, *Praep. ev.* 7.8; *dedicatio:* Augustine, *Civ.* 15.19).[62]

It can be seen from this list that Christian interpretations of Enoch varied widely. Some (*a, b, e, f, h*) were dependent on already existing Jewish Enoch literature and traditions; some (*c, d, g*) were developed *de novo.* Two (*f* and *g*) become especially prominent in Egyptian Christian literature and traditions, and it is on these that I wish to focus in what follows.

We take up first Enoch's role as opponent of the antichrist, a tradition which develops based on interpretation of Revelation 11, on the "two witnesses" of the end time.[63] While the most plausible interpretation of Revelation 11 would have the two witnesses as Moses and Elijah, Enoch soon supplants Moses in early Christian interpretation of that passage.[64] The earliest attestation of this tradition is found in the *Apocalypse of Peter,* probably composed in Egypt in the early second century. In chapter 2 of the Ethiopic version, Christ predicts the coming of the antichrist, when there will be many martyrs:

> Enoch and Elijah will be sent to instruct them that this is the deceiver who must come into the world and do signs and wonders in order to deceive. And therefore shall they that are slain by his hand be martyrs and shall be reckoned among the good and righteous martyrs who have pleased God in their life.[65]

---

62. Ibid., 273–75. *h* is in addition to the seven "functions or characteristics," *a–g.*

63. For an extensive discussion of this tradition see Richard Bauckham, "The Martyrdom of Enoch and Elijah: Jewish or Christian?" *JBL* 95 (1976): 447–58. Bauckham (pp. 447–49) provides a table featuring twenty-four texts which attest to the tradition.

64. See VanderKam, "1 Enoch," 89–92. According to Bauckham ("Martyrdom," 452) this happens under the influence of "an independent tradition of the return of Enoch and Elijah in the light of which Revelation 11 was interpreted." For a possible source see *1 Enoch* 90.31; cf. VanderKam, "1 Enoch," 99. Cf. also *4 Ezra* 6:26.

65. Translation in *NTApoc* 2.626 (slightly modified).

To be sure, it is not explicitly stated here that Enoch and Elijah will be martyred; that is made more explicit in a later ("Clementine") Ethiopic version of the *Apocalypse of Peter*.[66]

The tradition is much elaborated in the *Apocalypse of Elijah*, probably composed in Upper Egypt in the third century.[67] The appearance of the antichrist ("the Shameless One," chap. 3) is followed by a prophecy concerning a virgin named Tabitha, who will reprove the Shameless One, suffer martyrdom at his hands, and then rise again from the dead (4.1–6).[68] This episode is followed by the return of Elijah and Enoch, who upon reproving the Shameless One will be killed by him. They will spend three and a half days in the marketplace and then rise from the dead to give further reproof (4.7–15; cf. Rev. 11:7–11). After a lengthy treatment of the martyrdoms that will take place at that time and the rewards that the martyrs will receive, the text prophesies a time of tribulation, a final battle, and a judgment. Elijah and Enoch will come down again to kill the Lawless One (5.32–35), and Christ will descend to reign on earth for a thousand years (5.36–39, end). The influence of the Book of Revelation on the *Apocalypse of Elijah* is clear; in addition, there is very probable influence from the Animal Apocalypse of *1 Enoch* (chaps. 85–90, part of the Book of Dreams).[69]

The *Apocalypse of Elijah* apparently gained considerable circulation in Egypt, for its influence can be seen in a number of later texts.[70] The Coptic versions of the *History of Joseph the Carpenter* have Christ prophesy the death of Enoch and Elijah at the hands of the antichrist (chaps. 31–32). The influence of the *Apocalypse of Elijah* is clearer in the Arabic version, in which Tabitha is added, together with another woman, Sibyl.[71] Sibyl, sister of Enoch, is absent from the *Apocalypse of Elijah*, but she is featured in the Pierpont Morgan apocryphon. In one fragment (p. 14, fol. 9v) she tells Enoch of two other people who will be taken up to heaven in their bodies, Elijah and Tabitha. Reflected here, no doubt, is the antichrist tradition in the *Apocalypse of Elijah*.[72] While the end-time testimony of Enoch and Elijah is not found in the extant portions of the Coptic apocryphon, I do not doubt that it was present originally, in material that is now lost.

It is in his role as "scribe of righteousness" that Enoch gains the most currency

---

66. Bauckham, "Martyrdom," 455–56.

67. See now David Frankfurter, *Elijah in Upper Egypt: The Apocalypse of Elijah and Early Egyptian Christianity* (SAC 7; Minneapolis: Fortress, 1993). Frankfurter, in an appendix to his book, supplies a synoptic translation of the Sahidic and Akhmimic versions (pp. 301–28). I use his translation here.

68. On Tabitha, see Pearson, "Coptic Apocryphon," 241–43; David Frankfurther, "Tabitha in the Apocalypse of Elijah," *JTS* 40 (1990): 13–25.

69. So VanderKam, "*1 Enoch*," 98.

70. In addition to those cited here, see the *Tiburtine Sibylline Oracle* and Pearson, "Coptic Apocryphon," 243, n. 45; the *Apocalypse of Ps.-Shenoute*; and Bauckham, "Martyrdom," 456.

71. See Forbes Robinson, *Coptic Apocryphal Gospels*, TS 4/2 (Cambridge: Cambridge University Press, 1896), 146–47, 229. See my discussion in "Coptic Apocryphon," 241–43.

72. Pearson, "Coptic Apocryphon," 270–71 (text, translation), 239–43 (discussion).

in Coptic tradition: in literary sources, nonliterary texts (inscriptions), and in monastery wall paintings. Specifically, Enoch's scribal activity has as its purpose to record the deeds of humankind in connection with the judgment, and eventually to serve as a witness before the bar. The origins of this conception of Enoch's role as scribe lie in the earliest Jewish Enochic literature: He is already identified as "scribe of righteousness" in *1 Enoch* 12.3. This role is made more specific in *2 Enoch* 53.2, where he is said to be writing down the deeds of everyone. The specific association of Enoch with the judgment probably occurred in the original Jewish version of the *Testament of Abraham*, which was presumably composed in Greek in Alexandria in the late first century;[73] it is attested in recension B of what we now have as the *Testament of Abraham*, chapters 10 and 11.

It is in the Pierpont Morgan apocryphon (fifth to sixth centuries), in which the Coptic tradition is fully elaborated. Unfortunately, that apocryphon is far from complete, but in the extant fragments the following details are seen: Enoch records the sins and good deeds of humankind (p. 15, fol. 1r; p. 18, fol. 7v). Enoch is urged not to write down sins too hastily; he can even erase them (p. 17, fol. 7r). The judgment involves the use of "balances of righteousness" (p. 16, fol. 1v) on which are weighed sins and good deeds (p. 18, fol. 7v).[74] Considerations of space prevent further discussion of the apocryphon; the reader is referred to my article for the Coptic text, translation, and an extensive discussion.[75]

The influence of the Coptic Enoch apocryphon, or at least of the traditions concerning Enoch found there, are considerable in later Coptic literature: martyrological,[76] homiletic,[77] and magical.[78] One of the most interesting examples of the elaboration of these traditions is found in the aforementioned *Encomium on the Four Bodiless Living Creatures*, attributed (pseudonymously) to John Chrysostom.[79] The occasion for the encomium is the Feast Day of the Living Creatures on Hathor 8 (still observed in the Coptic Church today). At a eucharistic celebration prominent biblical figures are asked why they rejoice. When Enoch is asked, he replies:

---

73. See E. P. Sanders's introduction to, and translation of, *T. Ab.* in *OTP* 1.871–902.

74. Use of a scale in the judgment is also found in *T. Ab.*, rec. A, chap. 13. It is also reflected in the older Enochic literature; see esp. *1 Enoch* 61.8; *2 Enoch* 52.15.

75. Pearson, "Coptic Apocryphon."

76. *Martyrdom of Apa Anub*, in *Acta Martyrum* (ed. I. Balestri and H. Hyvernat; CSCO 43), 236, on which see Pearson, "Coptic Apocryphon," 246.

77. *Encomium of Theodosius on Saint Michael the Archangel*, in *Miscellaneous Coptic Texts in the Dialect of Upper Egypt*, by E. A. W. Budge (London: British Museum, 1915), 345–46 (text), 909 (translation); cited by Milik, *Books of Enoch*, 105.

78. Texts discussed in Pearson, "Coptic Apocryphon," 245.

79. Cited above and in n. 55. This homily was composed in Coptic no earlier than the mid–sixth century. See Tito Orlandi, "John Chrysostom, Saint," *Coptic Encyclopedia* (New York: Macmillan, 1991), 1357–59, esp. 1358.

I rejoice today since God transformed me and gave me the penholder of salvation and the tomes which were in the hand of the angel Mefriel, scribe of old. I copied them in six days and six nights according to the eons of light. After that the Lord issued a command to a cherub, one of the four creatures. After he had taken me to the land of my relatives, I gave orders to my children and my relatives and was taken up to heaven again. God established me before the throne of the cherub, namely the human-faced one. Because of this I rejoice today. (Chap. 11)[80]

This passage represents a revision of older traditions relating to Enoch as scribe and his ascent to heaven.[81] Later in the text, Christ delivers to his apostles, gathered on the Mount of Olives, a revelation concerning the mystery of the four living creatures. At one point the Savior explains that the four creatures play a role in assuaging the wrath of God against the sins of humankind (chaps. 25–26). He continues:

Because of this my Father has assigned Enoch, the scribe of righteousness, to the creature with the human face. Whenever a human being sins . . . , one of the creatures, the human-faced one, cries out and urges Enoch the scribe of righteousness, "Do not hurry to write down the sins of the children of humankind, but be patient a little and I will call the archangel Michael and he will implore the Father of mercy together with me. Restrain yourself a little and I will call Gabriel and he will implore the Father of all good people together with me. . . . O Enoch, because of this I have been established near you, since my likeness and yours are one, so that I might remind you. For I am bodiless, but you are of flesh and earth. Indeed, God who loves humankind, has made plans in this way. After he removed Mefriel the angel, who was scribe from the beginning, because he is bodiless, he established you in his place, having given you the spiritual penholder so that you might take into account the weakness of people of flesh and blood." (Chap. 27)[82]

This passage reveals some influence from the Coptic Enoch apocryphon, particularly in the exhortation to Enoch to be lenient in recording human sins. As to Enoch's bodiless predecessor, Mefriel,[83] I have so far not found him attested elsewhere in Coptic literature.[84]

In his role as "scribe of righteousness," Enoch became a patron saint of the monks in the Monastery of Apa Jeremias in Saqqara. As can be determined

80. Wansink's translation, pp. 30–31 (see n. 55 above).
81. See, e.g., 1 Enoch 81.5–6; 2 Enoch 22–23; 67.1–2.
82. Parts of this passage are found in Cairo MS 48085, frgs. 2v and 3r. Cf. discussion above.
83. Cf. "Vrevoil"/"Vereveil" in 2 Enoch 22.10.
84. His name is not found in the "Katalog der Engelnamen" by J. Michl in RAC 5.200–39; nor is it found in the index of angel names in C. Detlef G. Müller, *Die Engellehre der koptischen Kirche* (Wiesbaden: Otto Harrossowitz, 1959).

from the excavations conducted at the site from 1906 to 1910, the monastery was founded toward the end of the fifth century and was finally destroyed in the ninth century.[85] The excavations turned up three wall paintings with Enoch represented,[86] and numerous inscriptions invoking him and other saints.

In a niche in chapel D, Enoch is represented in a painting above the altar, at far right, with a scroll in his hand. The other figures in the painting are the Madonna, the two archangels (Michael and Gabriel), and Apa Jeremias, the monastery's founder, at the far left.[87] In a niche in cell 1725, Enoch and Apa Jeremias are represented in the sides, with the Madonna and Child as the central figure. Above the Madonna are the two archangels, and at the top of the apse the heads of the virtues are represented. In a painting in the oratory of cell 1727, the same figures appear, with Enoch at the right. He is carrying a scroll labeled in Coptic, "The Book of Life."[88] Enoch's role as a patron saint, coupled with the monastery's founder, Apa Jeremias, is made clear in these pictures.

Numerous Coptic inscriptions found in the monastery, mostly grave stelae and painted graffiti, testify to the same thing.[89] Indeed, one can speak of a Saqqara "triad" of saints, who appear repeatedly in invocations in the inscriptions: Apa Jeremias, Apa Enoch, and Ama ("Mother") Sibylla (the Sibyl).[90] The same "triad" appears less frequently in the Monastery of Apollo at Bawit, which seems to have been closely related to Apa Jeremias at Saqqara.[91] The invocations of the Saqqara triad typically include Father, Son, and Holy Spirit, Saint Mary, Saints Michael and Gabriel, Apa Jeremias, Apa Enoch, Ama Sibylla, and other saints; indeed, many of them begin with Jeremias and Enoch.[92] These invocations probably have a liturgical origin as "litanies," perhaps used in connection with services for the dead or other memorial services, for example, feast days of saints, observed at

---

85. J. E. Quibell, *Excavations at Saqqara* (vols. 2 [1906–7], 3 [1907–8], and 4 [1908–9, 1909–10]; Cairo: Institut Français d'Archéologie Orientale, 1908–12). The final statement on the dates of the monastery appears in vol. 4, p. i.

86. Another painting was found in 1899 at Tebtunis, in the Fayum. In that one Enoch is part of a judgment scene involving the punishment of sinners. He is represented as seated, with an open scroll in his left hand in which is inscribed in Coptic, "Enoch the scribe writing down the sins of mankind." In his right hand he holds a reed pen. See C. C. Walters, "Christian Paintings from Tebtunis, *JEA* 75 (1989): 191–208, esp. 200–202, and plates 25–29.

87. Quibell, *Excavations*, 2.67, plate 59.

88. Ibid., 3.23, plates 22, 24.

89. The inscriptions, some four hundred of them, are published in Quibell, *Excavations*, vols. 3 and 4, edited by Herbert Thompson. The dated ones range from 695 to 849 C.E. (see Thompson's introduction in Quibell, *Excavations*, 4.47).

90. See n. 49, above.

91. The Bawit triad, which also occurs in a few inscriptions at Saqqara, features Apollo, Phip, and Anoup. Cf. Thompson's discussion in Quibell, *Excavations*, 4.48. In addition to Bawit, Enoch is coupled with Apa Jeremias at Esna and Wadi Sarga; so Cäcilia Wietheger, *Das Jeremias-Kloster zu Saqqara unter besonderer Berücksichtigung der Inschriften* (Arbeiten zum Spätantiken und koptischen Ägypten 1; Altenburg, Germany: Oros Verlag, 1992), 213, n. 15; 225; and references cited.

92. See Wietheger's discussion in *Jeremias-Kloster*, 210–19.

Saqqara.[93] The monks at Saqqara even devised feast days for Enoch himself, as
attested in an inscription in ink on the wall of a room at Saqqara: Enoch's birthday
was observed on Hathor 11 (= November 20), and his translation probably on
Epep 20 (= July 27).[94]

The remarkable status achieved by Enoch at Saqqara is, unfortunately, not attested in literary sources. For example, there is no liturgical book which includes
litanies featuring the Saqqara triad. And evidence in Coptic sources for the observance of feast days in honor of Enoch is very meager, at best.[95] It would appear
that such honors accorded to our biblical patriarch ceased with the destruction
of the Monastery of Apa Jeremias in the ninth century.

Concluding Observations

In the foregoing discussion I have noted that books associated with Enoch circulated widely in Egypt. The text of *1 Enoch* may have achieved its current fivefold
form in Egypt in a Greek version, and continued to be used in many of Egypt's
monasteries, both in Greek and in Coptic, long after it was proscribed by Athanasius in his famous paschal letter of 367. It would appear that at least two books
of Enoch (*2 Enoch* and the Coptic Enoch apocryphon) were composed in Egypt,
the former in the Jewish community of first-century Alexandria, and the latter in
a Coptic monastery somewhere in Upper Egypt. The eschatological roles of the
biblical patriarch as opponent of the antichrist and as "scribe of righteousness"
in the judgment came to be featured in a number of works circulating in Coptic
in Egypt's monasteries. And in one important monastery, that of Apa Jeremias at

93. Ibid. Wietheger cites the work of Umberto Benigni, "Litaniae defunctorum Copticae," *Bessar-
ione* 4/6 (actually vol. 6, fourth year of publication, 1899): 106–21; and C. M. Kaufmann, *Handbuch
der altchristlichen Epigraphik* (Freiburg im Breisgau: Herder, 1917), 149–52.

94. Inscription no. 91, Quibell, *Excavations*, 3.54–55. The same inscription provides the dates of
Apa Jeremias's birth, tonsure, ordination, and death. See Thompson's discussion in Quibell, *Excava-
tions*, 4.47–48. For a convenient exposition of the Coptic calendar, with dates given in their Julian
and Gregorian equivalents, see Otto F. A. Meinardus, *Christian Egypt, Ancient and Modern* (Cairo:
American University in Cairo, 1977), 72–130. Enoch does not appear in the various editions of the
Synaxary cited by Meinardus. See n. 95.

95. Thompson (Quibell, *Excavations*, 4.48) cites calendars printed by John E. Selden, *De synedriis*
(Amsterdam: Henricus & Theodorus Boom, 1679), 3.219 and 224, for the feast of Enoch's translation
on Epiphi (Epep) 28 or 25. In the edition of Selden's work that I could obtain, *De synedriis &
praefecturis juridicis veterum ebraeorum* (London: Jacob Flesher, 1655), 3.407, Abib (=Epep) 25 is
given as the day of the ascension of Enoch into heaven. Selden relied on a Muslim informant,
who got his information from an unnamed Christian (p. 347). Wietheger (*Jeremias-Kloster*, 225) cites
Benigni, "Litaniae," 119, for Tobe 27 as the Feast Day of Enoch. Benigni is relying on Nicolaus
Nilles, *Kalendarium manuale utriusque ecclesiae orientalis et occidentalis* (2d ed.; Oeniponte: F. Rauch,
1897; repr., Farnborough, England: Gregg, 1971), 2.714, in which a "commemoration of Henoch the
righteous" is included among those of Tobi 27. The calendar given by Nilles is that of the Copts
in union with the Roman Catholic Church. Enoch's name is absent from the Egyptian Synaxary,
extant in Arabic. See Jacob Forget, *Synaxarium Alexandrinum* (CSCO 47, 48, 49, 78, 67, 90; Louvain:
Catholic University, 1905–26). On the other editions, see Meinardus, *Christian Egypt*, 74–75.

Saqqara in the shadow of Egypt's oldest pyramid (Djoser's "step pyramid"), the ancient patriarch was honored as a patron saint.

Curiously enough, from the ninth or tenth century on, all of that changes in Egypt. Enoch's books begin to disappear, and his memory fades virtually into oblivion in the lives of Egypt's faithful. In contrast to the situation in the sister church of Ethiopia, where 1 Enoch is still virtually part of that church's Old Testament, and where the patriarch's feast day is still observed,[96] there is no trace of Enoch in Coptic piety.

What happened? It could be that use of the books of Enoch and cultivation of Enoch as a saint was confined mostly to those ancient monasteries which did not survive into the present, monasteries such as that of Apa Jeremias at Saqqara, and many others, destroyed in the ninth and tenth centuries. Why Enoch plays no role at all in such monasteries as those of the Wadi Natrun, or those of Antony and Paul in the Eastern Desert near the Red Sea and others, I do not know. Perhaps, finally, the Bible's terse comment is true: "He was no more, because God took him."

---

96. The day of Enoch's ascension is Hamle (= Coptic Epep) 24 in the Ethiopic calendar. See Ignacio Guidi, Mois de Hamlè (vol. 2 of Le Synaxaire Éthiopien; PO 7/3; Paris: Firmin-Didot, 1911), 403. Cf. Thompson, in Quibell, Excavations, 4.48. In a version of the Ethiopian Synaxary published by Budge, another date is given: Ter (= Coptic Tobe) 27. See E. A. W. Budge, The Book of the Saints of the Ethiopian Church (Cambridge: Cambridge University Press, 1928), 2.555–57. As noted above, no note of Enoch is taken in the various versions of the Egyptian Synaxary.

20

Elijah, the Son of God, and Jesus: Some Issues in the Anthropology of Characterization in Mark

———— ◆ ————

Norman R. Petersen
Williams College

Mark has a number of things to say about Elijah that collectively raise some interesting questions about his characterization of both John the Baptizer and Jesus of Nazareth, each of whom is identified, rightly or wrongly, as Elijah (6:14–16; 8:28; 9:13). Three points are focal: in Mark, Elijah is an independent character who preexists John and Jesus historically and is an "angel" who resides in heaven; while some people in Mark's story think that Jesus is Elijah, Mark claims that it was John who was Elijah and that John's appearance marked the "coming" of Elijah, an expectation that is said to be a "scribal" view, that is, one that antedated the coming of both John and Jesus (9:11–13); after John's death, Elijah appears as recognizably himself in the transfiguration story (9:2–8). The principal question raised by these three points has to do with how we are to understand the proposition that either John or Jesus *was* Elijah, who both preexisted them and appeared as himself after John's death.

Precisely because Mark conceives of Elijah as a separable being from John and Jesus, both before and after their lives, the answer to this question cannot simply be that either of them was merely the fulfillment of scriptural expectations. That answer still begs the question of the denotation of the copula in the equative proposition that John or Jesus *was* Elijah. What is true of this proposition is also true of another proposition fundamental to Mark's characterization of Jesus, namely that he *is* the Son of God (e.g., 1:11; 9:7). My thesis is that the relationship

This paper owes much to discussions I have had with George Nickelsburg over the years, but especially to sessions at the University of Iowa in 1986 with George and an undergraduate student, Aaron Halstead, who was working on parallels between John and Jesus in Mark. Suffice it to say that the discussions raised problems about my argument that have taken all too long to resolve. Thank you, George, and many congratulations, my friend.

between Elijah ("my angel," 1:12)[1] and John the Baptizer is critically significant for understanding the relationship between the Son of God ("my son," 1:11; 9:7) and the (son of) man, Jesus of Nazareth. John and Jesus, I will argue, are for Mark human beings who relatively late in their lives are inhabited by divine beings, Elijah and the Son of God, who preexisted them as heavenly characters and continued to exist after their deaths. While it is not my present concern to discuss the literature and religious history relative to this inhabitation model, it should be noted that the model is widely evident in texts from Mark's broader cultural environment.[2] For example, it is present in stories of Athena's appearances in the form of already existing humans, Mentes and Mentor, in Homer's *Odyssey* (bks. 1–4), and in Ovid's story of Hermes and Zeus appearing in human form in *Baucis and Philemon,* which is remarkably similar to the idea of those gods appearing as Barnabas and Paul in Acts 14:8–19. The model is also fundamental to the story in Tobit of the angel Raphael appearing in the form of Azarias, a man known to Tobias. Interestingly, numerous later Jewish legends delight in telling about appearances of the angel Elijah in the forms of a variety of human beings.[3]

Needless to say, the evidence for my thesis from Mark is not overwhelming. Yet I think that considerably more exists in Mark than has thus far met the critical eye, especially in view of some anthropological possibilities Mark poses for construing human beings. Two of these possibilities call for attention before we turn to the core of my argument, because they both document an inhabitation model in Mark's characterization and illuminate some of the issues posed by his characterization of John and Jesus.

Some Anthropological Possibilities

The question, "Who then is this?" (4:41b), not only permeates Mark's narrative, but also receives numerous answers, each suggesting a different possibility for interpreting the actions of Jesus, a man whose biography before his public activities provided no clue as to how he could do what he came to do (cf. 3:31–35; 6:1–3). Indeed, questions about Jesus arose only after he began to do the things Mark tells about in his narrative. What he did led people to ask who he really was, and to provide a variety of answers. The two answers most interesting for Mark's anthropology are that Jesus was John the Baptizer raised from the dead (6:14–16;

1. For more on the identity of Elijah as "my angel," see below.

2. I have discussed related literary and comparative matters in two previous articles: " '*Literarkritik*': The New Literary Criticism, and the Gospel according to Mark," in *The Four Gospels, 1992, Festschrift Frans Neirynck* (ed. F. VanSegbroeck et al.; Louvain: Louvain University Press, 1992), 936–48; "Can One Speak of a Gospel Genre?" *Neotestamentica* 28 (1994) (special edition; Willem Vörster Festschrift): 137–58.

3. See the collection of legends about Elijah in Louis Ginzberg, *The Legends of the Jews,* vol. 4 (Philadelphia: Jewish Publication Society, 1968 [1913]), 194–235, esp. 201–33. Notes appear in vol. 6, 316–42.

8:28), and that "he has Beelzebul and casts out demons by the ruler of demons" (3:22, my translation). The answer also appears in Jesus' response to this charge — that Satan cannot cast out Satan (3:23b) — and in a reference to Satan rising up against himself (3:26a). Mark himself sees the charge as a claim that Jesus had an "unclean spirit," whereas he really had "the Holy Spirit" (3:29–30). Both charges entail the notion of inhabitation, but so also does Mark's response.

That Jesus is John redivivus is a notion some offer to explain the source of the powers at work in him (6:14b). Anthropologically, this explanation presupposes the belief that at least some recently deceased people can inhabit the bodies of other living human beings and do wondrous things through them. For our purposes, the present case is of interest not only as an explanation of Jesus' deeds, but also because his activities commenced only after John's death. Until then, Jesus had done nothing remarkable — according to Mark — and after John's death it was not Jesus who acted, but John working in and through him. Consequently, by virtue of being inhabited by John, Jesus' biographical identity would have been displaced by John's. Surprisingly or not, the charge of demonic possession is quite similar.

Nowhere in Mark is inhabitation more clearly evident than in his understanding of unclean spirits or demons as inhabiting humans, as acting and speaking through them, and as being cast out of them (1:21–28; 1:32–34; 3:11–12; 5:1–13; 6:7–13; 7:24–30; 9:14–27). However, of equal interest is that Mark's exorcism stories say as much about Jesus as they do about demons. According to Mark, Jesus addresses the unclean spirits, but when they speak to him they claim to know who he really is, namely the Son or Holy One of God (1:24; 3:11; 5:7; cf. 1:34), an identification otherwise made in Mark only by God to Jesus at his baptism (1:11) and to three disciples at Jesus' transfiguration (9:7).[4] Significantly, this knowledge is not granted to characters other than Jesus, because he (or the Son of God?) silences the demons to prevent them from making his real identity known (3:11–12). The three disciples also do not understand what they experienced (9:5–6) and are not permitted by Jesus to speak about what they saw until after the Son of Man, Jesus, has been raised from the dead, which they do not understand either (9:9–10). I will take up this matter later, but I mention it now to suggest that the demons' knowledge about Jesus' true identity is a central issue both in Mark's characterization of him and in the plot. In the present context, the demons' knowledge of Jesus as the Son of God leads back to the charges that "Beelzebul" and an "unclean spirit" inhabit him, for these suggest that the inhabitation model also applies to Jesus, both in the scribes' charges and in Mark's response.

The model applies doubly to Jesus because Mark responds to the charge that

---

4. The centurion's statement that Jesus is "a Son of God" (15:39) is problematic and is at best ironically correct, because the centurion knows nothing of what the reader knows.

Jesus had, that is, was inhabited by, an "unclean spirit" by citing the charge as blasphemy against the "Holy Spirit" (3:29–30). Jesus received the Holy Spirit at his baptism, when God told him that he was his Beloved Son (1:10–11). So for Mark, Jesus' baptism by John was both the moment when he was first identified as God's Son and when he received the Spirit that initiated his new role. As in the notion that Jesus was John redivivus, Jesus does not begin to act until after John's arrest (1:14). Also of interest in the reception of the Spirit and the identification of Jesus as God's Son is that these two occurrences parallel charges that Jesus "had" (*echei*) an unclean spirit and that he "had" (*echei*) Beelzebul. That the latter pair entails inhabitation is clear from the fact that unclean spirits are cast out of people, and from the fact that Beelzebul=Satan is also cast out (3:23). I see no alternative to understanding Jesus' having the Spirit as inhabitation, but that understanding leaves open whether the Son of God inhabits Jesus in the manner that Beelzebul/Satan inhabits people (as in Luke 22:3; John 13:27; cf. 7:70, 13:2).[5] I think so, but to make the case we must return to the relationship among Elijah, the Son of God, and Jesus.

"My Angel," "My Son"

Critics agree that "my angel" (1:2) refers to Elijah and derives from a conflated quotation attributed to Isaiah in 1:2–3.7.[6] As is well-known, v. 2 is a conflation of Exod. 23:20 and Mal. 3:1. In the former, God tells the people, "Behold, I send an angel before you...."; in the latter, God says, "Behold, I send my messenger (*mlkh, angelos*) to prepare the way before me...," which is reformulated in Mal. 4:5 as, "Behold, I will send you Elijah the prophet before the great and terrible day of Yahweh comes."[7] Mark 1:3 comes from Isa. 40:3. Critics also agree that both the Hebrew *mlkh* and the Greek *angelos* denote either an angel or a messenger, but that in the first century the Greek word refers predominantly to heavenly messengers, that is, angels. One of the few exceptions to this rule has been said to be Mark 1:2, where "angel" refers to John the Baptizer, who is a human being.[8] But this conclusion misses that 1:2 refers to Elijah, who only subsequently appears as John. The first question, therefore, is whether Mark understands Elijah to be

---

5. See also the *Testament of Job* (ca. 100 C.E.), in which Satan disguises himself as beggars (6–7), the king of Persia (17), and a bread seller (23). See also *Asc. Isa.* 2:1–4; 3:11; 4:4.

6. The Old Testament texts I consider are fully discussed in more traditional terms by Joel Marcus, *The Way of the Lord: Christological Exegesis of the Old Testament in the Gospel of Mark* (Louisville: Westminster/John Knox, 1992).

7. The same conflation of Exod. 23:20 and Mal. 3:1 occurs in the Q tradition in Luke 7:26–27//Matt. 11:9–10. Here the conflated texts refer to John the Baptizer. Only Matthew explicitly identifies John as Elijah (11:14). In both versions, however, the quotation explains why John is "more than a prophet" (Luke 7:26–27) and suggests that he is such because he is Elijah. But he would really be "more than a prophet" if he were the *angel* Elijah.

8. See Gerhard Kittel, "*Angelos*," *TDNT* 1.74–87, especially p. 83, for the views cited.

a heavenly, that is, angelic, messenger or a human messenger. The relationship between Elijah and John is yet another question, one that can only be answered after we have answered the first.

Linguistically, 1:2 is the only place Mark uses the singular *angelos*. Otherwise, his use of the plural always refers to heavenly beings (1:13; 8:38; 12:25; 13:27, 32). Conceptually, on the other hand, we must remember that Elijah had ex-isted as a human being in times long past, but that when last "seen" in Jewish texts he was being taken up into heaven by a whirlwind (2 Kings 2:11; cf. Sir. 48:9), whereupon he necessarily became a heavenly being. However, Elijah was seen subsequently, in Mark's transfiguration story (9:2–8), where he and Moses suddenly appear alongside a metamorphosed Jesus and, also suddenly, disappear, the way angels usually do (e.g., Judg. 6:21; 13:3, 10, 20, 21; Dan. 8:15; 9:21; 10:5; Tob. 12:19–23). Elijah and Moses are not their living historical selves, any more than the metamorphosed Jesus is the carpenter from Nazareth. Each of the three appears in a heavenly form, which can only be angelic form. In this light we need to remember that later Jewish legends contain numerous stories of the angel Elijah appearing in the guise of various human beings. I suggest that Mark's rendering of Elijah's appearances, both as his angelic self and as John the Baptizer, is on a trajectory with other biblical stories of angels appearing in human form (Judg. 6:11–24; 13:1–25; cf. Tobit) that culminate in the rabbinic stories about appearances of the angel Elijah.

If Mark understands Elijah to be an angel, we can identify Elijah's relationship to John as one of angelic inhabitation, such as the angel Raphael's inhabitation of Azarias in Tobit and the angel Elijah's inhabitation of Rabbi Hayyah in Jewish legend.[9] Moreover, because angels often take on the form of already existing humans, we can conclude that Elijah assumed John's form when John began to do what Elijah had been sent to do in 1:2–3. It is no coincidence that Elijah begins to act through John at a time chronologically and literarily related to the time when the Son of God began to act through Jesus, who is now empowered by the Holy Spirit.

Because "Jesus" begins to act only after the baptismal episode, and from that time raises questions about who he really is, our focus must not be on Jesus, but on the independent and prior existence of the Son of God. As with Elijah and John, we need to establish the nature of the Son of God in Mark before we ask about the Son's relationship to Jesus. Three texts are critical.

The most important text is, not coincidentally, the one in which God speaks about sending an angel, for the "thou" to whom God speaks in 1:2–3 can only be God's Son. Were God speaking to Jesus of Nazareth, "the carpenter, the son of Mary and brother of James and Joses and Judas and Simon" (6:3), Jesus, long before his birth as Jesus, would have required a prior existence in heaven. For

---

9. See Ginzberg, *Legends*, 4.209, and 6.328 for sources.

1:2–3 is not merely a quotation from Isaiah's writings; it also describes a heavenly event that Isaiah wrote about. In heaven, God addressed the Son on sending an angel to prepare God's Son's way. Not only is there no evidence in Mark for the preexistence of Jesus, but Mark specifically depicts Jesus as beginning to act only after being identified as God's Son. It is only after he begins to act that he encounters demons or unclean spirits, who claim to know that he is really the Son of God, not just the carpenter from Nazareth.

The evidence in Mark is that it is the Son of God about whom "Isaiah" wrote. But if this is the case, we have new questions: Whom is God addressing in 1:11 if the Son of God becomes/inhabits Jesus at his baptism? Who acts following the baptism, the man from Nazareth or the Son of God in him? We have already seen the beginnings of answers in reflection on Jesus as the Baptizer redivivus, on the charge that Jesus had Beelzebul and an unclean spirit, and in asking who acts when people are inhabited by demons. Comparative texts lead to the same conclusion: Athena acts through Mentes and Mentor; Zeus and Hermes act through Barnabas and Paul; and Raphael acts through Azarias. All evidence points to the Son of God as the one who acts through Jesus and as the one who has become Jesus, whom God addresses; this is not for the Son's sake or Jesus' sake, but for the reader's sake, to inform the reader that the Son has become Jesus. Mark 1:2–11 lets the reader know — dating from the beginnings of their public activity — that John is the angel Elijah and that Jesus is the preexistent Son of God.

The second text is 12:36, another case in which scripture represents a heavenly event from the past. Here David refers to God speaking to David's "Lord," the "Christ" of 12:35, telling him to sit at God's right hand until Christ's enemies have been put under his feet. Because, for Mark, "Christ" and "Son of the Blessed" (= Son of God) are synonymous expressions (14:61), God is for a second time addressing the Son well before the time of Jesus.

The last text reflecting the Son of God's preexistence is Mark's allegory of the wicked tenants in 12:1–12. For readers, the allegorical referents of a number of terms will be self-evident. Yet none of the allegorical elements is found in a more strictly parabolic version of the story in the *Gospel of Thomas* 65. In Mark's allegory, the owner of a vineyard (= God) sets it up, lets it to tenants (= the Jewish people), and goes to another country (= heaven). Some time later, from this other country, he sends servants to get fruit. But the tenants reject the servants, killing at least one of them (= John the Baptizer?), whereupon the owner sends his "beloved son" (= Jesus), whom they also kill. It is clear that the murdered son is Jesus, but because the Son is sent from heaven, which, for Mark, is where God resides, and because the Son only becomes Jesus at baptism, the allegory represents the Son's heavenly existence prior to his appearance as Jesus.

The heavenly nature of the Son of God suggests another understanding of a statement in 13:32, in which, after referring to "the Son of Man coming in clouds with great glory" and to "the angels" (13:26–27), Jesus says, "But of that day or that hour no one knows, not even the angels in heaven, nor the Son, but only the Father." The last time we saw an angel, the Son, and the Father in heaven was in 1:2–3 (cf. 12:1–12); here the angels and the Father are clearly in heaven. Is 13:32 a reference to the Son of God? "The Son" in 13:32 usually is understood as the "Son of Man" referred to in 13:26f. I do not want to disagree, but to suggest that in the light of what we have seen, 13:26–27, 32, raises new issues about the relationship between the preexistent Son of God and the (son of) man, Jesus. Mark 13 first speaks about a time after Jesus' death, which raises the question of what happens to the Son of God after Jesus dies. Second, 13:26f., like other passages in Mark, refers to *seeing* the (son of) man, Jesus, after his death, which reinforces the question about the Son of God. If the Son of God is to Jesus what Elijah is to John, it is the Son of God who should appear or be seen after Jesus' death, not a risen Jesus. This apparent contradiction requires that we address the relationship between what we know about the Son of God and what Mark says about the (son of) man, Jesus.

The Son of God and the Son of Man — Jesus

In 12:36, David heard God telling "the Christ" (12:35) that he was to sit at God's right hand until his enemies had been put under his feet. In 14:61–62, on the other hand, the high priest asks Jesus if he is "the Christ, the Son of the Blessed." Jesus responds affirmatively (cf. 8:29), but then says, "And you will see the son of man sitting at the right hand of Power, and coming with the clouds of heaven," an image just seen in 13:24–27 (cf. 8:38–9:1). Three points are noteworthy in the juxtaposition of these two texts. First, because "the Christ" and "Son of the Blessed" (= Son of God) are here synonymous, the preexistent Christ/Son had in the past been seated at the right hand of God. Second, because Jesus speaks about events after his own death and resurrection, it is the risen Jesus who will be seated at God's right hand and who will come with the clouds. Third, because Jesus is the Christ/Son, he will be seen in that capacity, in his resurrection form. In other words, the preexistent Christ/Son of God, who became Jesus, returned to the right hand of God as the risen Jesus and will be recognized as such. It would seem that we have found the missing Son of God, but let us look further at other things Mark says about the risen Jesus.

Mark 16:7 posits yet another vision of the risen Jesus at a projected meeting between Jesus and his disciples in Galilee. An angel in Jesus' empty tomb tells the women who came to anoint Jesus' body that "Jesus of Nazareth, who was crucified...has risen" (16:6). The angel directs them to tell Jesus' disciples and Peter that the risen Jesus is going before them to Galilee, where they will see Jesus as he had said. This refers to 14:26–31, in which Jesus tells his disciples, "After I am raised up, I will go before you to Galilee" (14:28). The literarily self-conscious reference to a previous announcement of a postresurrection appearance, an appearance prior to Jesus' being seen in heaven, resonates with another curious reference. Following the transfiguration episode, Jesus tells the three disciples, including Peter, not to tell anyone "what they had seen, until the son of man should have risen from the dead" (9:9). It is not odd that Jesus suppresses his disciples, nor that they fail to understand what they had seen or what Jesus meant about "rising from the dead" (9:10). Both are functions of the plot. The curious element is the implication that something would happen after Jesus' resurrection that would make it possible for the disciples both to understand and to speak about what they had seen *in the transfiguration episode*. The only such event in Mark is the twice-repeated reference to Jesus' postresurrection appearance to his disciples "and Peter" in Galilee. Presumably, then and there, they would see the risen Jesus, understand what they had not understood, and be able to tell what they had seen on the mountain of the transfiguration.

Before inquiring into what the disciples saw and understood, let us note some of the issues in 8:27f. that lead into the transfiguration story and its immediate aftermath in 9:9–13. One should keep in mind, too, that, for Mark, "Christ" and "Son of God" are not only synonyms; the terms are distinguished in 8:29, where Peter identifies Jesus as "the Christ," and in 9:7, where God tells Peter and his two companions that Jesus is his Son.

In 8:27f., Jesus asks his disciples who people say that he is, whereupon they reiterate the three options already recounted in 6:14–16: John the Baptist, Elijah, one of the prophets. When Jesus then asks who they think he is, Peter responds, "You are the Christ." Curiously, however, Jesus "charges" (*epitimao*) them "to tell no one about him" (8:30), using the same verb of rebuke employed in his silencing of demons, to prevent them from making his real identity as the Son of God known (1:25; 3:12; 9:25; cf. 4:39; 10:48). But Jesus immediately begins to teach the disciples about the necessity (*dei*) of his impending fate, ending with his death and resurrection (8:31), whereupon Peter rebukes (*epitimao*) Jesus, who in turn rebukes (*epitimao*) Peter, saying "Get behind me Satan..." (8:33), confirming the demonology at issue in the verb of rebuke. Something is not right about the disciples' understanding either of Jesus as the Christ or of the (son of) man, Jesus, having to suffer, die, and rise from the dead, the last term cited explicitly in 9:10; they did not understand, the narrator says, "what the rising from the dead meant." But it is also the case that they do not understand what is entailed in Jesus being the Son of God. Remember that none of the characters in Mark's story knows about Jesus' sonship, because he silenced the only ones who did know, the demons or unclean spirits. When God addresses Peter and the two disciples, informing them that Jesus is his Son, there is no hint of understanding; Jesus even requires the disciples to keep quiet, until after the resurrection, about what they saw. The transfiguration story occurs in this context.

The question, "Who then is this?" is clearly at issue in 8:27–9:13, which concludes with the assertion that Elijah *has* come, as the reader knows from 1:2f., and that now the (son of) man, Jesus, is to suffer, as the reader learned in 8:31. But what does the reader learn from the transfiguration story? It cannot be that Jesus is the Son of God, because the reader learned that from 1:11, from the exorcism stories, and from what Mark says about them. The answer has to relate to the most distinctive feature of the story, namely the metamorphosis (9:2, *metamorphoō*) of Jesus and what God says about him. For it is the *metamorphosed* Jesus whom God identifies as God's Son. This is critical: the "one" (*houtos*) whom God calls God's Son is the metamorphosed Jesus. The Greek word denotes a change of form, which critics often relate to the son of man coming in the "glory" (*doxa*) of his Father (8:38; cf. 13:26), with "glory" referring to the luminosity surrounding God. Critics also largely agree that Jesus' momentary transformation represents the form to be taken by the risen Jesus, a form probably like that of angels (cf. 12:24–25). Accordingly, and now going beyond critical consensus, what the disciples were to see in Galilee was what they had seen on the mountain of transfiguration; seeing that form again, Peter and the disciples would understand not only what they had failed to understand on the mountain, but also what it means to say that Jesus is the Christ (cf. 8:29–33): *the Son of God/Christ was a heavenly being who assumed the form of Jesus, but who also retained the form of the risen Jesus after his death*. Most striking is that the Son of God not only inhabited the form of Jesus at his baptism, but that the Son of God also retained the form of the risen Jesus. This fact leads to the resolution of the apparent contradiction arising from the appearance of the risen Jesus. Like Elijah's appearance after John's death, the Son of God *did* appear after Jesus' death, but in the form of the risen Jesus.

Conclusion

My thesis is that the relationship between Elijah ("my angel") and John the Baptizer contributes to understanding the relationship between the Son of God ("my Son") and Jesus of Nazareth. For Mark, John and Jesus are human beings who, relatively late in life, were inhabited by divine beings, Elijah and the Son of God, who both preexisted them and continued to exist after their deaths. The resolution of the problem posed by the post-resurrection appearances of Jesus — rather than appearances of the Son of God — leads to the following observations. First, unlike Elijah and Moses, the Son of God has no form of his own. Second, John died but was not raised from the dead; Jesus *had* to die and be raised (8:31). Third, like Elijah, who appeared as himself after John's death, the Son of God is to appear after Jesus' death, but he will do so in the form of the risen Jesus. One might conclude that the (son of) man, Jesus, had to die so that the Christ/Son of God could appear.

21

The Bones of Adam and Eve

———— ◆ ————

Michael E. Stone
Hebrew University of Jerusalem

In this article I publish for the first time an apocryphal fragment, preserved in
Armenian. Virtually nothing can be said of its origin or date, unless we identify
its author with an obscure, post-seventh-century Armenian writer. What is intriguing about it for a student of the Pseudepigrapha, and George Nickelsburg is
quintessentially that, is its evocation of biblical themes. Moreover, the working-
out of the double typology, of the Old Testament in the New and, in detail, of
the old Adam and Eve and the new is striking. Such a typology and the integrated view of the history of salvation that it presupposes, lie behind much of the
Christian interest in and transmission of the Pseudepigrapha. Even Enoch, one
might maintain, was of such interest because of his assumption, because he was
a prefiguration of Christ. It is noteworthy, moreover, that this fragment makes
much of the bones of Eve. Not only is Adam related to Christ's crucifixion, but
Eve is related to the nativity and thus to Mary.

This text occurs on fols. 254r–255v of manuscript no. 6617, in the Mate-
nadaran Institute of Ancient Manuscripts, in Erevan, Armenia. The manuscript
was written in 1618, at an unknown place.[1] It is a *Miscellany* containing apocryphal, theological, and some philosophical works. The text we are publishing is
attributed to one Marut'a (see below) and our microfilm also contains another
work attributed to him. It is entitled, *T'uē zbazmut'iwn astełac'*, "He numbers the
multitude of the stars." This text is found on fols. 254v–255v and nothing can be
said at present to help identify it.

The text dealing with the bones of Adam and Eve connects their disposition
with the life of Jesus. That Adam was buried on Golgotha where the cross of Christ
was set is commonplace, and the very name "Golgotha" ("skull" in Aramaic) is

———————————

1. One should not be discouraged by the late date of the manuscript. Many significant texts are
preserved in Armenian only in manuscripts produced during the revival of Armenian manuscript
copying in the sixteenth and seventeenth centuries.

241

related to Adam's skull, which is traditionally shown in Christian art at the foot
of the cross.[2] Our text, however, also relates Eve's burial to the life of Christ, and
particularly to the Virgin Mary. Christ is the new Adam, reversing Adam's sin,
and Mary is in a similar typological relationship with Eve.

The particular story related is an embellishment on an old theme also reflected
in Armenian miniature paintings of the nativity of Christ. In these paintings, Eve
is shown, often without a halo, but sometimes with one, present at the nativity.
In our text, not only is Adam buried at Golgotha, but Eve's bones are eventually
interred at the entry of the Grotto of the Nativity. The parallel between the two
burials and its implications are absolutely clear.

The manuscript is in *notrgir*, late minuscule script; note the form of *k'ē*; the
form of *tiwn* is inconclusive, but it seems to be the longer form. These two factors indicate a date after the sixteenth century.[3] The manuscript has a single
column, with visible vertical ruling. It is of paper. Old folio numeration in Armenian characters may be observed at the top right-hand corner and modern
folio numeration, to which we refer, in the lower margin. Folio 254 opens a new
fascicle and has what is apparently a fascicle number in the lower margin, in a
frame. The running head and the first two lines of the text are in red ink, and
the remainder is in black ink. Abbreviations are limited in number, and mainly
of standard character.

The running head at the top of the page is *Marut'ai asac'eal*, "Spoken by
Marut'a," and I have already noted that the text following *Concerning the Bones
of Adam and Eve* has the same header. It seems most likely that this was not
Marutha of Maipherkat, a Syrian bishop who died before 420, some of whose
writing was translated into Armenian.[4] A better candidate is the writer of this
name mentioned by H. Ačaṛean.[5] He was the author of *Bank' i veray zanazan
niwt'oc' hin ew nor ktakaranac', ayl ew i veray žołovoc' ew herjuacołac' omanc' ew
yaytnut'ean Mahmeti ew bažanman Vrac' ew Hayoc'* (Discourses concerning various subjects of the Old and New Testaments, and also concerning Councils and
certain heretics and the appearance of Mohammed and the division between the
Armenians and Georgians). Nothing is known about his identity or when he
lived. The reference to the separation of the Armenian and Georgian churches

2. Observe also that the branch Seth took out of the garden was planted at the head of Adam's
grave. It became the tree of the cross. See *Adam Fragment 2* in M. E. Stone, *Armenian Apocrypha
Relating to Patriarchs and Prophets* (Jerusalem: Israel Academy of Sciences, 1982), §8, 10–11.

3. M. E. Stone, "The History of Armenian Writing," in *Album of Armenian Paleography* (ed. M. E.
Stone, D. K. Kouymjian, and H. Lehmann; Aarhus, Denmark: Aarhus University Press, forthcoming),
§3.4.5.

4. See Robert W. Thomson, *A Bibliography of Classical Armenian Literature to 1500 A.D.* (Corpus
Christianorum; Turnhout, Belgium: Brepols, 1995), 69.

5. H. Ačaṛean, *Hayoc' Anjnanunneri Baṛaran* (Dictionary of Armenian proper names) (repr.,
Beirut: Sewan Press, 1972), 3.270.

and the mention of Mohammed imply that the document must be later than the early seventh century,[6] which excludes Marutha of Maipherkat.

Elsewhere we have observed that another tradition concerning the bones of Adam exists. In the Armenian version of *Chronicle of Michael the Syrian*, we read, concerning Maniton (Ionṭon), the fourth son of Noah, as follows:[7]

> For after the flood they say that Noah had a son, Manitos by name, who took his borders on the other side of the sea. And he besought some of the bones of Adam from his father, and he gave him the knee bones [?] as a memorial.

It is difficult to know what function these bones of Adam play in the *Chronicle of Michael the Syrian*, but it is of interest that they are mentioned. According to *Cave of Treasures*, after Adam's death, his body was buried in the Cave of Treasures (Bezold, 1.10). The responsibility for Adam's body was transmitted in the antediluvian generations (ibid., 1, 13, 16). Noah took Adam's body with him into the ark (ibid., 20, 21f.). After the flood, Shem put it at the middle of the earth, that is, in Golgotha, under angelic guidance (ibid., 28). In this tradition, which is much older than *Michael the Syrian*, Adam's body, in particular, is stressed.[8]

Following the section on the bones of Adam and Eve there is approximately one page of text dealing with eschatological prophecy. This page relates to that which precedes it through the image of a woman in labor. The labor of childbirth is one of the curses of Eve which the birth of Christ canceled. Similarly, the birth of the messianic age, the revelation of divine glory and the coming of joy, is inevitable and painful. The image of the pangs of childbirth leading up to the messianic age is ancient and widespread.[9] Similarly, the inevitability of the eschaton and the signs presaging it are common themes from the Second Temple period on.

---

6. See M. Ormanian, *L'Eglise arménienne* (Antelias, Turkey: Catholicossate of Cilicia, 1954), 32.

7. See M. E. Stone, *Armenian Apocrypha Relating to Adam and Eve* (SVTP 14; Leiden: Brill, 1996), 116, where Armenian texts and variant versions of this passage are given.

8. Observe that the bones, as such, are not mentioned.

9. *2 Apoc. Baruch* 25.2; *Soṭa* 9.1; etc.

Յաղագս ոսկերացն ադամայ եւ եւայի։

1. Եբրայեցոցն պատմեն գիրք եւ ասեն. Թէ գոսկերան ադամայ. եւ. եւայի։ նախախՀայրքն ունէին եւ ընդ իրեանս շրջեցուցանէին։ Օրպէս գյովսեփայն իսրայէղացիքն

եւ եկին մի<ն>չեւ ի մելքիսեդեկ. եւ նորա լծեալ գերինչան. եւ եղեալ ի վերայ սայլիցն. անցուցանել ընդ բեթղահՀեմ.

եւ բերեալ մինչեւ ի յայր մի երինչըն նստան. եւ առեալ գոսկերան եւայի թաղեցին առ դուրան այրին։ Ուր սուրբ կոյան ծնաւ գքրիստոս. եւ լուծան անէծքն եւայի.

եւ գոսկերան ադամայ բերեալ ի գողգոթայ եւ էր անդ ուր քրիստոս խաչեցաւ.

եւ էբարձ գմեղս նախաՀաւրն։ քանզի շիրիմ ասէ գնայ դաւիթ փիլիստփայն առաջին մարդոյն։

2. Կին յորժամ ծնանի տրտմութիւնն[10] է նմայ զի Հասեալ ժամ նորայ. զի յորժամ ծնանի կին շարժի ամենայն մարմին նորայ ցաւաւք եւ խայյւտարակին անդամաւք. եւ գգայութիւնք նորայ լիմարին եւ մոռանայ գխնդումն եւ գՀոգս իւր եւ խասարի լոյս աշ<ա<g>[11] նորայ։

[fol. 254v] եւ ունին գնայ անՀնարին ցաւք եւ առ վշտին եւ շարժման ցաւոց իւրոց ճռշիցէ. եւ բանին դրունք յարգանդի[12] նորայ։ եւ ելցէ մանուկն ի լույս։

Նոյնպէս եւ յաւուրն յետնումն լինիցի։[13] Շարժի երկիր ի Հիմանէ իւրմէ. եւ որոտմունք եւ շարժմունք. եւ արՀաւիրք. եւ խատատակին ամենայն փառատրութիւնք մարդկան. եւ բանա երկիր գարգանդ իւր եւ ծնանի գամենայն ազգս. եւ յայժամ տրտմութիւնք մարդկան յուրախուոթիւնն[14] դառնան։

---

10. Abbreviation mark is omitted.
11. The letter c' is largely obliterated.
12. *yi* below line, *prima manu*.
13. Written over an illegible word, *prima manu*.
14. *hiwn* 1° above line, *prima manu*.

Concerning the Bones of Adam and Eve

1. The books of the Hebrews relate and say that they had the bones of the forefathers Adam and Eve and moved them around with them[15] just as the Israelites [did] with those of Joseph.[16]

And they came to Melchisedek and he, having yoked heifers, put them upon the wagon[17] to transfer [them] to Bethlehem.

And having brought [them] as far as a cave, the heifers sat down.[18] And taking the bones of Eve they buried [them] by the entrance of the cave where the holy Virgin bore Christ, and the curse of Eve was undone.[19]

And they brought the bones of Adam to Golgotha, and he was there where Christ was crucified and removed the sins of the first father.[20] Wherefore David the Philosopher said it was the sepulchre of the first man.[21]

2. A woman, when she gives birth, has pain, for her hour has arrived. For when a woman gives birth, her whole body is shaken by pains and it is shamed by [its] limbs. And her senses are deranged and she forgets [her] pleasure and her care and the light of her eyes is darkened. And intolerable pains take hold of her and in distress and the movement of her pains, she screams out and the gates of her womb are opened and the child goes forth into the light.

Similarly it will also be on the last day. The earth is moved from its foundation and [there are] thunders and earthquakes and terrors.[22]

And all the glories of humans will be put to shame and the earth opens its womb and gives birth to all the nations.[23] And then the sadnesses of humans turn into joy.[24]

---

15. This contradicts the tradition in the *Cave of Treasures* mentioned above.

16. Exod. 13:19.

17. Based on 1 Samuel 5–6, esp. 6:7–8. It cannot be determined whether the dependence is on the Greek or Armenian Bible.

18. Indicating that this was the appointed spot.

19. Many Jewish traditions put the burial of Adam and Eve in the cave of Machpelah in Hebron. The recurrence of caves in the traditions mentioned here is notable.

20. Adam's curse is thus nullified by the crucifixion and, similarly, Eve's curse, the pain of childbirth, through the Virgin.

21. The source being referred to is unknown. In the Armenian tradition, "David the Philosopher," or "David the Invincible Philosopher," is a famous, if somewhat obscure, figure. See Thomson, *Bibliography*, 107–11. Nothing like this tradition occurs in the genuine writings of David, but other works were ascribed to him, as Thomson notes.

22. Compare the text *Signs of the Judgment*, in M. E. Stone, *Signs of the Judgment, Onomastica Sacra, and the Generations from Adam* (University of Pennsylvania Armenian Texts and Studies 3; Chico, Calif.: Scholars Press, 1981).

23. Or: generations.

24. This is already a biblical theme; see Isa. 35:10; Jer. 31:13; etc.

22

Jesus' True Family:
The Synoptic Tradition
and Thomas

◆

Fred Strickert
Wartburg College

A dozen years ago I wrote a dissertation for George Nickelsburg in which I ana-lyzed the impact of the *Gospel of Thomas* (hereafter GT) on the issue of rewriting scripture in the Gospel tradition. My conclusions were mixed: in certain cases, Thomas preserves early material; in others, Thomas's work provides a later rewrit-ing of the Synoptic Gospels. Thus statements implying the priority of Thomas as a whole are oversimplifications and at best misleading. In this article I have chosen to revisit a part of my dissertation in view of the work of the Jesus Seminar.

The episode of "Jesus' True Family" provides an excellent case study since it occurs in three extracanonical sources as well as in all three of the Synoptics. Here the Jesus Seminar and the publication of *Five Gospels* have taken the opposite track, arguing for the priority of GT 99. In their voting on the various versions the following results are noteworthy:[1]

Version	Red	Pink	Gray	Black	Average	Color
Matthew 12:46–50	30	40	10	20	0.60	Pink
Thomas (GT 99)	22	44	0	33	0.52	Pink
Luke 8:19–21	10	50	22	20	0.50	Gray
2 Clement (2C)	22	22	33	22	0.48	Gray
Gospel of the Ebionites (GE)	22	22	22	33	0.44	Gray
Mark 3:31–35	21	28	10	41	0.43	Gray

1. Robert W. Funk, Roy W. Hoover, and the Jesus Seminar, *The Five Gospels: The Search for the Authentic Words of Jesus* (New York: Macmillan, 1993), 551. A more complete record of the voting is included in *Forum* 6 (1990): 3–55.

Not surprisingly, the Thomas version of the saying has received high ratings (the pink rating means that Jesus probably said something like this). On the other hand, Mark is printed in gray (Jesus did not say this, but the ideas contained in it are close to his own). More surprising is that the Matthean version has the highest rating (pink) and that Luke receives a rating just below Thomas, even though both are clearly dependent on Mark. The question is quite complicated.

A Proposed Pre-Synoptic Form of the Saying

According to Mahlon H. Smith, who prepared the formative study for the Jesus Seminar, the earliest form of the saying was a simple two-part dialogue between the disciples and Jesus.[2] In response to the disciples' statement that Jesus' family is standing outside, Jesus identifies his true family in clever repartee as those doing the will of the Father.

> When some told Jesus, "**Your mother and brothers** are standing outside," he said to them, "Behold, these are [my mother and] **my brothers,** who do the will of my Father."

The simple dialogue, in which the mothers and brothers of Jesus are mentioned in two different senses, stands in contrast to the more complicated synoptic forms which present a series of five statements (Mark); four (Matthew); or three (Luke).

The earlier form, however, concludes with a simple statement of Jesus, introduced by a simple οὗτοι εἰσιν structure. Accordingly, there are no less than three noncanonical witnesses to this authentic saying.

Gospel of Thomas 99	*Gospel of the Ebionites*[3]	*2 Clement 9:11*
	Moreover they deny that he was a man, evidently on the basis of the word the Savior spoke	
The disciples said to him, "Your brothers and your mother are standing outside."	when it was announced to him, "Behold, your mother and your brothers stand outside." —*namely: "Who are my mother and brothers?" And*	
He said to them,	*pointing to his disciples he said,* "These	For the Lord said, "These are my brothers
"Those here who do the will of my Father, they are my brothers and mother; *these are they who shall enter the kingdom of my Father."*	who do the will of my Father are my brothers and mother and *sisters.*"	those who do the will of my Father."

---

2. Mahlon H. Smith, "Kinship Is Relative: Mark 3:31–25 and Parallels," *Forum* 6 (March 1990): 80–94.

3. Epiphanius, *Haer.* 30,14,5.

There is much appeal to the idea of such a simple two-part dialogue, yet the matter itself is not so simple. First, one must face that not a single source preserves this simple two-part dialogue (additional material is included in italics). The text of 2 *Clement* preserves only the response of Jesus while GT 99 contains an additional saying about entering the kingdom at the end. The three-part GE form is quite complicated. The reference to "sisters" is clearly a later addition, since it produces an unusual order and is not linguistically consistent with the previous members (no article or possessive pronoun). The question of Jesus ("Who are my mother and brothers?"), and the comment about Jesus pointing to the disciples, comes directly from Matthew's version. The result when these elements are excised, however, as Smith notes, is the simple two-part saying which parallels that of GT 99. He argues that the Jewish Christian Gospel originally knew this form of the story, which was then later doctored by someone familiar with the Matthew version.

The Priority of the Markan Saying

This is impressive analysis and carries much appeal. However, one must ask whether such a proposal is necessary or whether the change is simply the natural later development of the synoptic tradition. The reason for this question is that both 2C and GE tend elsewhere toward Gospel harmonies. Ron Cameron has described GE as "a harmony, composed in Greek, of the Gospels of Matthew and Luke (and, probably, the Gospel of Mark as well)."[4] Likewise, Helmut Koester views 2C as dependent on a "harmonizing collection of sayings which was composed on the basis of those two Gospels [Matthew and Luke]."[5] It is possible that these works could have used additional sources. However, the question must be asked whether this use was necessary or even likely. If the development can be explained simply on the basis of the Synoptics, then one must hesitate when assuming that a tradition is earlier mainly because it is found in Thomas.

The most perplexing part of Smith's thesis is that all three of the Synoptics also depend on this earlier two-part dialogue. Although Mark is complicated, it is, according to Smith, a development from this early source. When one places the early source side by side with Mark, one can easily see the complications.

---

4. Ron Cameron, *The Other Gospels* (Philadelphia: Westminster, 1982), 103.

5. Helmut Koester, *Synoptische Überlieferung bei den Apostolischen Vätern* (TU 65; Berlin: Akademie Verlag, 1957), 78, and idem, *Introduction to the New Testament* (Minneapolis: Fortress, 1982), 2.235.

Pre-Synoptic Source	Mark 3:31–35
	a. Then **his mother and his brothers** came; and standing outside, they sent to him and called him.
	b. And a crowd was sitting around him;
When some told Jesus, **"Your mother and brothers** are standing outside,"	*c.* and they said to him, **"Your mother and your brothers**[6] are outside asking for you."
	d. And he replied, "Who are **my mother and my brothers?**"
he said to them, "Behold, these are my **mother and my brothers**	*e.* And looking at those who sat around him, he said, "Here are **my mother and my brothers!**"
who do the will of my father."	*f.* Whoever does the will of God is **my brother and sister and mother.**"

Robert Tannehill notes that the Markan version is the most dramatic of all the accounts.[7] In addition to the repetitive listing of family members, a number of details emphasize the contrast, such as "those outside" versus "those around him" and "standing" versus "sitting," so that the contrasting senses of mother and brothers "rub against each other." While this may be effective storytelling technique, others may reckon the resulting literary product as redundant and vague.

This is the position of Smith, who suggests that the introductory statement *c* of the simple dialogue was expanded, by Mark, through *a–b* to a well-developed narrative. Likewise Mark is credited with expanding the pronouncement of Jesus (*e, f*), first by adding a rhetorical question *d* and, second, by altering the final statement into an inclusive general principle *f* about discipleship. This general principle is constructed as a conditional sentence introduced by ὅς; it mentions sisters; and it changes the Semitic "will of my father" to "will of God."

This leads us to the crux of the problem in Mark. It has long been recognized that this final verse (35) stands at odds with the rest of the account. The previous four mentions of the family members are rendered in a consistent fashion:

$$\text{ἡ μήτηρ αὐτοῦ καί οἱ ἀδελφοί αὐτοῦ (v. 31)}$$
$$\text{ἡ μήτηρ σου καί οἱ ἀδελφοί σοῦ (v. 32)}$$
$$\text{ἡ μήτηρ μου καί οἱ ἀδελφοί μου (v. 33)}$$
$$\text{ἡ μήτηρ μου καί οἱ ἀδελφοί μου (v. 34).}$$

However, when it comes to the final verse, a different pattern appears.

$$\text{ἀδελφός μου καί ἀδελφή καί μήτηρ ἐστίν (v. 35).}$$

---

6. The NRSV adds "sisters." However, this reading occurs only in MSS K, A, D, and *alii* and should be rejected.

7. Robert Tannehill, *The Sword of His Mouth* (Minneapolis: Fortress, 1975), 166–71, esp. 168.

This final verse offers no less than five stylistic differences from the earlier four references:

1. the order is reversed;
2. the mention of sister occurs only here;
3. "brother" occurs in the singular;
4. no articles are used;
5. the possessive pronoun is used only with the first member.

Form critics have, therefore, long concluded that v. 35 did not originally belong with vv. 31–35. While Bultmann[8] and more recently Lambrecht[9] proposed that v. 35 reflects the original kernel out of which this apothegm developed, Dibelius[10] and later Crossan[11] have suggested that vv. 31–34 made up the original story. Thus the climax came with the gesture and statement of Jesus: "Here are my mother and brothers!" However, for purposes of preaching, the general principle was later developed: "Whoever does the will of God is my brother and sister and mother."

Smith and the Jesus Seminar present an interesting variation to the form critics' development theories. In some respects, one would have to say that the members of the Jesus Seminar have ignored the careful work of their own J. D. Crossan and have opted for the Bultmannian approach, since in their argument virtually the whole narrative derives from the dialogical saying of Jesus. However, the original saying, they argue, is not the one preserved in Mark 3:35 but the response of Jesus in GT 99. Here is where the proposal begins to fall apart, because it ignores the linguistic difficulties within the Markan account. If Mark is responsible for creating both framework material (vv. 31–32, 34) and the concluding statement of Jesus (v. 35), then why did he structure the latter so drastically different from the former? Why did the seminar separate the final saying from the core saying in GT 99, while they voted on the Markan text as a unit? Should not v. 35 be voted on separately from Mark 3:34? If the members cast the same votes for both segments of the Markan text, so be it. However, the method of voting itself was predetermined in favor of the Thomas version.

The reference to brother and sister and mother in Mark 3:35 is exactly what one would expect from Mark. In 10:29–30, Jesus speaks of leaving behind brothers and sisters and mother (same order) and receiving, in return, a hundredfold of brothers and sisters and mothers. Likewise it is Mark (6:3) who mentions the real sisters among the family of Jesus. One would expect for Mark to mention the sisters of Jesus among those standing outside in Mark 3:31–35, as later manuscripts recognized. The most reasonable explanation for the dichotomy between

---

8. Rudolf Bultmann, *The History of the Synoptic Tradition* (trans. John Marsh; Oxford: Blackwell, 1963), 29–31.

9. J. Lambrecht, "The Relatives of Jesus in Mark," *Novum Testamentum* 16 (1974): 241–58.

10. Martin Dibelius, *From Tradition to Gospel* (New York: Scribner, 1963), 56–57.

11. J. D. Crossan, "Mark and the Relatives of Jesus," *Novum Testamentum* 15 (1973): 81–113.

vv. 31–34 and v. 35 is that the former was already fixed, perhaps reflecting an actual incident remembered from the ministry of Jesus. The effectiveness of that early story was made possible through the repetition of Jesus' family members and the implicit climactic statement, "Here are my brothers and mother!" With time, however, the generalized inclusive statement in v. 35 was introduced for Christian preaching.

There is no question that both Matthew and Luke chose to rewrite the Markan account. Interestingly, both of the later evangelists played down the hostility of the earlier account. Mark had set the stage by noting that the family had gone to restrain Jesus, because some had said, "He has gone out of his mind" (Mark 3:21), and by sandwiching the Beelzebul story (Mark 3:22–30) to highlight opposition to Jesus. Both Matthew and Luke, however, omit the former and distance the account of Jesus' true family from the latter.

Matthew 12:46–50	Mark 3:31–35	Luke 8:19–21
[46]While he was still speaking to the crowds, his mother and his brothers were standing outside, wanting to speak to him.[12]	[31]Then his mother and his brothers came; and standing outside, they sent to him and called him. [32]A crowd was sitting around him; and they said to him, "Your mother and your brothers are outside, asking for you."	[19]Then his mother and his brothers came to him, but they could not reach him because of the crowd. [20]And he was told, "Your mother and your brothers are standing outside, wanting to see you."
[48]But to the one who had told him this, Jesus replied, "Who is my mother, and who are my brothers?" [49]And pointing to his disciples, he said, "Here are my mother and my brothers! [50]For whoever does the will of my Father in heaven is my brother and sister and mother."	[33]And he replied, "Who are my mother and my brothers?" [34]And looking at those who sat around him, he said, "Here are my mother and my brothers! [35]Whoever does the will of God is my brother and sister and mother."	[21]But he said to them, "My mother and my brothers are those who hear the word of God and do it."

Within the story, Matthew has made several changes. He has reduced the repetitions of family members to four by omitting the statement that informed Jesus of his family's presence. He has extended the rhetorical question by repeating the interrogative pronoun "who?" and has changed the culminating statement from doing "the will of God" to "the will of my Father in heaven" (a phrase unique to Matthew among the Synoptics; Matt. 7:21; 12:50; 18:14; 21:31). He designated those around Jesus as "the disciples," perhaps reflecting a later conflict

---

12. Verse 47 is omitted in both important fourth-century manuscripts, Sinaiticus (original hand) and Vaticanus, and in numerous other manuscripts and versions.

of the 80s and 90s.[13] While Mark had heightened the contrast between those "standing outside" and those "sitting" around Jesus (mentioned twice in Mark 3:32, 34), Matthew omits both references.

Luke has extended his editorial hand in even more radical fashion. Since Luke presents Mary as a model hearer of the word (Luke 1–2) and the entire family as the core of the early church (Acts 1:14), a less hostile atmosphere is expected. The reference to Jesus' family "standing outside" is spoken not by the narrator, but by the messenger. The family does not "send for him" or "call him" (Mark 3:31–32), but they announce that they "desire to see him." It is not that they choose to remain outside, but they are unable (οὐκ ἠδύναντο) to reach him because of the crowd. Other than this reference, there is no further mention of those around Jesus. There are none described as "sitting around" (Mark 3:32, 34). There is no pause in which Jesus "looked around" (Mark 3:34). There is no probing question, "Who are my mother and my brothers?" (Mark 3:34). There is no demonstrative ἴδε (Mark 3:34). The pronouncement of Jesus in v. 21, therefore, serves not to contrast Jesus' spiritual family with his physical family, but to show that his real family includes more than those related by blood. The contrast between a narrow interpretation of Jesus' family and a wider interpretation lends itself to a shorter episode. The mentions of "mother and brothers" are reduced to three. Aside from the narrative introduction, the messenger (representing the narrow view) mentions them once, and Jesus (representing the wide view) mentions them once. This final pronouncement in Luke 8:21, thus, combines two separate sayings brought together by Mark in 3:34 and 35. Luke's reference to "mother and brothers" is taken from Mark 3:34 (agreeing in number, order, use of possessive, and the omission of "sister"). Consistent with the decision to locate this story directly after the parable of the sower (where emphasis is on hearing the word; Luke 8:15), Luke alters "who do the will of God" to "who hear the word of God and do it." These elements from two separate sayings are linked by the construction οὗτοί εἰσιν, which reflects Mark's use of the pronoun οὗτος in v. 35.

The changes in Luke 8:19–21 reflect both Luke's theological interests and his literary tendencies. Typical Lukan features include παρεγένοντο (28 of 37 NT occurrences are in Luke-Acts); ἀπηγγέλη (27 of 45 NT occurrences are in Luke-Acts); ἰδεῖν θέλοντές (Luke 9:9; 19:3; 23:8); and τόν λόγον τοῦ θεοῦ (only once each in Matthew, Mark, and John, but 19 times in Luke-Acts). There is no hint that Luke has employed other sources.[14] Through his own literary abilities, Luke has reshaped this episode to present a version much different from Mark 3:31–35.

---

13. Funk, Hoover, and the Jesus Seminar, *Five Gospels*, 190.

14. Tim Schramm, *Der Markus-Stoff bei Lukas* (Cambridge: Cambridge University Press, 1971), 124.

Smith, however, has reached another conclusion: the changes in both Matthew and Luke are attributed to awareness of the Thomas-like early form. This is certainly possible in theory. We have an interesting parallel with the parable of the mustard seed, which is available in Mark and Q versions (and also Thomas). In this case, Matthew combined the two versions, but Luke opted to include only the Q parable. Nothing like this case exists in the rewriting of Mark 3:31–35 by Matthew and Luke. The changes can be explained entirely in view of Matthean and Lukan redactionary traits. To suggest that Luke made use of a Thomas-like version of the episode is even more unexpected, since Luke's purpose was, not to contrast the family of Jesus with those around Jesus, but to present them in a more positive light. Once again, Smith's proposal falls short of the critical analysis of the synoptic versions.

The Noncanonical Tradition as Later Development

This analysis of the synoptic versions of Jesus' true family does not in itself preclude an independent version preserved by Thomas and other sources. It only concludes that the Synoptics are not dependent on this version. At this point we can return to the other three sources of the saying. As noted earlier, both 2C and GE are generally included in the tradition of Gospel harmonies. Is there evidence in this particular saying that they are dependent on the canonical Gospels?

According to Smith, the three noncanonical sources have three major elements in common:

1. An οὗτοι εἴσιν structure for the pronouncement of Jesus.

2. The expression "will of my father."

3. A simple two-part dialogue format.

The first of these is paralleled by Luke; the second by Matthew; but the third no longer survives in any version, canonical or noncanonical.

The 2C version is especially important for Smith because it is the unique witness to a version of the saying in which only the brothers are mentioned. Thus the punch of the saying comes in the contrasting symbols of authority, the brothers of Jesus and his heavenly Father. However, closer investigation demonstrates that 2C is secondary, or, more accurately, tertiary. This is clear when the Greek text is compared with Lk 8:21.

Luke 8:21	μήτηρ μου καί ἀδελφοί μου οὗτοί εἴσιν οἱ τόν λόγον τοῦ θεοῦ
2 Clement	ἀδελφοί μου οὗτοί εἴσιν οἱ
Luke 8:21	ἀκούοντες καί ποιοῦντες
2 Clement	ποιοῦντες τό θέλημα του πατρός μου.

In the Lukan form, which mentions both mother and brothers (taken over from
Mark 3:34), the presumptive pronoun οὗτοι is quite natural. It is totally unnecessary in 2C ("my brothers these are . . .") and betrays a source — most certainly
Luke — which includes a compound subject. The reference to doing the will of
my Father is not Lukan. While Smith posits that it originates with the pre-Markan
source, there is difficulty. The other Greek witness to that hypothetical source,
GE, presents a plural reading, τά θελήματα, while 2C has the singular τό θέλημα
(like Matthew). In other words, the 2C version of the saying points clearly to a
harmonization of Matthew and Luke and not to any pre-canonical source.

Regarding the GE version, Smith has already recognized dependence in part
on Matthew (expressed below in italics).

> . . . when it was announced to him, "Behold, your mother and your brothers
> stand outside." — *namely; Who are my mother and brothers?" And pointing to
> his disciples he said,* "These who do the will of my Father, are my brothers
> and mother *and sisters.*"

The resulting material, however, he posits as evidence for the pre-canonical
source. Yet again, the similarity with Luke is striking.

| Luke 8:19 | ἀπαγγέλη δέ αὐτῷ   ἡ μήτηρ σου καί οἱ ἀδελφοι σου |
| GE | ἐν τῷ ἀναγγελῆναι αὐτῷ ὅτι ἡ μήτηρ σου καί οἱ ἀδελφοι σου |

| Luke 8:19 | ἐστήκασιν ἔξω. . . . |
| GE | ἔξω ἐστήκασιν. . . . |

Even more significant than the similarity between Luke and GE is that GT 99
differs on four points: (1) the questioners are identified as "disciples" (as in other
GT sayings); (2) the text is presented in active voice; (3) the verb is a simple
"said" rather than "report"; and (4) the text reverses the order of family members
"brothers and mother." In one significant reading, in which Luke 8:19 and GE
differ in word order (ἐστήκασιν ἔξω rather than ἔξω ἐστήκασιν), Luke is in
agreement with GT 99. In not a single case in this introductory statement does
GT 99 agree with GE, against Luke 8:19. Again, a closer look at the GE saying
shows evidence of harmonization on the basis of both Matthew and Luke.

GT 99 — Rewriting Scripture

The Thomas version then stands alone. There are no parallels for a pre-canonical
two-part dialogue form. Does the evidence hold for GT 99? Regarding the final
pronouncement of Jesus, there are some important variations from Lk 8:21.

GT 99	Gospel of the Ebionites	2 Clement
"Those here who do the will of my Father, they are my brothers and mother...."	"Those who do the will of my Father are my brothers and mother and sisters."	"These are my brothers those who do the will of my Father."

GT 99 and GE do agree at several points, against the Lukan version: (1) they refer to doing the "will of my Father" (although GE offers a plural); (2) they give priority to "brothers" over "mother." Interestingly, both of these elements can be found in Matt. 12:50. Likewise, the Matthean version does provide a parallel in one instance in which GT 99 differs from both GE and Luke 8:21 — the ordering of the sentence in mentioning the family members last.

The only case in which GT 99 preserves a unique reading is the adverb "here." Those "standing outside" in the introductory statement of the disciples are contrasted in the response of Jesus with "those here." This detail is necessary to provide contrast in the two-part dialogue version. In Luke, the context provides the contrast, and this detail is unnecessary. This is also the case with GE in its present form. However, might one expect such residue in the pronouncement of Jesus in either the GE version or, in fact, in any of the other versions, if they were dependent on this pre-canonical two-part dialogue? More likely the explanation is that GT 99 added this detail because all the other narrative details had been excised. Again, there is reason to think that GT 99 may be dependent on the canonical Gospels as is the case with the other noncanonical versions.

The question, then, is whether this contrast in GT 99 would be sufficient. One could ask after Jesus' saying, Outside of what? Why is the family outside and not inside? Why are they standing? Why is standing outside at odds with doing the will of the Father? The Thomas version provides no explanation. It is difficult to imagine the effect of this saying without prior knowledge of the more developed synoptic story.

The context of the *Gospel of Thomas* provides a negative view of Jesus' family. In GT 101, Jesus' biological mother is contrasted with his "true mother." In GT 105, he states that the one who knows his father and mother will be called "son of a harlot." Thus the exclusive view brought out by GT 99 is expected and is reinforced by the concluding statement:

These are they who shall enter the kingdom of my Father.

By separating the two parts of this pronouncement, the Jesus Seminar has missed an important clue concerning the development of the GT 99 version. The expression "to enter the kingdom" is relatively rare in the Synoptics, occurring only once in the triple tradition (Matt. 19:23–24=Mark 10:23–25=Luke 18:24–25) and three times in Matthew (Matt. 7:21; 18:3; 21:31). Most significant, the combination of "doing the will of my Father" and "entering the kingdom" occurs in Matt. 7:21.

Not everyone who says to me, "Lord, Lord," shall enter the kingdom of heaven, but only the one who does the will of my Father in heaven.

The combination of the two concepts in GT 99 is significant. While one would not readily associate Matthew 7 with GT 99, it is significant that this section of Thomas provides a number of parallels to this part of Matthew. GT 92 reflects 7:7–8; GT 93, Matt. 7:6; GT 94, Matt. 7:8.

How then does this unrelated saying from Matt. 7:21 join the saying about Jesus' true family? The answer comes from another Thomas saying, GT 75. When placed side by side, the parallel structure between GT 75 and GT 99 becomes apparent.

	GT 75	GT 99
A	Many	Your brothers and your mother
B	are standing at the door but	are standing outside.
A1	the solitary	Those here who do the will of my Father, they are my brothers and my mother,
B1	are the ones who will enter the bridal chamber.	these are they who shall enter the kingdom of my Father.

The allusion to Matt. 7:21 is more obvious in GT 75. Some are standing at the door and calling "Lord, Lord," but they will not enter the kingdom. The expression "standing outside" in GT 99 thus parallels "standing at the door" in GT 75. Yet the major change in GT 99 is that the family is now identified with the "many" who are excluded. Thus, in GT 99, it would be improper to mention the crowd as the reason that the family remains outside. In contrast to the many standing at the door, those who enter are identified as "the solitary." By solitary, Thomas means those who reject the traditional relationships of marriage and family.[15] Thus "the solitary" // "those doing the will of my Father" are contrasted with Jesus' real brothers and mother. The real family, representing those still in traditional relationships, are described as "many."

Matthew 7:21 is thus a fitting passage for the motifs expressed in GT 75 and 99. The "many" are outside because the door to life is narrow (Matt. 7:13–14). Those same "many" will call "Lord, Lord" as if they knew him (Matt. 7:22–23), but they will be cast out, while only the one doing his will shall enter the kingdom. It is Thomas's use of Matt. 7:21 in GT 99 that helps to explain the presence of the expression "doing the will of my Father," not a pre-synoptic source. GT 99 as a whole is very close to Luke. However, while Luke presented a relatively favorable

---

15. A. F. J. Klijn, "The 'Single One' in the *Gospel of Thomas*," *JBL* 81 (1962): 271–78; B. E. Gartner, *Theology of the Gospel of Thomas* (trans. Eric J. Sharpe; New York: Harper & Brothers, 1961), 249–57.

picture of Jesus' family, Thomas's purpose is different. Thus the simpler form is due to the extraction of Lukan details.

The *Gospel of Thomas* may sometimes be valuable in studying sayings of Jesus. The episode of Jesus' true family, however, is an example in which the Synoptics have been rewritten to attain a different theological goal.

23

Anti-apocalyptic Apocalypse

———— ◆ ————

Patrick Tiller

Introduction

I first met George Nickelsburg when I was just beginning my doctoral dissertation on *1 Enoch* at Harvard Divinity School. He eagerly and freely shared ideas and compared notes. He has become not only a guide into the mysteries of Enoch, but also a friend, whose concrete acts of encouragement have meant a great deal over the past twelve years. One of George's abiding interests concerns the function and meaning of the apocalyptic literature produced during Greek and Roman domination of Judea. He and I, along with many colleagues, are currently collaborating in research on the interrelatedness of apocalyptic and wisdom literature in both early Judaism and early Christianity. In this essay I investigate *4 Ezra*'s use of apocalypse, a use reminiscent both of earlier apocalypses and earlier wisdom traditions.

The text of *4 Ezra*, or *2 Esdras*, is Ezra's account of seven visions. In these visions Ezra either raises problems relating to theodicy, receiving various answers, or receives allegorical visions about the end of time.[1] In each case the problem is closely related to the Romans' recent and heartbreaking conquest and destruction of Judea. Most of the answers have to do with the future judgment, the coming of the Messiah, and the nearness of the end of the age. Notable among the visions are that of a woman in mourning for her only son and her transformation into the glorious city of Zion (9:26–10:59), and the historical vision of an eagle rising from the sea, which represents the Roman Empire (11:1–12:39).

The original Judean apocalypse (chaps. 3–14) is usually said to have been composed around 100 C.E.[2] This is based partly on the first verse of the text,

---

1. For a convenient introduction to *4 Ezra*, see G. W. E. Nickelsburg, *Jewish Literature between the Bible and the Mishnah* (Philadelphia: Fortress, 1981), 287–94; or B. M. Metzger, "The Fourth Book of Ezra," in *OTP* 1.516–59. All quotations from *4 Ezra* are taken from the NRSV. Quotations from *2 Baruch* are taken from A. F. J. Klijn, "2 (Syriac Apocalypse of) Baruch," in *OTP* 1.621–52.

2. M. E. Stone, *Fourth Ezra: A Commentary on the Book of Fourth Ezra* (Hermeneia; Minneapolis: Fortress, 1990), 9–10.

which states, "In the thirtieth year after the destruction of our city..." Although the city spoken of is Babylon, the text is probably a cryptic reference to the destruction of Jerusalem in 70 C.E. The ordinal number "thirtieth," however, could have been used in imitation of Ezek. 1:1, "In the thirtieth year, in the fourth month on the fifth day, while I was among the exiles by the Kebar River, the heavens were opened and I saw visions of God." Since 4 *Ezra* seems clearly to refer to the destruction of the temple and since it is quoted in Clement of Alexandria, *Stromata* 3.16 (quoting 4 *Ezra* 5:35), it must have been written after 70 C.E. and before the end of the second century. If the common identification of the three heads of the eagle with Vespasian, Titus, and Domitian is accepted, the book must have been written during the reign of Domitian (81–96 C.E.). Finally, Michael Stone cites two Hebrew expressions (*'wlm* and *qts 'chrwn*), assumed to have been used in ways which seem to fall midway between the usage of the Dead Sea Scrolls and that of Mishnaic Hebrew.[3]

Translation errors and the existence of Greek quotations of the text point to Greek as the language of the common *Vorlage* of the extant versions (Latin, Syriac, Ethiopic, Arabic, Georgian, and Armenian).[4] Most scholars, however, suppose that the original language was either Hebrew, or, less likely, Aramaic, on account of semiticisms.[5] The book was later expanded through the addition of a Christian framework consisting of chapters 1–2 (the call of Ezra and his vision of a multitude of Gentiles on Mount Zion, receiving a crown from the "Son of God") and chapters 15–16 (woes against the nations and warnings of impending tribulation; preserved only in Latin).

Literary Genre

The genre of the work is clearly that of apocalypse.[6] It is a narrative about visionary revelations of future and heavenly realities delivered or interpreted in part by the angel Uriel[7] (although Uriel is not always, strictly speaking, an *angelus interpres*).[8] It includes a symbolic, visionary review of history that begins in the past

---

3. M. E. Stone, *Features of the Eschatology of IV Ezra* (HSS 35; Atlanta: Scholars Press, 1989), 10–11, 149–80.

4. Stone, *Fourth Ezra*, 1–2.

5. Ibid., 10–11.

6. See the widely accepted definition of apocalypse in John J. Collins, "Introduction: Towards the Morphology of a Genre," *Semeia* 14 (1979): 9.

7. Various source theories have been proposed, but they are not generally accepted. The main evidence is the sudden appearance in 4:1 of "the angel that had been sent to me, whose name was Uriel" and of the lack of preparation for the first vision. Possibly some material has been lost from the end of chapter 3. There is also an unexplained reference to Ezra's being "taken up" in 8:19. Other anomalies could also be noted.

8. According to E. Brandenburger (*Die Verborgenheit Gottes im Weltgeschehen: Das literarische und theologische Problem des 4.Esrabuches* [ATANT 68; Zürich: Theologischer Verlag, 1981], 200), "Er trägt vielmehr in vielem die Züge einer himmlischen Offenbarerfigur, die den Offenbarungsempfänger im

and extends into the future (chaps. 11–12).[9] Its function, like that of the first, fourth, and fifth Books of 1 Enoch, is in part to provide answers to questions of evil and theodicy. As the works now collected in 1 Enoch were driven by the desire to come to terms with the seemingly unnatural events happening in and around Jerusalem, so the author of 4 Ezra writes to respond to the destruction of the Jerusalem temple by the Romans. He provides encouragement to remain faithful and hopeful and assures his readers that wisdom, understanding, and knowledge are still accessible, even if limited (14:47).

Although 4 Ezra is undoubtedly an apocalypse in form, its apocalyptic heart has been torn out. It is often said about apocalypses that they represent a pessimistic view. While that is true, it is equally true that in the "big picture" they are usually quite optimistic. The present world, with its cosmological, political, economic, social, and religious orders, is condemned and doomed to final judgment. But this world is viewed from a transcendent perspective gained by heavenly visions and angelic guides. From this heavenly point of view, everything is comprehensible and will work out properly. In 4 Ezra, however, all optimism has faded; the work does not understand present, aberrant, earthly realities from the perspective of heavenly realities. It is for 4 Ezra impossible to understand heavenly realities, and, indeed, Ezra makes little attempt to understand even earthly realities. Instead, assurance is given that things are the way they must be, that God loves creation, that the end is near, and that the final judgment will bring life to those who have been faithful to God and God's law. The text of 4 Ezra represents apocalyptic concession to the failure of an apocalyptic worldview. This can be seen most clearly in its view of the limits of human understanding and in the subject of its speculative discussions. The concession is also apparent in the book's final narrative of the rewriting of the ninety-four books, and in its symbolic treatment of history. Like Job, in the end Pseudo-Ezra can only affirm God's goodness and justice, but he cannot understand it; he leaves his readers unsatisfied.

The Limits of Human Understanding

One might expect to find discussion of cosmology, astronomy, meteorology, oura-nology, or angelology in an apocalyptic text. This is especially true of 4 Ezra since the angelic interpreter is Uriel, who, according to the Astronomical Book of 1 Enoch, revealed the astronomical secrets of the sun, moon, and stars to Enoch and who accompanied Enoch on his tours of the cosmos in chapters 17–36 of the

---

Gesamtgeschehen begleitet und die Stationen des Weges bestimmt" (He bears rather in many respects the features of a heavenly revealer who accompanies the recipient of revelation throughout the whole event and determines the stops along the way). The distinction between an interpreting angel and a revealing angel is not significant for generic classification.

9. The book also begins with a review of history (3:4–27), but it is entirely historical and not revelatory.

Book of the Watchers. But 4 *Ezra* has none of these elements. Michael Stone has analyzed what he calls "lists of revealed things" that occur in apocalypses and, in a different form, in much of the wisdom literature.[10] Stone analyzes lists found in *2 Baruch* 59.5–11; *1 Enoch* 41.1–7; 60.11–22; 93:11–14; *2 Enoch* 23.1; 40.1–13; *4 Ezra* 14:5, 7; Pseudo-Philo, *Liber antiquitatem biblicarum* 19.10; Job 28:25–27; 38; Sirach 43; and others. These lists occur in one of three forms: (1) a list of things revealed to the seer; (2) a list of divine secrets; and (3) a list of rhetorical questions designed to demonstrate the unbridgeable distance between divine and human understanding. Stone, following von Rad in part, traces the origin of these forms partly to earlier wisdom traditions.

Especially interesting for our purposes are recurring questions about measurements of fire, wind, rain, the abyss, paradise, and the future. In Ezra's first vision, after he complains about the "evil heart" inherited from Adam and the unfavorable treatment of Israel in comparison with Babylon, and after he asserts his ability "to comprehend the way of the Most High," he receives God's answer through Uriel.

> And he said to me, "Go, weigh for me the *weight of fire*, or measure for me a *blast of wind*, or call back for me the day that is past." I answered and said, "Who of those that have been born can do that, that you should ask me about such things?" And he said to me, "If I had asked you, 'How many dwellings are in the heart of the sea, or how many streams are at the source of the deep, or how many streams are above the firmament, or which are the *exits of Hades*, or which are the entrances of paradise?' perhaps you would have said to me, 'I never went down into the deep, nor as yet into Hades, neither did I ever ascend into heaven.'" (*4 Ezra* 4:5–7)

Similarly, in the list of things revealed to Moses in *2 Baruch* 59.5–11, we have the following items:

> ... the *measures of fire*, the depths of the abyss, the *weight of the winds*, the number of the raindrops, ... the height of the air, the greatness of Paradise, the end of the periods, ... the worlds which have not yet come, the *mouth of hell*, ... the multitude of the angels which cannot be counted, the powers of the flame, the splendor of lightnings, the voice of the thunders, the orders of the archangels, the treasuries of the light ...

The almost exact correspondence of the italicized phrases, their recurrence elsewhere, and the similarity of other phrases indicate that we are dealing with lists at least partly determined by traditional usage. Pseudo-Ezra's use of this list, however,

---

10. M. E. Stone, "Lists of Revealed Things in the Apocalyptic Literature," in *Magnalia Dei: The Mighty Acts of God* (ed. Frank Moore Cross, Werner E. Lemke, and Patrick D. Miller, Jr.; Garden City, N.Y.: Doubleday, 1976), 414–52.

is not only an innocuous adaptation of older wisdom lists, but a self-conscious rejection of the typical apocalyptic use. Pseudo-Baruch, on the other hand, embraces the older apocalyptic view. In 48:3–4, along with the admission that "you do not reveal your secrets to many," he prays, "You make known the multitude of the fire, and you weigh the lightness of the wind." The striking difference between the views expressed in 4 *Ezra* and 2 *Baruch* seems significant.

Stone suggests two possibilities for understanding the significance of these lists in apocalyptic literature. They may be merely "formulaic, traditional lists" that had only partial overlap "with the actual concerns of the apocalyptic authors."[11] But Stone prefers an alternate explanation of their "common function."

> They all occur at the high point of a revelation, where a brief statement of its contents is desired, or else as a summary of what is revealed to the seer. It seems likely, therefore, that by examining in detail the information which the lists claim to have been revealed to the seers, a view can be reached of what the writers of the apocalypses thought to lie at the heart of apocalyptic revelation itself.[12]

This explanation would be consistent with the origins of Enochic traditions in astronomical, angelological, and cosmological speculations. If true, then 4 *Ezra* represents the use of the apocalyptic genre by a writer who does not share the theoretical underpinnings of apocalypticism. If, however, the lists are merely formulaic and not representative of the speculative concerns of apocalyptic writers, then 4 *Ezra* still represents rejection of the form traditional in apocalyptic literature in favor of the form characteristic of wisdom literature.

For 1 and 2 *Enoch* and 2 *Baruch*, the list items are revealed either to Moses or to Enoch, but for 4 *Ezra*, as for Job, the items are mentioned as rhetorical questions that ask about the protagonist's knowledge. Neither Job nor Ezra is able to answer questions about these mysteries. Especially interesting in contrast is 1 *Enoch* 93:11–14. The form of this passage, like the passages in Job and 4 *Ezra*, is that of the rhetorical question. Whereas, in Job and 4 *Ezra*, the answer to be supplied is, "I do not know about these things," in 1 *Enoch* the reader is expected to understand that Enoch knows precisely these things. As Enoch confidently says in 2 *Enoch* 40:1, "I know everything."

In 4 *Ezra*, Uriel and Ezra agree that heavenly knowledge is inaccessible to human beings. Ezra goes so far as to wish that all knowledge and understanding were withheld from humans, since it only makes them miserable.[13] This conviction, however, is not simply representative of traditional Israelite wisdom traditions, but goes beyond such traditions in its pessimism concerning any kind of

---

11. Ibid., 419.
12. Ibid., 418.
13. 4 *Ezra* 4:22; 7:63.

understanding. Engaging in the old dispute between writers of wisdom and apocalyptic texts, 4 Ezra denies the possibility of receiving by revelation information which is the standard subject of revelation in other apocalypses.[14] In reference to 4 Ezra 5:36–37, Michael Stone concludes:

> When seen in this light, the passage receives its full dramatic dimension. It is a denial, daring, perhaps even polemical, of the availability of certain types of special knowledge, a denial therefore of a specific part of apocalyptic tradition.[15]

What is confidently asserted in other apocalypses as the basis for understanding the natural world and its implications for human society is rejected in 4 Ezra. The optimistic view that it is possible to come to terms with human experience, no matter how overcome by evil, is explicitly rejected. The only understanding of interest to Ezra is understanding what is on earth (4 Ezra 4:21). In 4 Ezra, the form of apocalypse is used to deny the possibility of apocalypse.

Speculative Interests

While 4 Ezra denies the possibility of knowing traditional objects of speculative investigation, it has its own speculative interests. The only cosmological speculation in 4 Ezra is the claim that one-seventh of the earth is water and the rest dry land (6:42). There are, however, other kinds of speculation. Note the tradition that the ancient monster Behemoth lives in the mountains, Leviathan lives in the water, and both will be eaten by people of God's choice. This may refer to some kind of messianic banquet. There is also a lengthy discussion of the state of the dead before the last judgment. The souls of the unrighteous dead, 4 Ezra states, will immediately (after seven days of observation) enter torment, but the souls of the righteous will immediately enjoy rest after the same seven-day period (7:75–101). There is also speculation about the appearance and nature of the messianic period (7:26–31); the timing and signs of the end; the efficacy of prayer for the ungodly (7:102–15); and the attributes of God (7:132–40). Other similar speculations may be found, but cosmological speculations are absent. More significant is that these speculations have almost no practical implications. The author is keenly interested in signs of the end of the age and other eschatological issues, but the only significance seems to be that this information illustrates the ways of God. This information is useful in understanding the justice and goodness of God, but there do not seem to be many moral or other behavioral consequences.

---

14. See R. A. Argall, *1 Enoch and Sirach: A Comparative Literary and Conceptual Analysis of the Themes of Revelation, Creation, and Judgment* (SBLEJL 8; Atlanta: Scholars Press, 1995), 249–55, for some interesting suggestions about the possibility that Sirach may have been written partly to dispute the apocalyptic claims of some of his contemporaries.

15. Stone, "Lists of Related Things," 420.

Meaning of History

The 4 *Ezra* text includes, in the fifth vision of the eagle, visionary review of a brief bit of Roman history, but there is no attempt to explain the meaning of history. Nor is there implicit theodicy in the symbols of the vision. Nothing in the vision prepares the reader to find meaning under Rome's jurisdiction. The vision serves only to identify a period in Roman history as the time when the Messiah would destroy the wicked and deliver the saved remnant of his people.

There is no attempt to make sense of the present predicament, only assurance that it will soon be over. In fact, Pseudo-Ezra is advised not to "be quick to think vain thoughts concerning the former things, lest you be hasty concerning the last times" (6:34). The bulk of the first three visions asserts that it is impossible to understand the meaning of the past or the reasons for God's actions; only the future is certain, and even that is obscure in its details. This is contrary to some of the older apocalypses (Daniel; Animal Apocalypse; Apocalypse of Weeks) that review history in the form of *vaticinium ex eventu*. In those cases the purpose is not only to establish the competence of the pseudepigraphic seer, but also to explain the significance of past events. But 4 *Ezra* knows of no such significance.

Scripture

Instead of the revelation of heavenly secrets by way of heavenly tablets (as in *1 Enoch* and *Jubilees*), Ezra is permitted to rewrite the twenty-four books of the scriptures, along with seventy other books to be reserved for "the wise among your people" (14:46). Seen in the light of the previous discussion, this permission takes on new meaning. No doubt the seventy books to be secretly delivered to the wise are full of esoteric wisdom. Indeed, even in 12:37–39, Ezra was instructed to write the eagle vision (and presumably its interpretation) in a book, which was also to be delivered secretly to the wise. In this final episode, Ezra functions precisely as a scribe, but not quite as a sage. Ezra increased in wisdom and understanding, but most notably in memory retention. There are a few hints to the content of these seventy books. First, we may assume that the eagle vision was included, given the parallels with 12:37–39. Second, Ezra's prescribed preparation is to put away human thoughts, burdens, and nature. If one assumes that the doubts and intellectual struggles described in the first three visions represent such thoughts and burdens, then one may also assume that the seventy secret books do not go further than the rest of 4 *Ezra* in answering those thoughts. Third, God's directions to Ezra in 14:17–18 and Ezra's instructions to the people in 14:34–36 concern the future: the final ages of human history and the final judgment. It seems likely, then, that the esoteric wisdom contained in the seventy books should be presumed the same sort promoted in the rest of 4 *Ezra*: faithful resignation and acceptance of God's justice and wisdom.

The significance of Ezra rewriting scripture cannot be overstated. This episode focuses the reader on revelation of the past. It is the preservation and remembrance of past revelation that eventually brings meaning to Ezra's quest for understanding. New revelation, such as that contained in 4 Ezra, brings assurance, but not new understanding.

Conclusions

Pseudo-Ezra is no longer able to make sense of this world in the light of heavenly and future realities. The most compelling part of 4 Ezra is the depth of Ezra's despair at the unlikelihood of finding answers to his questions about evil and the sufferings of God's people. According to Michael Stone, the apparent lack of correspondence between the rationally ordered questions in the first part of the book and the eschatological answers in the second part is due to "the author... not really thinking in 'logical' terms, not interested in reaching an answer to his questions by means of reasoned, propositional argument."[16] Nevertheless, the urgency and forcefulness of Ezra's questions and complaints in the first three visions lead the reader to look for an equally forceful and satisfying answer.

Revelations about wicked or good angels, the cosmos, the divine throne room, or the future are unable to satisfy the author's intense desire to understand. Like Job, in the end Pseudo-Ezra can only affirm God's goodness and justice, but he cannot understand it; thus, he leaves his readers unsatisfied.[17] Only by accepting Pseudo-Ezra's transformation of his queries into eschatological questions, for which answers are forthcoming, can the reader gain satisfaction. This satisfaction, however, is not based on the feeling that life makes sense, but on the feeling that, in the end, everything will be all right and that, in the meantime, the evils are necessary, incomprehensible evils.

Ezra's movement from dispute and doubt in the first three visions to acceptance, it is often noted, culminates the elevation of Ezra to a second Moses. Indeed, 4 Ezra shares the common apocalyptic conviction that earthly troubles can be resolved by reference to heavenly wisdom. What is new is the conviction that this wisdom is inaccessible to human understanding, and must simply be accepted on the basis of written tradition. No new revelation is meaningful; focus on the scriptures of Israel provides meaning.

---

16. Stone, *Features*, 25.

17. E. Brandenburger asserts that 4 Ezra solves the dual problems of the way of God and of the evil heart by rejecting earthly wisdom and accepting heavenly wisdom. The heavenly wisdom as revealed forces earthly wisdom out of the recipient, resulting in the experience of the way of God (*Die Verborgenheit Gottes*, 197–201). Even in this explanation, however, the reader is asked to suspend rational judgment (which leads only to despair) and simply to accept the rightness of the way of God.

24

Studies on the Prologue and *Jubilees* 1

——— ◆ ———

James C. VanderKam
University of Notre Dame

The *Book of Jubilees* is a prominent early member of the group of ancient Jewish writings often labeled the Rewritten Bible. The author closely follows the text of Genesis and Exodus, beginning with the story of creation in Genesis 1 and continuing to the arrival of the Israelites at Mount Sinai in Exodus 19 and to the meeting between the Lord and Moses in Exodus 24. As we might expect, the author has not simply reproduced the authoritative scriptural base; rather, he has added, subtracted, and otherwise modified source material as he wrote.

Jubilees 1 is unique in the *Book of Jubilees* in that it is not set in the order of the scriptural narrative and does not continue the story. The writer supplies a preface, introductory words that allow him to characterize the text that will follow and to contextualize it for the benefit of readers. Genesis and Exodus do not, of course, furnish an introduction that identifies the speaker, the standpoint of the author, and the situation from which he wrote. The writer of *Jubilees*, through the addition of chapter 1, overcame the lack of context at the beginning of the scriptural narrative and thus made it possible for readers to perceive how he viewed the revelatory materials that follow. Not only did he fashion an introduction, but he also placed much of it in the mouth of God — unlike the rest of the book, which is revealed to Moses by an angel. As a consequence, the chapter is of great importance for grasping what happens.

The understanding of the revelation to Moses as presented in *Jubilees* 1 forms the subject of the present essay. It is now possible to carry out exegetical study of the chapter on a more secure textual base, because the fragments of 4Q216 (4QJub[a]) preserve a relatively large amount of the original Hebrew text.[1] After introductory comments, *Jubilees'* presentation is treated under two headings that consider the content and the date of the revelation.

---

1. See J. VanderKam and J. Milik, "216: 4QJubilees[a]," in *Qumran Cave 4: VIII, Parabiblical Texts, Part I* (J. VanderKam, consulting editor; DJD 13; Oxford: Clarendon Press, 1994), 1–22. Apart from the Hebrew fragments, only the Ethiopic version preserves this section of the text.

Introductory Comments

In the prologue, the writer of *Jubilees* alerts the reader that the setting for the revelation is a meeting on Mount Sinai between God and Moses. After this summary statement, he continues by reproducing the Lord's order to Moses to ascend the mountain, the latter's compliance, and the encounter that transpired. The author does not allow readers to forget the Sinaitic setting; on the contrary, he has inserted periodic reminders throughout (e.g., 2:26, 29; 6:11, 13, 19, 20, 32; etc.) so that is it never far from mind. In the prologue and in 1:1–4 he makes it clear, through allusions and quotations, that Exodus 24 in particular was the inspiration for the setting.

This much is obvious, but what is less clear is how the writer uses the material in Exodus 24 and how he modifies it. The Sinai episode in the Bible served as the basis for much reflection and for many exegetical treatments in ancient Jewish commentaries. *Jubilees* stands at a very early point in that exegetical tradition and evidences some of the interests and concerns found elsewhere, but in a number of respects the author seems to have gone his own way as he used the story to present his teachings.

A glance at the structure of the prologue and chapter 1 will highlight the author's dependence on and independence from Exodus 24 and its context.

Prologue: summary statement about ascending the mountain to receive the tablets and what the tablets contained. Exod. 24:12 is the major source.

1:1–4: narrative introduction giving the date (3/16), God's command, Moses' ascent, and a statement about the duration of his stay (see Exod. 19:1; 24:12, 15–18).

1:5–18: God's speech to Moses predicting the apostasy and punishment of Israel and their eventual return and reunion with God. These verses depart almost completely from Exodus and contain a heavy Deuteronomic flavor, with Deuteronomy 31 especially influential.

1:19–21: Moses' intercession for Israel. In the Bible, Moses is often presented as an intercessor for the people, who are deserving of judgment (see, e.g., Exod. 32:11–14, 30–32). Here the text draws particularly from Deut. 9:25–29.

1:22–25: the Lord's response in which God cites the need for the people to acknowledge their sin and to return to God, and the provisions God will make so that they never again turn away.[2]

---

2. For an analysis of *Jub.* 1:4b–26 and its biblical sources, see G. Davenport, *The Eschatology of the Book of Jubilees* (SPB 20; Leiden: Brill, 1971), 19–29. Davenport also draws attention to 1Q22 (*The Words of Moses*), which adopts the setting in Deuteronomy but offers a number of parallels to

1:26–29: provisions for writing the revelation:

> 1:26: the Lord first commands Moses to write "all these words" (see Exod. 34:27; cf. 24:4).

> 1:27–28: the Lord next commands the angel of the presence to dic-tate the material to Moses. There seems to be some connection with Exod. 23:20–33a (cf. 32:34), although nothing is said there about this angel's dictation.

> 1:29: the angel of the presence takes the tablets; their message is summarized.

It should be evident that only the first two sections (the prologue and 1:1–4) and part of the last (vv. 26–29) are based on the Sinai narratives in Exodus. The remainder of chapter 1 includes material largely external to the Sinai stories and is added to create the author's introductory message. The initial parts of the chapter, that is, the prologue and 1:1–4, are especially rich about the way the author understood his book. They should be examined for what they convey about the nature of the revelation and the timing of the meeting between God and Moses.

The Nature of the Revelation to Moses

There are several statements in the opening chapter regarding the character of the disclosures made to Moses and contained in *Jubilees*.

The prologue of *Jubilees* reads:

> These are the words regarding the divisions of the times of the law and of the testimony, of the events of the years, of the weeks of their jubilees throughout all the years of eternity as he related (them) to Moses on Mount Sinai when he went up to receive the stone tablets — the law and the commandments — on the Lord's orders as he has told him that he should come up to the summit of the mountain.[3]

The clause "these are the words" echoes Deut. 1:1 (*'lh hdbrym*) and may have been chosen purposely to remind the reader of that second presentation of the Torah, which plays a major role in the language and thought of *Jubilees* 1, especially in vv. 5–25. The phrase "divisions of the times" seems to have served as an early title for *Jubilees*, because it is used already in CD 16:3 to refer to the book (*spr*

Jubilees 1. He thinks *Jub.* 1:4b–26 belongs to a different redaction of the book than the verses that precede and follow, but it is difficult to see convincing reasons for the source division.

3. English translations of *Jubilees* are from J. VanderKam, *The Book of Jubilees* (2 vols.; CSCO 510–11; Scriptores Aethiopici 87–88; Louvain: Peeters, 1989), vol. 2. Textual evidence other than 4Q216 is cited from vol. 1.

mḥlqwt h'tym). It highlights the paramount importance attached to chronology and its arrangement in the entire composition.[4] The sequel mentions the units of time employed: years, weeks, and jubilees.

Within the statement about time divisions are two terms to which those divisions relate — "law" and "testimony." Although little of the prologue has survived in 4Q216, there is no doubt that the Hebrew for the first term was *twrh* (see col. 1:6 = *Jub.* 1:1 for the same equivalence between Ethiopic *ḥegg* and Hebrew *twrh*) and there is great likelihood that for the second (Ethiopic *sem'*) it was *t'wdh*. The same word pair appears in 1:4, where the Hebrew is lost; but, for the similar expression in *Jub.* 1:26, 4Q216 4:4 reads *ltwr]h wlt'w[dh*. These two nouns are important for understanding how the writer conceived of the revelation contained in his book.

As commentators have noted, both words are present in Isa. 8:16 ("Bind up the testimony, seal the teaching")[5] and 8:20, where they appear to be poetic parallels (*Jubilees* follows the order of the two terms in 8:20; they are reversed in 8:16). After noting that Ruth 4:7 is the only other passage in the Hebrew Bible where *t'wdh* occurs, H. Wildberger writes about the related verb, *'wd:*

> As is shown by Pss. 50:7 and 81:9 (see also 1 Sam. 8:9), the verb can be used when one paraphrases to describe the activity of the speaker at a covenant festival, the one who confronts the people with the will of Yahweh. The verb was apparently considered to be apt for describing the entire scope of prophetic responsibilities, and it would not be at all surprising if *t'wdh* (admonition) was in frequent use as a way to depict the prophetic task.[6]

The term *t'wdh* appears not only in the prologue of *Jubilees* and *Jub.* 1:4, 26, but also in 1:8, where the writer, basing himself on Deut. 31:21,[7] substitutes it for a different word in Deuteronomy: where Deuteronomy has *w'nth hšyrh hz't* ("this song will confront them as a witness"), *Jubilees*, in repetitive fashion, has *w'nth h[t'wdh 'l] ht'wdh hz't* ("And the [testimony] will respond [to] this testimony" [4Q216 2:5]). That is, the writer seems to highlight the term *t'wdh* by repeating it and by using it to replace the scriptural *hšyrh*. G. Brooke has noted this change and writes about its function: "Through this clever word substitution..., the author of *Jubilees* combines Isaiah 8 with Deuteronomy 31 as a secondary text which he will use to provide the vocabulary for what he wants to say to illustrate how God's position in Deuteronomy 31 will be vindicated. Israel will indeed go

---

4. On this subject see VanderKam, "Das chronologische Konzept des Jubiläenbuches," *ZAW* 107 (1995): 80–100.

5. Scriptural translations are from the NRSV.

6. H. Wildberger, *Isaiah 1–12: A Commentary* (Continental Commentaries; Minneapolis: Fortress, 1991), 366–67.

7. Deut. 31:16–22 is a divine speech to Moses with a character similar to the one in *Jub.* 1:5–18.

astray as predicted."[8] He goes on to show that Isa. 8:14–16 strongly influenced the vocabulary of *Jub.* 1:9–11.[9] Other uses of *t'wdh* in the Qumran texts allow Brooke to conclude that it

> has a breadth of connotation which suits the author of *Jubilees* very well. The testimony is in effect to be understood as another way of talking about the secrets of the heavenly realm, which are disclosed only to the chosen few. In particular they are the "signs of heaven," "the ordained times." Since the use of Isa. 8:12–16 allows for the understanding that the *t'wdh* is synonymous with the *twrh* (Isa. 8:20), the extended meaning of the term allows the author to imply what is the prime content of the Law itself as it is now being dictated to Moses by the angel of the presence: it has to do with the knowledge of the calendar and the periodisation of history.[10]

It seems, however, that more can be said about *t'wdh* in *Jubilees*. Elsewhere, the author distinguishes between what is being revealed to Moses in *Jubilees* and what appears in the Pentateuch. This is expressed most clearly in 6:22: "For I have written (this) in the book of the first law which I wrote for you . . ."; here the angel of the presence is speaking about the Festival of Weeks and the legislation for when and how it was to be observed, as recorded in Lev. 23:15–21 and Num. 28:26–31, for example. The angel also refers to his earlier written work in 30:12, 21; 50:6. It is reasonable to suppose that when the writer of *Jubilees* uses the term *twrh* he has the Pentateuch in mind.[11] But what is the referent for *t'wdh*? It may be that the author draws from Exod. 24:12, which is quoted in the prologue and in 1:1, where the Lord tells Moses: "I will give you the tablets of stone, with the law and the commandment, which I have written for their instruction." The MT reads *'t lḥt h'bn whtwrh whmṣwh* (literally: "the tablets of stone *and* the Torah and the commandment"), while the Samaritan Pentateuch and the LXX lack the conjunction between *h'bn/htwrh*.[12] The MT reading possibly suggests that the *twrh* and *mṣwh* were an addition to the contents of the tablets, although the *waw*

---

8. G. Brooke, "Exegetical Strategies in *Jubilees* 1–2: New Light from 4QJubilees[a]," in *Studies in the Book of Jubilees* (ed. M. Albani, J. Frey, and A. Lange; TSAJ 65; Tübingen: Mohr [Siebeck], 1997), 50–51.

9. Ibid., 51–53.

10. Ibid., 52.

11. R. H. Charles (*The Book of Jubilees or the Little Genesis* [London: Adam and Charles Black, 1902], 7, note to v. 26) thought that, according to *Jubilees*, the angel wrote down the first law, that is, the Pentateuch, but that Moses wrote down the second law, that is, *Jubilees*. As Charles indicated, however, this explanation of the conflicting statements about who wrote *Jubilees* — Moses or the angel — is not very satisfactory (see p. 8, note to v. 27). It is quite likely that in the original Hebrew text of *Jubilees* there was no conflict on this point and that it consistently pictured the angel dictating to Moses, who did the writing. On this see VanderKam, "The Putative Author of the Book of Jubilees," *JSS* 26 (1981): 209–17; and 4Q216 4:6 (= *Jub.* 1:27).

12. See J. T. A. G. M. van Ruiten, "The Rewriting of Exodus 24:12–18 in Jubilees 1:1–4," *BN* 79 (1995): 28.

could be taken as an explicative conjunction. *Tg. Ps.-J.* Exod. 24:12 expands with *yt lwḥy 'bn' dbhwn rmyz š'r pytgmy 'wryyt' wšyt m'h wtlysyry pyqwdy'* ("the tablets of stone in which the rest of the words of the law are intimated and the 613 commands" [my translation]).[13]

That more than the Ten Commandments or the laws from Exodus 20 through Numbers 10 had been revealed to Moses on Sinai is a common claim in the exegetical traditions, a claim that could be based on Exod. 24:12 or on other pentateuchal passages that use multiple terms for the revelation. Commenting on Exod. 24:12, *b. Ber.* 5a records R. Shimon b. Resh Laquish's teaching that the word "tablets" referred to the Ten Commandments, "law" to the Pentateuch, and "commandment" to the Mishnah, adding that the word "written" intends the Prophets and Writings and that "instruction" points to the Talmud. The familiar tradition that both the Written and Oral Torahs were revealed to Moses on Mount Sinai could be attached to a verse such as Lev. 26:46 ("These are the statutes and ordinances and laws that the Lord established between himself and the people of Israel on Mount Sinai through Moses"), where the plural *twrwt* lent itself to such a reading, as in *Sifra b-ḥqwty* 8: "'. . . the statutes': this refers to the exegeses of Scripture '. . . and ordinances': this refers to the laws '. . . and Torahs': this teaches that two Torahs were given to Israel, one in writing, the other oral."[14]

It seems that *Jubilees* belongs in some such tradition, but the author, through parallel formulations, shows that he understands the two revelations to Moses to be the law and the testimony. As seen, he twice quotes Exod. 24:12 (prologue; 1:1) where the two terms are "law" and "command," but in four passages (prologue; 1:4, 26, 29) he pairs "law" and "testimony," and does so with similar wording:

Prologue: the words regarding the divisions of the times of the law and of the testimony.

1:4: he related to him the divisions of all the times — both of the law and of the testimony.

1:26: during all the divisions of time that are in the law and which are in the testimony.

1:29: the tablets (which told) of the divisions of the years from the time the law and the testimony were created.

All four passages occur in contexts connecting them with what was revealed on Sinai to Moses. The author may have been encouraged to associate the term *t'wdh*

---

13. For the text see E. G. Clarke, ed., *Targum Pseudo-Jonathan of the Pentateuch: Text and Concordance* (Hoboken, N.J.: Ktav, 1984).

14. The translation is taken from J. Neusner, *SIFRA: An Analytical Translation* (BJS 140; Atlanta: Scholars Press, 1988), 3.375.

with law and the tablets by Exod. 32:15, which speaks about the two tablets of *h'dt* (the testimony).

It is possible, as J. Kugel has written, that *t'wdh* designates *Jubilees* or what the author intends the *Book of Jubilees* to be: "[H]e took 'Torah' to be a reference to the written text of the Pentateuch, and used 'testimony' (he actually understood this word more in the sense of 'solemn warning') to refer to his own book. *Jubilees* was presented as the solemn warning that God's angel had delivered to Moses on Mount Sinai, a warning about, among other things, the dire consequences of failing to observe the proper calendar ('the divisions of all the times')."[15] Kugel's understanding of the word is in line with Brooke's conclusion from the word's use in *Jubilees* and in the Qumran literature. The central section of *Jubilees* 1 (vv. 5–25) allows for an interpretation also consistent with this proposed meaning. There the Lord addresses Moses in strongly Deuteronomic language,[16] warning about the people's apostasy from the laws (calendrical ones are prominent, but others are included). *Jubilees* is meant to be a solemn warning about violation of covenantal stipulations, and this warning was revealed to Moses in the form of the *Book of Jubliees*.

The four passages in which *Jubilees* 1 pairs Torah and testimony add information about what is covered in the revelation to Moses.

Prologue: of the events of the years, of the weeks of their jubilees throughout all the years of eternity.

1:4: what (had happened) beforehand as well as what was to come. He related to him the divisions of all the times.[17]

1:26: what is first and what is last and what is to come during all the divisions of time.

1:29: for the weeks of their jubilees, year by year in their full number, and their jubilees from [the time of the creation until] the time of the new creation.

These statements about the time covered by the revelation, as commentators have long noted, do not fit well with the Pentateuch nor even with most of *Jubilees.* They may, however, refer to passages such as *Jub.* 23:8–31, which predicts what will happen at the end.[18] Whatever their referent, the author of *Jubilees*

---

15. J. Kugel, *The Bible as It Was* (Cambridge and London: Harvard University Press, Belknap Press, 1997), 405–6, n. 23. On pp. 402–6, Kugel has collected a number of texts that speak about what was revealed to Moses on Mount Sinai.

16. See K. Berger, *Das Buch der Jubiläen* (JSHRZ 2/3; Gütersloh: Gütersloher Verlagshaus, 1981), 314, note *a* to v. 6.

17. Space considerations in 4Q216 1:10–11 may indicate that the Hebrew text contained the longer formulation found in v. 26, including the phrase "and what was to come." See DJD 13.5, 7.

18. See, for example, Charles, *Book of Jubilees,* 7–10.

was not the only expositor who thought that God had revealed the future to Moses. B. Beer drew attention to *b. Meg.* 19b; *b. Men.* 29b; *Leviticus Rabbah,* chap. 26; and especially to *Exodus Rabbah,* chap. 40: "He [= God] brought to him [= Moses] the book of the first Adam and showed him all the generations that would arise from the beginning until the resurrection of the dead" (my translation).[19] Or, *4 Ezra* 14:4–5 says: "... and I led him up to Mount Sinai. And I kept him with me many days; and I told him many wondrous things, and showed him the secrets of the times and declared to him the end of the times"[20] (see also *Apoc. Mos.* 1:1; *2 Apoc. Bar.* 59:4). The presence of this motif in *Jubilees* 1 may be another effect of Deuteronomic influence, since a number of passages in that book, in connection with the revelation to Moses, predict what will happen if the people do or do not remain faithful to the covenant (see esp. Deuteronomy 27–31).[21] Moses' testimony in the *Book of Jubilees* covers the present and as far as the distant future, just like his testimony in Deuteronomy (cf. Deut. 3:24–29).[22]

The Date of the Revelation

It is no surprise that the author of *Jubilees* dates the revelation that functions as his source. The first verse indicates the time when Moses encountered the Lord: "During the first year of the Israelites' exodus from Egypt, in the third month — on the sixteenth of the month — the Lord said to Moses: 'Come up to me on the mountain. I will give you two stone tablets of the law and the commandments which I have written so that you may teach them'" (1:1). How did the writer arrive at this dating, and what is its significance?

The date in the third month is related to Exod. 19:1, where "[o]n the third

---

19. B. Beer, *Das Buch der Jubiläen und sein Verhältniss zu den Midraschim* (Leipzig: Wolfgang Gerhard, 1856), 25.

20. The translation is from M. Stone, *Fourth Ezra* (Minneapolis: Fortress, 1990), 414; see his explanation on pp. 418–19, where he refers to other passages containing a similar theme.

21. Kugel (*The Bible as It Was,* 404) cites *Midrash Tanhuma Yitro* 11 as a text which associates such a view with Deut. 29:13–14.

22. The words in the prologue translated "on the Lord's orders" reflect *bdbr yhwh* in the Hebrew original (4Q216 1:3). Brooke ("Exegetical Strategies in Jubilees 1–2," 45), after surveying the instances of this phrase in the Hebrew Bible (*dbr yhwh* occurs usually in connection with prophets and prophetic books; the specific phrase with the preposition *b* appears most frequently in connection with the man of God in 1 Kings 13), has astutely remarked that the author "understood the content of the *Book of Jubilees* not primarily as law but as prophecy. Such an understanding has broad ramifications for how the book as a whole should be viewed and how the basis of its authority should be portrayed. Moses' prophetic authority with eschatological implications is stressed in the use of Samaritan Exodus 20 (= MT Deut. 5:28–29 + 18:18–19) in 4Q158 6 and in 4QTestimonia (4Q175 1–8)." He also refers to 4Q375 1 i 1, "[You will do all that] your God has commanded you from the mouth of the prophet," where "prophet" could refer to Moses. It would be natural for the writer of *Jubilees* to understand Moses as a prophet on the basis of Deut. 18:18–19, but he does not call him that; rather, he uses language commonly associated with prophecy as he introduces the divine revelation to Moses.

new moon after the Israelites had gone out of the land of Egypt, on that very day, they came into the wilderness of Sinai." *Jubilees* goes beyond the scriptural text in specifying that it was the first year of the exodus (an obvious inference from the context). It is important to be clear about exactly what the writer is dating. The sixteenth day of the third month (= 3/16) in *Jubilees* is, of course, not the time of entry into the Sinai wilderness but of the Lord's command that Moses ascend. As seen, the wording of that command is derived from Exod. 24:12: "The Lord said to Moses, 'Come up to me on the mountain, and wait there; and I will give you the tablets of stone, with the law and the commandment, which I have written for their instruction.'" The only item that *Jubilees* adds is the number "two" for the tablets, a detail available in several scriptural passages (Exod. 31:18; 32:15; 34:29 [from the story about the second set of tablets]; Deut. 4:13; 5:22; 9:10, 11).[23] In other words, the author in *Jub.* 1:1 has combined information from Exodus 19 and 24 (with a detail perhaps from Exodus 34).

It is not unusual to find combinations of Exodus 19 and 24 in ancient treatments of the Sinai event. These two chapters, which encase the revelation of the law (Exodus 20–23), give an odd appearance. Not only does Moses ascend the mountain an inordinate number of times (without always being allowed to descend between ascents), but the two chapters are parallel to a considerable degree: Moses climbs the mountain or is told to do so, proclaims the divine covenantal word to the people, and the people give virtually the same response (19:8; 24:7). In both chapters, the deity descends upon the mountain with smoke and fire, and Moses meets him on the summit. As Childs comments about 19:3b–8, the "passage actually anticipates by way of summary the action of the next chapters, and presupposes the ratification of the covenant which only comes in 24:3ff."[24] Naturally, these similarities did not escape ancient commentators, who often viewed the two chapters as parallel accounts of the same events. There may be a hint of this already in 4Q364 (4QReworked Pentateuch[b]) frg. 14, where it appears that two words from the end of Exod. 19:17 figure in line 2, while line 3 begins with Exod. 24:12. The editors comment: "The most likely explanation is that the fragment does not represent a sequence of Exod. 19:17 and 24:12, but constitutes a freely rewritten text using elements of 19:17 before 24:12. In many ways Exodus 19 and 24 supplement each other, presenting parallel versions of the Mt. Sinai episode, so that this fragment probably reflects a version in which elements from both chapters have been combined."[25] According to *'Abot de Rabbi Nathan*, R. Akiva thought that Exod. 24:15–16 was a repetition of chapters 19–

---

23. See van Ruiten, "Rewriting," 28.

24. B. Childs, *The Book of Exodus* (OTL; Louisville: Westminster, 1974), 360.

25. E. Tov and S. White, "364. 4QReworked Pentateuch[b]," DJD 13.221–22. See also van Ruiten, "The Relationship between Exod 31,12–17 and Jubilees 2,1.17–33," in *Studies in the Book of Exodus: Redaction-Reception-Interpretation* (ed. M. Vervenne; BETL 126; Louvain: Peeters, 1996), 567.

20, while Rashi, commenting on Exod. 19:11, identified the covenantal ceremony in chapter 24 with what occurs in 19:3–8.[26]

Jubilees may belong somewhat in the tradition of blending Exodus 19 and 24, but the author is surprisingly unconcerned with the timing of events before Israel arrived at Sinai and during its stay; in fact, the narrative at the end of the book lacks reference to Exod. 19:1 and to either the covenantal ceremony in Exodus 19 or Exodus 24. *Jubilees* 49:1 speaks about celebrating Passover by sacrificing it on 1/14, so that it can be eaten during the evening (that is, the beginning) of 1/15. It also refers to having celebrated the Festival of Unleavened Bread in haste "when you were leaving Egypt until the time you crossed the sea into the wilderness of Sur, because you completed it on the seashore" (49:23). This is the last dated event in the book. Thus, the writer omits the time indicators from the crossing of the sea to the arrival at Sinai, including Exod. 16:1, which places entry into the wilderness of Sin on 2/15. In fact, he does not mention the date in Exod. 19:1 when Israel reached Sinai; it is reflected only indirectly in *Jub.* 1:1 in the reference to the third month. How, then, did the author conclude that Exod. 24:12 was to be dated to 3/16?

Several attempts to determine the date of the Sinai events are recorded in the ancient exegetical sources, and the starting point is the date in Exod. 19:1. The wording there is *bḥdš hšlyšy lṣ't bn yśr'l m'rṣ mṣrym bywm hzh*. Addition of the last phrase (*bywm hzh*) implies that the writer had a specific day in mind, not simply some unspecified date in the third month. M. Noth concluded that this was the case and that the formulation pointed to the first day of the month; that is, *ḥdš* here means the new moon;[27] Childs agrees.[28] A problem with this view is that the text is not explicit and that the Priestly writer is capable elsewhere of expressing the date in an unmistakable way, as he did in Exod. 16:1 (*bḥmšh 'sr ywm lḥdš hšny*); hence, some have argued that the specific date has dropped from the text, thus allowing exegetes to connect the covenant at Sinai with the Festival of Weeks, which also occurs in the third month.[29] *Tg. Ps.-J.* Exod. 19:1 solved the problem by mentioning the first day of the month explicitly after the reference to "this day" (*bḥd lyrḥ'*). In fact, the Targum continues to provide dates elsewhere in Exodus 19: in v. 3, it places Moses' ascent on the second day (his summoning the people in v. 7, is located on the same day); in v. 9, the Lord speaks to him on the third day; in v. 10, the Lord speaks to him on the fourth day, telling him to consecrate the people and to prepare them for the third day (in v. 14 he descended on the same day). The targumic version of 19:16 identifies that third day as the sixth day in the third month. It also reports that the event

---

26. See Childs, *Book of Exodus*, 364.
27. M. Noth, *Exodus* (OTL; Philadelphia: Westminster, 1962), 155.
28. Childs, *Book of Exodus*, 342.
29. For references to those who hold this view, see ibid., 342; Childs himself rejects the thesis.

in 24:1 occurred on the seventh day (of the month). This way of reading the text reflects the rabbinic view that the Festival of Weeks occurred on 3/6.

One can find similar readings in other rabbinic texts. For example, *Pirqe R. El.* 46 says: "On the sixth of Sivan the Holy One, blessed be He, was revealed unto Israel on Sinai...."[30] Moreover, the Israelites are said to have stood at Sinai on the eve of the Sabbath.[31] In the same work Rabbi Chanina is quoted as saying: "In the third month the day is double the night, and the Israelites slept until two hours of the day, for sleep on the day of the (feast of) 'Azereth is pleasant, the night being short."[32] Later we learn that Rabbi Eleazar said: "On Friday, on the 6th of the month, at the sixth hour of the day, Israel received the Commandments." In the *Mek.* 48 *bḥdš,* chap. 2, Moses' ascent to God is dated to a Monday,[33] while in *Mek.* 49 *bḥdš,* chap. 3, the Lord's command that Moses consecrate the people occurs on a Wednesday; thus, the morrow is a Thursday and the decisive third day a Friday, "when the Torah was given."[34] The *Mekilta* then says that, on that Thursday, Moses rose early in the morning and built an altar (Exod. 24:4), thus showing that in this text, too, Exodus 19 and 24 were conflated. More details about these datings and discussions appear in *b. Shabbat* 86b–87a, where the standard view that the Ten Commandments were given on 3/6 is contrasted with the position of R. Jose that this happened on 3/7. All are said to agree that Exod. 19:1 refers to the first of the month; the disagreement arises from deciding whether it was a Monday (so the rabbis) or a Sunday (so R. Jose). In both calculations the Torah was given on the Sabbath.

The *Mekilta* and other sources thus illustrate how one could begin with Exod. 19:1 and, despite an absence in the text of specific time indicators, still arrive at a date such as 3/6, the date of the Festival of Weeks, for the giving of the Torah. The writer of *Jubilees,* however, had a more difficult problem, because he had to place the event on 3/15. A fundamental theme in *Jubilees* is that the Festival of Weeks was the holiday on which the one covenant was made (6:17) and renewed (14:10; 15:1); one can infer that it occurred on 3/15.[35] Hence, the covenant between God and the people on Mount Sinai was made on 3/15, which is a Sunday in the solar calendar of *Jubilees* and in the Dead Sea Scrolls. The Priestly source of Exodus

---

30. The translation is from G. Friedlander, *Pirke de Rabbi Eliezer* (repr., New York: Hermon, 1970), 318.

31. Ibid., 321.

32. Ibid., 322. 'Azereth is another name for the Festival of Weeks.

33. See J. Neusner, *Mekhilta according to Rabbi Ishmael* (BJS 154; Atlanta: Scholars Press, 1988), 2.47.

34. Ibid., 53.

35. Despite the importance of the Festival of Weeks in *Jubilees,* the author never states the date on which it is to be celebrated, contenting himself with the phrase "in the middle of the month." The only passage from which one can demonstrate that the date was 3/15 is 44:1–5, where Jacob celebrates the holiday after the first fourteen days of the month have elapsed, and before the Lord appears to him on the sixteenth.

indicated that Israelites had entered the wilderness of Sinai in the third month, but it did not specify the exact date. For a source such as *Jubilees*, one must assume that the arrival at Sinai did not occur on a Sabbath; otherwise the ban on travel would have been violated. As a consequence, the Israelites could not have entered the wilderness on 3/14. This eliminates the idea that the author read the word *ḥdš* in Exod. 19:1 as the third period of thirty days after 1/14, the date of the exodus. But it is also likely that he did not take it in the sense of "new moon" or, in his case, "first of the month."[36] In Exodus 19, once the people are at the mountain, Moses is told: "Consecrate them today and tomorrow. Have them wash their clothes and prepare for the third day, because on the third day the Lord will come down upon Mount Sinai in the sight of all the people" (19:10–11). Moses did consecrate the people, and they washed their clothes on the first day — an activity that could not have been done on the Sabbath. Nothing is then said about the second day of their stay at Sinai, but the people were thus prepared for the third day, when the deity descended on the mountain in thunder, lightning, and thick cloud (19:16). The Ten Commandments and the covenant code follow.

In Exodus 24 (there are no indicators of time passing in chaps. 20–23), the first three verses recount the people's unanimous affirmation of the covenantal arrangements revealed to Moses and which he had related to them. All of this is apparently still happening on the third day mentioned in Exodus 19, the day of the covenant, which for *Jubilees* would have been 3/15. It is not until we reach Exod. 24:4 that we find another time indicator: "And Moses wrote down all the words of the Lord. He rose early in the morning..." If the covenantal arrangement was revealed and ratified on 3/15 (the Festival of Weeks), the reference to the morning should be to 3/16. More covenantal ceremonies take place in vv. 4b–8, and in vv. 9–11, Moses, Aaron, Nadab, and Abihu ascend the mountain and see God. This brings us to 24:12, which is the verse that *Jub.* 1:1 uses as the book's setting and that it dates to 3/16. Consequently, it seems that the author would have placed Israel's arrival at Sinai on 3/13 or, more likely, 3/12,[37] so that they would have had a chance to settle down before the events in Exod. 19:2–25. This means that 3/13 would have been the first day of the three-day period mentioned in Exod. 19:10. Nothing is said to have occurred on the second day (3/14), which would have been a Sabbath in *Jubilees'* calendar, and, on the third day, the one for which the people were to be prepared, the covenant was revealed and ratified (= 3/15). Following these three days, that is, on 3/16,[38] the Lord summoned Moses to the mountain to receive the revelation contained in *Jubilees*.

---

36. See Childs, *Exodus*, 342, who notes the old exegetical problem of what the term means — "month" or "new moon." He defends the meaning in 19:1 of "new moon."

37. In *b. Shabbat* 86b–87a, both calculations of the date for giving the Ten Commandments allow for rest on the date of people's arrival, because they would have been exhausted from their journey.

38. *L.A.B.* 23:2 dates the covenant between Joshua and the people at Shiloh to 3/16 and connects it with the covenant made with their fathers at Horeb. See Berger, *Buch der Jubiläen*, 297. H. Jacobsen

A suggestion about how the writer concluded that Israel arrived at the Sinai wilderness on 3/12 relates to the curious *bayyôm hazzeh* in Exod. 19:1. As seen, the phrase makes little sense when attached to a nonspecific date such as "the third month." It seems that the author of *Jubilees* took the consonants *z* and *h* of *hzh* as numerals (7+5) and thus understood the phrase to mean "on the twelfth day." This seems a plausible suggestion, because gematria appears to have been practiced by this time,[39] and the suggestion makes sense of a feature in *Jubilees*, whose author was a very careful reader of scriptural details.

Regardless of the way in which the writer arrived at his dating of events at Mount Sinai, he does place Moses' encounter with God on 3/16. What is accomplished by doing this? It may be that in doing so he provided a more powerful context in which to situate his testimony. By means of the date 3/16, he draws the reader's attention to the previous day, the day when the covenant was made. He does not describe the covenantal ceremonies in *Jubilees* 1, but the chapter does contain a few uses of the word "covenant" (1:5,[40] 10), and the language of covenant permeates it (see, e.g., 1:15–18, 23–25). The specific references to covenant highlight that Israel is going to stray from the agreement and that terrible consequences will follow. The covenant receives treatment elsewhere, particularly in 6:4–22. In that passage the angel emphasizes the connection between the covenant with Noah and the covenant at Sinai (6:11). The angel also refers to the Festival of Weeks as the time when one is "to renew the covenant each and every year" (6:17). According to the angel, the festival had been celebrated from creation to the time of Noah, and during the patriarchal period, but in Moses' time "the Israelites had forgotten (it)" until it was renewed at the mountain (6:19).

Against this background, one can see that the writer pictures a new beginning for the covenantal relationship. Now that the Festival of Weeks has once again been properly observed, as in the days of Noah and the patriarchs, the

---

(*A Commentary on Pseudo-Philo's* Liber Antiquitatum Biblicarum [2 vols.; AGJU 31; Leiden: Brill, 1996], 2.711) claims, however, that the date is to be corrected to 3/6.

39. See S. J. Lieberman, "A Mesopotamian Background for the So-Called *Aggadic* 'Measures' of Biblical Hermeneutics?" *HUCA* 58 (1987): 157–225. Lieberman adduces Mesopotamian examples from the eighth to seventh centuries B.C.E. (he calls them "Gamatria-Like Hermeneutics in Cuneiform," 174–76) and cites as biblical examples Abram's 318 servants (the numerical value of the letters in the name of his servant and potential heir Eliezer; see Gen. 14:14) and the 666 of Rev. 13:18 as the numerical value of Neron Caesar (167–70). Lieberman could also have mentioned the numerical correspondences in Proverbs between the sum of the letters in Solomon's name and the number of units in the clearly defined section Prov. 10:1–22:16, or between Hezekiah's name and 25:1–29:27. I wish to thank Prof. M. Bernstein for discussing this issue with me and for pointing me to Lieberman's essay.

40. It seems almost certain in *Jubilees* that the covenant of Sinai takes place on 3/15, but this verse, apparently set on the seventh day, when Moses entered the cloud, mentions "the covenant between me and you which I am making today on Mount Sinai for their offspring" (the word "today" is confirmed by *hywm* in 4Q216 1:14 [DJD 13.5]). However, in this verse the writer is echoing the rhetoric of Deut. 29:11, 13, and the repetition of the covenant found there; perhaps it should be understood as referring generally to the present time, not to a specific day.

relationship between God and Israel enters a new phase. With the revelation to Moses, the nation would have the benefit of full disclosure of the law, not just the limited number of laws available in earlier periods of sacred history. Those laws, recorded in the "first law," are now fortified in *Jubilees* with a powerful exhortation (especially *Jub.* 1:5–25), so that contemporary readers could avoid the disasters of the past. Thus *Jubilees* presents itself as a covenantal testimony, a prophetic proclamation and endorsement of the covenantal law that bound Israel and God in a unique relationship.

25

The Curses of the Covenant Renewal Ceremony in 1QS 1.16–2.19 and the Prayers of the Condemned

◆

Rodney A. Werline
Emmanuel School of Religion

As K. Blatzer argues, the covenant renewal ceremony in 1QS 1.16–2.19 contains the basic elements of the covenant formulary as presented in the Hebrew Bible.[1] While Deuteronomic language abounds in much of the ceremony, it does not occur in the blessings and curses. The blessings, as many interpreters have noted, draw their language from the Aaronic blessing in Num. 6:24–26, with some embellishments.[2] The source of the curses' language is not as obvious. B. Nitzan, in her fine book *Qumran Prayer and Religious Poetry*, notes that each of the three blessings in the ceremony has a corresponding curse and argues that the curses reverse the ceremony's blessings.[3] In this instance, though, Nitzan's proposed threefold correspondence between the blessings and the curses is not as neat as she suggests.

A better possibility for understanding the curses' language lies in a comparison of the curses to traditional scenes of the judgment of the wicked in Second Temple Jewish texts, especially those that include prayer. The curses themselves invite this comparison by inclusion of the phrase: "May God not heed when

---

This essay is a revised version of a paper that I gave at the 1997 SBL Annual Meeting in San Francisco, in the Prayer in the Greco-Roman World Group.

1. K. Baltzer, *The Covenant Formulary in Old Testament, Jewish, and Early Christian Writings* (trans. D. Green; Oxford: Blackwell, 1971), 49–50.

2. E.g., G. W. E. Nickelsburg, *Jewish Literature between the Bible and the Mishnah* (Philadelphia: Fortress, 1981), 135; A. R. C. Leaney, *The Rule of Qumran and Its Meaning* (Philadelphia: Westminster, 1966), 129–30; P. Wernberg-Møller, *The Manual of Discipline* (Leiden: Brill, 1957), 51–52; M. Knibb, *The Qumran Community* (Cambridge: Cambridge University Press, 1987), 86; B. Nitzan, *Qumran Prayer and Religious Poetry* (trans. J. Chipman; Leiden: Brill, 1994), 133–35.

3. Nitzan, *Qumran Prayer*, 151–53.

you *call* on him" (1QS 2.8). The word "call" in the Hebrew Bible and Second Temple literature sometimes means "to pray to God."[4] Further, the content of the *Community Rule*'s curses imagines a context for the "call": a future moment of severe crisis when God's punishment has descended upon the wicked. In some judgment scenes in Second Temple Jewish texts, the "call," that is, prayer, to God becomes an appeal for relief or a commuted sentence. The texts that exhibit these features include *Jubilees* 23 (a historical apocalypse that describes events leading up to the eschaton); *1 Enoch* 12–16 (an apocalyptic scene in which the condemned watchers cry for release from punishment); and *1 Enoch* 62–63 (the condemnation and confession of the kings and the mighty). In each of these scenes, the condemned do not get their wishes, and their punishment continues. In order to establish the relationship between these scenes and the curses in the covenant renewal ceremony in 1QS, the following discussion analyzes these judgment/prayer scenes and then compares them to the imagery of the curses.

1 Enoch

1 Enoch 12–16: The Confession of the Watchers

The text in *1 Enoch* 6–11 records the story of the rebellion of the watchers. Binding themselves by an oath, these heavenly beings revolt against God by forsaking their divinely ordained station in the cosmic order and by having intercourse with human women. They also reveal to humans the divine secrets of magic, metallurgy, and cosmetics.[5] As a result of the sexual union, giants are born who wreak violence upon the earth. After cries from the oppressed reach the angels, the angels petition God on behalf of the suffering humans. God responds by commissioning Michael to bind the rebellious watchers until the final judgment, when they will be "led away to the fiery abyss, and to the torture, and to the prison where they will be confined forever" (10:13).[6]

Later in the narrative, God commissions Enoch to pronounce judgment on them, that they will have "no peace," "forgiveness," or "mercy" (12:4, 6; 13:1). When the watchers hear their judgment, they ask Enoch to "write a memorandum of petition" that they might receive forgiveness and present it to God (13:4). In other words, they have engaged Enoch as an intermediary to deliver a petitionary prayer to God. As mentioned, earlier in the story the angels functioned as mediators for humans who had suffered and died at the hands of the giants

---

4. Patrick D. Miller, *They Cried to the Lord: The Form and Theology of Biblical Prayer* (Minneapolis: Fortress, 1994), 32–54.

5. For more about the myth, the history of this text, and possible meanings, see G. W. E. Nickelsburg, "Apocalyptic and Myth in *1 Enoch* 6–11," *JBL* 96 (1977): 383–405; L. Hartman, *Asking for a Meaning: A Study of "1 Enoch" 1–5* (ConBNT 12; Lund: CWK Gleerup, 1979).

6. All translations of *1 Enoch* are from G. W. E. Nickelsburg, *The Book of Enoch or "1 Enoch"* (privately published, 1994).

(9:11). Besides making their petition, the watchers' behavior resembles that of penitents in other texts. They are afraid and trembling (13:3; cf. Isa. 66:2; Ezra 9:4; 10:3), and they recognize their shame so that they cannot lift their eyes to heaven (13:3). This posture appears in several penitential scenes which describe suppliants as experiencing shame: for example, Ezra (Ezra 9:6); Azariah (Pr. Az. 10, 19); Baruch (Bar. 1:15; 2:6); and Daniel (Dan. 9:7).[7]

Continuing his role as intermediary, Enoch delivers the petition to God, who refuses to reverse the judgment. Indeed, God is furious that divine beings have engaged a human to mediate a petition for them when it was the watchers' job to petition on behalf of humans (15:2). God gives Enoch some final words for the watchers: "You will have no peace," the same words of judgment in the commissioning scene in 12:4–13:1.

This judgment and petitioning scene has several features in common with the introductory chapters in 1 Enoch, in which God indicts the wicked for transgressing divine order and pronounces judgment against them: "[Y]ou have turned aside, you have spoken proud words. . . . Hard of heart! There will be no peace for you! . . . And there will be no mercy or peace for you!" (5:4–5; cf. Isa. 57:19–21).

1 Enoch 62–63: *The Judgment of the Kings and the Mighty*

The "Parables of Enoch" (1 Enoch 37–71) contains a scene of judgment of the kings and the mighty in which these two condemned parties make supplication. These chapters of 1 Enoch, of course, do not appear among the Qumran scrolls. Nevertheless, the judgment scene in these chapters contributes in filling out the picture of this tradition in Second Temple Jewish literature and consequently contributes to the interpretation of 1QS 1.16–2.19.

After carrying out a lifetime of oppression and exploitation of the righteous, the kings and the mighty see the formerly hidden Son of Man (1 Enoch 62). At the sight of this figure, they experience pain like labor pains, terror seizes them, and they cast down their faces (vv. 4–5). As Nickelsburg shows, their responses resemble the reactions of humans in Isaiah 13 who sense their impending doom on the Day of YHWH:[8]

> Pangs and agony will seize them
> they will be in anguish like a woman in labor;
> They will look aghast at one another
> their faces will be aflame. (v. 8)[9]

---

7. See R. Werline, *Penitential Prayer in Second Temple Judaism: The Development of a Religious Institution* (SBLEJL 13; Atlanta: Scholars Press, 1998), 46–53, 90–91, 172–74.

8. G. W. E. Nickelsburg, *Resurrection, Immortality, and Eternal Life in Intertestamental Judaism* (HTS 26; Cambridge: Harvard University Press, 1972), 72–73.

9. Translation is from the NRSV.

Like those who recognize their guilt in Ezra 9, Daniel 9, *Prayer of Azariah*, and *1 Enoch* 13, the text describes the kings and the mighty as having their "faces filled with shame" and "darkness" (*1 Enoch* 62:10; cf. 63:11).

Attempting to undo their destiny, the kings and the mighty "supplicate and petition for mercy" from the Son of Man (v. 9), but it is too late. The Lord of the Spirits himself forces them from his presence and delivers them to the angels for punishment (v. 11), the same angels whom Enoch saw in his vision of the Valley of Punishment. Drawing on imagery from the Divine Warrior mythology, the author pictures God's wrath falling on these wicked. God's sword becomes "drunk with them" (v. 12; cf. Isa. 63:1–6).

In the midst of suffering at the hands of the angels, the kings and the mighty petition God a second time, on this occasion for a respite from their tortures (63:1–11). They wish to confess their sins in God's presence, because they understand that their failure to recognize God's sovereignty and their sins have brought this punishment upon them. So, from their place of torment, they do what they did not do during their lives on earth — bless God and acknowledge God's power. However, like the previous petitions, these pleas do not alter their fate (63:11–12).

This same image from Isaiah 13 probably also influences several other Second Temple texts in which the unrighteous recognize that destruction is upon them because of their deeds. First Maccabees 6 and 2 Maccabees 9 depict Antiochus IV doing this just before his death. Both stories agree that Antiochus dies after failing in an attempt to rob a temple in Persia, and after learning that his armies have suffered a critical loss in Palestine. Further, both stories understand Antiochus's death as a result of his blasphemous deeds against the temple, the Jews, and God. In 1 Maccabees 6, Antiochus, who is in deep despair, confesses to his "friends" and then soon dies. Second Maccabees 9 states that God assaults Antiochus's body with a torturous "scourge" of worms. This breaks his arrogance, and he submits to God's sovereignty (vv. 5–12). Desperate, he vows to God that he will change his policies toward the Jews and the Jerusalem temple and will himself convert to Judaism (vv. 13–18). None of these actions, though, changes his situation. In a case of such wickedness, God's judgment is irrevocable (v. 18). Antiochus dies a painful, humiliating death.

The final judgment of the wicked in Wisdom of Solomon 5 also resembles *1 Enoch* 62–63. The wicked, who in life have oppressed and killed the righteous, must confront the righteous at the time of judgment. The wicked learn that the righteous who have died have actually been kept in God's "hand" (cf. 3:1–9; 5:1). Being "shaken with dreadful fear," the wicked confess to one another that they lived a lawless life and oppressed the righteous. Now annihilation awaits them.[10]

---

10. See Nickelsburg, *Jewish Literature*, 175–79. He also notes the similarities between Wisdom of Solomon 4:20–5:14 and the vindication of the servant in Isa. 52:13–53:12. See also Nickelsburg, *Resurrection, Immortality, and Eternal Life in Intertestamental Judaism*, 68–92; J. J. Collins, *Jewish Wisdom in the Hellenistic Age* (OTL; Louisville: Westminster/John Knox, 1997), 182–89.

Jubilees 23

Jubilees 23[11] contains a scene in which neither rebellious divine beings nor powerful men experience judgment, but unfaithful Jews. A prayer to God is explicitly
part of the narrative. This chapter, which probably dates to the period just prior
to Antiochus IV's decree in 167 B.C.E.,[12] begins with the description of Abraham's death and burial, digresses about why human life spans have shortened,
and concludes with a description of the events that will lead to a new era.
Human sinfulness has decreased life spans. Jubilees speaks of this sinfulness as
transgression of the commandments and forsaking of the covenant. As events
move toward the eschaton, a reform movement emerges among the young. They
indict the evil generation, the parents, for committing injustices and forsaking
Torah and its proper interpretation (vv. 16–17, 19). The disagreement turns violent (vv. 19–21). Because of their sin, God punishes the wicked through the
"sword," "captivity," "pillage," and "destruction" at the hands of "the sinners of
the nations" (v. 23). Now the magnitude of human sinfulness has decreased life
spans to the point that even children have white hair and babies look like the
elderly (v. 25). In the midst of punishment, the wicked begin "to cry out," "call,"
and "pray" for deliverance from the punishment. Their request goes unanswered:
"In those days, they will cry out and call and pray to be saved from the hand
of the sinners, the Gentiles, but there will be no one who will be saved" (v. 24).
The story reaches its turning point when a penitential group, "children," begins
to study Torah and the commandments.[13] Human life spans increase. As in other
penitential scenes, God provides "healing" and "peace" for this righteous group
(v. 30).

Summary

From the examination of these texts, a basic pattern emerges: (1) a group has
sinned; (2) God pronounces judgment; (3) the condemned sinners call to God in
prayer, confess their sins, and seek an end to their punishment; (4) God refuses
to respond, and punishment continues. The lifting of judgment is not guaranteed.
Thus far, the investigation shows that the pattern fits well within apocalyptic and
eschatological judgment scenes. Antiochus IV's deathbed confessions in 1 Maccabees 6 and 2 Maccabees 9 testify to the pattern's flexibility as these two texts
incorporate the tradition into a "historical" narrative. As with many other types
of traditions in Second Temple literature, the identity of the condemned sinners

---

11. For the Ethiopic text, see J. C. VanderKam, The "Book of Jubilees": A Critical Text (Scriptores Aethiopici 87; Louvain: Peeters, 1989). Aramaic fragments exist for Jubilees 23. See M. Kister,
"Fragments of the Book of Jubilees," RevQ 12 (1987): 529–36.

12. See Nickelsburg, Jewish Literature, 77.

13. See Werline, Penitential Prayer in Second Temple Judaism, 113–14. Cf. Jubilees 1:7–25.

changes from text to text. In the texts above, the condemned can be rebellious divine beings, kings and the mighty, or groups within Judaism. The discussion below returns especially to consider this last manner of identifying the wicked.

The Curses in the Covenant Renewal Ceremony in 1QS

With this basic pattern of judgment in mind, my attention turns to the covenant renewal ceremony in 1QS. The ceremony actually contains two sets of curses. The first set is against Jews who are not members of the community,[14] while the second is pronounced upon apostates from the community.[15] The first set is most important for the present study.

As in Deut. 27:14, the Levites pronounce the curses at Qumran (1QS 2.4), which here fall on "the men of the lot of Belial" for their "guilty deeds of wickedness."[16] In accordance with the dualism that pervades this document, the cursed are opposite "the men of the lot of God," who received the blessings in 1QS 2.2.

As mentioned in the introduction, the curses display no contact with the language of Deuteronomy, with two exceptions. First, the phrase "object of terror" might indicate influence from Deut. 28:25 (cf. Jer. 24:9 and 29:18).[17] Second, in Deut. 27:26 the people respond to Moses' words with a single "Amen."[18] Perhaps the double "Amen" (1QS 2.10) from those entering the covenant may have developed from Deuteronomy. However, both these similarities are slight and are too insubstantial to permit a claim that the author of the ceremony was depending primarily on Deuteronomy. The dependence lies elsewhere.

Several elements of the curses suggest that the author imagines the scenes of the condemned like those that appear in *1 Enoch* and *Jubilees*. The Levites invoke upon the wicked the curse of being turned over to "terror by the hand of all those who carry out acts of vengeance" and "destruction by the hand of all those who accomplish retribution" (lines 5–7). The references are to the angels of torture, like those in the "Book of the Watchers" and the "Parables of Enoch" (*1 Enoch* 12–16, 62–63), who punish the wicked.[19] These creatures appear in the *Damascus Document* as the "Angels of Destruction," whose job is to punish "those who departed from the way" (CD 2.6). The Enochic scene and the 1QS

---

14. Knibb (*Qumran Community*, 86) believes that the text might have backsliders in mind.

15. Leaney, *Rule of Qumran and Its Meaning*, 130; Wernberg-Møller, *Manual of Discipline*, 52; Knibb, *Qumran Community*, 86. However, both the priests and the Levites pronounce the curses on the community's apostates in 1QS 2.11.

16. Cf. 1QM 4.2; 13.2.

17. Gottstein points out that the spelling of z'wh in Jer. 29:18 matches the Qere in the Bible (from Wernberg-Møller, *Manual of Discipline*, 52). Cf. also the watchers and other sinners who tremble or are filled with terror when they recognize that their sin is upon them as judgment.

18. Leaney (*Rule of Qumran and Its Meaning*, 134) notes that a twofold "Amen" appears in Num. 5:22. Cf. also 1QS 1.20; 2.18.

19. Cf. Wernberg-Møller, *Manual of Discipline*, 52; *1 Enoch* 53:3; *T. Levi* 3:2–3.

ceremony also agree that the place of punishment contains both darkness and fire (*1 Enoch* 63:6, 10).

The ceremony's curses anticipate that on the day of judgment and punishment the wicked will "call out" to God for mercy, which is most likely a reference to prayer. This appeal to God was a fixed part of the judgment scenes from *1 Enoch* and *Jubilees,* and from the portions of the Hebrew Bible from which they draw. While the curses do not explicitly state that the wicked confess their sins, the Levites' pronouncement that God will not "pardon" them by "atoning" for their "sins" seems to imply a confession. In *1 Enoch,* both the watchers and the kings and the mighty confess their sins and hope for forgiveness. In the case of the watchers, God explicitly declares that they will not receive forgiveness (*1 Enoch* 12:4, 6; 13:1).

According to the ceremony's curses, God's wrath is against, literally, "all who hold fast to the fathers" (*kwl 'hzy 'bwt*). At first glance, the author seems to be identifying the condemned group in much the same manner that *Jubilees* 23 spoke of the wicked. In *Jubilees,* the fathers hold to the old improper way of interpreting the Bible. This improper interpretation, and the resulting sinful activity, causes God to send judgment.

Another possible interpretation of the phrase exists. Claiming that the language in 1QS parallels a Syriac idiom, Wernberg-Møller translates it "in the mouth of those who intercede." His position and translation seem to be obtaining a consensus.[20] He traces the idiom's origin to Akkadian and proposes that it was adopted into Aramaic and occurs in Syriac as *'hd 'bwt'*, which means, "to seize fatherhood," i.e., to assume the role of intercessor. It occurs in a hymn of Ephraim the Syrian and almost certainly has this meaning of "intercession" as the author speaks of Christ as intercessor.[21] Reading the phrase in 1QS as an idiom with the meaning "those who intercede" neatly fits the context and stays within the traditions of the condemned calling out to God in the midst of judgment. Certainly angels can intercede on behalf of humans (see *1 Enoch* 9:3; *T. Dan* 6:1; *T. Levi* 3:6).[22]

One other phrase in the ceremony's curses is reminiscent of the scenes of the condemned. As in the judgment of the watchers in *1 Enoch* 12:5 and 13:1, the ceremony's curses say that the wicked will "have no peace" (see also Isa. 57:21). Only the righteous in *Jubilees* 23 can experience "peace" (v. 30). The wicked must suffer.

Finally, the "Teaching of the Two Ways" in 1QS 3–4 further confirms that the covenant ceremony is drawing from these traditional scenes of punishment of the

---

20. Cf. Leaney, *Rule of Qumran,* 133; Knibb, *Qumran Community,* 87; See also J. H. Charlesworth, ed., *The Dead Sea Scrolls: Hebrew, Aramaic, and Greek Texts with English Translation* (Tübingen: Mohr [Siebeck], 1994), 11.

21. See Wernberg-Møller, *Manual of Discipline,* 52. I also especially thank my colleague at the Emmanuel School of Religion, Robert Owens, a Syriac specialist, for researching this idiom and explaining its meaning to me.

22. See R. H. Charles, *The Book of Enoch or "1 Enoch"* (Oxford: Clarendon, 1913), 21.

wicked. In this section of the *Community Rule*, the text divides all of humanity into two groups: the "sons of light" and the "sons of darkness." God has appointed two spirits over these two groups of humans and has preordained who would be in each group. Likewise, God has predetermined their destinies. According to 1QS, the "sons of darkness" face the following future:

> And the visitation of all those who walk in it will be for an abundance of afflictions at the hands of all the angels of destruction, for eternal damnation by the scorching wrath of the God of revenges, for permanent terror and shame without end with the humiliation of destruction by the fire of the dark regions. And all the ages of the generations [they shall spend] in bitter weeping and harsh evils in the abysses of darkness until their destruction, without being a remnant or a survivor among them. (4.11–14)[23]

This description of the fate of the wicked is reminiscent of the commissions to imprison 'Asael and Shemihazah and his associates in *1 Enoch* 10. Raphael is to bind 'Asael and to cast him into outer darkness to await the final day of judgment, when he will be led into "the burning conflagration" (10:4–8). God commissions Michael to bind Shemihazah and his companions and to place them in "the valleys of the earth" for "seventy generations" until the time of judgment (v. 12). After the judgment, they will go to the "fiery abyss," where they are tortured and confined forever (v. 13). The place of punishment for the fallen stars in chapter 21 also is reminiscent of chapter 10. However, the language in the *Community Rule* resembles in particular Enoch's tour of the mountain of the dead in *1 Enoch* 22. There, dead sinners are gathered in great pits and kept until the day of judgment. At that time, God delivers them over to "judgment, scourges, and tortures" and binds them forever (v. 11).

Conclusions and Questions

Several Second Temple Jewish texts contain traditional material about the condemned calling out to God in the moment of punishment. Various authors drew from these traditions and assimilated them into new literary and ideological contexts. As a result, the identities of the righteous and the wicked change with each new historical and sociological setting. The author of the covenant renewal ceremony in 1QS used this well-developed tradition of the condemned who call out to God. Taking the various elements of judgment scenes — the punishing angels, the call to God, the darkness of punishment, the condemned who call, God's refusal to alter the judgment, and the pronouncement that the wicked will find "no peace" — the author remolds them into the form of curses.

---

23. Translation is from F. G. Martínez and E. J. Tigchelaar, *The Dead Sea Scrolls Study Edition* (vol. 1; Leiden: Brill, 1997).

In the process, important transformations have occurred in 1QS in regard to those who constitute the cursed. The curses of Deuteronomy 28 are for the nation as a whole. As several have noticed, including Nitzan, the curses in 1QS no longer apply to the nation as a whole as they did in Deuteronomy, but to a group *within* Israel. Likewise, the blessings are not for Israel as a whole, but for those *within* the *Yahad* community. Thus the material of the condemned calling to God now fits within the rigid Qumran dualism of insiders and outsiders. *Jubilees* 23 displays a similar tendency.

A final question arises from examination of these texts: Why do the penitential prayers not work in these scenes and in the imagined scene behind the curses in 1QS? Several possible answers arise. First, the authors may have understood the sins of the wicked as "committed with a high hand and proud heart," that is, with such intentional rebelliousness and insolence that they had gone beyond the possibility of forgiveness. This idea may be suggested in the rebellion of the watchers, especially if one reads the story in connection with *1 Enoch* 1–5.

Second, as Kugel proposes in his examination of *Jubilees* 23, the tradition as a whole may rely on the prophetic notion of "fair warning."[24] According to this idea, the people of Israel always had some figure, usually a prophet, who would warn them that their sin would bring punishment. Once the prophet made the proclamation, God considered the people duly warned, and God would not revoke the punishment. This is played out in Jeremiah as God prohibits the prophet from interceding on behalf of the people because they have persistently rejected the message of the prophets (Jer. 7:16–34; 11:1–17; 14:1–15:9). God declares that their punishment has been fixed. In another text, Micah pronounces judgment against Israel's rulers (chap. 3). In the midst of their punishment they cry to God, but they receive no answer: "Then they will cry to the Lord, but he will not answer them; he will hide his face from them at that time because they have acted wickedly" (v. 4). Micah follows this with a pronouncement of judgment against the prophets, who, also upon crying out, find no comfort (v. 7).

Third, some Second Temple authors may have come to believe that the hope for change is only possible within history. Once removed from history, a person's lot was fixed. This suggestion may give partial explanation to the condemnation of the kings and the mighty in the "Parables of Enoch" and to the curses of 1QS.

Fourth, the prayers in *Jubilees* 23 and 1QS are subject to a more dominant schema — a deterministic eschatological dualism. That is, God has in place a predetermined schema for history, which includes not only various periods or events but also the fate of various humans or groups. If a person is in the group of the wicked to be condemned, no possibility may exist for moving into the group of the blessed, not even by prayer.

---

24. J. Kugel, "The *Jubilees* Apocalypse," *DSD* 1 (1994): 322–37.

Notes on 4Q391 (papPseudo-Ezekiel^e) and Biblical Ezekiel

————— ◆ —————

Benjamin G. Wright III
Lehigh University

From the initial excitement surrounding the discovery of the Dead Sea Scrolls to the flurry of publications in recent years, one issue that has continually interested scholars is the reuse in many Qumran texts of what we now call biblical literature. One such text, called "Pseudo-Ezekiel," exists in multiple copies and takes the form of a dialogue between Ezekiel and God, often using first-person speech by the prophet. Pseudo-Ezekiel recasts a number of sections of the biblical Book of Ezekiel, most notably the Merkabah vision of chapters 1 and 10 and the dry-bones vision of chapter 37, although it adapts material from all over the biblical book. Pseudo-Ezekiel does not simply incorporate passages from the biblical Ezekiel mechanically; it also reinterprets them. Perhaps the clearest example of such reinterpretation is the way that Pseudo-Ezekiel understands the dry-bones vision (see 4Q385 2 and 12) as concerning resurrection of the righteous rather than community restoration, as in the biblical text.[1]

As currently understood by Devorah Dimant, its primary editor, Pseudo-Ezekiel exists in several fragmentary copies. In the recently published *Encyclopedia of the Dead Sea Scrolls* she provides her most current assessment of the extent of

---

Almost twenty years ago, at the SBL meetings in New York City, my teacher, Robert Kraft, introduced me to George Nickelsburg. I am honored to contribute to a volume celebrating someone who, in these past twenty years, has been a mentor, colleague, and friend.

1. On 4Q385 2, see John Strugnell and Devorah Dimant, "4Q Second Ezekiel," *RevQ* 13 (1988): 45–58. On 4Q385 12, see Benjamin G. Wright III, "Qumran Pseudepigrapha and Early Christianity: Is *1 Clement* 50:4 a Citation of 4QPseudo-Ezekiel (4Q385 12)?" in *Pseudepigraphic Perspectives: The Apocrypha and Pseudepigrapha in Light of the Dead Sea Scrolls* (ed. Michael E. Stone and Esther G. Chazon; STDJ 31; Leiden: Brill, 1999), 183–93.

Pseudo-Ezekiel. She identifies four copies of the work in her lot: 4Q385 1–6, 12, previously numbered 1–5, 12, 24 (=PsEzek[a]); 4Q386 (=PsEzek[b]); 4Q387, eight fragments previously numbered 6, 19, 24–27, 30, 38 (=PsEzek[c]); and 4Q388 1–7, previously numbered 7–14 (=PsEzek[d]).[2]

4Q391, published by Mark Smith in DJD 19, is comprised of seventy-eight papyrus fragments, many of which are, unfortunately, too small to be of very much use.[3] Even though none of the 4Q391 fragments shares any common text with the other copies of Pseudo-Ezekiel, Smith has, in his publication of 4Q391, shown that at least one of the fragments reworks material from biblical Ezekiel. Thus 4Q391 most likely represents a fifth copy (Pseudo-Ezekiel[e]) of this Qumran pseudepigraphon.[4] In my own examination of the fragments published by Smith, I have discovered several others that apparently rework passages from the biblical book. I offer some notes below that (*a*) show the possible connections between 4Q391 and the biblical Ezekiel; (*b*) note possible connections between 4Q391 and the other copies of Pseudo-Ezekiel from Cave 4; and (*c*) confirm Smith's conclusion that all of 4Q391 is from a Pseudo-Ezekiel text.

Fragment 1 (Smith, 156). Smith notes that this "fragment" is actually five smaller pieces joined together. In the three lines of useful text extant here, there are no clear contextual affinities with biblical Ezekiel. Two surviving snippets of text in lines 1 and 2 suggest a possible context for this fragment — biblical Ezekiel's oracles against the nations, especially those against Egypt. Line 1 preserves the term *śmḥtm*. The noun *śmḥh* occurs twice in Ezekiel (35:15 and 36:5) in oracles against Mount Seir and Edom. Line 2 contains the phrase *mlk mṣrym*, which appears in the anti-Egypt oracles of Ezek. 29:2; 30:21, 22; 31:2; 32:2. Hostile references to Egypt occur elsewhere in Pseudo-Ezekiel (cf. 4Q385 24; 4Q386 ii), but the phrase "king of Egypt" only appears here among the extant Pseudo-Ezekiel fragments.

Fragment 2 (Smith, 156). This fragment contains the beginning of two lines. The verb in line 1 is clearly *wyqlql*. In the Hebrew Bible the verb only occurs three times, once in Ezek. 21:21. There the image is of the king of Babylon who

---

2. Devorah Dimant, "Pseudo-Ezekiel," in *Encyclopedia of the Dead Sea Scrolls* (ed. Lawrence H. Schiffman and James C. VanderKam; New York: Oxford University Press, 2000), 1:282. The numbers 4Q385–4Q388 given in this essay reflect the older fragment numbers since Dimant has not yet published the text of Pseudo-Ezekiel with the new numbers. For a recent discussion of the status of research on what various scholars have thought constitutes Pseudo-Ezekiel, see my paper, "The Apocryphon of Ezekiel and 4QPseudo-Ezekiel: Are They the Same Work? How Do We Know?" presented at an international congress, "The Dead Sea Scrolls — Fifty Years after Their Discovery," The Israel Museum, Jerusalem, July 20–25, 1997.

3. Mark Smith, "H. Pseudo-Ezekiel," in *Qumran Cave 4: XIV, Parabiblical Texts, Part 2* (ed. Magen Broshi et al.; DJD 19; Oxford: Clarendon Press, 1995), 153–93. Henceforth referred to in text as "Smith."

4. I will argue below that 4Q391 is probably another copy of Pseudo-Ezekiel. But, since no text overlaps with the other known copies of Pseudo-Ezekiel, it could theoretically be another Ezekiel apocryphon altogether.

shakes arrows, but that is probably not the context in this fragment. Because this verb appears only infrequently, one might, however, consider a connection with 4Q385 24 4, which uses this verb in a section that clearly relies on the opening verses of Ezekiel 30.

Fragment 4 (Smith, 157–58). This four-line fragment contains little to aid in its identification. It does, however, use the word *śkrk*, "your wages." In Ezek. 29:18–19, which also contains this term, the word is used to indicate the wages or spoil the Babylonian army will take in its plunder of Egypt. Another Pseudo-Ezekiel fragment, 4Q386 iii 1, may depend on this same biblical chapter as well. This text refers to Babylon as "a cup in the hand of the Lord." Rather than an indictment of Babylon, as some have argued, this passage may have Ezekiel 29 in the background. This chapter claims that God will use Babylon as an agent of destruction against Egypt.[5]

Fragments 6–7 (Smith, 158–59). Smith argues that fragments 6 and 7 fit together, and he treats them as one.[6] Three words bear investigation: *wypr'h* (line 2),[7] *k'sw* (line 3), *yr'm* (line 3). The verb *pr'* only occurs one time in Ezekiel (24:14), where it is used to mean "refrain." Ezek. 20:28 uses the noun *k's* in a context completely different from 4Q391. Ezek. 27:35 refers to the faces of kings that are "convulsed" (*r'mw*), but that context does not help here. The phrase *lkl 'mw* in line 2 is paralleled in the *kl h'm* of 4Q385 12 1, another Pseudo-Ezekiel manuscript.

Fragment 9 (Smith, 159–60). This small fragment of four lines shares some of the vocabulary of Ezekiel's vision of the abominations taking place in the Jerusalem temple (8:1–18) and appears to be a rewriting of that biblical chapter. The critical phrase is in line 3, *w'r'h zqnym* ("and I saw elders"), which accords with Ezekiel's vision in 8:12 of the Israelite elders worshiping images in the darkness of their rooms. The term *ṭm'w* in line 2 may also be a reference to the *tw'bwt* of the biblical text (Ezek. 8:6, 9, 13). Not enough text is extant to get a clear picture of how 4Q391 rewrites the biblical passage, but the use of *drk* in line 3 (cf. Ezek. 8:5) may suggest that 4Q391 contained a shorter version of this episode.

Fragment 10 (Smith, 160–61). Smith suggests that this fragment may possibly be joined with fragments 11 and 12, because the top stroke of the *kap* in fragment 10 4 may line up with the bottom stroke in 11 1.[8] 4Q391 10 contains the word *rglyhm*, a word that occurs numerous times in the biblical Ezekiel. The only possible suggestion of a context comes if indeed fragments 11 and 12 do belong

---

5. See Wright, "Apocryphon of Ezekiel and 4QPseudo-Ezekiel."

6. Smith, "H. Pseudo-Ezekiel," 159.

7. Smith (ibid., 159) notes that what he reads as *resh* here could possibly be read as *yod*. After examination of PAM 43.470 in Timothy H. Lim, ed., *The Dead Sea Scrolls Electronic Reference Library* (Oxford: Oxford University Press, 1997), I am convinced that the letter is a *resh*.

8. Smith, "H. Pseudo-Ezekiel," 161.

with this one. Fragment 12 is a small fragment of two lines and has the phrase *rp' 'tkm*. Both the verb *rp'* and the noun *rgl* occur in Ezekiel 34, a chapter that condemns Israel's leaders for being poor shepherds and that claims God as the true shepherd of Israel.[9]

The phrase in 10 4, *hlkw bhyyhm*, "they went in their lives," is a strange conjunction, but the two words do come together in Ezek. 33:15 in the phrase "walk in the statutes of life." That context, however, does not seem to fit 4Q391.[10]

Fragment 16 (Smith, 163). This tiny piece contains the words *mhnhw* and *krb*. Ezekiel 4:2 uses the word *mhnh*, but the most important and suggestive word in fragment 16 is *krb*, "cherub." While most occasions of *krb* in the biblical text are in the plural, the singular does occur several times in Ezekiel 10. 4Q385 4, the other Pseudo-Ezekiel fragment that preserves the Merkebah vision, uses the word *hyh* exclusively when referring to the creatures that Ezekiel saw. In the two visions of God's chariot throne in Ezekiel 1 and 10, *hyh* is more characteristic of the form recorded in Ezekiel 1, while *krb* is typical of Ezekiel 10. The appearance of *hyh* in 4Q385 4 without overt reference to the cherubim prompts John Strugnell and Devorah Dimant to remark, "The most glaring omission in this respect is the complete absence from our fragment [4Q385 4] of the identification of the living creatures with the Cherubim, an identification central to *Ez* 10 but absent from *Ez* 1."[11] 4Q391 16 makes it clear that Pseudo-Ezekiel did refer to cherubim, but, due to the small size of this fragment, one cannot tell with any certainty whether it was in a recounting of the Merkebah vision or not.

Fragment 25 (Smith, 167). This fragment has five extant lines with a relatively large amount of text. Smith notes that the phrase in line 3, *'lyk qynwt wbky*, "laments over you and weeping," parallels the idiom *nś' 'lyk qynh* in Ezek. 27:32.[12] In fact, the entire fragment matches up well with Ezekiel 27:27–28:2. The following textual outline demonstrates with reasonable certainty that 4Q391 25 is a rewriting of this section of biblical Ezekiel (similar or common words between the two texts are underlined).

---

9. An "Apocryphon of Ezekiel" that circulated in Greek also included a reworking of this biblical chapter. On the Greek "Apocryphon of Ezekiel," see James R. Mueller, *The Five Fragments of the "Apocryphon of Ezekiel": A Critical Study* (JSPSup 5; Sheffield: Sheffield Academic Press, 1994), and Benjamin G. Wright, "Talking with God and Losing His Head: Extrabiblical Traditions about the Prophet Ezekiel" in *Biblical Figures outside the Bible* (ed. Michael E. Stone and Theodore A. Bergren; Harrisburg, Pa.: Trinity Press International, 1998), 290–315.

10. In his reconstruction of fragment 10 2, Smith has *m]lkym bhyyhm*. Given the certainty of the phrase *hlkw bhyyhm* in line 4, another possible reconstruction might be *h]lkym bhyyhm*, "those who go in their lives," a participial phrase matching the vocabulary of the later line.

11. John Strugnell and Devorah Dimant, "The Merkebah Vision in Second Ezekiel (4Q385 4)," *RevQ* 14 (1990): 346.

12. Smith, "H. Pseudo-Ezekiel," 167.

25 1	]h bqrbk yplw kl h [	Ezek. 27:27	wbkl qhlk 'šr btwkk yplw blb ymym
25 2	]'l h'rs wy'lw'pr [	Ezek. 27:29–30	'l h'rs ... wy'lw 'pr 'l r'šyhm b'pr ytplšw
25 3	]w'lyk qynwt wbky [	Ezek. 27:32	wnś'w 'lyk bnyhm qynh wqwnnw 'lyk
25 4	]l'bdn [	No parallel text in Ezekiel	
25 5	['mwr lml [k	Ezek. 28:2	'mwr lngyd ṣr

Except for the term 'bdn in line 4, the fragment shares with Ezek. 27:27–28:2 the same or similar vocabulary in an identical verse sequence. Abaddon, meaning "destruction," is also found in 4Q385 24 2 in a passage which speaks of the destruction of the Gentiles. A reference to destruction would be appropriate in a passage that depends on Ezekiel 27–28, especially since the destruction of the city of Tyre is mentioned in 27:32 and destruction is implied in 27:34, 36. The apparent skipping-over in this fragment of five biblical verses, from Ezek. 27:32 to 28:2, may indicate that the rewriting of the section in 4Q391 shortened the biblical passage somewhat.

Fragment 31 (Smith, 170). Although this fragment contains only two readable words, one can suggest a possible context in Ezekiel. The word hmwn in line 2 is a common term in Ezekiel, occurring twenty-two times in the book. Line 1 of the fragment consists solely of the prepositional phrase b'š. In two places, 30:8–10 and 30:14–15, biblical Ezekiel uses these two words in oracles prophesying God's judgment against Egypt. As I noted above, Ezekiel 30 is an important chapter elsewhere in Pseudo-Ezekiel (4Q385 24 and 4Q386), and this biblical chapter seems to be a good candidate in which to find a context for this fragment.

Fragment 36 (Smith, 172–73). This is a fragment that, despite its five lines of text, provides only a few clues to its contents. Smith remarks that the text "might suggest a dialogue between God and a prophetic figure told in the first person."[13] Line 2 apparently refers to the "feet of YHWH," an image found in Ezek. 43:7 (as well as other places in Hebrew scripture). What is tantalizing about this fragment is that a number of the vocabulary words occur in Ezekiel 43, and that chapter may provide its context. These are: rgly • • • • (line 1)[14]//rgly (meaning God's feet, Ezek. 43:7);]r'h (line 2)//r'yty (Ezek. 43:3); ydbr • • • • 'ly (line 4)//'šm' mdbr 'ly (Ezek. 43:6); bny yśr'l (line 5)//bny yśr'l (Ezek. 43:7). The only major exceptions are the phrases w'wmr 'lyw in line 2 and qšt • • • • in line 3. The noun qšt occurs twice in Ezekiel 39, but neither refers to God; it does not occur elsewhere in the extant Pseudo-Ezekiel manuscripts. The first-person speech of line 2, although not in Ezekiel 43, evidences the dialogue form so common to Pseudo-Ezekiel.

Fragment 52 (Smith, 179). This fragment is very faded and has few words that help in identifying a possible context in Ezekiel. One finds the prepositional phrase 'lyw in lines 2 and 3. It may presume the kind of first-person speech found

---

13. Ibid., 173.
14. The Tetragrammaton is represented in 4Q391 by four dots.

in 4Q391 36 2 and thus indicate the dialogue form typical of Pseudo-Ezekiel. Line 6 contains *wy'mr* at the end. This verb appears numerous times in biblical Ezekiel in the phrase *wy'mr 'ly bn 'dm*. The only legible phrase appears in line 5, *ml'k* • • • •, but this phrase, although common in the Hebrew Bible, is not found in Ezekiel.

Fragment 55 (Smith, 180–81). This piece is intriguing if for nothing more than the amount of text that is extant. Upon close examination, it is very difficult to find any language characteristic of the biblical Ezekiel. Of the six lines extant in this fragment, lines 3–5 are the most extensively preserved. The most interesting phrase is in line 4, *npšwt bnykm w* [ ] *'wbdwt*. This language is very close to the phrase *l'bd npšwt* in Ezek. 22:27. The context in the biblical text, however, is a diatribe against the leaders of Israel. From the text preserved in this fragment, one cannot determine if such is the context here, but 4Q391 55 does seem to contain a threat against the sons (and perhaps daughters?) of Israel. Line 5 ends with the verb *ydbr*. This same verb is found in 4Q391 36.

Fragment 56 (Smith, 181–82). According to Smith, this fragment "might refer to human revivification in the manner inspired by Ezekiel 37 in 4Q385 2."[15] Indeed, the use of this chapter in 4Q385 2 (cf. also 4Q386 i; 4Q388 8) and 4Q385 12 indicates its importance for Pseudo-Ezekiel. Does this fragment have Ezekiel 37 in focus?

The most important phrase to examine is *'wlh mrwḥwtykm* ("will go up from your spirits/winds" [?]) in line 4 (the same verb may also be present in lines 1 and 2). The verb *'lh* appears several times in Ezekiel 37. In vv. 6 and 8 it is used to describe the reconstitution of flesh on the dry bones. This use is also reflected in 4Q385 2 6, which closely represents the biblical phrase. The verb in Ezekiel 37 and 4Q385 2, however, comes in conjunction with the preposition *'l* and means "come upon." Later, Ezek. 37:12, 13 use the hiphil of *'lh* in a speech of God, who says, "I will raise you up out of your graves." In this case, *'lh* is used with the preposition *mn*, but only in the phrase "raise you up out of your graves." This same verb/preposition combination comes in 4Q391 56 4; the object of the preposition is not graves, however, but *rwḥwtykm*. One does find *'lh* and *rwḥ* used together in Ezek. 20:32, but there the verb is accompanied by the preposition *'l* to mean "to come to one's mind."

Despite the difficult Hebrew syntax, a couple of arguments might be made in favor of some connection to Ezekiel 37. First, that the same verb, *'lh*, probably appears in lines 1 and 2 might indicate a context like Ezekiel 37, where the verb is used on several occasions. Unfortunately, because of the bad state of preservation of these first two lines of the fragment, the context of *'lh* in them cannot be determined. Second, line 3 consists of the phrase *byt yśr'l*, which is a phrase used in the dry-bones vision in Ezek. 37:11 (*bny yśr'l* is used in the rewriting

---

15. Smith, "H. Pseudo-Ezekiel," 181.

of the vision in 4Q385 2 4; cf. above, 4Q391 36) and several times in the context surrounding that vision. Thus, the several occasions of *'lh* in combination with the phrase "house of Israel" could indicate some reworking of Ezekiel 37 in this fragment.

Fragment 62 (Smith, 184–85). Portions of two columns survive on this piece. Column one contains only one word; column two preserves five lines with readable text. The condition of the fragment does not provide a lot of context, but several phrases do appear. Jerusalem is mentioned in line 1. The only readable words in line 2 are *šlmwt kbwd*, which Smith translates "glorious acts of retribution." The term *šlmwt* is not used in the biblical Ezekiel. Line 3 preserves a two-word phrase, *qr' bšmk*. To call on God's name, as is apparently happening here, is an idiom not found in Ezekiel nor in the other Pseudo-Ezekiel manuscripts as Dimant has delineated them. Smith does the best that one can do with this phrase when he says, "Elsewhere, Pseudo-Ezekiel attaches importance to the divine name."[16]

Smith reconstructs the end of line 4 as *k'šr ktwb*, "as it is written." He notes that if this reconstruction is correct, and it is by no means certain, then Pseudo-Ezekiel contains a formula for quoting authoritative texts. The utilization of scriptural quotation may run counter to the kind of pseudonymous dialogue so characteristic of the rest of Pseudo-Ezekiel.[17]

Fragment 65 (Smith, 186–88). This fragment, which preserves text on ten lines, is the largest in the corpus of 4Q391 fragments and arguably the most important. It preserves the fragmentary remains of a vision of Ezekiel. The river Chebar, the site of Ezekiel's vision of the Merkebah, is mentioned in line 4 followed by the verb *w'r'h*, "and I saw." Smith remarks that the verb is "the converted form, in accordance with the biblical style which this work evokes."[18] Line 5 also contains a converted form in the phrase *'d'h ky* • • • •, "I knew that YHWH..." This phrase, as Smith notes, recalls Ezek. 10:20 and may indicate the report of a vision.[19]

The following lines (6–8) contain measurements. There is a mention of thirteen cubits, the height (*gbwh*) of something measuring five (presumably cubits), a base, and a "postern." Smith notes that all these vocabulary words fit Ezekiel's vision of the new temple in chapter 40.[20]

One word in particular, *hmšpš* in line 8 (the word translated "postern" by Smith), has an Aramaic cognate, *špšy'*, in 5Q15, a text that has been titled "The Description of the New Jerusalem." 5Q15 is known to depend on Ezekiel 40–48,

---

16. Ibid., 185.
17. Ibid.
18. Ibid., 188.
19. Ibid.
20. Ibid.

and the cognate vocabulary in 4Q391 65 reinforces its connection with these same chapters.[21]

The fragment, then, most likely represents some reworking of Ezekiel's vision of the new temple. The mention of the river Chebar may be part of a recollection of another vision, as it sometimes is in the biblical Ezekiel (cf. 3:23; 10:15, 20; 43:3), or it may denote the site of the vision itself, as in Ezekiel 1. If the latter is the case, it would be especially interesting, since in the biblical text Ezekiel's vision of the new temple takes place in the land of Israel (Ezek. 40:1–2). As it is, there can be little doubt that this fragment, and therefore most probably the entirety of 4Q391, belongs to Pseudo-Ezekiel.

Fragment 77 (Smith, 192). Although there is little text extant on this fragment, one word, *gwltw* ("its captivity"), is important. Of the forty total uses of this term in the Hebrew Bible, eleven are in Ezekiel and eleven in Jeremiah. It is thus a word one might expect to find in an Ezekiel pseudepigraphon. The phrase *wyš' bnym l...,* "and he will raise up sons for...," is not a biblical phrase. One raises hands, heads, and so on in the Hebrew Bible, but not sons.

Miscellaneous Fragments. The fragments that I treated above are those for which, because of their extant vocabulary and amount of text preserved, I could make some suggestions about where they intersect the biblical Book of Ezekiel. Simply because the work concerns the prophet Ezekiel, however, does not preclude either the use of other biblical texts, or perhaps none at all. Both of these possibilities can be found elsewhere in the Pseudo-Ezekiel manuscripts. In several places, for example, Pseudo-Ezekiel either alludes to passages from Isaiah or utilizes language characteristic of that prophet.[22] 4Q385 3, a text in which Ezekiel asks God to hasten the days so that "it be said by all men, indeed the days are hastening on in order that the children of Israel may inherit,"[23] does not appear to depend on any particular biblical text.

Accordingly, a number of 4Q391 fragments have some extant text, but I can discover no apparent connections to biblical Ezekiel. These may either depend on other biblical texts or comprise sections of Pseudo-Ezekiel that do not have any particular biblical passage in view. I include some comments for the sake of completeness, but also in the expectation that others may be more perceptive in discovering any possible biblical or other literary connections in these fragments.

Fragment 5 (Smith, 158). There is little to go on in the four lines of this fragment. The text refers to drunkenness, a word not used in Ezekiel, but which appears a number of times in Jeremiah and Isaiah (see also 4Q391 37, which

21. Ibid.

22. See, for example, Strugnell and Dimant, " Merkebah Vision," 334, and Wright, "Qumram Pseudepigrapha."

23. The translation comes from M. Kister and E. Qimron, "Observations on 4Q *Second Ezekiel* (4Q385 2–3)," *RevQ* 15 (1992): 598.

preserves only one complete word, "drunk"). Line four contains a mention of Egypt, the subject of a number of Pseudo-Ezekiel fragments.

Fragment 8 (Smith, 159). Line 2 of this small fragment contains the phrase *kl ywšb[y*. References to those who live in various places abound in the exilic-period prophets, including Ezekiel.

Fragment 19 (Smith, 164). This small fragment of three lines contains the infinitive *lrwm*, which occurs in Ezekiel's vision of the Merkebah in Ezek. 10:16. The only full word in line 2, *hrbh*, provides no additional information.

Fragment 24 (Smith, 166). This fragment preserves three lines. Line 2 has the word *kwḥ*, "strength." This word does not occur in Ezekiel, although it is common in Isaiah, Daniel, the Books of Chronicles, and Job.

Fragment 26 (Smith, 168). The four words in this fragment give no indication of context, but the use of first person (line 1, *'tn nym*) and second person (line 2, *twmr 'ly*) indicates the dialogue form characteristic of Pseudo-Ezekiel.

Fragment 28 (Smith, 168–69). This piece has only one recognizable word, *nkr*, which appears a number of times in the biblical Ezekiel, but always in the phrase *bn* or *bny nkr*. This phrase is definitely not in use here.

Fragment 32 (Smith, 170). This small fragment makes reference to "proud ones" (*g'ym*) and to someone "killed on the way" (*whrwg bdrk*). Jeremiah and Isaiah use the adjective "proud," but Ezekiel does not. The verb *hrg* is found a number of times in Ezekiel and Jeremiah, but none with *drk*.

Fragment 33 (Smith, 171). This fragment preserves the verb "he will wash" (*wyšṭp*) and the noun "curse" (*qllh*). Biblical Ezekiel uses this verb, and it is also common in Isaiah. The noun "curse" does not appear at all in Ezekiel, but is most frequently found in Deuteronomy and Jeremiah.

Fragment 38 (Smith, 174). Although this fragment preserves four lines, only three complete words survive. Line 4 refers to what Smith translates as "curses of a name" (*qlly šm*). The notion of cursing parallels 4Q391 33.

Fragment 48 (Smith, 177). Smith reconstructs the end of line 2 of this fragment as *]lmzbhy mṣ[rym* (he translates, "altars of Egypt"). If the reconstruction of the name Egypt is correct, this would certainly fit other contexts in Pseudo-Ezekiel which speak against Egypt (cf. 4Q385 24; 4Q386 ii). The major difficulty with Smith's reconstruction, however, is that the plural of *mzbh* is normally *mzbhwt*.[24] An additional difficulty is that in the biblical Ezekiel the term *mzbh* always refers to the temple of YHWH in Jerusalem. The reference here seems to me more likely to be God speaking about "my altar" (cf., for example, Isa. 56:7, 60:7). If this were the case, then Smith's reconstructed reference to Egypt would be difficult to sustain.

---

24. S.v. *"mzbh"* BDB, and in Marcus Jastrow, ed., *A Dictionary of the Targumin, the Talmud Babli and Yerushalmi, and the Midrashic Literature* (New York: Judaica Press, 1982).

Conclusion

The notes that I have made above, together with Smith's analysis in his DJD publication, provide the basis for a number of conclusions concerning 4Q391. The presence in a significant number of 4Q391 fragments of language characteristic of the biblical Book of Ezekiel and the high probability that several fragments rework specific biblical passages confirm the conclusion that the entirety of 4Q391 belongs to an Ezekiel pseudepigraphon.

When one asks whether this text is another copy of the same Ezekiel pseudepigraphon identified by Dimant or a separate work, the answer is not altogether certain. 4Q391 does share with 4Q385, 386, 387, 388 the form of a dialogue between Ezekiel and God. The prophet clearly speaks in the first person in a number of fragments, and the preserved text of some smaller pieces seems to presume some kind of first-person speech. A number of the 4Q391 fragments have language in common with other Pseudo-Ezekiel fragments, or they depend on the same texts as the other Pseudo-Ezekiel texts. Most significant in this regard is that several 4Q391 fragments look as if they rework the biblical Ezekiel's oracles against Egypt, oracles that are a prominent feature of the other Pseudo-Ezekiel manuscripts. So, even if 4Q391 shares no common text with the other Pseudo-Ezekiel copies, one can reasonably conclude that it is the same work.

With regard to the scope of Pseudo-Ezekiel's dependence on biblical Ezekiel, 4Q391 65 is an important fragment. This fragment is the first indication that Pseudo-Ezekiel included material from the biblical prophet's vision of the new temple, since none of the other Pseudo-Ezekiel copies shows any use of chapters 40–48. These chapters were important to a number of other Qumran works, which, although not written in Ezekiel's name, depend heavily on this vision.[25]

The mounting evidence suggests that the community who lived at Qumran valued Pseudo-Ezekiel highly. It is one of a number of important pseudepigrapha that purport to come from the mouth or pen of a biblical figure and that rework and reinterpret biblical texts. As such it will continue to garner more attention for the light it sheds on the use of the Hebrew Scriptures both at Qumran and in the larger landscape of Second Temple Judaism.

---

25. On this issue, see Devorah Dimant, "The Apocalyptic Interpretation of Ezekiel at Qumran," in *Messiah and Christos: Studies in the Jewish Origins of Christianity* (ed. Ithamar Gruenwald, Shaul Shaked, and Gedaliahu G. Stroumsa; Tübingen: Mohr [Siebeck], 1992), 31–51, and George J. Brooke, "Ezekiel in Some Qumran and New Testament Texts," in *Proceedings of the International Congress on the Dead Sea Scrolls — Madrid, 18–21 March 1991* (ed. J. Trebolle Barrera and L. Vegas Montaner; STDJ 10; Madrid: Universidad Complutense; Leiden: Brill, 1992), 317–37.

George W. E. Nickelsburg Publications

Books

Resurrection, Immortality, and Eternal Life in Intertestamental Judaism. HTS 26. Cambridge: Harvard University Press, 1972.

Jewish Literature between the Bible and the Mishnah: A Historical and Literary Introduction. Philadelphia: Fortress, 1981. [Paperback edition, 1987.]

Faith and Piety in Early Judaism: A Reader of Texts and Documents (with Michael E. Stone). Philadelphia: Fortress, 1983. [Paperback edition, New York: Trinity Press International, 1991.]

Collaborative Books

A Complete Concordance to Flavius Josephus 2. Edited by K. H. Rengstorf. Leiden: Brill, 1975.

A Complete Concordance to Flavius Josephus 3. Edited by K. H. Rengstorf. Leiden: Brill, 1979.

Books Edited

Studies on the "Testament of Moses." SBLSCS 4. Cambridge, Mass.: Society of Biblical Literature, 1973.

Studies on the "Testament of Joseph." SBLSCS 5. Missoula, Mont.: Scholars Press, 1975.

Studies on the "Testament of Abraham." SBLSCS 6. Missoula, Mont.: Scholars Press, 1976.

Ideal Figures in Ancient Judaism: Profiles and Paradigms (with John J. Collins). SBLSCS 12. Missoula, Mont.: Scholars Press, 1981.

Christians among Jews and Gentiles: Essays in Honor of Krister Stendahl on His Sixty-fifth Birthday (with George W. McRae). HTR 79/1–3. Philadelphia: Fortress, 1986.

Early Judaism and Its Modern Interpreters (with Robert A. Kraft). Atlanta: Scholars Press, 1986.

The Future of Early Christianity: Essays in Honor of Helmut Koester (with Birger A. Pearson [principal editor], A. Thomas Kraabel, and Norman R. Petersen). Minneapolis: Fortress, 1991.

Dictionary of Judaism in the Biblical Period (associate editor with Jacob Neusner and William Scott Green, editors). 2 vols. New York: Macmillan, 1995.

Articles

"1 and 2 Maccabees: Same Story, Different Meaning." *Concordia Theological Monthly* 42 (1971): 515–26.

"Eschatology in the *Testament of Abraham*: A Study of the Judgment Scenes in the Two Recensions." Pages 180–227 in *1972 Proceedings*. Edited by Robert A. Kraft. SBLSCS 2. Missoula, Mont.: Scholars Press, 1972.

"An Antiochan Date for the *Testament of Moses*." Pages 33–37 in *Studies on the "Testament of Moses."* Edited by George W. E. Nickelsburg. Cambridge, Mass.: Society of Biblical Literature, 1973.

"Narrative Traditions in the *Paraleipomena of Jeremiah* and *2 Baruch*." CBQ 35 (1973): 60–68.

"Enoch 97–104: A Study of Greek and Ethiopic Texts." Pages 90–156 in *Armenian and Biblical Studies*. Edited by Michael E. Stone. Supplementary volume to Sion 1. Jerusalem: St. James, 1976.

"Enoch, Book of." *IDBSup* 265–68.

"Eschatology in the *Testament of Abraham*." Pages 23–63 in *Studies on the "Testament of Abraham."* Edited by George W. E. Nickelsburg. SBLSCS 6. Missoula, Mont.: Scholars Press, 1976.

"Future Life in Intertestamental Literature." *IDBSup* 348–51.

"Miscellaneous Small Finds." Pages 101–2 and seven plates in *Discoveries in the Wâdi ed-Dâliyeh*. Edited by Paul W. Lapp and Nancy L. Lapp. AASOR 41. Cambridge, Mass.: American Schools of Oriental Research, 1976.

"Review of the Literature." Pages 9–22 in Nickelsburg, *Studies on the "Testament of Abraham."*

"The Roman Occupation and Pottery of 'Arâq en-Na'saneh (Cave II)" (with Nancy L. Lapp). Pages 49–54 and eight plates in Lapp and Lapp, *Discoveries in the Wâdi ed-Dâliyeh*.

"Simon: A Priest with a Reputation for Faithfulness." BASOR 223 (1976): 67–68.

"Structure and Message in the *Testament of Abraham*." Pages 85–93 in Nickelsburg, *Studies on the "Testament of Abraham."*

"Summary and Prospects of Future Work." Pages 289–98 in Nickelsburg, *Studies on the "Testament of Abraham."*

"Apocalyptic and Myth in *1 Enoch* 6–11." JBL 96 (1977): 383–405.

"The Apocalyptic Message of *1 Enoch* 92–105." CBQ 39 (1977): 309–28.

"Good News/Bad News: The Messiah and God's Fractured Community." *Currents in Theology and Mission* 4 (1977): 324–32.

"Reflections upon Reflections: A Response to John Collins' 'Methodological Issues in the Study of *1 Enoch*.'" Pages 311–14 in *SBL Seminar Papers, 1978*. Edited by Paul J. Achtemeier. Missoula, Mont.: Scholars Press, 1978.

Review of Charlotte Klein, *Anti-Judaism in Christian Theology. RelSRev* 4 (1978): 161–68.

"Riches, the Rich, and God's Judgment in *1 Enoch* 92–105 and the Gospel according to Luke." *NTS* 25 (1979): 324–44.

"The Genre and Function of the Markan Passion Narrative." *HTR* 73 (1980): 153–84.

"Resurrection." Pages 447–48 in volume 23 of *The Encyclopedia Americana,* international edition. Danbury, Conn.: Encyclopedia Americana, 1980.

"Enoch, Levi, and Peter: Recipients of Revelation in Upper Galilee." *JBL* 100 (1981): 575–99.

"Good and Bad Leaders in Pseudo-Philo's *Liber Antiquitatum Biblicarum.*" Pages 49–65 in *Ideal Figures in Early Judaism.* Edited by John J. Collins and George W. E. Nickelsburg. Missoula, Mont.: Scholars Press, 1981.

Review of *The Books of Enoch in Recent Research. RelSRev* 7 (1981): 210–17.

"Some Related Traditions in the *Apocalypse of Adam,* the *Books of Adam and Eve,* and *1 Enoch.*" Pages 515–39 in *Sethian Gnosticism.* Vol. 2 of *The Rediscovery of Gnosticism.* Edited by Bentley Layton. Studies in the History of Religions 41. Leiden: Brill, 1981.

"The Epistle of Enoch and the Qumran Literature." *JJS* 33 [essays in honor of Yigael Yadin] (1982): 333–48.

"The Bible Rewritten and Expanded." Pages 89–156 in *Jewish Writings of the Second Temple Period.* Edited by Michael E. Stone. CRINT 2/2. Philadelphia: Fortress, 1983.

"Reading the Hebrew Scriptures in the First Century: Christian Interpretations in Their Jewish Context." *WW* 3 (1983): 238–50.

"Social Aspects of Palestinian Jewish Apocalypticism." Pages 641–54 in *Apocalypticism in the Mediterranean World and the Near East: Proceedings of the International Colloquium on Apocalypticism, Uppsala, August 12–17, 1979.* Edited by David Hellholm. Tübingen: Mohr [Siebeck], 1983.

"Stories of Biblical and Early Post-biblical Times." Pages 33–87 in Stone, *Jewish Writings of the Second Temple Period.*

"The God of the Bible in a Nuclear Age?" *Currents in Theology and Mission* 11 (1984): 213–24.

"Aaron." Columns 1–11 in *RAC,* supplementary volume 1. Stuttgart: Anton Hiersemann, 1985.

"Revealed Wisdom as a Criterion for Inclusion and Exclusion: From Jewish Sectarianism to Early Christianity." Pages 73–91 in *To See Ourselves as Others See Us.* Edited by Jacob Neusner and Ernest S. Frerichs. Atlanta: Scholars Press, 1985.

"*1 Enoch* and Qumran Origins: The State of the Question and Some Prospects for Answers." Pages 341–60 in *SBL Seminar Papers, 1986.* Edited by Kent Harold Richards. Atlanta: Scholars Press, 1986.

"An *Ektroma*, Though Chosen from the Womb: Paul's Self-Description in 1 Cor 15 and Gal 1." Pages 198–205 in *Christians among Jews and Gentiles*. Edited by George W. E. Nickelsburg. Philadelphia: Fortress, 1986.

"Introduction: The Modern Study of Early Judaism" (with Robert A. Kraft). Pages 1–30 in *Early Judaism and Its Modern Interpreters*. Edited by Robert A. Kraft and George W. E. Nickelsburg. Philadelphia: Fortress, 1986.

"Salvation without and with a Messiah: Developing Beliefs in Writings Ascribed to Enoch." Pages 49–68 in *Judaisms and Their Messiahs*. Edited by Jacob Neusner, William S. Green, and Ernest Frerichs. New York: Cambridge University Press, 1988.

"Tobit." *HBC* 791–803.

"Tobit and Enoch: Distant Cousins with a Recognizable Resemblance." Pages 54–68 in *SBL Seminar Papers, 1988*. Edited by David J. Lull. Atlanta: Scholars Press, 1988.

"Introduction to the Apocrypha." Pages 3–11 in volume 2 of *The Books of the Bible*. Edited by Bernhard W. Anderson. New York: Scribner, 1989.

"The Apocalyptic Construction of Reality of 1 Enoch." Pages 51–64 in *Mysteries and Revelations: Apocalyptic Studies since the Uppsala Colloquium*. Edited by John J. Collins and James H. Charlesworth. JSPSup 9. Sheffield: Sheffield Academic Press, 1991.

"The Incarnation: Paul's Solution to the Universal Human Predicament." Pages 348–57 in *The Future of Early Christianity: Essays in Honor of Helmut Koester*. Edited by Birger A. Pearson et al. Minneapolis: Fortress, 1991.

"Patriarchy with a Twist: Men and Women in Tobit" (with Beverly Bow). Pages 127–43 in *Women Like This*. Edited by A. Levine. Atlanta: Scholars Press, 1991.

"The Qumran Fragments of 1 Enoch and Other Apocryphal Works: Implications for the Understanding of Early Judaism and Christian Origins." Pages 181–95 in *Jewish Civilization in the Hellenistic-Roman Period*. Edited by Shemaryahu Talmon. JSPSup 10. Sheffield: Sheffield Academic Press, 1991.

"The Qumranic Radicalizing and Anthropologizing of an Eschatological Tradition (1QH 4:29–40)." Pages 423–35 in *Ernten, was man sät: Festschrift für Klaus Koch zu seinem 65*. Edited by Dwight R. Daniels, Uwe Glessmer, and Martin Rösel. Neukirchen-Vluyn: Neukirchener, 1991.

"Two Enochic Manuscripts: Unstudied Evidence for Egyptian Christianity." Pages 251–60 in *Of Scribes and Scrolls: Studies on the Hebrew Bible, Intertestamental Judaism, and Christian Origins*. Edited by H. W. Attridge, J. J. Collins, and T. H. Tobin. Resources in Religion 5. Lanham, Md.: University Press of America, 1991.

"Enoch, First Book of." *ABD* 2.508–16.

"Eschatology: Early Jewish Literature." *ABD* 2.579–94.

"Jeremiel." *ABD* 3.722–23.

"Passion Narratives." *ABD* 5.172–77.

"The Qumranic Transformation of a Cosmological and Eschatological Tradition (1QH 4:29–40)." Pages 648–59 in volume 2 of *The Madrid Qumran Congress: Proceedings of the International Congress on the Dead Sea Scrolls, Madrid, 18–21 March 1991*. Edited by Julio Trebolle Barrera and Luis Vegas Montaner. 2 vols. STDJ 11. Leiden: Brill, 1992.

"Resurrection: Early Judaism and Christianity." *ABD* 5.684–91.

"Son of Man." *ABD* 6.137–50.

Annotations for "The Book of Tobit." *Harper Study Edition* of the New Revised Standard Version of the Bible. New York: HarperCollins, 1993.

"Jews and Christians in the First Century: The Struggle over Identity." *Neotestamentica* 27 (1993): 365–90.

"Dealing with Challenges and Limitations: A Response." *DSD* 1 (1994): 229–37.

"The First Century: A Time to Rejoice and a Time to Weep." *Religion & Theology/ Religie & Teologie* 1 (1994): 4–17.

"Wisdom and Apocalypticism in Early Judaism: Some Points for Discussion." Pages 715–32 in *SBL Seminar Papers, 1994*. Edited by Eugene H. Lovering. Atlanta: Scholars Press, 1994.

"Why Study the Extra-canonical Literature: A Historical and Theological Essay." *Neotestamentica* 28 [special edition: essays in honor of Willem Vorster] (1994): 181–204.

"The Jewish Context of the New Testament." *NIB* 8.27–42.

"Scripture in *1 Enoch* and *1 Enoch* as Scripture." Pages 333–54 in *Texts and Contexts: Biblical Texts in Their Textual and Situational Contexts, Essays in Honor of Lars Hartman*. Edited by Tord Fornberg and David Hellholm. Oslo: Scandinavian University Press, 1995.

"Son of Man." Columns 1510–20 in *Dictionary of Deities and Demons in the Bible*. Edited by Karel van der Toorn et al. Leiden: Brill, 1995.

Various articles in *The Dictionary of Judaism in the Biblical Period*. Edited by Jacob Neusner and William Scott Green. 2 vols. New York: Macmillan, 1995.

"The Search for Tobit's Mixed Ancestry: A Historical and Hermeneutical Odyssey." *RevQ* 17/65–68 (hommage à Jozef T. Milik; ed. F. García Martínez and Emile Puech; Paris: Gabalda, 1996): 349–59.

"4Q551: A *Vorlage* to Susanna or a Text Related to Judges 19?" *JJS* 48 (1997): 349–51.

"Abraham the Convert: A Jewish Tradition and Its Use by the Apostle Paul." Pages 151–75 in *Biblical Figures outside the Bible*. Edited by Theodore Bergren and Michael E. Stone. Harrisburg, Pa.: Trinity Press International, 1998.

"Enochic Wisdom: An Alternative to the Mosaic Torah?" Pages 123–32 in *Hesed ve-emet: Studies in Honor of Ernest S. Frerichs*. Edited by Jodi Magness and Seymour Gitin. Brown Judaic Studies 10. Atlanta: Scholars Press, 1998.

"Patriarchs Who Worry about Their Wives: A Haggadic Tendency in the *Genesis Apocryphon.*" Pages 137–58 in *Biblical Perspectives: Early Use and Interpretation of the Bible in Light of the Dead Sea Scrolls. Proceedings of the First International Symposium of the Orion Center for the Study of the Dead Sea Scrolls and Associated Literature, 12–14 May 1996.* Edited by Michael E. Stone and Esther G. Chazon. Leiden: Brill, 1998.

"Response to Paolo Sacchi's *Jewish Apocalyptic and Its History.*" *Henoch* 20 (1998): 89–106.

"Revisiting the Rich and the Poor in *1 Enoch* 92–105 and the Gospel according to Luke." Pages 579–605 in *SBL Seminar Papers, 1998.* Atlanta: Scholars Press, 1998.

"The Books of Enoch at Qumran: What We Know and What We Need to Think About." *ZNW* 97 (Antikes Judentum und Frühes Christentum: Festschrift für Hartmut Stegemann zum 65 Geburtstag; Berlin: de Gruyter, 1999): 99–113.

"Currents in Qumranic Research: The Interplay of Data, Agendas, and Methodology." Pages 79–99 in *The Dead Sea Scrolls at Fifty.* Edited by Robert A. Kugler and Eileen Schuller. Atlanta: Society of Biblical Literature, 1999.

"'Enoch' as Scientist, Sage, and Prophet: Content, Function, and Authorship in *1 Enoch.*" Pages 203–30 in *SBL Seminar Papers, 1999.* Atlanta: Scholars Press, 1999.

"The Nature and Function of Revelation in *1 Enoch, Jubilees,* and Some Qumranic Documents." Pages 91–119 in *Pseudepigraphical Perspectives: The Apocrypha and Pseudepigrapha in Light of the Dead Sea Scrolls. Proceedings of the International Symposium of the Orion Center for the Study of the Dead Sea Scrolls and Associated Literature, 12–14 January 1997.* Edited by Esther G. Chazon and Michael E. Stone. STDJ 31. Leiden: Brill, 1999.

"Religious Exclusivism: A World View Governing Some Texts Found at Qumran." Pages 45–67 in *Das Ende der Tage und die Gegenwart des Heils: Begegnungen mit dem Neuen Testament und seiner Umwelt, Festschrift für Heinz-Wolfgang Kuhn zum 65 Geburtstag.* Edited by Berndt Kollmann. Leiden: Brill, 1999.

"Seeking the Origins of the Two-Ways Tradition in Jewish and Christian Ethical Texts." Pages 95–108 in *A Multiform Heritage: Studies on Early Judaism and Christianity in Honor of Robert A. Kraft.* Edited by Benjamin Wright. Scholars Press Homage Series 24. Atlanta: Scholars Press, 1999.

"Judgment, Life-After-Death, and Resurrection in the Apocrypha and the Non-apocalyptic Pseudepigrapha." Pages 141–62 in *Death, Life-After-Death, Resurrection, and the World to Come in the Judaisms of Antiquity.* Edited by Alan J. Avery-Peck and Jacob Neusner. Judaism in Late Antiquity 4. Leiden: Brill, 1999.

"Apocalyptic Writings." Pages 29–35 in *Encyclopedia of the Dead Sea Scrolls.* Edited by Lawrence H. Schiffman and James C. VanderKam. New York: Oxford University Press, 2000.

"Daniel, Additions to." Pages 174–76 in Schiffman and VanderKam, *Encyclopedia of the Dead Sea Scrolls.*

"Enoch, Books of." Pages 249–53 in Schiffman and VanderKam, *Encyclopedia of the Dead Sea Scrolls.*

"Eternal Life." Pages 270–72 in Schiffman and VanderKam, *Encyclopedia of the Dead Sea Scrolls.*

"Resurrection." Pages 764–67 in Schiffman and VanderKam, *Encyclopedia of the Dead Sea Scrolls.*

"Revelation." Pages 770–72 in Schiffman and VanderKam, *Encyclopedia of the Dead Sea Scrolls.*

Articles in Press

"*1 Enoch*": *A Critical and Exegetical Commentary* [Editor and contributor], Hermeneia; Minneapolis: Fortress Press

"Prayer of Manasseh." *Oxford Bible Commentary.* Oxford: Clarendon.

"Tobit." *Harper's Bible Commentary.* Rev. ed. San Francisco: Harper & Row.

"Tobit and the *Odyssey*: A Complex Web of Intertextuality." *Proceedings of the Conference on Mimesis and Intertextuality in Early Christian Literature, Claremont Graduate School, 4–5 June 1998.* Forthcoming from Trinity Press International in *Mimesis and Intertextuality in Antiquity and Christianity,* edited by Dennis MacDonald.

Book Reviews

Matthew Black, *An Aramaic Approach to the Gospels and to Acts. The Pulpit* (1968): 27.

Raymond E. Brown et al., *The Jerome Biblical Commentary. Christian Century* 86 (1969): 754.

Reginald C. Fuller, *A New Catholic Commentary on Holy Scripture. Christian Century* 87 (1970): 214.

Wolfgang Harnisch, *Verhängnis und Verheissung der Geschichte: Untersuch zum Zeit- und Geschichtsverständnis im 4 buch Esra und in der Syr Baruchapokalypse. JBL* 89 (1970): 486.

Erling Jorstad, *That New-Time Religion: The Jesus Revival in America. Christian Century* 89 (1972): 1197–98.

Otto Plöger, *Aus der Spätzeit des Alten Testaments: Festschrift für Otto Plöger, Studien zu seinem 60 Geburtstag. CBQ* 34 (1972): 102–3.

M. Didier, ed., *L'Evangile selon Matthieu: Rédaction et théologie. CBQ* 35 (1973): 525–27.

Gerhard Maier, *Mensch und freier Wille: Nach den jüdischen Religionsparteien zwischen Ben Sira und Paulus. JBL* 92 (1973): 293–96.

Günther Stemberger, *Der Leib der Auferstehung: Studien zur Anthropologie und Eschatologie des palästinischen Judentums im neutestamentlichen Zeitalter.* CBQ 35 (1973): 555–56.

Hans Cavallin, *Life after Death: Paul's Argument for the Resurrection of the Dead in I Cor. 15.* JSJ 6 (1975): 100–102. [Also appeared in *Interpretation* 31 (1977): 331–32.]

John H. Hayes, *Son of God to Superstar: Twentieth-Century Interpretations of Jesus.* *Christian Century* 93 (1976): 501–2. [Also appeared in *Currents in Theology and Mission* 3 (1975): 250–51.]

W. Stewart McCullough, *The History and Literature of the Palestinian Jews. Currents in Theology and Mission* 3 (1976): 368–69.

Raymond F. Surburg, *Introduction to the Intertestamental Period.* CBQ 38 (1976): 600–601.

William Barclay, *Jesus of Nazareth* (reviewed with Marilyn M. Nickelsburg). *Christian Century* 94 (1977): 664–66.

"Book Notes." *RelSRev* 3 (1977): 58, 120, 122, 177, 178, 180.

John Dart, *The Laughing Savior.* *Christian Century* 94 (1977): 306–7.

David L. Edwards, *Today's Story of Jesus* (reviewed with Marilyn M. Nickelsburg). *Christian Century* 94 (1977): 664–66.

David M. Rhoads, *Israel in Revolution. Currents in Theology and Mission* 4 (1977): 313.

"Book Note." *JAAR* 46 (1978): 580.

"Book Notes." *RelSRev* 4 (1978): 57–59, 134, 214.

M. de Jonge, ed., *Studies on the "Testaments of the Twelve Patriarchs."* CBQ 40 (1978): 438–40.

J. T. Milik, *The Books of Enoch.* CBQ 40 (1978): 411–19.

The Oxford Annotated Apocrypha. PSB 2 (1978): 58–59.

James M. Robinson, *Nag Hammadi Library. Christian Century* 95 (1978): 595–96.

"Book Notes." *JAAR* 47 (1979): 665–66, 670.

"Book Notes." *RelSRev* 5 (1979): 221, 297.

Luke Johnson, *The Literary Function of Possessions in Luke-Acts.* JAAR 47 (1979): 670.

E. P. Sanders, *Paul and Palestinian Judaism: A Comparison of Patterns of Religion.* CBQ 41 (1979): 171–75.

E. Best and R. M. Wilson, eds., *Text and Interpretation: Studies in the New Testament Presented to Matthew Black.* JAAR 48 (1980): 603–4.

"Book Notes." *JAAR* 48 (1980): 277–78, 603–4.

"Book Notes." *RelSRev* 6 (1980): 73, 155, 239–40.

J. D. M. Derrett, *Studies in the New Testament.* JAAR 48 (1980): 277.

Hans Kosmala, *Studies, Essays, and Reviews.* JAAR 48 (1980): 604.

D. S. Russell, *Apocalyptic Ancient and Modern.* JAAR 48 (1980): 277–78.

James C. VanderKam, *Textual and Historical Studies in the "Book of Jubilees."* JAOS 100 (1980): 83–84.

"Book Note." *JAAR* 49 (1981): 536.

"Book Note." *RelSRev* 7 (1981): 83.

Ferdinand Dexinger, *Henochs Zehnwochenapokalypse und offene Probleme der Apokalyptikforschung.* JBL 100 (1981): 669–70.

Michael A. Knibb and Edward Ullendorff, eds., *Ethiopic Book of Enoch.* CBQ 43 (1981): 133–35.

"Book Note." *JAAR* 50 (1982): 296.

"Book Notes." *RelSRev* 8 (1982): 194, 380, 389.

Lars Hartman, *Asking for a Meaning: A Study of "1 Enoch" 1–5.* CBQ 44 (1982): 327–28.

Eckhard von Nordheim, *Die Lehre der Alten I: Das Testament als Literaturgattung im Judentum der hellenistisch-römischen Zeit.* JAAR 50 (1982): 296.

Paul J. Kobelski, *Melchizedek and Melchiresa.* CBQ 45 (1983): 492–93.

"Book Notes." *RelSRev* 10 (1984): 78–79, 186, 188.

G. H. R. Horsley, *New Documents Illustrating Early Christianity, vol. 1: A Review of Greek Inscriptions and Papyri Published in 1976.* CBQ 46 (1984): 348–49.

John C. Meagher, *Five Gospels: An Account of How the Good News Came to Be. Christian Century* 101 (1984): 24–25.

Otto Neugebauer, *The "Astronomical" Chapters of the Ethiopic Book of Enoch (72–82).* JBL 103 (1984): 457.

Ryszard Rubinkiewicz, *Die Eschatologie von Henoch 9–11 und das Neue Testament.* JBL 106 (1987): 535–37.

Roger Beckwith, *The Old Testament Canon of the New Testament Church and Its Background in Early Judaism.* CBQ 50 (1988): 706–7.

Matthew Black, ed., *The Book of Enoch or "1 Enoch."* JBL 107 (1988): 342–44.

James H. Charlesworth, ed., *The Old Testament Pseudepigrapha, vol. 1: Apocalyptic Literature and Testaments.* CBQ 50 (1988): 288–91.

James H. Charlesworth, ed., *The Old Testament Pseudepigrapha, vol. 2: Expansions of the "Old Testament" and Legends.* CBQ 50 (1988): 288–91.

H. F. D. Sparks, ed., *The Apocryphal Old Testament.* CBQ 50 (1988): 288–91.

Margaret Barker, *The Older Testament: The Survival of Themes from the Ancient Royal Cult in Sectarian Judaism and Early Christianity.* JBL 109 (1990): 335–37.

John Dominic Crossan, *The Cross That Spoke: The Origins of the Passion Narrative.* JAAR 59 (1991): 159–62.

Albert M. Denis, *Concordance grecque des Pseudépigraphes d'Ancien Testament: Concordance, Corpus des textes, Indices.* CBQ 53 (1991): 463–65.

Michael E. Stone and David Satran, eds., *Emerging Judaism: Studies on the Fourth and Third Centuries* B.C.E. CBQ 54 (1992): 199–200.

Michael E. Stone, *A History of the Literature of Adam and Eve.* JR 74 (1994): viii, 163.

Florentino Garcia Martinez, *Qumran and Apocalyptic: Studies on the Aramaic Texts from Qumran. DSD* 2 (1995): 235–38.

James C. VanderKam, *The "Book of Jubliees." JSP* 13 (1995): 110–12.

John J. Collins, *The Scepter and the Star: The Messiahs of the Dead Sea Scrolls and Other Ancient Literature. JR* 77 (1997): 457–58.

Merten Rabenau, *Studien zum Buch Tobit. JBL* 116 (1997): 348–50.

Magen Broshi et al., *Qumran Cave 4, XIV, Parabiblical Texts, Part 2: Discoveries in the Judean Desert, XIX. JSP* 17 (1998): 120–23.

James C. VanderKam and William Adler, eds., *The Jewish Apocalyptic Heritage in Early Christianity. CBQ* 60 (1998): 104–6.

George Brooke et al., *Qumran Cave 4, XVII, Parabiblical Texts, Part 3: Discoveries in the Judean Desert, XXII. DSD* 6 (1999): 194–99.

Research and Writing in Progress

"1 Enoch": A Critical and Exegetical Commentary. Vol. 2.

Jewish Literature between the Bible and the Mishnah. Rev. ed. Philadelphia: Fortress Press.

Refocusing the Images: Paradigm Shifts in the Study of Early Judaism. Trinity Press International.

Resurrection, Immortality, and Eternal Life in Intertestamental Judaism. [Enhanced version of dissertation.]

Contributors

William Adler is Professor of Early Christianity and Judaism, North Carolina State University.

Randal A. Argall is Assistant Professor of Religion, Jamestown College, Jamestown, North Dakota.

Theodore A. Bergren is Associate Professor of Religion, University of Richmond.

Beverly Bow is Adjunct Professor of Religion, Cleveland State University.

Esther Chazon teaches in the Department of Hebrew Literature, Hebrew University of Jerusalem.

John J. Collins is Holmes Professor of Old Testament, Yale University.

Marinus de Jonge is Professor Emeritus of New Testament and Early Christian Literature at the University of Leiden.

Jonathan A. Goldstein is Emeritus Professor, University of Iowa.

Martha Himmelfarb is Professor of Religion, Princeton University.

Richard A. Horsley is Distinguished Professor of Liberal Arts and the Study of Religion, University of Massachusetts Boston.

Ralph Klein is Christ Seminary-Seminex Professor of Old Testament, Lutheran School of Theology at Chicago.

Ross S. Kraemer is Professor of Religious Studies, Brown University.

Robert A. Kraft is Berg Professor of Religious Studies, University of Pennsylvania.

J. Kenneth Kuntz is Professor of Religion, University of Iowa.

Dennis R. MacDonald is John Wesley Professor of New Testament and Christian Origins, Claremont School of Theology and Claremont Graduate University.

James F. McCue is Emeritus Professor, School of Religion, University of Iowa.

Jacob Neusner is Research Professor of Religion and Theology, Bard College.

ELAINE H. PAGELS is Harrington Spear Paine Foundation Professor of Religion, Princeton University.

BIRGER A. PEARSON is Professor Emeritus of Religious Studies, University of California, Santa Barbara.

NORMAN R. PETERSEN is Washington Gladden Professor of Religion, Emeritus, Williams College.

MICHAEL E. STONE is Gail Levin de Nur Professor of Religious Studies and Professor of Armenian Studies, Hebrew University of Jerusalem.

BISHOP KRISTER STENDAHL is Andrew W. Mellon Professor Emeritus, Harvard Divinity School.

FRED STRICKERT is Professor of Religion, Wartburg College.

PATRICK TILLER is an independent scholar living in Sharon, Massachusetts.

JAMES C. VANDERKAM is John O'Brien Professor of Theology, University of Notre Dame.

RODNEY WERLINE is Assistant Professor of Hebrew Bible and Early Judaism, Emmanuel School of Religion.

BENJAMIN G. WRIGHT III is Associate Professor of Religion Studies, Lehigh University.

Index of Ancient Sources

Index of Modern Authors